NATIONAL INDEX OF PARIS

A Guide to Anglican, Roman Catholic
and Non-Conformist Registers
together with information on Bishop's Transcripts,
modern copies and Marriage licences.

VOLUME   8

PART 5

DEVON

Compiled by
Anthony Wilcox M.A. M.Phil F.S.G.

General Editor
C R Webb M.A. F.S.G.

SOCIETY OF GENEALOGISTS

Published by
Society of Genealogists
14 Charterhouse Buildings
Goswell Road
London EC1M 7BA

ⓒ 1999 Society of Genealogists

ISBN 1 85951 605 X

Volumes of the National Index of Parish Registers already published

Volume 1   *General Sources of Births, Marriages and Deaths before 1837*
            Parish Registers, Marriage Licences, Monumental Inscriptions,
            Newspapers, Clandestine Marriages, Divorce, Mediaeval Sources,
            Other Records. General Bibliography.

Volume 2   *Sources for Nonconformist Genealogy and Family History*
            The Three Denominations (Presbyterians, Independents
            and Baptists), Society of Friends, Moravians, Methodists,
            Foreign Churches, Other Denominations.

Volume 3   *Sources for Roman Catholic Genealogy and Family History*
            With a short section on Jewish Records contributed by Edgar
            Samuel. Index to Volumes 1, 2 and 3.

Volume 4   *South East England*
            Kent, Surrey and Sussex.
            A revised edition of Surrey has appeared as Volume 4 Part 1.

Volume 5   *South Midlands and Welsh Border*
            Gloucestershire, Herefordshire, Oxfordshire, Shropshire,
            Warwickshire, Worcestershire.

Volume 6   *North and East Midlands*
            Part 1: Staffordshire.
            Part 2: Nottinghamshire.
            Part 3: Leicestershire and Rutland.
            Part 4: Lincolnshire.
            Part 5: Derbyshire.

Volume 7   *East Anglia*
            Cambridgeshire, Norfolk, Suffolk.

Volume 8   *The West of England*
            Part 1 : Berkshire.
            Part 2 : Wiltshire.
            Part 3 : Somerset.
            Part 4 : Cornwall.
            Part 5 : Devon.

Volume 9   *Home Counties (North of the Thames) and South-East Midlands*
            Part 1 : Bedfordshire and Huntingdonshire.
            Part 2 : Northamptonshire.
            Part 3 : Buckinghamshire.
            Part 4 : Essex.
            Part 5 : London and Middlesex.

Volume 10   *North West England*
            Part 1 : Cheshire.
            Part 2 : Lancashire
            Part 3 : Cumberland and Westmorland

Volume 11   *North East England*
            Part 1: Durham, Northumberland.
            Part 2: Yorkshire (North and East Ridings and York).
            Part 3: Yorkshire (West Riding).

Volume 12   *Sources for Scottish Genealogy and Family History*
            Historical background, Parish Registers, Ancillary Sources
            Nonconformists, Bibliography.

Volume 13   *Parish Registers of Wales*

Volume 14   *Nonconformist Registers of Wales*

VOLUME 8

PART 5

CONTENTS

ABBREVIATIONS FOR RECORD REPOSITORIES, LIBRARIES AND SOCIETIES

Researchers are advised to make a preliminary telephone enquiry about opening times and conditions of admission.

A. **National**

AAB   Archives of the Archbishop of Birmingham
Cathedral House, St Chad's Ringway, Birmingham B4 6EX

AAW   Archives of the Archbishop of Westminster,
16a Abingdon Road, Kensington, London W8 6AF

AFCC   Armed Forces Chaplaincy Centre, Amport House, Amport,
Andover, Hampshire SP11 8BG. Registers for RAF station chaplaincies, when completed, or when station closes.

BL   The British Library, Euston Road, London NW1 2DB
A reader's ticket is required

Bod   Department of Western Manuscripts, Bodleian Library,
Broad Street, Oxford OX1 3BG.

BRS   British Record Society, c/o College of Arms, below.

C of A   College of Arms, Queen Victoria Street, London
EC4V 4BT. The Library is not open to the public.

GL   Guildhall Library, Aldermanbury, London EC2P 2EJ.

Harl Mss   Harleian Manuscripts, in the Department of Manuscripts,
The British Library.

MoD   [Army registers] Ministry of Defence Chaplains (Army), Trenchard Lines, Upavon, Pewsey, Wiltshire SN9 6BE
[Naval registers] Central Services (Records Management) Room 1/07, 3-5 Great Scotland Yard, London SW1A 2HW. Registers will be moved to PRO, new class ADM 338, in due course.

Phil Mss   Manuscript copies of parish registers in the possession of Phillimore and Co. Ltd, Shopwyke Manor Barn, Chichester, West Sussex PO20 6BG. A fee is normally charged.

PRO   Public Record Office, Ruskin Avenue, Kew, Richmond TW9 4DU
Non-parochial registers in the PRO may be seen on microfilm at: Family Records Centre, 1 Myddleton Street, London EC1R 1UW

RCRO   Roman Catholic Records Office, Bishopric of the Forces, AGPDO, Middle Hill, Aldershot, Hampshire GU11 1PP.
Registers of RC chaplaincies to the Royal Navy, Army and RAF, in Britain and abroad.

SG   Society of Genealogists, 14 Charterhouse Buildings,
Goswell Road, London EC1M 7BA.
The library is open to non-members on payment of hourly, half-daily and daily fees.

SLC   The Genealogical Society of Utah, 35 North West
Temple Street, Salt Lake City, Utah 84150 U.S.A.

B.   **Local repositories holding Devon records**

BG/PCL   Baring-Gould Collection at PCL (see below, and Other Copies p.11)

CRO   Cornwall Record Office, County Hall, Truro TR1 3AY
           Tel: 01872 273698

DCRS/WSL Collections of the Devon and Cornwall Record Society
           at Westcountry Studies Library, Castle Street, Exeter EX4 3PQ
           Tel: 01392 384216. Available to Society members only. Temporary
           membership may be taken out in the Library.

DFHS   Devon Family History Society: Headquarters and library at
           Tree House, Unit 3b-4b 7-9 King Street, Exeter (no correspondence).
           Secretary: Mrs E.Wilmot, 8 King Henry's Road, Exeter EX2 6AL

DLS   Devon Library Services, North Devon Local Studies Centre,
           Tuly Street, Barnstaple EX31 1EL Tel: 01271 388607

DRO   Devon Record Office, Castle Street, Exeter EX4 3PU
           Tel: 01392 384253

NDA   North Devon Athenaeum, Tuly Street, Barnstaple EX31 1EL
           Tel: 01271 342174

NDRO   North Devon Record Office, Tuly Street, Barnstaple EX31 1EL
           Tel: 01271 388607

PCL   Plymouth Central Library, Drake Circus, Plymouth PL4 8AL
           Tel: 01752 385909

PWDRO   Plymouth and West Devon Record Office, Unit 3, Clare Place,
           Coxside, Plymouth PL4 0JW Tel: 01792 305940

RIC   Courtney Library, Royal Institution of Cornwall, Royal Cornwall
           Museum, River Street, Truro TR1 2SJ Tel: 01872 272205

WSL   Westcountry Studies Library, as DCRS/WSL, above

C.   **Other local abbreviations**

CFHS   Cornwall Family History Society, 5 Victoria Square, Truro TR1 2RS

Cresswell   see Monumental Inscriptions p.14

DCNQ   *Devon [and Cornwall] Notes and Queries* 1900+

DCRS   Devon and Cornwall Record Society (publications)

DFH   *Devon Family Historian* Journal of DFHS, above

DNQ   *Devon Notes and Queries*

DRMI   see Monumental Inscriptions p.14

Dwelly   see Monumental Inscriptions p.14

Granville   see Bishop's Transcripts p.10

Incledon   see Monumental Inscriptions p.14

SP   Service Point. see p.9

TDA   *Transactions of the Devonshire Association*

Whitmore   see Monumental Inscriptions p.14

B	Burials
Bapt	Baptists (never Baptisms)
Boyd	Marriage index complied by late Percival Boyd (*see* p.12)
Boyd Misc	Boyd's Marriage Index: Miscellaneous Volumes
BT	Bishop's Transcript
c.	*circa*
C	Baptisms; christenings; adult baptisms.
Cem	Cemetery
Ch Sec	Church Secretary (see current yearbook of denomination)
CMI	Catholic Marriage Index
Cong	Congregationalist
Cong Fed	Congregational Federation
Cons.	Consecrated
Cop	Modern copies
CRS	Catholic Record Society publication
Cy	Churchyard
D	Deaths
Extr	Extracts
f	Founded
FFHS	Federation of Family History Societies
FIEC	Fellowship of Independent Evangelical Churches
fl.	Flourished
Gen Bapt	General Baptist
Gent.Mag.	*Gentleman's Magazine*
I	Index(ed)
IGI	The International Genealogical Index (*see* p.11)
Inc	Incumbent (i.e. rector, vicar, parish priest etc)
Ind	Independent (Congregationalist)
Lady Hunt Conn	Countess of Huntingdon's Connexion
LBA	London Baptist Association
M	Marriages
Mf	Microfilm
Mfc	Microfiche
M Lic	Marriage Licences
MM	Monthly Meeting (Society of Friends)
Ms	Manuscript
n.d.	No date
NIPR	National Index of Parish Registers
Nonc	Nonconformist
OR	Original Registers
Part Bapt	Particular Baptist
PCC	Prerogative Court of Canterbury
Phil	Phillimore's printed Marriage Series; with volume number
Pres	Presbyterian
Prim Meth	Primitive Methodist
Ptd	Printed
QM	Quarterly Meeting (Society of Friends)
RC	Roman Catholic
S of F	Society of Friends (Quakers)
Ts	Typescript
U Meth	United Methodist Church
UMFC	United Methodist Free Church
URC	United Reformed Church
VCH	Victoria County History
Wes	Wesleyan Methodist
Z	Births
+	Onwards. Normally, up to the present day

ACKNOWLEDGEMENTS

For the help and advice which have made this volume possible I am most grateful to John Draisey, County Archivist of Devon, to John Brunton, Senior Archivist at Exeter, and Tim Wormleighton, Senior Archivist at Barnstaple; to Ian Maxted, County Studies Librarian at the Westcountry Studies Library; to Paul Brough, City Archivist, and Rachel Bloomfield at Plymouth and West Devon Record Office; to Les Franklin of the North Devon Athenaeum; to Joyce Brown, Local and Naval Studies Librarian, Plymouth Central Library; to Alison Campbell of Cornwall Record Office; to Eileen Wilmot of Devon Family History Society; to Jack Jacobs of the LDS Family History Centre, Ipswich; and to Susan Lumas for information from the Public Record Office.

I am no less indebted to the following incumbents, churchwardens, church secretaries, librarians, curators and others, who have taken the time and trouble to reply to my letters: Roger Adams, Moira Andrews, Linda Ashman, R.W.Bamberg, Geoffrey Bamsey, Paul Barrett, Peter Berry, Bill Blakey, Peter Bottrill, Peter Bowers, Mike Brown, Norman Buckle, Mark Butchers, Roger Carlton, Barry Champion, Elsa Churchill, John Cochrane, Gordon Cooper, S.Dawe, John Doonan, John Edwards, Margaret Foulkes, Colin Furness, Sue Gibbons, Yvonne Gray, Paul Hambling, Michael Hart, Paul Hawkins, Caroline Hayman, A.Howard, Martin Hunnybun, Louis Irwin, Giles King-Smith, Phyllis Langdon, David Lee, Alan Lewin, Geoff Lloyd, C.A.Losey, W.A.McCoubrey, P.J.Milton, Jackie Morten, David Morris, Derek Newport, J.Ottaway, Susan Peters, Philip Ringer, L.D.Roberts, Harold Roche, Derek Sanford, Eric Shapland, Barbara Softly, Andrew Sowden, Victor Standing, Monnica Stevens, John Sweatman, Brian Thayer, Brian Tubbs, Alan Voce, R.Ware, Dame Margaret Wheeler, John Williams, Pru Williams, Nick Woodcock and Timothy Woods.

Cliff Webb, General Editor of this series, has as always given me valuable support.

Anthony Wilcox
Ipswich
July 1999

THE COUNTY OF DEVON

Devon, or Devonshire, lies in the south-west of England. It is bounded on the west by Cornwall, from which it is separated by the River Tamar, on the north and north-west by the Bristol Channel, on the north-east by Somerset, on the east by Dorset, and on the south by the English Channel. It is the third largest ancient county in England, after Yorkshire and Lincolnshire, covering some 2700 square miles, with 300 miles of coastline. Among its most distinctive physical features is Dartmoor, with its granite tors, extensive bogs, and a bleaker climate contrasting with the milder and more relaxing south coast. With Somerset the county shares Exmoor.

The population of the county in 1831 was 493,308; at present it is just over one million, concentrated mainly on the southern coast. The principal towns are Exeter, Plymouth and Torbay, the latter an amalgamation of Torquay, Paignton and Brixham. The city of Exeter, on the river Exe, is the county town, settled by the Romans as Isca Damnoniorum. It was captured in 1068 by William the Conqueror, who erected a castle at Rougemont. The cathedral, as it now stands, was completed around 1400, but there were earlier Saxon and Norman buildings on the site. A number of medieval parish churches still stand.

The city of Plymouth is rich in maritime history. Located in the south-west corner of the county, on the estuaries of the Tamar and the Plym, it benefits from a vast protected anchorage, and from the earliest times has been an important port and naval base. From here Sir Francis Drake, born in Tavistock, set sail on his *Golden Hind* in 1577 to circumnavigate the globe, and in 1588 with Sir John Hawkins, a Plymouth man, he left here to defeat the Spanish Armada. Of other great Elizabethan navigators, Sir Walter Raleigh was born at East Budleigh, and Sir Richard Grenville at Bideford. From Plymouth the Pilgrim Fathers set sail in 1620 on the *Mayflower*, an event with extensive genealogical repercussions. In 1941 much of the old city was destroyed by German bombs, with the loss of many early buildings and some ecclesiastical records, but it has been rebuilt.

Torbay, east-facing on the southern coast, has become known as the English Riviera and is a major holiday centre. Among the historic market towns and boroughs inland are Okehampton and Tiverton, each with the remains of a castle; Tavistock, where once stood an abbey which came into the hands of the Dukes of Bedford; Honiton, celebrated for lace-making; and Totnes, at the highest tidal point on the Dart, whose charter dates from 1205. Princetown, on Dartmoor, is best known for its remote and forbidding prison, first used in the Napoleonic and American wars. On the north coast the ancient boroughs of Bideford and Barnstaple lie near the meeting point of the estuaries of the Taw and Torridge, and Ilfracombe to the north is a seaport and watering place. On the south coast Dartmouth is well known for the Royal Naval College, and Kingsbridge is at the centre of the fertile agricultural area of the South Hams. Brixham is an ancient fishing port and the place where William of Orange landed in 1688. To the north-east of Torbay lie the holiday resorts of Teignmouth, Exmouth and Sidmouth.

Historically the economy of the county depended on fishing, agriculture, the woollen industry, and the extraction of china clay, copper and tin, and the quarrying of granite. In the modern period tourism has also become very important, together with a range of manufacturing and service industries.

ECCLESIASTICAL DIVISIONS

Devon parishes are in the Diocese of Exeter, which, until the formation of the Diocese of Truro in 1876, also included Cornwall as an Archdeaconry. The parishes of St Giles in the Heath, Virginstow and Werrington (the latter transferred to Cornwall in 1966) are in the Truro Diocese. The Diocese of Exeter is now divided into the Archdeaconries of Exeter, Totnes, Barnstaple and Plymouth. There are suffragan bishops of Crediton and Plymouth.

ORIGINAL PARISH REGISTERS

Of the parishes whose original registers are deposited in one of the three record offices, 51 have registers starting in 1538-40. Exceptionally, the parish of Charles has deaths recorded from 1531. Registers of 161 other parishes now start later in the sixteenth century. A further 205 begin in the seventeenth, 38 in the eighteenth, and 83 in the nineteenth.

By the time of the survey of registers of ancient parishes made in connection with the 1831 Census, some from Aveton Gifford, Belstone, High Bickington, Cadbury, Clayhidon, Tamerton Foliot, Woodleigh and West Woolfardisworthy had been lost by fire. After 1831 the same fate befell some registers of Ashbury, Bondleigh, Knowstone and Sidbury. Those of Thorverton were said to have suffered flood damage in 1821, and it was stated that early registers of Aveton Gifford had been 'accidentally burnt', but they are now in the Exeter Record Office, apparently undamaged.

Volumes missing or having lost leaves, since 1831, for the usual reasons including physical decay and simple negligence, include some from Ashcombe, Abbots Bickington, Bickleigh near Tiverton, Bittadon, Bratton Fleming, Bridgerule, Down St Mary, Eggesford, Exbourne, Haccombe, Hollacombe, Kingskerswell, Marwood, West Ogwell, Poltimore, Poughill, East Putford, Salcombe Regis, Sampford Spiney, Stockleigh Pomeroy and Welcombe. Some volumes from Exeter Allhallows Goldsmith Street, St Lawrence, St Martin. St Paul and St Stephen are now unfit for production. Some registers for Clyst St George and Exeter St Martin were destroyed by bombing in the 1940s. Two volumes from Sampford Spiney disappeared in the early years of the 20th century and were believed to have been destroyed, but reappeared eventually in the hands of a bookseller and are now in the Record Office. To a limited extent some of the more recent losses are compensated for by the availability of modern copies.

All deposited registers are available on microfiche at all three record offices. Service Points have been established at various locations in the county, where microfilm or microfiche copies of parish registers for the local area are held, with copies of other parochial records. At present [1999] they are at: North Devon Maritime Museum, Appledore; Local History Centre, Colyton; Museum of Dartmoor Life, Okehampton; Public Library, Tavistock; Tiverton Museum; Local Studies Library, Torquay; and Totnes Museum. The appropriate Service Point for each parish is shown in our lists under the heading **Cop (Mf)**, in the form **(Appledore SP)**. Precise dates of these microform holdings should be obtained from the Record Office or Service Points.

BISHOP'S TRANSCRIPTS

Bishop's transcripts for Devon are held at the Devon Record Office, Exeter, with microfilm copies up to 1812 at Exeter, Barnstaple and Plymouth. They are arranged and filmed by parish. There are BTs for 460 ancient parishes. Of these, only 39 are fully listed to 1812. Of the remaining 421, 158 are listed to 1699-1701, 67 to 1715, and the rest to a variety of dates in the 17th and 18th centuries. This situation is reflected in the present volume by the use of round brackets around the unlisted period. It is believed that most parishes have a more or less complete set from around 1770. BTs antedate surviving registers in no fewer than 226 parishes, but sporadic coverage makes them a less than adequate substitute for the missing years. In the post-1812 period the coverage is more complete, and listing is broken down into baptisms, marriages and burials, but for a few parishes there are no BTs listed. The latest are for Whitestone in 1885 and Topsham in 1887, but in most parishes the series ends considerably earlier.

All years in the 17th century are represented in the collection, except those from 1645 to 1660 inclusive, during the Civil War and Commonwealth period. The earliest in date are 65 returns for 1596 or 1597. There are no pre-1812 BTs listed for the parishes of Templeton, a peculiar of the manor of Templeton. Those for Uffculme, a peculiar of the prebend of Uffculme in Salisbury Cathedral, are at Wiltshire Record Office, but those after 1812 are at Exeter,

Where possible under the BT heading we give full lists rather than terminal dates, to avoid the false impression one might get, for example, at Buckland in the Moor where 1624-1780 would represent 1624, 1634, 1636, 1664, 1750, 1754-80. Terminal dates are given, however, for modern copies of BTs. A few returns are noted in search-room lists as fragmentary, torn, faded or illegible; we give dates, but do not repeat this information here. Some are undated, and are not noted here.

Extracts from early BTs of 37 parishes are included in the following volume, referred to in our parish lists as **Granville**:

R.Granville and W.E.Mugford: *Abstracts of the existing transcripts of the lost Parish Registers of Devon, 1596-1644, and short notes on all the extant pre-restoration registers of all the parishes in the county...*(Vol 1: A-Bra) 1908

Early BTs from one parish were printed in J.Cole *Morchard Bishop, Devon, Bishop's Transcripts 1606-44*: 1995)

PRINTED COPIES

The Devon and Cornwall Record Society has published transcripts of the early registers of Branscombe, Colyton, Exeter (Cathedral, Allhallows, St Pancras, St Paul), Halberton, Hartland, Hemyock, Lapford, Lustleigh, Ottery St Mary, Parkham, Parracombe, Plymouth St Andrew, Plymtree, Topsham (including some nonconformist churches) and Widecombe in the Moor. The Parish Register Society printed those of Clyst St George. Those of Barnstaple, and Huntsham were published privately. Significant parts of those of Churston Ferrers, Membury and Venn Ottery have also appeared in print. Marriages for Countisbury, Ipplepen, Kingskerswell, Martinhoe, Trentishoe, Uffculme, and Werrington were published in Phillimore's Marriage Series.

The Devon Family History Society, in an ongoing programme, has published over 60 parish volumes of Marriage Books for 1813-37, and some 160 Burials Books, mostly for the same dates.

Most printed registers may be found in the Westcountry Studies Library, the library of the Society of Genealogists, and in other libraries elsewhere in the county and outside.

OTHER COPIES

The only ancient parishes for which no complete or partial modern transcript appears to have been made, and for which entries are not extracted onto the International Genealogical Index (see below), are Bittadon, Calverleigh and Chawleigh, though any surviving records of marriages from 1754 to 1837 may be found in the indexes kept by Devon FHS. (see p.12)

The Westcountry Studies Library, Exeter, has numerous modern copies of registers, including those in the collections of the Devon and Cornwall Record Society (see p.5) Many of these are also found in the library of the Society of Genealogists.

Apparently extensive copies for 122 Devon parishes, in 19 manuscript volumes (1-12, 14-20) of transcriptions made by the Rev. Sabine Baring-Gould (1834-1924) and held at Plymouth Central Library, were mostly listed by K.Blomfield and H.K.Percy Smith in *National Index of Parish Register Copies* (Society of Genealogists 1939). The same references also appeared in the first edition of the Society's *Parish Register Copies Part 2: Other than the Society of Genealogists Collection* (1971). A note in the 1974 reprint of the latter work states that these are in fact scanty extracts mainly relating to gentry and clergy. They are listed in the present work, with more detailed dates provided by Plymouth Library, and noted, with the volume number, as **BG/PCL**. They include the following parishes, not listed in the 1974 reprint: Cornwood, Clyst St George, Dittisham, Dunterton, Kenton, Lustleigh, Molland, Ottery St Mary, Poughill, Totnes, Widecombe, Withycombe Raleigh and Uffculme.

THE INTERNATIONAL GENEALOGICAL INDEX

Baptisms and marriages of 425 parish churches and nonconformist chapels in Devon, for various periods, extracted from registers and bishops transcripts, are to be found in the International Genealogical Index of the Genealogical Society of Utah, U.S.A., held on computer and published on microfiche. Since May 1999 the Index may also be searched on the internet at **www.familysearch.org**. Print-outs may also be obtained from family history societies and elsewhere. It should be noted, however, that the IGI has no entries from as many as 222 ancient parishes in Devon, and that, of nonconformist registers held at the Public Record Office, the contents of those of all the Quaker meetings, and of five other chapels in the county, are not included.

This useful but incomplete source of information should be used with caution, and original registers should always be checked. This is particularly the case with the 1992 edition of the IGI. A key to which parishes are represented, and the years covered, is to be found in the Parish and Vital Records List. Instructions for the 1992 IGI contain the note : '*Changes have been made in the way names are added to the International Genealogical Index. As a result, the Parish and Vital Records List does not coordinate with the current [1992] edition of the*

International Genealogical Index exactly as it did in the past, the relationship between the two sources will continue to evolve over the next few years... .You can no longer tell by using the Parish and Vital records List whether a name will be listed in the International Genealogical Index. You must look in the index....the Parish and Vital records Index does not indicate gaps in the records.'

For the purposes of this volume we have used a copy of the PVRL dated July 1998 and have included those entries which are marked with a double asterisk, indicating that *'records in this batch and period are not in the 1988 edition of the IGI'*. It may therefore be safer to take the IGI dates given in this volume as indicating the availability in general of genealogical material from a variety of Mormon sources, accessible through the PVRL, rather than the certain presence of entries in the IGI itself.

Some care should be exercised in interpreting in particular the terminal dates of nineteenth century extracts, and especially those deriving from Nonconformist registers held in the Public Record Office. A recent survey has shown that early printed lists of these registers are inaccurate, and it appears that the terminal dates quoted for IGI extracts were taken from those early lists. The same must apply to details given in this volume for the holdings in the Genealogical Society Library at Salt Lake City, Utah, of microfilmed print-outs of parish indexes derived from the IGI.

For the location of copies of the IGI consult the latest edition of:
J.Gibson and M.Walcot *Where to find the International Genealogical Index* (FFHS, 1985)

The resources of the Family History Library at Salt Lake City are available also to the general public at over 1,600 Family History Centres in 57 countries, where the IGI and microfilm copies of all available records may be ordered and consulted. An appointment should always be made before visiting these centres.

Church of the Latter-Day Saints, Mannamead Road, Hartley, Plymouth
Tel: 01752 668666

MARRIAGE INDEXES

Devon FHS Indexes

Marriages 1754-1812 (as complete as possible) and 1813-37 (complete).

1754-1812: Mr J. Glanville, 3 Highclere Gardens, Widewell, Roborough,
Plymouth PL6 7EA
1813-1837: Mr I. Guthrig, 11 Trelawny Road, Plympton PL7 4LH

A fee is charged.

Boyd   **Boyd's Marriage Index**

Marriages from 170 out of 472 ancient parishes, for various periods, taken mainly from transcripts held by the Devon and Cornwall Record Society, which holds a copy of the index in its collections at the Westcountry Studies Library (see p.5), as does the Society of Genealogists. Covering dates in our parish lists are taken from:
A List of Parishes in Boyd's Marriage Index: Society of Genealogists 1987

Pallot   **Pallot's Marriage Index**

Marriages from 25 Devon parishes, mostly 1790-1812 or 1790-1837. Covering
dates in our parish lists are taken from:
C.Humphery-Smith *The Phillimore Atlas and Index of Parish Registers*
1984 edition.

Institute of Heraldic and Genealogical Studies, Northgate, Canterbury,
Kent CT1 1BA   A fee is charged.

Fursdon Marriage Index

In the DCRS collections at Westcountry Studies Library (see p.5).
25 parishes indexed in 9 volumes. Mainly Exeter area. No postal enquiries.

Dartmoor

Indexes to pre-1754 marriages in 27 Dartmoor parishes, edited by M.Brown,
were published by Dartmoor Press in 14 volumes in 1999.

MARRIAGE LICENCES

Devon Record Office has marriage licence records for the Diocese of Exeter
1523-1837, for which there are 20 volumes of calendars and indexes in the
Devon and Cornwall Record Society archives at the Westcountry Studies
Library in the same building. Copies of these volumes covering 1631 to 1762
are held by the Society of Genealogists. Licence records for parishes which
were Peculiars of the Dean and Chapter of Exeter are at Exeter Cathedral
Library, Diocesan House, Palace Gate, Exeter EX1 1HX.

An index by J.L. Vivian of licences for the years 1523 to 1631 was published
in 1887, with additions for 1598-99 appearing in an article by J.F.Chanter
in DCNQ 10, 1918-19.

PROBATE RECORDS

Until 1857 Devon was under the probate jurisdiction of the Diocese of
Exeter. There were also a number of peculiars subject either to the Bishop
of Exeter or to the Dean and Chapter of Exeter. When a parish did not come
under the diocese, parish entries in the present volume include a note of
the peculiar jurisdiction.

Most of the records of the courts at Exeter were destroyed by enemy action
during the Second World War. A few were edited and published at an earlier
date, and indexes can reveal whether a will was made and proved, even though
the text will not be available. The following volumes may prove useful:

E.A.Fry *Calendars of wills and administrations...Devon and Cornwall, proved
        in the Court of the Principal Registry of the Bishop of Exeter
        1559-1799, and of Devon only, proved in the Court of the Archdeacon
        of Exeter 1540-1799*:   Index Library 35: BRS: 1908

E.A.Fry as above, *Consistory Court of the Bishop of Exeter 1532-1800*:
        Index Library 46: BRS: 1914

H.Tapley-Soper *'Devon and Cornwall wills not in the calendar of wills at the
        Exeter Probate Office'*: DCNQ: 9: 1916-17: pp.57-58

C. Worthy *Devonshire wills: a collection of annotated testamentary abstracts* 1896

M. Cash *Devonshire inventories of the sixteenth and seventeenth centuries*: DCRS New series 2: 1966

P.Wyatt *The Uffculme Wills and Inventories, 16th to 18th centuries*: DCRS: New series 40: 1997

Wiltshire Record office has the probate records for Uffculme 1528-1857. Those from parishes formerly in Cornwall may be found at Cornwall Record Office. Copies of a typescript index of the lost wills and administrations of the Consistory Court of the Archdeacon of Barnstaple 1563-1857 are held at WSL, NDA, Exeter University Library and New York Public Library. Copies of wills from various sources are held at Exeter Record Office, including Estate Duty Office copy wills from all Devon courts 1812-57. The Public Record Office, Kew, has abstracts of wills and administrations 1796-1811 in the Estate Duty Registers. Devon testators of substance may have had their wills proved at the Prerogative Court of Canterbury, 1383-1858, records of which are also held at Kew.

MONUMENTAL INSCRIPTIONS

References to the following sources of monumental inscriptions are given in our parish lists:

DFHS An ongoing alphabetical index of names from about 170 churches and chapels, held for the Devon FHS by:
Miss B.Slocombe, 13 Temple Road, Exeter EX2 4HG
A fee is charged.

DRMI Dartmoor Region Monumental Inscriptions Indexes: in 23 volumes by Mike Brown, publlshed by Dartmoor Press

NDA A card index held by the North Devon Athenaeum, of inscriptions for 54 burial grounds in the north of the county, made in 1986-88. This consists of a surname index with age and date of death, keyed to a separate index with full details of the inscription.

Incledon: Transcriptions of MIs from 128 Devon parishes, made by Benjamin Incledon, Thomas Bremridge and Rev. John Sydenham, 1769-93, held by North Devon Athenaeum, and indexed in
T.Wainwright *An index to the names of persons found in the monumental inscriptions of Devonshire churches, copied in the years 1769-93*: TDA 36 1904

Cresswell B.F.Cresswell *Notes on the Churches of the Deanery of Kenn, Devon*: 1912

Dwelly E.Dwelly *Dwelly's Parish Records* vol.6: 1918

Whitmore J.B.Whitmore *Devonshire Monumental Inscriptions*: Ms at Society of Genealogists: 1951

Other useful publications include:

W.H.Hamilton Rogers *The antient sepulchral efficies and monumental and memorial sculpture of Devon* 1877

W.R.Crabbe   *An account of the monumental brasses remaining in the churches of the county of Devon* 1859

B.F.Cresswell   *Exeter Churches,,,*1908

A.Guy   *An index of brass rubbings in the Westcountry Studies Library:* 1991

M.Brown   *Heraldic and genealogical notes from Dartmoor churches:* 1997

A short collection of epitaphs from Plymouth churchyards: n.d.

OTHER DENOMINATIONS

Major sources of information about the existence of these chapels include Kelly's Directories, various denominational yearbooks, and a return of registered chapels made to Parliament in 1882, hereafter referred to as the 1882 Return. Although every effort has been made to include in the present volume a reference to every church or chapel that has existed in each parish, it is clear that many ephemeral foundations and some existing modern ones have been inadvertently left out.

A total of 167 volumes of earlier registers from 120 chapels and Methodist circuits in Devon (excluding those from Quaker meetings) were surrendered to the Registrar General and are now in the Public Record Office at Kew. Of these the 159 authenticated registers in class RG 4 may also be seen on microfilm at the Family Records Centre and the Westcountry Studies Library, and in most cases are extracted onto the IGI (see p.11). The eight unauthenticated registers in class RG 8 can only be seen at Kew, as can the thirty-three deposited Quaker registers in class RG 6. Early officially published lists of all these registers contain some inaccurate dates and provenances, and for the purposes of this volume corrections, based on a recent PRO survey, have been made, where necessary, to IGI datings, and those of microfilm copies.

Devon Record Office has a large collection of registers and other records of nonconformist churches and chapels in the county, mainly for the period after 1837. In a number of cases early registers, or copies of those in the PRO, are still at the chapel.

Returns made voluntarily at the time of the 1851 Census contain details of churches and chapels. Those for Devon are printed by M.J.L. Wickes in: *Devon in the Religious Census of 1851: a transcript of the Devon section of the 1851 Church Census:* c.1990

In the case of Plymouth, details of registrations of the churches and chapels of the various nonconformist denominations are given in two articles by Edwin Welch in the *Transactions of the Devonshire Association.* The period up to 1852 is covered in volume 94 (1962) and from 1852 to 1939 in volume 99 (1967).

Roman Catholics

From 1688 Catholics in Devon came under the authority of the Vicars Apostolic of the Western District, until 1850 when the diocese of Plymouth was founded, embracing Devon, Cornwall and Dorset. A Return of Papists in 1767 showed that there were only 235 Catholics in Devon. The leading families were the Chichesters of Arlington, the Carys of Cockington and

Torre Abbey, the Cliffords of Ugbrooke and the Rowes of Kingston. They and others supported Mass centres on their estates. The earliest urban missions founded before 1800 (technically not parishes until the early 20th century) were those at Exeter and Plymouth.

Almost all registers are still at the churches. The earliest extant volumes are those of the mission at Ugbrooke, in the parish of Chudleigh, dating from 1736 and printed by the Catholic Record Society in 1925, followed by those of Exeter in 1774, Arlington 1778, Dartmouth 1782, Torre Abbey 1785, and Plymouth 1793.

Michael Gandy   *Catholic Missions and Registers 3: Wales and the West of England*: 1994

George Oliver   *Collections, illustrating the history of the Catholic religion in the counties of Cornwall, Devon, Dorset... etc.*: 1857

Plymouth Diocesan Directory

Journal: *South-Western Catholic History*

Methodists

The immediate impact of John Wesley's visits to Devon was in no way as dramatic as it was in Cornwall, and took effect mainly in the south of the county. The Methodist movement expanded significantly in Devon as a whole in the mid-nineteenth century. The Bible Christians, a distinctively south-western branch of Methodism, were founded in Shebbear in 1815 by a Cornishman, William O'Bryan, born in Luxulyan in 1778. They were also popularly known as Bryanites, Shouters, Trumpeters or Free Willers, and spread rapidly in Devon and Cornwall.

The relative strengths of the branches of Methodism by the later 19th century may be seen in the return to Parliament made in 1882 of registered nonconformist chapels. Of these 191 were Wesleyan and 125 were Bible Christian, while the Primitive Methodists had 22 and the United Methodist Free Church had 8.

The Public Record Office has registers of 22 Wesleyan circuits or chapels, of which the only pre-1800 ones are those of Morrice Street, Devonport, from 1787. There are Bible Christian registers from Shebbear (1818), Ashreigney (1820), Buckfastleigh (1820), Plymouth (1820) and Chagford (1822). There are none for any other branch of Methodism.

The record offices at Exeter, Barnstaple and Plymouth are authorised places of deposit for Devon Methodist records, and have a large collection of registers from all branches of Methodism, the earliest of which is of baptisms in the Ashburton Circuit from 1801. Those for Totnes from 1802, and for Bovey Tracey from 1813, have no equivalent in the Public Record Office. A few chapels near the border with Cornwall were in Launceston circuits, for which registers are held at Cornwall Record Office.

Roger Thorne   *Methodism in Devon - A Handlist of Chapels and their Records* 1983. [in the present volume chapels listed by Thorne are marked *fl c.1970*; many still exist in 1999]

Michael Wickes   *The Westcountry preachers: a new history of the Bible Christian Church (1815-1907)*: 1987

Baptists

The surrendered registers of 19 chapels are held in the Public Record Office. Earliest in date are those of Tiverton (1767), Devonport, Morice Square (1770), Bovey Tracey (1778), Devonport, Liberty Street (1779), Kingsbridge (1785), Exeter (1786), Plymouth, How Street (1786) and Culmstock (1787).

The *Baptist Handbook* for 1861 listed sixty chapels in the county, of which thirty-one belonged to Devon Baptist Association. Those of Bampton, Exeter South Street, Kingsbridge, Plymouth George Street, Tiverton and Upottery dated their erection back to the 17th century. In the 1882 Return seventy-seven chapels were listed.

County record offices have registers of 20 chapels, including for periods before 1837 those of Cullompton, Dartmouth, East Dartmoor, Exeter (Bartholomew Street and South Street), Kilmington, Thorverton and Tiverton.

G.L.W.Beards *A short history of the Devon and Cornwall Baptist Associations* c.1975

Independents, Congregationalists, Presbyterians, Unitarians

The earliest surviving nonconformist registers in the Public Record Office are those of the Presbyterian, later Unitarian churches at Moretonhampstead (from 1672), Plymouth (1672), Exeter, Bow Meeting (1687), Tavistock, Abbey Chapel (1692) and Cullompton (1693). Other registers from churches that later became Unitarian are those of Exeter, Mint (1719), Crediton (1735), Topsham (1744), Sidmouth, Higher Meeting (1753), Colyton (1773) and Woodbury (1773).

Chapels later in the Independent/Congregational tradition are represented at Honiton (1697), Barnstaple (1701), Plymouth, Batter Street (1704), Chudleigh (1711), Dartmouth (1726), Newton Abbot (1726), Ilfracombe (1729), Ottery St Mary (1746), Exmouth (1751), Bideford (1753), Sidbury (1757), South Molton (1758), East Budleigh (1762), Devonport, Princes Street (1763), Tiverton (1766), Stokenham and Chivelstone (1772), Stokenham (1772), Exeter, Combe Street (1775), Kingsbridge (1775), Axminster (1786), Stonehouse, Corpus Christi (1786), Buckfastleigh (1787), Beer (1788), Uffculme (1790), Stonehouse, Emma Place (1794), Totnes (1794), Tavistock (1796), Exeter, Castle Street (1798), Plymouth, Norley Street (1798) and Okehampton (1799).

The *Congregational Yearbook* of 1851 listed ninety-two chapels and mission stations, divided between the North, South and East Devon Congregational Unions. Present-day member-churches of the United Reformed Church claiming descent from seventeenth century foundations include those of Appledore, Axminster, Barnstaple, Braunton, Dartmouth, Ilfracombe, Newton Abbot, Ottery St Mary, Tavistock, Tiverton and Uffculme.

The three Devon record offices hold Unitarian registers from Cullompton, Exeter, Lympstone, Sidmouth, Tavistock and Topsham; and Congregational registers, mainly of later date, from some twenty-eight chapels.

Society of Friends

George Fox was present at a general meeting of Quakers from Devon and Cornwall at Exeter in 1657. Devon Quarterly Meeting was established in 1668. In 1870 it became Devon and Cornwall Quarterly Meeting. Its constituent Monthly Meetings in 1668 were Topsham (later Exeter), Crediton, Sticklepath, Cullompton and Spiceland, Membury, and Plymouth. Kingsbridge MM was established by 1676. Crediton was united with Exeter in 1696. Membury joined Cullompton in 1742, and both were joined to Exeter in 1785.

The Public Record Office holds 33 volumes of surrendered Quaker registers for Devon, but published 19th century listings of these are sometimes less than accurate in describing their provenance and giving their terminal dates. Digests or indexes of the entries in these registers are available on microfilm at Friends House, London and at the Society of Genealogists. Hugh Peskett provides a useful list of meetings and their registers in his *Guide to the parish and non-parochial registers of Devon and Cornwall 1538-1837*: DCRS: 1979.

Devon Record Office at Exeter has a collection of Quaker records including registers for the Eastern Division of the county, including Exeter, Culmstock, Newton Tracey, Spiceland and Topsham.

Huguenots

French and Flemish protestant refugees from religious persecution came to England from the seventeenth century onwards. Some conformed, and were absorbed into the Church of England, and in Devon references to them are found in the parish registers of, for example, Bideford, Barnstaple, Dartmouth, Exeter and Plymouth. French churches were established at Plymouth and Devonport, the registers of which have been printed by the Huguenot Society of London in a volume edited in 1912 by C.E.Lart.

see also: I. Rogers *Huguenots in Devonshire*: 1942

N.Currer-Briggs and R.Gambier *Huguenot Ancestry*: 1998

Moravians

The Moravians, members of a Protestant Episcopal church descended from the Bohemian Brethren of the fifteenth century, came to England in the early eighteenth. John Cennick, a Moravian missionary, preached at Plymouth in 1746. Two foundations were made around 1768, one at the Mitre Inn, Plymouth, which amalgamated in 1805 with the other at Devonport. For the latter, which from 1771 to 1916 was at James Street, the Public Record Office has a register of births and baptisms 1785-1834, duplicated and continued by volumes to 1914 held in the archives at Moravian Church House, 5 Muswell Hill, London N10 3TJ.

Brethren

The Brethren originated in Ireland among Anglicans who rejected sectarianism and a separate paid ministry. J.N.Darby, their founder, came from Dublin to Plymouth in 1830, and the sect became known as the Plymouth Brethren because of this local association. The first meeting was founded at Raleigh Street in 1831. In the 1840s they split into 'exclusive' and 'open' brethren. The movement still survives, but its history and records are difficult to trace.

Jews

Ashkenazi Jews from Germany and Central Europe came to Devon in the early 18th century. The synagogue at Plymouth was erected in 1762 and that at Exeter in 1763. For Exeter, see their web-site: www.eclipse.co.uk/exeshul/

see B.Susser *The Jews of South-West England*: 1993
     D.Black   *The Plymouth Synagogue 1761-1861*:1961
'The Plymouth Aliens List 1798 and 1803' *Proc. Jewish Hist Soc of England* 6.

CENSUSES

The earliest local census for Devon, with parishioners names, is an incomplete record for Sowton, 1696, in Devon Record Office. The British Library has a list for Buckfastleigh and Ringmore, with names and ages, for 1698. Devon Record Office has late eighteenth and early nineteenth century returns, with names, for Wembworthy (1779), Sandford (1790, 1793, 1800), Bickleigh near Tiverton (1801), Exeter St Mary Steps, and St Paul (1803), Doddiscombeleigh (1811), Clyst St George (1821) and Sidbury (1829), as well as lists of householders' names with household numbers for Ottery St Mary (c.1700), Sandford (1776, 1783), Axminster, Dean Prior, Exeter Holy Trinity and Rewe (1821). North Devon Record Office has returns for Mortehoe (1801), Barnstaple (1803) and Fremington (1821). All the adult men of Tavistock are named in a document of c.1760 at Devon Record Office. Both offices have later lists.

J.Gibson, M. Medlycott *Local Census Listings 1522-1930*: FFHS: 3rd edit.1997

The original Census returns for 1841 to 1891, for the whole country, may be seen on microfilm at the Family Records Centre, London, and those for Devon, and some border parishes in neighbouring counties, at the Westcountry Studies Library. The libraries at Plymouth, Torquay, Barnstaple and Exmouth have them for their local registration districts.

For computer users an index to the 1851 Census for Devon (with Norfolk and Warwickshire), and the complete 1881 Census for Great Britain, may be purchased on CD-ROM from the Church of Jesus Christ of Latter-Day Saints, or may be seen at their Family History Centres. Print-outs from the 1851 and 1881 censuses may be obtained through Devon FHS and other county societies. Indexes to parishes in the 1851 Census have been published by Devon FHS.

J.Gibson, C.Rogers *Marriage, Census and other Indexes for family historians:* FFHS: 6th edit. 1996

NEWSPAPERS

Files of the *Western Flying Post* are available at the British Library, Colindale, and at the Westcountry Studies Library from pre-1750 to 1867. This circulated in all the south-western counties. The *Exeter Flying Post* from 1768 is held at the Westcountry Studies Library, and from 1807 at the British Library. Devon Record Office has an index of personal names in this paper, 1763-1835. Full details of these and many other publications are contained in: Jeremy Gibson: *Local Newspapers 1750-1920:* FFHS 1987

Devon Library and Information Services issue a comprehensive list (L 15) of newspapers in local studies collections in the county. This is also available on their web-site: www.devon-cc.gov.uk

see also:

Bibliography of British Newspapers: Devon; county editor: Ian Maxted; British Library, c.1991

Lorna Smith   *Devon Newspapers: A Finding List:* Standing Conference on Devon History: 1973, revised 1975.

DIRECTORIES

Kelly's Directories for the Devon were published in 1856, 1866, 1873, 1883, 1889, 1893, 1897, 1902, 1906, 1910, 1914, 1919, 1923, 1926, 1930, 1935, and 1939. *Pigot's Directory* appeared earlier, in 1823-24, 1830 and 1844. Pigot's 1830 directory may be purchased on microfiche from the Society of Genealogists.

Trewman's directory for Exeter is available at the Westcountry Studies Library for a variety of different years betwen 1788 and 1857, and Besley's for the same city from 1828 to 1955. For Plymouth the Westcountry Studies Library and Plymouth Central Library have directories issued by several publishers, from 1795 to 1967. Devon Library and Information Services issue a comprehensive list (L 14) of directories in local studies collections in the county, either in hard copy on on microfilm, up to about 1975. This is also available on their web-site, as above. A published *Handlist of local directories in Devon libraries* may also be purchased from the Westcountry Studies Library or Exeter Central Library.

J.E.Norton   *Guide to the National and Provincial Directories of England and Wales...before 1856*:   Royal Historical Society: 1950

G.Shaw and A.Tipper   *British Directories 1850-1950*:   1988

L.W.L.Edwards   *Directories and Poll Books in the Library of the Society of Genealogists* 1989

POLL BOOKS AND ELECTORAL REGISTERS

The earliest extant county poll book, for 1712, was published in the *Transactions of the Devonshire Association*, vol.106: 1974. Others are in Devon Record Office, dating from 1790 to 1830. A variety of books for Plymouth, Exeter and Barnstaple are held at the local record offices. A few exist for the 18th century, but most are for the first half of the 19th. Guildhall Library, London, has a copy of a book for Honiton, 1763. The Bodleian Library has one for Okehampton, 1802. The Institute of Historical Research, in London, has a small collection for Totnes, 1812-65.

An incomplete series of electoral registers for the county is held at the Exeter record office for 1832-1915, 1918-39 and 1945 onwards. A series for 1832-95 is on microfilm at the Barnstaple record office. At Plymouth the earliest surviving registers are from 1885, but most are of the 20th century. These offices and some libraries in the county have collections of local registers relating mainly to the 20th century. Burgess rolls for Barnstaple in 1639, 1674-75, 1729, 1758 and later are held at Barnstaple record office.

see also J.Gibson and C.Rogers *Poll Books c.1696-1872*: FFHS: 3rd edit: 1994
Electoral Registers since 1932: FFHS: 1989

MILITARY AND NAVAL HISTORY

A military survey of the City of Exeter in 1522, containing 1363 names, was published in *Tudor Exeter: Tax Assessments 1489-1595*, edited by Margery Rowe: DCRS: NS 22: 1977. Early county muster rolls, with 15,000 names by hundred and parish, were printed in A.J.Howard and T.L.Stoate's *Devon Muster Rolls for 1569*: 1977. The Public Record Office and Devon Record Office have other muster rolls from Tudor times and later.

J.Gibson and A.Dell *Tudor and Stuart Muster Rolls*: FFHS: 1989

Devon Record Office at Exeter has militia muster rolls for Exeter from 1758-76 and later; for Barnstaple in 1792, for Cullompton 1797-1804; and for the county 1808-73. It also holds other local militia records. North Devon Record Office has ballot lists for Barnstaple and Pilton 1791, and provisional cavalry levy lists for the Hundreds of Fremington, Hartland and Shebbear, 1797. The Public Record Office at Kew has various militia returns for the county, dating from 1780 to 1876. A *levée en masse* list for the City of Exeter was published in: W.G.Hoskins edit. *Exeter Militia List 1803*: 1972

J. Gibson and M. Medlycott *Militia Lista and Musters 1757-1857*: FFHS: 1994

J.D.C.Sullock *Militia of the South Hams* Parts 1-3: *c.*1993

J.D.C.Sullock *Militia of Roborough Hundred 1569*: 1996

There is a Royal Devon Yeomanry Museum at the Museum of North Devon, The Square, Barnstaple.

The Devonshire Regiment took its origins in the 11th of Foot raised as The Duke of Beaufort's Regiment on 16 June 1685 to fight in The Duke of Monmouth's rebellion. The 11th were first officially referred to as The Devons on 2 April 1786. Later they became the 11th (North Devon) Regiment of Foot and finally The Devonshire Regiment. Their battle honours include Dettingen (in Flanders) 1743; Salamanca 1812, after which they were nicknamed 'The Bloody Eleventh'; Wagon Hill, in Ladysmith, South Africa, 1900; and Bois des Buttes in 1918, where the battalion was virtually wiped out, losing nearly 550 officers and men. In 1958 they amalgamated with the Dorsetshire Regiment to become The 1st Battalion The Devonshire and Dorset Regiment. The regimental headquarters is at Wyvern Barracks, Exeter. The Military Museum of Devon and Dorset is at The Keep Museum, Bridport Road, Dorchester, Dorset.

The Bloody Eleventh: history of the Devonshire Regiment vol.1 1685-1815 R.E.R.Robinson; vol.2 1815-1914 and vol.3 1914-1969 W.J.P. Aggett

J.Taylor *The Devons... the Devonshire regiment 1685-1945:* 1951

Soldiers Died in the Great War 1914-19. Part 16 *The Devonshire Regiment* 1989

S.Fowler *Army Records for Family Historians*: PRO: 1992

Casualties in the First World War who were buried in Devon cemeteries and churchyards are listed in two volumes published by the Imperial War Graves Commission in 1924 and 1930. The first lists those buried in Plymouth Old Cemetery, and Efford and Weston Mill cemeteries; the second those in other places in Devon. Those who died in the Second World War and are buried in Devon are listed in two volumes published by the Commonwealth War Graves Commission in 1960. Names, places of burial and some other details of 1.7

million members of the Commonwealth forces who died in both wars, and some civilian casualties, may also be found on the Roll of Honour Register on the Commission's web-site: www.cwgc.org.

The Royal Naval War Memorial at Plymouth, like identical memorials at Chatham and Portsmouth, bears the names of 23,191 sailors for whom this was the home port, who died in the two World Wars, but who had no known graves. Also included for 1914-18 were sailors from Australia and South Africa, and for 1939-45 were added those from other parts of the Commonwealth. Their names may also be seen in registers kept at Plymouth Central Library and at the local Tourist Information Office.

For service records of officers and ratings in the Royal Navy, held at the Public Record Office, see:

N.A.M.Rodger *Naval Records for Genealogists*: PRO: 1988, revised 1998

Registers for Royal Navy and Royal Air Force chaplaincies in Devon are held by the Ministry of Defence, the Armed Forces Chaplaincy Centre and the Roman Catholic Records Office (see p.4).

For a description of records of mariners in the merchant service, including a section on births, marriages and deaths at sea, see:

K.Smith, C.Watts and T.Watts *Records of Merchant Shipping and Seamen* Public Record Office 1998

The record offices in Devon have a range of sources for maritime history. A summary list is available. Crew lists for Devon ports, 1863-1914, are held at Exeter.

SELECTIVE BIBLIOGRAPHY

Stuart Raymond *Devon: a genealogical bibliography*: 2nd edit. 1994

W.G.Hoskins *Devon*: 1954; new edition 1972. A history of the county, with short descriptive accounts of each parish, and a comprehensive bibliography including parish histories

Ian Maxted *In pursuit of Devon's history*: 1997

Michael Duffy edit. *The new maritime history of Devon*: 2 vols 1992-1994

Abbots Bickington to Zeal Monachorum: a handlist of Devon parish histories: Devon County Council Libraries, 1994

Library Listing and Tree House Resources - a guide to the books, documents and microfiche: Devon FHS: 1998

Mike Brown *The Devon Family History Researchers' Essential Mini-Guide to Dartmoor Region MIs, Surname Distributions and Parish registers etc* Revised edition 1997

Devon Family Historian: published quarterly: Devon FHS; 1977+

Exeter Diocesan Directory: published annually

N.Pevsner and B.Cherry *Devon*: Buildings of England: 2nd edit 1989

The Devon Village Book: Devon Federation of Women's Institutes: 1990

Sabine Baring-Gould *Devonshire*: The Little Guides 1907; 10th edit. revised H.R.Hicks 1949

A.Grigg   *Place Names in Devon and Cornwall*: 1988

David Postles *The surnames of Devon*: English Surnames Series: 1995

Crispin Gill   *Plymouth - A New History*: 2nd edit 1979

Brian Little   *Portrait of Exeter*: 1983

J.C.Trewin   *Portrait of Plymouth*: 1973

Vian Smith   *Portrait of Dartmoor*: 1969

        The following are published by Phillimore:

Robin Staines *A History of Devon*: Darwen County Histories: 1985

Hazel Harvey   *Exeter Past*: 1996

W.G.Hoskins   *Two Thousand Years in Exeter*: 1979

Hugh Meller   *Exeter Architecture*: 1989

John Whitham   *Ottery St Mary - A Devonshire Town*: 1984

Ann Born   *The Torbay Towns*: 1989

Guy Fleming   *Plymouth: A Pictorial History*: 1995

Duncan Fielder *A History of Bideford*: 1985

Mary de la Mahotière *Tiverton - A Pictorial History*: 1990

USEFUL WEB SITES

Devon Family History Society   **www.devonfhs.org.uk**

Devon Record Office   **www.devon-cc.gov.uk/dro/homepage.html**

Public Record Office, Kew   **www.pro.gov.uk**

Society of Genealogists, London   **www.sog.org.uk**

Genuki   **www.genuki.org.uk**
A useful all-purpose genealogical site for the United Kingdom, providing a great deal of national and local research information, with a link to Devon, including a gazetteer of place names in the county.

Devon Library and Information Services   **www.devon-cc.gov.uk**
A gazetteer, bibilographical information, and a variety of lists and information sheets of use to genealogists and local historians.

PARISH LISTS

For the purposes of this volume, modern parishes and chapelries founded in the nineteenth century are grouped with the mother parish from which they were formed. Ancient chapelries with registers before the mid-eighteenth century are treated as separate parishes, even if they did not in fact gain independence from the mother-parish until after 1800.

Parishes and their ancient chapelries are cross-referred. The figure in square brackets at the head of each parish is its population in 1831.

ABBOTS BICKINGTON *see* BICKINGTON, ABBOTS

ABBOTSBURY *see* NEWTON ABBOT

ABBOTSHAM St Helen [Shebbear Hundred; Bideford Union] [387]
Now with HARTLAND COAST
OR C 1653-1878 M 1653-1939 B 1653-1920 (NDRO)
BT CMB 1597-1602, 1607, 1610, 1614-16, 1617, 1630-31, 1636, 1668, 1670,
    1672, 1674, 1678-79, 1682-83, 1685, 1688-91, 1694-97, 1699-1700,
    1702-05, 1707-12, 1714-15, 1725-27, 1732-37, 1739, 1741-43, 1745,
    1747-51, 1754, 1756, 1762, 1754-65, 1767, 1768-75 (1776-1812 ?)
Cop CMB 1597-1602, 1607-36 from BT (Ptd Granville); B 1813-37 (Ptd DFHS);
    CMB 1597-1636 from BT, 1653-1812 (DCRS/WSL); Extr CMB 1597-1637 (SG);
    B 1813-37 (WSL,SG); M 1597-1636 from BT (Boyd)
Cop (Mf) (Appledore SP); Extr C 1598-1636, 1653-1875 M 1597-1875 (IGI);
    C 1598-1636, 1653-1875 M 1597-1875 (Mf I SLC)
MI (I, NDA); Incledon 721 (NDA)

ABBOTSHAM (Bapt) Rehoboth [1882 Return] Greencliff Road f 1852

ABBOTSHAM (Wes)
OR for *c.* 1807-37 *see* BARNSTAPLE CIRCUIT (RG 4/954 PRO) and BIDEFORD
    (RG 4/955 PRO)

ABBOTSKERSWELL Blessed Virgin Mary [Haytor Hundred; Newton Abbot Union]
[442]
OR C 1607-1876 M 1607-1842 B 1607-1919 ((DRO)
BT CMB 1606, 1610-11, 1614-15, 1617, 1619, 1629-30, 1632, 1634-35, 1663-64,
    1669-72, 1675-79, 1681, 1688, 1697, 1699-1700 (1701-1812 ?)
Cop B 1813-37 (Ptd DFHS); CMB 1607-1837 (DCRS/WSL); M 1607-43 (C of A);
    B 1813-37 (WSL, SG); Extr C 1613-1701 M 1718 B 1608-1740 (Vol 19,
    BG/PCL)
Cop (Mf) (Torquay SP); Extr C 1607-1837 M 1607-79, 1699-1837 (IGI);
    C 1607-1837 M 1607-79, 1699-1837 (Mf I SLC)
MI Extr (Whitmore MS, SG)

ABBOTSKERSWELL (RC) St Augustine's Priory 1863. Canonesses of St Augustine
MI (I, DFHS)

ABBOTSKERSWELL (Wes) A house [1851 Religious Census] [1882 Return]
OR for c.1811-37 see BRIXHAM CIRCUIT, TEIGNMOUTH (RG 4/842,1220 PRO)

ABBOTSKERSWELL (S of F) fl c.1764. Burial ground. Part of EXETER MM

ALFINGTON see OTTERY ST MARY

ALLERBRIDGE see COLDRIDGE

ALLINGTON, EAST or NORTH ALLINGTON St Andrew [Stanborough Hundred;
Kingsbridge Union] [677] Now with MODBURY
OR C 1554-1852 M 1555-1968 B 1554-1890 (DRO)
BT CMB 1608-09, 1614-15, 1617, 1622, 1628, 1641, 1664, 1666, 1668-69,
1671-82, 1686-90, 1695-97, 1700 (1701-1812 ?)
Cop M 1837-1968 with index (PWDRO); Extr C 1557-1764 M 1561-1764 B 1562-1789
(Vol 15, BG/PCL)
MI (Ptd A.Lancefield 'Some notes on the brasses, heraldry and monuments in
East Allington church': DNQ 2: 1902-3: 97-105)

ALLINGTON, EAST (Ind) East Allington Chapel [1882 Return]

ALLINGTON, EAST (Wes) f 1850 [1851 Religious Census]
OR for c.1813-37 see KINGSBRIDGE (RG 4/1088 PRO)

ALLINGTON, EAST (Prim Meth) Erected 1865. fl c.1970
OR C 1861 (DRO)

ALMINSTONE see WOOLFARDISWORTHY, WEST

ALPHINGTON St Michael and All Angels [Wonford Hundred; St Thomas Union]
[1236]
OR C 1603-1977 M 1603-1994 B 1603-1986 (DRO)
BT CMB 1606, 1609, 1626, 1634-36, 1638, 1644, 1664?, 1668-70, 1672-75,
1678-79, 1683, 1687, 1690, 1695-97, 1699-1837 (DRO)
Cop CMB 1603-1837 with index (DCRS/WSL); M 1603-1837 (Boyd)
Cop (Mf) Extr C 1603-1837 M 1603-43, 1657-1837 (IGI); C 1603-1837 (Mf I SLC)
MI (I, DFHS); Ch extr (Ptd Cresswell 15-17)

ALPHINGTON (Wes) Chapel Lane. Rebuilt 1895. fl c.1970
OR for c.1818-37 see EXETER Mint (RG 4/1207, 1208 PRO)

ALSCOTT see ALVERDISCOTT

ALSWEAR see MARIANSLEIGH

ALVERDISCOTT All Saints [Fremington Hundred; Torrington Union] [339]
Now with TWO RIVERS
OR C 1602-1998 M 1602-1978 B 1602-1989 (NDRO)
Noted in 1831: gap CMB 1615-26
BT CMB 1607-08, 1614, 1617, 1624, 1630, 1632, 1634-35, 1641, 1668, 1672-74,
1679, 1682-83, 1685, 1689-91, 1694-95, 1697, 1699-1700, 1702-04,
1708-12, 1714-19, 1723, 1725, 1727-28, 1730, 1732-35, 1737, 1739-40
(1741-1812 ?)

ALVERDISCOTT *cont.*
Cop CMB 1617, 1674 from BT (Ptd Granville); CMB 1617-18, 1624 (SG);
    C 1602-49, 1653-60 M 1602-60 B 1609-59 (DLS)
Cop (Mf) (Appledore SP); C 1602-1896 M 1602-1837 B 1602-1812 (Mfc SG)
MI (I, NDA); Incledon 844 (NDA)

ALVERDISCOTT (Wes) Stoney Cross. Erected 1833 [1851 Religious Census]
[1882 Return] New chapel 1909. fl *c.*1970
OR for *c.*1819-37 *see* BIDEFORD (RG 4/955 PRO)

ALVINGTON, WEST All Saints [Stanborough Hundred; Kingsbridge Union] [872]
see also chapelries of MALBOROUGH, SOUTH MILTON, SOUTH HUISH. Now with
MALBOROUGH, SOUTH HUISH, CHURCHSTOW
OR C 1558-1853 M 1558-1990 B 1558-1943 (DRO)
BT CMB 1602, 1605-06, 1610, 1614-15, 1620, 1624, 1628, 1663, 1666, 1668-69,
    1671, 1675-77, 1678-81, 1682?, 1686-88, 1695, 1697, 1699 (1700-1812 ?)
Cop CMB 1628 from BT (Ptd Granville); CMB 1628 (SG); M 1627-28 from BT
    (Boyd); Extr C 1559-1655, 1663-1771 Z 1656-62 M 1559-1749 B 1564-1807
    (Vol 15, BG/PCL)
Cop (Mf) C 1558-1853 M 1558-1947 B 1558-1943 (Mfc SG)
MI (I, DFHS)

ALVINGTON, WEST Bowringsleigh House. Home of Ilbert family from 17th cent.
Private chapel.

ALVINGTON, WEST (Wes)
OR for *c.*1813-37 *see* KINGSBRIDGE Ebenezer (RG 4/1088 PRO)

ALVINGTON, WEST (S of F) Woolston. Home of Pollexfen family. fl 1659 to
late-18th cent. Part of KINGSBRIDGE MM
OR Z 1655-1813 M 1659-1815 B 1661-1824 (RG 6/1596 PRO)

ALVINGTON, WEST (Free Grace Gospel Christians) The Refuge [1882 Return]

ALVINGTON, WEST (Calv) Trinity Chapel. Erected 1847 [1851 Religious Census];
Refuge Chapel [1882 Return]

ALWINGTON St Andrew [Shebbear Hundred; Bideford Union] [486]
Now with HARTLAND COAST
OR C 1550-1903 M 1553-1978 B 1549-1970 (NDRO)
BT CMB 1597-1602, 1607, 1614, 1624, 1628, 1630-31, 1634, 1668, 1670, 1672,
    1674, 1678-79, 1682-83, 1688-91, 1694-97, 1699-1700, 1702, 1704,
    1706-97, 1709-1712, 1714-15, 1741, 1751 (1752-1812 ?)
Cop CMB 1628-31 from BT (Ptd Granville); CMB 1550-1812 (DCRS/WSL);
    CMB 1596-1644 (Great Card Index, SG); Extr C 1578-1799 M 1586-1753
    B 1551-1796 (SG); M 1555-1812 (Boyd)
Cop (Mf) (Appledore SP); Extr C 1550-1812 M 1554-1812 (IGI); C 1550-1812
    M 1554-1812 (Mf I SLC)
MI (I, NDA); (Ptd A Messenger '*Heraldry in Alwington church*': DCNQ 20:
    1938-39: 324-27); Incledon 202 (NDA)

ALWINGTON (Wes) Ford Hamlet. Erected *c.*1831 [1851 Religious Census] Rebuilt
1897 fl *c.*1970
OR for *c.*1807-37 *see* BARNSTAPLE CIRCUIT (RG 4/954 PRO) and BIDEFORD
    (RG 4/955 PRO)

ALWINGTON (Wes) Ford [1882 Return]

ALWORTHY   *see* BRADWORTHY

ANSTEY, EAST or **ANSTEY CRUWYS** St Michael [South Molton Hundred; South Molton Union] [166] Rebuilt 1870. Now with OAKMOOR
OR C 1596-1650, 1688-1947 M 1596-1989 B 1596-1812 (NDRO) Noted in 1831:
     M gap 1680-92
BT CMB 1607, 1610, 1614, 1617, 1624, 1633, 1668, 1670, 1672, 1674, 1678-79,
     1682, 1694-97, 1699, 1705-06, 1708, 1712, 1714-15 (1716-1812 ?);
     C 1813-14, 1822-24, 1828, 1830, 1832, 1834, 1836-40 M 1813-14, 1823-24,
     1830, 1834, 1836-38 B 1813-14, 1823-24, 1830, 1834, 1836-37, 1839-40
     (DRO)
Cop M 1607-33 from BT (Ptd Granville); CMB 1610 (SG); CMB 1607-82 from BT,
     1596-1812 (DCRS/WSL); M 1610-1812 (Boyd)
Cop (Mf) Extr C 1596-1812 M 1610, 1668-1812 (IGI); C 1596-1812 (Mf I SLC)
MI (I, NDA)

ANSTEY, WEST St Petrock [South Molton Hundred; South Molton Union] [226]
Now with OAKMOOR
OR C 1653-1982 M 1654-1988 B 1653-1987 (NDRO)
BT CMB 1608, 1614, 1623, 1629, 1631, 1635, 1668, 1670, 1672, 1674, 1679-80,
     1683, 1685, 1688-89, 1712, 1714-15 (1716-1812 ?); CMB 1838-39 (DRO)
Cop CMB 1608-35 from BT, 1653-1812 (DCRS/WSL); Extr CMB 1608-36 (SG);
     M 1608-1812 (Boyd)
Cop (Mf) Extr C 1608-1812 M 1608-31, 1654-1809 (IGI); C 1608-1812 M 1608-31,
     1654-1809 (Mf I SLC)
MI (I, NDA)

ANSTEY, WEST (Wes) [1882 Return]

ANVIL CORNER   *see* HOLSWORTHY

APPLEDORE   *see* NORTHAM

APPLEDORE   *see* BURLESCOMBE

ARLINGTON St James [Shirwell Hundred; Barnstaple Union] [235] Rebuilt 1846.
United 1944 with EAST DOWN. Now with SHIRWELL
OR C 1640-1994 M 1671-1944 B 1598-1996 (NDRO)
BT C 1640 M 1671 B 1598 CMB 1597-1602, 1607, 1610-11, 1616?, 1619, 1626,
     1631, 1636, 1638, 1641, 1668, 1670-72?, 1674, 1678-79, 1682, 1690-91,
     1694, 1696-97, 1700, 1702-03, 1712, 1714-15 (1716-1812 ?); C 1813-26,
     1830, 1833-34 M 1813-15, 1820-24, 1833 B 1814, 1817, 1819-24, 1826,
     1833-35 (DRO)
Cop B 1813-37 (Ptd DFHS); C 1640-1849 M 1671-1850 B 1598-1850 (I, NDA);
     CMB 1598-1850 (DCRS/WSL); CMB 1596-1644 (SG); B 1814-37 (SG);
     M 1597-1638 from BT (Boyd)
Cop (Mf) Extr C 1640-1849 M 1671-1850 (IGI); C 1640-1849 M 1671-1850
     (Mf I SLC)
MI (I, DFHS); Incledon 172 (NDA)

ARLINGTON (RC) Domestic chapel of Chichester family, f by 1730. Closed 1795,
succeeded by CALVERLEIGH
OR B 1778+ M 1766+ Confirmations 1793+ (Plymouth Diocesan Archives)
     Earliest register at Sacred Heart, Exeter, includes entries 'copied from
     Arlington register'

ASH MILL   *see* ROSE ASH

ASH THOMAS   *see* HALBERTON

ASHBURTON St Andrew [Teignbridge Hundred; Newton Abbot Union] [4165]
see also chapelries of BUCKLAND IN THE MOOR and BICKINGTON, with which it is
now united
OR C 1603-1948 M 1603-1966 B 1603-1950 (DRO)
BT CMB 1608-09, 1614, 1616, 1622, 1624, 1633, 1636 (1637-1812 ?);
    CMB 1813-21, 1823-25, 1827, 1830, 1832, 1837-41, 1843, 1845, 1850,
    1861-64, 1868-71 M 1813-21, 1823-25, 1827, 1830, 1832, 1837 M 1813-21,
    1823-25, 1827, 1830-32, 1837-46 (DRO)
Cop B 1813-37 (Ptd DFHS); CMB 1603-1837 (DCRS/WSL); B 1813-37 (SG);
    M 1603-1837 (Boyd); Extr C 1603-1736 M 1604-1743 B 1603-1728 (Vol 16,
    BG/PCL)
Cop (Mf) (Totnes SP); Extr CM 1603-1837 (IGI); CM 1603-1837 (Mf I SLC)
MI (I, DFHS); Extr (Whitmore MS, SG)

ASHBURTON St Laurence Chapel. Later used as grammar school

ASHBURTON (RC) Our Lady of Lourdes and St Patrick, East Street 1912

ASHBURTON (Bapt) f 1798. Erected 1800. New chapel purchased from Wes 1837
[1851 Religious Census] [*Baptist Handbook* 1861]

ASHBURTON (Bapt) Zion erected 1827 [1851 Religious Census]

ASHBURTON (Presb/Ind/Cong) Great Meeting fl 1665-1946. Erected 1739 ?
[1851 Religious Census] A building in front of the Independent Chapel, North
Street [1882 Return]
OR ZC 1817-37 (RG 4/951 PRO); C 1777-1881, 1910-24, 1940-78 M 1909-69
    B 1911-23, 1949-62 (DRO) For 1693-98 *see* CULLOMPTON.
Cop ZC 1817-37 (SG)
Cop (Mf) ZC 1817-37 (Mf DCRS/WSL, SG); Extr ZC 1817-37 (IGI); ZC 1817-37
    (Mf I SLC)

ASHBURTON (Wes) Circuit
OR C 1801-36 (RG 4/840,1763 PRO); C 1801-1980 (DRO) *see also* TOTNES -
    ASHBURTON Circuit
Cop C 1801-36 (SG)
Cop (Mf) C 1801-36 (Mf DCRS/WSL, SG); Extr C 1801-36 (IGI); C 1801-36
    (Mf I SLC)

ASHBURTON (Wes) West Street. Erected 1835 [1882 Return] fl *c.*1970

ASHBURTON (S of F) fl *c.*1773

ASHBURY St Mary [Black Torrington Hundred; Okehampton Union] [74] In grounds
of Ashbury House, home of Woollacombe family. Rebuilt 1872-73. Now redundant
OR None deposited. Said to have been destroyed by fire at Ashbury House in
    1877. Noted in 1831: CMB 1615-1812; *see* copies below
BT CMB 1610, 1613-14, 1629, 1635, 1663-64, 1670-72, 1674-82, 1685-88, 1695,
    1699, 1713 (1714-1812 ?); C 1838-44 B 1838-40, 1842-44 (DRO)
Cop CMB 1610-35 from BT (Ptd Granville); CMB 1610-35 (Great Card Index and
    Ts, SG); M 1610-13 from BT (Boyd)
Cop (Mf) (Okehampton SP)

ASHCOMBE St Nectan [Exminster Hundred; St Thomas Union] [320]
Now with HALDON
OR CB 1732-1992 M 1732-1991 (DRO) Noted in 1831: CMB 1583-1653, 1661-1812
    in three volumes. Missing since 1932 or earlier ? *see* copies below
BT CMB 1609, 1620, 1624, 1633-36, 16??. 1663-64, 1668-72, 1675, 1677-79,
    1683, 1687, 1690, 1695-97 (1698-1812 ?); CMB 1813-14, 1819-20, 1831-32
    C 1837-65 B 1837-47, 1849-65 (DRO)
Cop CMB 1609-36 from BT (Ptd Granville); C 1581-1640, 1653-1837 M 1581-1638,
    1654-1837 B 1581-1640, 1651-52, 1655-1837, with MIs: transcribed
    pre-1932, 3 copies only (Ts DCRS/WSL, SG, Inc); M 1633-36 from BT
    (Boyd); M 1790-1837 (Pallot)
Cop (Mf) Extr C 1562, 1581-1836 M 1583-1836 (IGI); C 1562, 1581-1836
    M 1583-1836 (Mf I SLC)
MI (I, DFHS); Ch extr (Ptd Cresswell 20); ch cy (Ts SG)

ASHFORD St Peter [Braunton Hundred; Barnstaple Union] [99] Rebuilt 1854.
United 1945 with PILTON . Now with BARNSTAPLE
OR C 1701-77, 1813-1964 M 1701-1943 B 1701-1966 (NDRO)
BT CMB 1596-1601, 1607-08, 1610, 1612, 1614, 1630-31, 1640, 1668, 1670,
    1672, 1674, 1679, 1682-83, 1688-91, 1694-97, 1700, 1702-04, 1712,
    1714-15 [film covers 1678-79, 1743-44 only. 1744 missing] (1743-1812 ?);
    CB 1842 (DRO)
Cop CMB 1596-1640 from BT (Ptd Granville); CMB 1597-1812 from BT, 1774-1966
    (DCRS/WSL); CMB 1596-1640 (Great Card Index, SG); C 1596-1641, 1813-1964
    M 1597-1640, 1774-1964 B 1597-1641, 1813-1966 (SG); M 1597-1640 from BT
    (Boyd)
Cop (Mf) Extr C 1813-1964 M 1774-1875 (IGI); C 1813-75 M 1774-1875
    (Mf I SLC)
MI (I, NDA); (Ptd A.Shilling *St Peter's, Ashford, Monumental Inscriptions*:
    1993); Incledon 463 (NDA)

ASHFORD (Bapt) Erected 1835 [1851 Religious Census]

ASHFORD (Wes)
OR for *c.*1807-37 *see* BARNSTAPLE CIRCUIT (RG 4/954 PRO) and LANDKEY
    (RG 4/1213 PRO)

ASHILL   *see* UFFCULME

ASHPRINGTON St David [Coleridge Hundred; Totnes Union] [549]
Now with CORNWORTHY, DITTISHAM
OR C 1607-1940 M 1607-1856 B 1607-1908 (DRO)
BT CMB 1597-1602, 1608-10, 1612, 1614-15, 1620, 1623-24, 1626-27, 1663,
    1666, 1670-72, 1674, 1676-81, 1684, 1686-90, 1696, 1697, 1700, 1750-80
    (1781-1812 ?); CB 1813-41 M 1813-33, 1835-41 (DRO)
Cop CMB 1597-1602 from BT (Ptd Granville); CMB 1596-1644 (Great Card Index
    and Ts, SG); M 1597-1601 from BT (Boyd); Extr C 1607-1762 B 1607-1811
    (Vol 7, BG/PCL)
Cop (Mf) (Totnes SP); C 1607-1940 M 1607-1856 Banns 1824-1925 B 1607-1908
    (Mfc SG)

ASHPRINGTON St John the Baptist, Painsford. Private chapel of Kelland
family; licensed 1400, rebuilt 1683-87. Closed mid-18th cent. Demolished
19th cent ?

ASHPRINGTON (Wes) Circuit
OR for *c.*1801-36 *see* ASHBURTON Circuit (RG 4/840,1763 PRO)

ASHPRINGTON (Cong/Prot Diss) (Cong) Tuckenhay [1851 Cong Year Book]; (Prot Diss) Building in the occupation of John Symons Esq, Tuckenhay [1882 Return]

ASHREIGNEY or **RING ASH** St James [North Tawton and Winkleigh Hundred; Torrington Union] [1038]
OR C 1653-1838 M 1654-1837 B 1653-1867 (NDRO)
BT CMB 1607-08, 1610, 1612-13, 1623-24, 1626-27, 1629-30, 1636, 1664, 1668, 1670, 1672, 1674, 1676, 1678, 1680, 1682-83, 1688, 1690-91, 1695-97, 1702. 1712, 1714 (1715-1812 ?); CMB 1814-16, 1818-24 C 1826, 1828-29 M 1828-29 B 1826, 1829 (DRO)
Cop CMB 1607-36 from BT (Ptd Granville); C 1607-1838 Banns 1754-1825, 1860-1981 M 1607-1837 B 1607-1839 (DRO); CMB 1596-1644 (Great Card Index, SG); C 1607-1981 M 1607-1978 Banns 1754-1981 B 1607-1982 (SG); CMB 1607-1839 (WSL); M 1607-36 from BT (Boyd)

ASHREIGNEY (Ind) Bridge Reeve [1882 Return]

ASHREIGNEY (Bible Christian) Churchwater. Erected 1906. fl *c.*1970

ASHREIGNEY (Bible Christian/U Meth) Ringsash Circuit
OR ZC 1820-37 (RG 4/338 PRO); C 1837-1948 (NDRO)
Cop (Mf) ZC 1820-37 (Mf DCRS/WSL, SG); ZC 1820-37 (Mf SG); Extr ZC 1820-37 (IGI)

ASHREIGNEY (Bible Christian) Zion, Ringsash [1882 Return]

ASHREIGNEY (Bible Christian) Zion, Chinghey Water. Erected 1840 [1851 Religious Census]

ASHTON St John the Baptist [Exminster Hundred; St Thomas Union] [333]
Now with CHRISTOW, TRUSHAM, BRIDFORD
OR C 1547-1907 M 1547-1979 B 1547-1992 (DRO)
BT CMB 1609, 1615, 1617-18, 1620, 1630, 1633, 1636, 1641, 1663-64?, 1669-70, 1672-73, 1675, 1677-79, 1683, 1687, 1690, 1695-97, 1699, 1701 (1702-1812 ?); CMB 1813, 1815-17 CB 1819-24, 1827-28, 1830-33, 1838-53, 1855-56 M 1819-22, 1827-28, 1830-33, 1838 (DRO)
Cop B 1740-1837 (Ptd DFHS); Extr CMB 1547-1808 (Vol 6, BG/PCL)
MI (I, DFHS); (Ptd H.Watkin '*Ashton parish church of St John the Baptist*': DCNQ 9: 1916-17: 101-7); Ch extr (Ptd Cresswell 27-28); ch, cy (Ptd Dwelly 197-210)

ASHTON (Wes) A house, Brinscott [1851 Religious Census]

ASHWATER St Peter ad Vincula [Black Torrington Hundred; Holsworthy Union] [862] Now with HALWILL, BEAWORTHY, CLAWTON, TETCOTT, LUFFINCOTT
OR C 1558-1862 M 1559-1837 B 1558-1875 (DRO)
BT CMB 1606, 1609, 1614, 1626-27, 1634, 1638, 1663-64, 1668-72, 1674-81, 1695 (1696-1812 ?); C 1813-39 M 1813-37, B 1813-53, 1855-59 (DRO)
Cop B 1813-37 (Ptd DFHS); CMB 1558-1837 (DCRS/WSL); M 1559-1837 (Boyd); B 1813-37 (SG); Extr CMB 1558-1747, said to be 'muddled' (Vol 17, BG/PCL)
Cop (Mf) Extr C 1558-1837 M 1559-79, 1591-1837 (IGI); C 1558-1837 M 1559-79, 1591-1837 (Mf I SLC)

ASHWATER (Bapt) Muckworthy. Erected 1826 [1851 Religious Census] [*Baptist Handbook* 1861]
OR Z 1828-37 (RG 8/5 PRO); for *c.*1817-37 *see* HOLSWORTHY (RG 4/1210 PRO)
Cop (Mf) Z 1828-37 (Mf DCRS/WSL); Extr Z 1828-37 (IGI)

ASHWATER (Bapt) Cottage Chapel. Erected 1840 [1851 Religious Census]

ASHWATER (Bible Christian) Erected 1865. fl c.1970

ASHWATER (Bible Christian) Buckhorn. Erected 1849 [1851 Religious Census]
[1882 Return] fl c.1970

ASHWATER (Bible Christian) Gilgall, Presticot. Erected c.1837
[1851 Religious Census] [1882 Return]

ATHERINGTON St Mary [North Tawton and Winkleigh Hundred; Barnstaple Union]
[592] Now with TWO RIVERS
OR C 1538-1966 M 1548-1973 B 1570-1917 (NDRO)
BT CMB 1596-1601, 1607, 1610-11, 1613-14, 1618-20, 1632, 1638?, 1641, 1644,
    1668, 1670, 1674, 1678-79, 1682-83, 1685, 1688-90, 1694-97, 1699,
    1701-02, 1706-07, 1709-12, 1714-15 (1716-1812 ?): CMB 1813-15, 1817,
    1819, 1821-23, 1825-35 (DRO)
Cop CMB 1607 from BT (Ptd Granville); C 1538-1812 M 1548-1812 B 1570-1812
    (DCRS/WSL); CMB 1596-1644 (Great Card Index, SG); M 1548-1812 (Boyd);
    Extr C 1539-1705 M 1550-1763 B 1570-1763 (Vol 12, BG/PCL)
Cop (Mf) Extr C 1541-1812 M 1549-1812 (IGI); C 1541-1812 M 1548-1812
    (Mf I SLC)

ATHERINGTON (Bapt) f 1833. Connected with BARNSTAPLE [1882 Return]

ATHERINGTON (Presb) fl c.1672-90

ATHERINGTON (Bible Christian) Langridgford [1882 Return]

ATWORTHY   see BRADWORTHY

AVETON GIFFORD St Andrew [Ermington Hundred; Kingsbridge Union] [939]
Bombed in 1943. Rebuilt 1951-57. Now with MODBURY
OR C 1613-1919 M 1603-1970 B 1603-1986 (DRO) Noted (inaccurately) in 1831:
    'all the registers of Bap Bur prior to 1678 and of Marr prior to 1754
    have been accidentally burnt'
BT CMB 1608-09, 1614, 1617, 1620, 1628, 1633, 1636, 1663-66, 1668-69, 1671,
    1674-82, 1686, 1690, 1695, 1697, 1699 (1700-1812 ?); CMB 1814, 1820-25,
    1827-28, 1831-34 CB 1838-43, 1845 (DRO)
Cop CMB 1608-10 from BT (Ptd Granville); M 1661-80 (DFHS); CMB 1596-1644
    (Great Card Index, SG)
Cop (Mf) (Totnes SP)
MI Ch (Ptd DCNQ 4:1906-07: 5-7)

AVETON GIFFORD (Bapt) [1882 Return]

AVETON GIFFORD (Presb) fl c.1672-90

AVETON GIFFORD (Ind) Erected 1816 [1851 Religious Census]

AVETON GIFFORD (Wes) Erected 1837; rebuilt 1901 [1851 Religious Census]
[1882 Return] fl c.1970
OR for c.1813-37 see KINGSBRIDGE (RG 4/1088 PRO); M 1906-88 (DRO)

AVETON GIFFORD (Bible Christian) Erected 1832 [1851 Religious Census]
[1882 Return]

AVONWICK   see DIPTFORD

AWLISCOMBE St Michael and All Angels [Hemyock Hundred; Honiton Union]   [598]
Now with HONITON
OR   C 1559-1657, 1690-1902 M 1559-1640, 1690-1979 B 1559-1645, 1690-1812
     (DRO)
BT   CMB 1606, 1611, 1614, 1616, 1625, 1633, 1638, 1663, 1667, 1669-70, 1672,
     1675, 1678, 1683, 1685, 1687, 1690, 1696-97, 1699, 1701-1812; CB 1813-36
     M 1813-33, 1835-36 (DRO)
Cop B 1813-37 (Ptd DFHS); B 1813-37 (SG)
Cop (Mf) (Colyton SP); C 1559-1657, 1690-1855 M 1559-1640, 1690-1837
     B 1559-1645, 1690-1812 (Mfc SG)
MI   Ch cy extr (Ptd *Gent.Mag.*:1817 I: 492-3); Incledon 216 (NDA)

AWLISCOMBE (Presb) Licensed 1672; fl *c.*1715; closed by 1772

AWLISCOMBE (Wes) A house [1851 Religious Census]
OR   for *c.*1809-37 *see* AXMINSTER (RG 4/512 PRO)

AXMINSTER   United benefice including AXMINSTER, CHARDSTOCK St Andrew,
CHARDSTOCK All Saints, COMBE PYNE, WOODBURY

AXMINSTER St Mary [Axminster Hundred; Axminster Union 1836-1915]   [2719]
see also chapelries KILMINGTON, MEMBURY
OR   C 1566-1580, 1648-1948 M 1695-1943 B 1559-1569, 1648-1920 (DRO)
BT   CMB 1606, 1612, 1614, 1617, 1625, 1629, 1634-35, 1669, 1672, 1675, 1677,
     1682-83, 1685, 1687, 1690, 1698-99 (1700-1712 ?); CMB 1813-15, 1818-20,
     1822-23, 1825-26 C 1830-31, 1833-34, 1836-38, 1840-63 M 1830-31,
     1833-34, 1836-37 B 1831, 1833 (DRO)
Cop CMB 1606-36 from BT (Ptd Granville); M 1813-37 (Ptd DFHS); CMB 1606-36
     from BT, 1598-1812 (DCRS/WSL); CMB 1596-1644 (Great Card Index and Ts,
     SG); M 1606-35 from BT (Boyd)
Cop (Mf) (Colyton SP); Extr C 1598-1812 M 1559-1812 (IGI); C 1598-1812
     M 1559-1812 (Mf I SLC)
MI   Ch, cy (Ptd Pulman: *Book of the Axe* 1875; reprint 1969); (I, DFHS);
     Ch cy 1909 (A.W.Matthews *Ye Olde Mortality* vol.8: Ms SG); Incledon 308
     (NDA)

AXMINSTER Holy Cross, Woodbury Erected 1898. Mission church in parish of
Axminster

AXMINSTER (RC) Hilary House, domestic chapel of Knight family 1763-1831.
St Mary, Lyme Road. Erected 1831;1862 [1851 Religious Census] [1882 Return]
OR   C 1829+ M 1833+ B 1830+ Confirmations 1830+ (Inc) Later confirmations at
     Plymouth Diocesan Archives

AXMINSTER (Cong, later URC) Wykecroft and Chard Street f 1660. Rebuilt
*c.*1827 [1851 Religious Census]
OR   ZC 1786-1837 (RG 4/511,841 PRO)
Cop ZC 1786-1837 (SG)
Cop (Mf) ZC 1786-1837 (Mf DCRS/WSL, SG); Extr C 1788-1837 (IGI); C 1788-1837
     (Mf I SLC)

AXMINSTER (Wes) Circuit
OR   C 1842-1877 (DRO)
Cop (Mf) C 1842-1977 (Mfc Colyton SP)

AXMINSTER (Wes) Castle Street erected 1796; Back Lane [1882 Return]
OR ZC 1809-37 (RG 4/512 PRO); *and see* HOLSWORTHY (RG 4/1210 PRO)
Cop ZC 1809-37 (SG)
Cop (Mf) ZC 1809-37 (Mf DCRS/WSL, SG); Extr ZC 1809-37 (IGI); C 1809-37
    (Mf I SLC)

AXMINSTER (Wes) Smallridge. Erected 1813 [1851 Religious Census]

AXMINSTER (Wes) Lyme Road. Erected 1894. fl *c.*1970

AXMINSTER (S of F) f by 1693, part of MEMBURY MM; united with MEMBURY
meeting 1705

AXMINSTER (Brethren) Gospel Hall, Castle Hill [1882 Return]

AXMINSTER Registration district
OR Marriage notices 1838-1916 (DRO)

AXMOUTH St Michael [Axminster Hundred; Axminster Union] [646]
Now with UPLYME
OR C 1603-1908 M 1603-1978 B 1603-1992 (DRO)
BT CMB 1620, 1626, 1629, 1635, 1668-72, 1675, 1678, 1683, 1685, 1687, 1690,
    1695-97, 1699 (1700-1812 ?); CMB 1815-18, 1822, 1824, 1826, 1828,
    1830-31, 1833 (DRO)
Cop M 1813-37 (Ptd DFHS); B 1813-37 (Ptd DFHS); B 1813-37 (WSL,SG);
    CMB 1603-1837 (DCRS/WSL); M 1603-1837 (Boyd)
Cop (Mf) (Colyton SP); Extr C 1605-1837 M 1603-1837 (IGI); C 1605-1837
    M 1603-1837 (Mf I SLC)
MI Ch, cy (Ptd Pulman: *Book of the Axe* 1875; reprint 1969); Extr (Whitmore
    MS, SG); Cy 1909 (A.W.Matthews *Ye Olde Mortality* vol.8: MS SG); Incledon
    390 (NDA)

AXMOUTH St Pancras, Rousdon (or St Pancras, or Down St Pancras) Ancient
chapel rebuilt 1872. United 1935 with COMBE PYNE. Redundant. Costume museum,
Allhallows School
OR C 1872-1967 M 1873-1968 B 1872-1988 (DRO)

AXMOUTH Bindon Manor house chapel, licensed 1425

AXWORTHY *see* THRUSHELTON

AYLESBEARE Blessed Virgin Mary [East Budleigh Hundred; St Thomas Union]
[437, excluding Newton Poppleford] Now with ROCKBEARE, FARRINGDON, CLYST
HONITON, SOWTON
OR C 1580-1867 M 1580-1837 B 1580-1883 (DRO)
BT CMB 1609, 1611, 1616, 1624, 1633-35, 1639, 1662-63, 1669-70, 1672-73,
    1675, 1678-79?, 1683, 1687, 1690, 1696, 1699, 1701 (1702-1812 ?);
    C 1813, 1815, 1817-20, 1830-31, 1833, 1836, 1838-84 M 1813, 1815,
    1817-18, 1820, 1830-31, 1833, 1836 B 1813, 1815, 1817, 1819-20, 1830-31,
    1833, 1836, 1838-84 (DRO)
Cop B 1813-37 (Ptd DFHS); CMB 1580-1854 (DCRS/WSL); C 1580-1867 M 1580-1837
    Banns 1754-1874 B 1580-1883 (SG); CMB 1580-1854 (WSL); B 1813-37 (WSL,
    SG)
Cop (Mf) Extr C 1581-1854 M 1580-1639, 1653-1837 (IGI); C 1581-1854
    M 1580-1639, 1653-1837 (Mf I SLC)
MI (I, DFHS); Incledon 573 (NDA)

AYLESBEARE St Luke, Newton Poppleford. Ancient chapelry and tything in
Aylesbeare [588] Separate parish 1862. Now with HARPFORD, COLATON RALEIGH
OR   C 1580-1678 M 1581-1630 B 1580-1622 in Aylesbeare registers, separately
     listed (DRO); M 1862-1970 B 1862-1955 (DRO); C 1862+ (Inc)
Cop (Mf) Newton Poppleford: Extr C 1580-1678 M 1581-1630, 1654-70 (IGI);
         C 1580-1678 M 1581-1630, 1654-70 (Mf I SLC)

AYLESBEARE (Ind) Newton Poppleford. Erected 1816 [1851 Religious Census]
[1882 Return]

AYLESBEARE (Ind/Cong ? later URC)) The Village f 1893

AYLESBEARE (Wes) Newton Poppleford. Erected 1936. fl *c.*1970

BABBACOMBE   *see* TORQUAY

BAMPTON St Michael and All Angels (formerly St Mary) [Bampton Hundred;
Tiverton Union]   [1961] Now with MOREBATH, CLAYHANGER, PETTON
OR   C 1653-1813, 1844-1989 M 1653-1813, 1837-1983 B 1653-1812, 1867-1937
     (DRO)
BT   CMB 1609-10, 1616, 1637, 1675, 1678, 1683, 1685, 1687, 1696, 1701,
     1713-35, 1737, 1739, 1740-47, 1750 (1751-1812 ?); CM 1814, 1822,
     1829-31, 1833, 1837-38 B 1814, 1829-31, 1833, 1837-38 (DRO)
Cop CMB 1609-17 from BT (Ptd Granville); CMB 1609-17 (Great Card Index and
     Ts, SG); M 1609-16 from BT (Boyd)
Cop (Mf) (Tiverton SP)

BAMPTON St Petrock, Petton. Chapelry in Bampton. Rebuilt 1848. Separate
parish 1879-82. Now with BAMPTON, MOREBATH, CLAYHANGER
OR   C 1701-1926 M 1701-1739 B 1701-1812 (DRO)
BT   *see* BAMPTON
Cop CMB 1701-1837 (DCRS/WSL)
Cop (Mf) (Tiverton SP); Extr C 1701-1837 M 1701-50 (IGI); C 1701-1837
         (Mf I SLC)

BAMPTON Shillingford. Ruins of an ancient chapel [Kelly 1889]
OR   C 1701-1812 M 1701-1739 B 1701-1812 catalogued with PETTON (DRO)
BT   none

BAMPTON (Bapt) High Street. Erected 1690 [1851 Religious Census]
[1882 Return]
OR   ZCB 1807-36 (RG 4/957 PRO); M 1934 (DRO)
Cop Z 1807-37 B 1827 (SG)
Cop (Mf) Z 1807-37 B 1827 (Mf DCRS/WSL, SG); Extr Z 1807-37 (IGI)

BAMPTON (Bapt) Bethel Cottage, Shillingford [1882 Return]

BAMPTON (Bible Christian) Mary Lane. Erected 1862. fl *c.*1970

BAMPTON (Bible Christian) Petton. Erected 1901. fl *c.*1970

BARBROOK   *see* LYNTON

BARNSTAPLE   United benefice including PILTON, BARNSTAPLE St Mary, St Peter,
Holy Trinity, BISHOP'S TAWTON, GOODLEIGH, NEWPORT, STICKLEPATH, ROUNDSWELL

BARNSTAPLE St Peter, High Street [Braunton Hundred; Barnstaple Union]
[6840] Now with BARNSTAPLE united benefice
OR C 1538-1979 M 1538-1959 B 1538-1962 (NDRO)
BT CMB 1596-1602, 1606-08, 1610, 1612-13, 1619, 1623, 1632-36, 1685,
1688-89, 1691, 1714-15 (1716-1812 ?) ; C 1813-27, 1829-36, 1845-49
M 1813-18, 1819-27, 1829-36 B 1813-27, 1829-36, 1849 (DRO)
Cop CMB 1538-1812 (Ptd edit.T.Wainwright: 1903); M 1813-37 (Ptd DFHS);
B 1813-26, 1827-37 (Ptd DFHS); C 1813-1979 M 1813-1957 B 1813-1962
(NDA); CMB 1538-1812 (Great Card Index and Ts, I, SG); CMB 1538-1812
(WSL); B 1813-37 (SG); M 1538-1812 (Boyd); M 1790-1812 (Pallot)
Cop (Mf) Extr CM 1538-1812 (IGI); CM 1538-1812 (Mf I SLC)
MI (Ptd J.Chanter *Memorials descriptive and historical of the church of St
Peter, Barnstaple*: *c.*1882); Incledon 9 (NDA)

BARNSTAPLE St Mary Magdalene, Bear Street. Parish created 1844 from
Barnstaple. Erected 1844-46. United with Barnstaple St Peter. Now with
BARNSTAPLE. Church demolished
OR C 1846-1975 M 1846-1977 B 1846-1963 (NDRO)
Cop C 1846-1975 M 1846-1976 B 1846-1963 (NDA)

BARNSTAPLE Holy Trinity, Barbican Road. Parish created 1846 from Barnstaple
St Peter. Erected 1847; rebuilt 1867. Now with BARNSTAPLE
OR C 1845-1976 M 1846-1972 B 1847-1957 (NDRO)
MI (I, NDA)

BARNSTAPLE St Paul, Sticklepath. Parish created 1956 from BARNSTAPLE,
FREMINGTON, TAWSTOCK. Now with BARNSTAPLE
OR (Inc)

BARNSTAPLE St Anne's Chapel. Used by Huguenots 1685-1785. Later a museum

BARNSTAPLE Roundswell Conventional District. Now with BARNSTAPLE

BARNSTAPLE (RC) The Immaculate Conception, Higher Church Street f 1845
[1882 Return]
OR C 1855+ M 1858+ B 1856+ Confirmations 1859+ (Inc) Register from 1836
missing

BARNSTAPLE (Bapt) Ebenezer Chapel, Vicarage Lane f 1817. Erected 1824
[1851 Religious Census]
OR C 1821-37 (RG 4/953 PRO)
Cop Z 1821-37 (NDRO, SG)
Cop (Mf) Z 1821-37 (Mf DCRS/WSL, SG); Extr Z 1819-37 (IGI)

BARNSTAPLE (Bapt) Boutport Street. Erected 1833 [1851 Religious Census]
[1882 Return]

BARNSTAPLE (Cong, later URC) Cross Street f 1662 [1851 Religious Census]
[1882 Return]; Christ Church
OR ZC 1701-68, 1777-1837 (RG 4/68,513.952,2026 PRO); C 1851-1900
M 1896-1904, 1978-97 B 1840-1858 (NDRO)
Cop ZC 1701-68, 1777-1837 (NDA, SG)
Cop (Mf) ZC 1701-68, 1777-1837 (Mf DCRS/WSL, SG); Extr C 1701-1837 (IGI);
C 1701-1837 (Mf I SLC)

BARNSTAPLE (Wes) Circuit
OR   ZC 1807-37 (RG 4/954 PRO); C 1837-1880 (NDRO); for *c.*1811-37 *see also*
    BIDEFORD, BRIXHAM, TIVERTON (RG 4/955,842,342 (PRO)
Cop ZC 1807-37 (SG)
Cop (Mf) ZC 1807-37 (Mf DCRS/WSL, SG); Extr ZC 1807-37 (IGI); ZC 1807-37
    (Mf I SLC)

BARNSTAPLE (Wes) Boutport Street. Erected 1815 [1851 Religious Census]
Rebuilt 1868
OR   M 1925-63 (NDRO); *see also* STICKLEPATH

BARNSTAPLE (Wes) Barnstaple and Ilfracombe Circuit
OR   C 1850-1877 (NDRO)

BARNSTAPLE (Bible Christian) Bear Street Circuit [1851 Religious Census];
OR   C 1866-1909 (NDRO)

BARNSTAPLE (Bible Christian) Thorne Memorial, later Central Barnstaple,
Bear Street. Erected 1876 [1882 Return] fl *c.*1970

BARNSTAPLE (Meth) Circuit
OR   C 1936-55 (NDRO)

BARNSTAPLE (Meth) Sticklepath, Rhododendron Avenue. Erected 1936. fl *c.*1970
OR   C 1955-69 (NDRO)

BARNSTAPLE (Prim Meth) Circuit *see* BIDEFORD

BARNSTAPLE (Evangelical) Whaddon Valley Evangelical Church FIEC

BARNSTAPLE (S of F) Two meeting houses existed 1729. High Street, a house,
erected pre-1800 [1851 Religious Census] Settled 1828. Cross Street [1882
Return]

BARNSTAPLE (Brethren) Grosvenor Street erected *c.*1840; Bear Street Meeting
House [1882 Return]

BARNSTAPLE (Salvation Army) Oxford Hall; and Music Hall [1882 Return]

BARNSTAPLE Poor Law Union Workhouse
OR   Z 1837-1913 D 1914-48 (NDRO)

BARNSTAPLE Cemetery
BT   B 1856-58 (DRO)

BARTON   *see* TORQUAY

BATTISBOROUGH *see* HOLBETON

BEAFORD All Saints [Shebbear Hundred; Torrington Union] [624]
Now with TWO RIVERS
OR   C 1653-1855 M 1653-1972 B 1653-1889 (NDRO)
BT   CMB 1597-1602, 1607, 1615, 1668, 1670, 1674, 1678-79, 1682-83, 1689-91.
    1696-97, 1699-1701, 1703, 1707-09, 1711-12, 1714-15 (1716-1812 ?);
    CMB 1813-37 C 1819-41 M 1820-28, 1830-36, 1838 B 1820-41, 1844 (DRO)
Cop CMB 1598-1615 from BT (Ptd Granville); B 1813-37 (Ptd DFHS);
    CMB 1653-1729 (DCRS/WSL); CMB 1598-1602, 1607, 1615 (SG); B 1813-37
    (SG); M 1598-1729 (Boyd)
Cop (Mf) Extr CM 1653-1729 (IGI); CM 1653-1729 (Mf I SLC)

BEAFORD Woolleigh Barton manor house. Remains of chapel [Kelly 1889]

BEAFORD (Bapt) Cross Cottage. f 1846 [1851 Religious Census]

BEAFORD (Bible Christian) Erected 1838 [1851 Religious Census] fl c.1970

BEAFORD (Bible Christian) Zion [1882 Return]

BEAWORTHY St Alban [Black Torrington Hundred; Okehampton Union] [339]
Now with ASHWATER, HALWILL, CLAWTON, TETCOTT, LUFFINCOTT
OR C 1759-1972 M 1758-1954 B 1760-1812 (DRO) No earlier registers noted in
    1831
BT CMB 1602-03, 1611, 1613-14, 1629, 1635, 1664, 1666, 1668-72, 1674-82,
    1684, 1686-88, 1694-95, 1697, 1699 (1700-1812 ?); CMB 1813-31, 1834,
    1836-44 M 1813-38, 1820, 1822-32, 1824-35 B 1813-22, 1824-35 (DRO)
Cop CMB 1602-35 from BT (Ptd Granville); Extr CMB 1602-36 (SG); M 1602-35
    from BT (Boyd)
Cop (Mf) (Okehampton SP)

BEAWORTHY (Bible Christian/U Meth) Bethlehem, Madworthy. Erected 1840
[1851 Religious Census] [1882 Return] Rebuilt 1922. fl c.1970

BEAWORTHY (Bible Christian) Farmhouse used since 1840 [1851 Religious
Census]

BEER   see SEATON AND BEER

BEESANDS   see STOKENHAM

BELMONT   see PLYMOUTH

BELSTONE St Mary [Black Torrington Hundred; Okehampton Union] [206]
Now with SOUTH TAWTON
OR C 1553-1659, 1703-1813 M 1553-1664, 1704-37, 1773-1906 B 1552-1626,
    1703-37, 1772-1812 (DRO) Noted in 1831: 'about 20 years ago some of
    the register books were burnt'
BT CMB 1608-09, 1613-14, 1623-24, 1635, 1641, 1664, 1666?, 1670-72,
    1674-81, 1684, 1686-88, 1695-97 (1698-1812 ?); C 1839-42, 1844-45, 1847
    B 1839-45, 1847 (DRO)
Cop CMB 1635-41 from BT (Ptd Granville); CMB 1609-1811 from BT, 1552-1837
    (DCRS/WSL); M 1553-1809 B 1635-41 (SG); M 1601-1837 (Boyd)
Cop (Mf) (Okehampton SP); Extr C 1553-65, 1578-1837 M 1553-1766, 1785-1835
        (IGI); C 1553-65, 1578-1837 M 1553-1766, 1785-1835 (Mf I SLC)
MI (Ptd DRMI 23: 1998)

BELSTONE (Ind) Zion. Erected 1841 [1851 Religious Census] [1882 Return]

BELSTONE (Wes) Erected 1890 fl c.1970 = ? Zion Chapel, owned by Robert
Reddaway [1882 Return]

BERE ALSTON   see BERE FERRERS

BERE FERRERS or BEER FERRIS St Andrew [Roborough Hundred; Tavistock Union]
[1876] Now with Bere Alston
OR C 1538-1979 M 1538-1945 B 1539-1968 (DRO)
BT CMB 1605-06, 1612-14, 1618, 1626, 1629, 1631, 1663, 1664, 1668, 1670-73,
    1675-77, 1679-82, 1684, 1686, 1688, 1690, 1695-97, 1699-1700?, 1712-15,
    1719-27, 1730, 1733-36, 1738, 1743-46, 1748, 1750, 1751, 1753-58,
    1760-99, 1801-04, 1806-11; none listed after 1811 (DRO)

BERE FERRERS cont.
Cop M 1813-37 (Ptd DFHS); B 1800-1900 (I, PWDRO); B 1813-37 (Ptd DFHS);
    CMB 1605-07 from BT (Ptd Granville); M 1661-1837 (DFHS); CMB 1605-06
    (SG); B 1814-37 (SG); M 1605-06 from BT (Boyd)
Cop (Mf) (Tavistock SP)
MI Extr (Whitmore MS, SG)

BERE FERRERS Holy Trinity, Bere Alston. Borough of Bere Alston in the parish
of Bere Ferrers. Chapel-of-ease erected 1848. Now with BERE FERRERS
OR see Bere Ferrers St Andrew
Cop B 1800-1900 (I, PWDRO)

BERE FERRERS (Ind/Cong, later URC) Higher Chapel, Bere Alston f 1811
[1851 Religious Census]
OR ZC 1813-37 (RG 4/514 (PRO)
Cop ZC 1813-37 (SG)
Cop (Mf) ZC 1813-37 (Mf DCRS/WSL, SG); Extr ZC 1813-37 (IGI); ZC 1813-37
    (Mf I SLC)

BERE FERRERS (Ind) Independent Meeting Room, Beerferris [1882 Return]

BERE FERRERS (URC) Fore Street, Bere Alston f 1989

BERE FERRERS (Wes)
OR for c.1817-37 see HOLSWOPRTHY (RG 4/1210 PRO)

BERE FERRERS (Wes) Cotts. Erected 1850 [1851 Religious Census]

BERE FERRERS (Wes) Mount Zion, Bedford Street, Bere Alston. Erected 1841
[1851 Religious Census] [1882 Return] fl c.1970
OR for c.1809-37 see TAVISTOCK (RG 4/341 PRO)

BERE FERRERS (Bible Christian) Erected 1868. fl c.1970

BERE FERRERS (Bible Christian) Ebenezer, Bere Alston. Erected 1850
[1851 Religious Census] [1882 Return]

BERE FERRERS (UMFC) Bere Alston [1882 Return]

BERRY POMEROY St Mary [Haytor Hundred; Totnes Union] [1186] see also TOTNES
St John Bridgetown. Now with TOTNES, BRIDGETOWN, DARTINGTON, BROOKING
OR C 1602-1877 M 1602-1957 B 1602-1909 (DRO)
BT CMB 1596-1602, 1608, 1613-14, 1619, 1623, 1626, 1629, 1634, 1663-64,
    1666, 1668-71, 1674-77, 1689-90 CM 1695 B 1696 CMB 1697 (1698-1812 ?);
    C 1813, 1819-25, 1829-35, 1838-48 M 1819-25, 1828-30, 1832-35 B 1813,
    1819-25, 1829-31, 1833-35, 1838-48 (DRO)
Cop CMB 1596-1602 from BT (Ptd Granville); B 1813-37 (Ptd DFHS);
    CMB 1596-1801 from BT, 1602-1837 (DCRS/WSL); Extr CMB 1596-1602 (SG);
    B 1813-37 (SG); M 1596-1837 (Boyd)
Cop (Mf) (Totnes SP); Extr CM 1596-1837 (IGI); C 1596-1837 (Mf I SLC)

BERRY POMEROY (Wes)
OR for c.1820-36 see ASHBURTON CIRCUIT (RG 4/840 9PRO)

BERRY POMEROY (Free Church) Bridgetown. Erected 1832 [1851 Religious Census]

BERRYNARBOR St Peter [Braunton Hundred; Barnstaple Union] [794] Now with
NORTH DEVON COAST
OR C 1550-1974 M 1540-1950 B 1540-1952 (NDRO)
BT CMB 1597-1601, 1607, 1610-11, 1613, 1623, 1629, 1635-38, 1641, 1643,
  1668, 1672-73, 1678-79, 1682-83, 1688, 1690-91, 1694-97, 1700, 1703-04,
  1706, 1712-16, 1720-27, 1731-39, 1741-42, 1744-49, 1751-56, 1762-76,
  1778 (1779-1812 ?); CMB 1823, 1825-26, 1828, 1831, 1833, 1835-36 (DRO)
Cop CMB 1599-1641 from BT (Ptd Granville); B 1813-37 (Ptd DFHS);
  CMB 1682-1704 from BT, 1540-1812 (DCRS/WSL); M 1540-1783 (WSL, SG);
  Extr CMB 1599-1642 (SG); C 1540-1702 M 1540-1703 (NDRO); C 1540,
  1551-1702 M 1540-1703 B 1540-99, 1610-35, 1642-81, 1696-1700 (Ts SG);
  B 1813-37 (SG); M 1540-1812 (DFHS); M 1540-1812 (Boyd)
Cop (Mf) Extr C 1550-1812 M 1540-1812 (IGI); C 1550-1812 M 1540-1812
  (Mf I SLC)
MI Incledon 831 (NDA)

BERRYNARBOR (Cong) [*Cong. Year Book* 1851]

BERRYNARBOR (Brethren) Erected 1850 [1851 Religious Census]

BICKINGTON   *see* FREMINGTON

BICKINGTON St Mary the Virgin [Teignbridge Hundred; Newton Abbot Union]
[351] Chapelry in ASHBURTON. Separate parish 1861. Now with ASHBURTON,
BUCKLAND IN THE MOOR
OR C 1603-1858 M 1603-1951 B 1603-1922 (DRO)
BT CMB 1620, 1622, 1633, 1636, 1736, 1750, 1752-95 (1796-1812 ?);
  C 1813-15, 1817-31, 1833-38, 1845 M 1813-31, 1833-37 B 1813-31, 1833-38,
  1845 (DRO)
Cop CMB 1620-36 from BT (Ptd Granville); B 1771-1837 (Ptd DFHS);
  CMB 1754-1851 (DCRS/WSL); CMB 1620-22, 1636 (SG); M 1631-36 from BT
  (Boyd); Extr C 1603-91 M 1605-87 B 1632-1700 (Vol 9, BG/PCL)
Cop (Mf) (Totnes SP)
MI Ch (Ptd A.C.Ellis *Some Ancient Churches around Torquay*: n.d. 89-94)

BICKINGTON (Wes) Erected 1814 [1851 Religious Census] [1882 Return]
Rebuilt 1885, closed 1984. Now a house
OR for *c.*1801-37 *see* ASHBURTON CIRCUIT, BARNSTAPLE (RG 4/840,1763,954 (PRO)

BICKINGTON, ABBOTS or LITTLE BICKINGTON St James [Black Torrington Hundred;
Holsworthy Union] [77] *see also* chapelry of BULKWORTHY, with which it is
now united
OR C 1717-1812 M 1717-1748, 1813-33 B 1717-1812 (DRO) Noted in 1831: 'the
  Parish being small, it is believed no Marriages were solemnized from
  1748-1759'. No earlier registers noted, but Vol.II contained M 1759-1812
BT CMB 1614-17, 1631, 1634, 1663, 1666, 1669, 1672-75, 1677, 1679-82, 1699
  (1700-1812 ?); C 1813-26, 1828-32 M 1813-15, 1817-20, 1828, 1831-32
  B 1813-15, 1817-32 (DRO)
Cop CMB 1609-34 from BT (Ptd Granville); CMB 1614-1811 from BT, 1716-1837
  (DCRS/WSL); CMB 1609-1837 (SG); M 1615-31 from BT (Boyd)
Cop (Mf) Extr C 1615-1836 M 1615-31, 1673-77, 1709-43, 1770-1833 (IGI);
  C 1615-1836 M 1615-31, 1673-77, 1709-43, 1770-1833 (Mf I SLC)
MI Extr (Whitmore MS, SG); Incledon 1027 (NDA)

BICKINGTON, ABBOTS (Wes)
OR for c.1817-37 *see* HOLSWORTHY (RG 4/1210 PRO)

BICKINGTON, HIGH   St Mary [North Tawton and Winkleigh Hundred; Torrington Union]   [853] Now with TWO RIVERS
OR   C 1707-1913 M 1754-1992 B 1707-1992 (NDRO) Noted in 1831: 'the former Registers are supposed to have been burnt'
BT   CMB 1597-1602, 1607, 1610, 1614, 1616, 1619-20, 1623, 1627, 1636, 1643-44, 1670, 1674, 1678-79, 1681, 1683-84, 1688-91, 1695-97, 1700-01, 1705-06, 1708-09, 1712, 1714 (1715-1812 ?); CB 1813-49 M 1813-37 (DRO)
Cop B 1813-37 (Ptd DFHS); B 1813-37 (WSL, DLS, SG); CMB 1597-1753 from BT, 1707-1837 (DCRS/WSL); M 1751-1837 (Boyd)
Cop (Mf) Extr C 1597-1812 M 1610-44, 1670-1837 (IGI)
MI   (I, NDA)

BICKINGTON, HIGH (Bible Christian) Erected 1834/1865. fl *c.*1970

BICKINGTON, HIGH (Brethren) [1882 Return]

BICKINGTON, HIGH (Christians) Baptist Chapel. Erected 1825 [1851 Religious Census]

BICKLEIGH near Plymouth St Mary the Virgin [Roborough Hundred; Plympton St Mary Union]   [466] *see also* chapelry of SHEEPSTOR. Now with ROBOROUGH united benefice
OR   C 1694-1985 M 1695-1980 B 1694-1943 (PWDRO)
BT   CMB 1609, 1614, 1616, 1620, 1633-34, 1639, 1641, 1664, 1666, 1668-72, 1674-78, 1680-81, 1683-84, 1686-87, 1689-90, 1694, 1697, 1699, 1750-51, 1754-95 (1796-1812 ?) 1816 (DRO)
Cop CMB 1609-42 from BT (Ptd Granville); B 1811-37 (Ptd DFHS); M 1609-1754 (I, Ptd, edit M.Brown, Dartmoor Press 1999); M 1837-1970 with Index (PWDRO); Extr CMB 1609-42 (SG); M 1609-41 from BT (Boyd)
MI   (Ptd DRMI 2: 1998); Ch (Ptd *The Genealogist* 5: 1881: 148-52); Ch cy 1974-75 (Ts SG)

BICKLEIGH near Plymouth St Anne, Glenholt. see PLYMOUTH Egg Buckland. Now with ROBOROUGH team ministry.

BICKLEIGH near Plymouth (Wes)
OR   for *c.*1813-37 *see* PLYMOUTH Ebenezer (RG4/1325 PRO)

BICKLEIGH near Plymouth (Meth) Blackeven Lane, Roborough. Erected 1960

BICKLEIGH near Tiverton St Mary [Hayridge Hundred; Tiverton Union]   [323] Now with SILVERTON, BUTTERLEIGH, CADELEIGH
OR   C 1570-1882 M 1571-1979 B 1569-1964 (DRO) Noted in 1831: CB 1538-1812 M 1538-1754; 1754-1812 missing. CMB 1538-70 now lost.
BT   CMB 1614, 1620, 1626, 1633, 1641, 1663-64, 1666?, 1668-70, 1672, 1675-76, 1678, 1683, 1685, 1687, 1690, 1695, 1697, 1699 (1700-1812 ?); CMB 1814-23 CB 1825-27, 1829-30, 1832-37, 1839-43 M 1825-26, 1829-30, 1832-36, 1839-40 (DRO)
Cop B 1800-37 (Ptd DFHS); B 1800-37 (SG); CMB 1570-1837 B 1813-37 (SG)
Cop (Mf) (Tiverton SP); as Bickleigh near Exeter: Extr C 1570-1837 M 1573-1836 (IGI); C 1570-1837 M 1573-1836 (Mf I SLC)
MI   (I, DFHS)

BICKLEIGH near Tiverton Bickleigh Castle. Restored medieval chapel of home of Courtenay and Carew families

BICTON St Mary [East Budleigh Hundred; St Thomas Union] [213] Rebuilt 1851 on new site. Old church a Rolle family mausoleum. United 1926 with EAST BUDLEIGH. Now also with OTTERTON
OR C 1642-1812 M 1557-1752, 1779-1926 B 1557-1681, 1725-1812 (DRO)
BT CMB 1620, 1625, 1627, 1630-31, 1638, 1663-64, 1668-73, 1676, 1679, 1683, 1687, 1690, 1695-96?, 1697, 1699 (1700-1812 ?); CB 1813-14, 1817-18, 1820-21, 1824, 1831-32, 1835, 1839 (DRO)
Cop CMB 1620-38 from BT (Ptd Granville); Extr CMB 1620-39 (SG); M 1620-38 from BT (Boyd)
Cop (Mf) C 1642-1812 M 1557-1926 Banns 1770-1974 B 1557-1812 (Mfc SG)
MI Incledon 688 (NDA)

BIDEFORD St Mary [Shebbear Hundred; Bideford Union] [4846] Rebuilt 1865. Now with TORRIDGE ESTUARY
OR C 1561-1951 M 1561-1972 B 1561-1968 (NDRO)
BT CMB 1607-08, 1610, 1612, 1614, 1617, 1668?, 1670, 1674, 1682-83, 1688-91, 1694-95, 1697, 1699-1700, 1702, 1707-12, 1714-16, 1783-86 (1787-1812 ?); CMB 1813-29, 1831-35 CB 1837-47, 1849 M 1837 (DRO)
Cop M 1813-37 (Ptd DFHS); B 1813-37 (Ptd DFHS); C 1813-26 (DRO, WSL, DLS); CMB 1561-1812 B 1813-37 (SG); M 1561-1812 (Boyd)
Cop (Mf) (Appledore SP); C 1561-1951 MB 1561-1968 (Mfc SG);
        Extr CM 1561-1812 (IGI); CM 1561-1812 (Mf I SLC)
MI (I, NDA); Old Town (I, DFHS)

BIDEFORD St Peter, East the Water. Chapel-of-ease erected 1889. Now with TORRIDGE ESTUARY
MI (I, NDA)

BIDEFORD Workhouse Chapel n.d. [1851 Religious Census]

BIDEFORD (RC) The Sacred Heart, North Road 1892

BIDEFORD (Bapt) Mill Street f 1821

BIDEFORD (Bapt) Bethesda, Lower Gunstone Street. Erected 1838 [1851 Religious Census] [1882 Return]

BIDEFORD (Ind/Cong, later URC) Great Meeting, Bridgeland Street f 1660. Erected 1696 [1851 Religious Census] Rebuilt 1859. United with NORTHAM and APPLEDORE
OR C 1753-1837 (RG 4/515 PRO); C 1695-1944 M 1854-1870, 1899-1985 B 1854-1870, 1897-1926 (NDRO)
Cop C 1753-1837 (SG); C 1690-1785 (DLS)
Cop (Mf) C 1753-1837 (Mf DCRS/WSL, SG); Extr C 1753-1837 (IGI); C 1753-1837 (Mf I SLC)

BIDEFORD (Presb) Little Meeting f 1693 by secession from Great Meeting, with which reunited 1760

BIDEFORD (Wes) Circuit
OR C 1819-1923 (NDRO)

BIDEFORD (Wes) Chapel Street, Erected 1816 [1851 Religious Census] [1882 Return]
OR ZC 1819-37 (RG 4/955 PRO); *and see* BARNSTAPLE CIRCUIT (RG 4/954 PRO)
Cop ZC 1819-37 (SG)
Cop (Mf) ZC 1819-37 (Mf DCRS/WSL, SG); Extr C 1819-37 (IGI); C 1819-37 (Mf I SLC)

BIDEFORD (Wes) Bridge Street. [1882 Return] Erected/rebuilt 1892
OR C 1923-65 M 1905-65 (NDRO)

BIDEFORD (Prim Meth) Barnstaple and Bideford Circuit
OR C 1836-48 (NDRO)
Cop C 1834-49 (DLS)

BIDEFORD (Bible Christian) Circuit
OR C 1847-92 (NDRO)

BIDEFORD (Bible Christian) Zion, Silver Street. Erected 1844 [1851 Religious
Census] [1882 Return]

BIDEFORD (Bible Christian/U Meth) High Street. Erected 1913. fl c.1970

BIDEFORD (Non-denominational) Bethel Chapel, East-the-Water
OR C 1885-98 (NDRO)

BIDEFORD (Evangelical) Town Mission Evangelical Church, Lime Grove FIEC

BIDEFORD (S of F) f 1773-74; no later information. Now at Honestone Street

BIDEFORD Old Town Cemetery
OR B 1841-1911 (NDRO)

BIDEFORD Public Cemetery
OR B 1899-1966 (NDRO)

BIGBURY St Lawrence [Ermington Hundred; Kingsbridge Union] [578]
Rebuilt 1872. Now with MODBURY
OR C 1691-1947 M 1678-1959 B 1691-1896 (DRO)
BT CMB 1613-14, 1617, 1620, 1622, 1624, 1626, 1663-64, 1666, 1668-74,
   1676-77, 1680-82, 1684, 1686-87, 1690, 1695, 1699-1700, 1714-15,
   1719-30, 1732-37, 1743-83, 1785-90 (1791-1812); CMB 1813, 1818-27
   CB 1829-39, 1841-45 M 1829-37 (DRO)
Cop CMB 1613-27 from BT (Ptd Granville); B 1813-37 (Ptd DFHS);
   Extr CMB 1613-27 (SG); B 1813-37 (SG); M 1613-26 from BT (Boyd)

BIGBURY (Bapt) Zion. Erected 1820 [1851 Religious Census]

BIGBURY (Presb) fl 1672-90

BIGBURY (Bible Christian) Tabernacle. Erected 1850 [1851 Religious Census]

BISHOP'S CLYST   see FARRINGDON

BISHOP'S MORCHARD   see MORCHARD BISHOP

BISHOP'S NYMPTON   see NYMPTON, BISHOP'S

BISHOP'S TAWTON   see TAWTON, BISHOP'S

BISHOPSTEIGNTON or TEIGNTON EPISCOPI St John the Baptist [Exminster Hundred;
Newton Abbot Union] [1085] Peculiar of the Bishop of Exeter until 1848.
see also chapelry of WEST TEIGNMOUTH. Now with HALDON
OR C 1558-1993 M 1558-1990 B 1558-1992 (DRO)
BT CMB 1609, 1612, 1614, 1617, 1624, 1633?, 1635-36, 1662-65, 1667-79,
   1681, 1683, 1685-86, 1688, 1690-92, 1694-96, 1698-1704, 1706 or 1708,
   1730, 1750-59, 1779-95 (1796-1812 ?); C 1813-33 MB 1813-32 (DRO)

BISHOPSTEIGNTON cont.
Cop B 1813-37 (Ptd DFHS); B 1813-37 (SG); CMB 1558-1812 (WSL)
Cop (Mf) C 1558-1812 M 1558-1949 B 1558-1863 (Mfc SG)
MI Ch extr (Ptd Cresswell 34-37); Extr (Whitmore MS, SG); Incledon 99 (NDA)

BISHOPSTEIGNTON St John the Evangelist, Luton. Parish created 1866 from Bishopsteignton. Now with HALDON
OR C 1853-1992 M 1856-1871 B 1854-1991 (DRO)
BT C 1866-69 M 1866-68 B 1866-67, 1869 (DRO)

BISHOPSTEIGNTON (RC) St Mary Magdalene, Cockhaven Street 1937

BISHOPSTEIGNTON (Wes) Fore Street. Erected 1850 [1851 Religious Census] [1882 Return] Rebuilt 1908. fl *c*.1970
OR for *c*.1813-37 *see* TEIGNMOUTH (RG 4/1220 PRO)

BISHOPSTEIGNTON (Prim Meth) Ridaway Street [1882 Return]

BISHOPSTEIGNTON (Prim Meth) Building occupied by William Howard, Luton [1882 Return]

BISHOPSTEIGNTON (Brethren) Rehoboth. Erected *c*.1835 [1851 Religious Census]

BITTADON St Peter [Braunton Hundred; Barnstaple Union] [57]
Now with ILFRACOMBE
OR CB 1813+ M 1790+ (Inc) Noted in 1831: CMB 1712-77, 1796-1812 'no other registers can be found'. These volumes now missing
BT CMB 1668, 1670, 1672, 1680, 1682-83, 1691, 1694, 1697, 1700, 1703, 1705, 1710, 1712, 1714-15 (1716-1812 ?); C 1813-21, 1823-32, 1834-36, 1838, 1840, 1842-43 M 1815, 1823, 1833, 1835 B 1815-16, 1823, 1827, 1830, 1835-36, 1838, 1843 (DRO)
MI Incledon 46 (NDA)

BITTAFORD   *see* UGBOROUGH

BLACK TORRINGTON   *see* TORRINGTON, BLACK

BLACKAWTON St Michael [Coleridge Hundred; Kingsbridge Union] [1477]
Now with STOKE FLEMNG, STRETE
OR C 1538-1856 M 1538-1618, 1653-1907 B 1538-1913 (DRO)
BT CMB 1597-1603, 1609, 1614-15, 1617-18, 1627, 1641, 1663, 1666, 1668-74, 1676, 1678-82, 1684, 1687-90, 1695-97, 1750-83, 1785-98 (1799-1812 ?); CM 1813-40 M 1813-37 (DRO)
Cop CMB 1609-18 from BT (Ptd Granville); B 1813-37 (Ptd DFHS); Extr B 1609-18 (SG)
Cop (Mf) (Totnes SP); C 1538-1856 M 1538-1837 B 1638-1812 (Mfc SG)

BLACKAWTON St Michael, Strete. Chapelry in Blackawton. Erected 1836. Separate parish 1881. Now with BLACKAWTON, STOKE FLEMING
OR C 1836-1952 M 1871-1968 B 1838-1987 (DRO)

BLACKAWTON (Wes) Blackawton and Strete. Ebenezer, Blackawton erected 1823 [1851 Religious Census] closed 1975. Strete erected 1830 [1851 Religious Census] [1882 Return]
OR for *c*.1811-37 *see* BRIXHAM CIRCUIT (RG 4/842 PRO)

BLACKAWTON (Wes) Bethel Chapel, adjoining the King's Arms [1882 Return]

BLACKAWTON (Object to be designated) A building, Blackpool [1882 Return]

BLACKBOROUGH   *see* KENTISBEARE

BLACKPOOL   *see* BLACKAWTON

BLAGDON   *see* PAIGNTON

BOASLEY   *see* BRATTON CLOVELLY

BOLHAM   *see* TIVERTON

BONDLEIGH St James the Apostle [North Tawton and Winkleigh Hundred; Okehampton Union] [339] Now with NORTH TAWTON, SAMPFORD COURTENAY, HONEYCHURCH
OR M 1754-1837 (DRO); C 1813+ Banns 1846+ M 1837-1977, 1980+ B 1813+ (Inc) Noted in 1831: CM 1734-1812 B 1742-1812. Missing registers believed to have been lost by fire at rectory 1915
BT CMB 1607, 1610, 1621, 1624, 1626, 1629, 1632, 1636, 1668, 1674, 1679, 1682-83, 1688-91, 1695, 1697, 1699-1700, 1707, 1711-12, 1715 (1716-1812 ?); CB 1813-37 M 1813-31, 1833-34, 1836-37 (DRO)
Cop CMB 1607-36 from BT (Ptd Granville); M 1770-90 (DFHS); Extr CMB 1607-37 (SG); M 1607-36 from BT (Boyd)
Cop (Mf) (Okehampton SP); M 1754-1837 (Mfc SG)
MI Extr (Whitmore MS, SG)

BONDLEIGH (Bible Christian) Ebenezer. Erected 1838 [1851 Religious Census]; Bondleigh Bridge [1882 Return]

BONDLEIGH (Brethren) Erected 1847 [1851 Religious Census]

BOTTREAUX MILL   *see* MOLLAND

BOVEY TRACEY St Peter, St Paul and St Thomas of Canterbury [Teignbridge Hundred; Newton Abbot Union] [1697] Now with HENNOCK
OR C 1538-1965 M 1539-1739, 1755-1960 B 1539-1973 (DRO) Some baptisms took place at LUSTLEIGH
BT CMB 1613-14, 1626, 1629, 1634, 1636, 1638, 1663-64, 1669-70, 1672, 1675-81, 1684, 1686-89, 1694-96, 1700 (1701-1812 ?); C 1813-48 M 1814-37 B 1813-29, 1831-48 (DRO)
Cop CMB 1613-39 from BT (Ptd Granville); CMB 1538-1837 (DCRS/WSL); Extr CMB 1613-39 (SG); M 1598-1836 (Boyd); Extr C 1541-1655 M 1539-1654 (Vol 19, BG/PCL)
Cop (Mf) C 1538-1965 M 1536-1960 B 1539-1973 (Mfc SG); C 1581-1655 B 1781-1849 (DRO); Extr C 1538-1837 M 1539-1837 (IGI); C 1538-1837 M 1539-1837 (Mf I SLC)
MI Incledon 141 (NDA)

BOVEY TRACEY St John the Evangelist. Erected 1852. Parish created 1895 from Bovey Tracey. Now with Chudleigh Knighton
OR M 1896-1922 (DRO)

BOVEY TRACEY St Paul, Chudleigh Knighton. Chapelry partly in Bovey Tracey, partly in HENNOCK. Erected 1841-42. Separate parish 1852. Now with Bovey Tracey St John
OR C 1875-1954 M 1880-1981 (DRO)

BOVEY TRACEY St Catherine, Heathfield. Chapel-of-ease, Now with St John Bovey Tracey, Chudleigh Knighton

BOVEY TRACEY Devon House of Mercy. Clewer Sisters f 1863

BOVEY TRACEY (RC) Holy Ghost, Ashburton Road 1904; 1936

BOVEY TRACEY (Bapt) Hen or Hind Street f 1773. Used an earlier Presbyterian building. Rebuilt 1824 [1882 Return] Part of East Dartmoor f 1976
OR Z 1778-1833 B 1784-1833 (RG 4/956 PRO)
Cop Z 1778-1833 B 1784-1833 (SG)
Cop (Mf) Z 1778-1833 B 1784-1833 (Mf DCRS/WSL, SG); Extr Z 1778-1833 (IGI)

BOVEY TRACEY (Cong)
OR C 1935-65 (DRO)

BOVEY TRACEY (Presb) f pre-1715, closed 1760s. Taken over by Baptists by 1773

BOVEY TRACEY (Wes) Hen Street, erected pre-1800 [1851 Religious Census] Fore Street [1882 Return] Cong chapel erected 1811, purchased 1969
OR C 1813-44 (DRO); for c.1801-36 see also ASHBURTON CIRCUIT (RG 4/840,1763 PRO)
Cop (Mf) C 1813-44 (Mfc Torquay SP)

BOVEY TRACEY (S of F) f c.1700; closed c.1766. Part of EXETER MM

BOVEY, NORTH St John the Baptist [Teignbridge Hundred; Newton Abbot Union] [609] Now with MORETONHAMPSTEAD, MANATON, LUSTLEIGH
OR C 1572-1954 M 1572-1837 B 1572-1812 (DRO)
BT CMB 1609, 1612, 1614, 1617, 1630, 1634, 1636, 1638, 1643, 1663-64, 1668-70, 1672, 1674-80, 1682, 1684, 1689-90, 1695-96, 1699 (1700-1812 ?); CB 1814-16, 1818, 1838-51, 1853, 1855-63 M 1814-16, 1818 (DRO)
Cop CMB 1612-30 from BT (Ptd Granville); M 1572-1754 (I, Ptd, edit M.Brown, Dartmoor Press 1999); CMB 1572-1791 (DCRS/WSL); CMB 1572-1840 (SG)
Cop (Mf) (Okehampton and Totnes SPs); Extr C 1572-1791 M 1572-1775 (IGI); C 1572-1791 M 1572-1775 (Mf I SLC)
MI (Ptd DRMI 20: 1998)

BOVEY, NORTH (Bible Christian) Lettaford. Erected 1860, closed 1980

BOVEY, NORTH (Wes) [1882 Return] and see HENNOCK and MORETONHAMPSTEAD

BOW or NYMET TRACEY, St Bartholomew, formerly St Martin [North Tawton and Winkleigh Hundred; Crediton Union] [962] Now with Broad Nymet. Not in ownership of Diocese of Exeter
OR C 1608-1871 M 1604-1638, 1732-1978 B 1604-1708, 1732-1960 (DRO)
BT CMB 1597-99, 1610, 1613-14, 1621, 1629, 1635, 1638, 1668, 1670, 1674-75, 1678-79, 1683, 1688-89, 1691, 1694, 1709, 1712, 1714?, 1715, 1719? (1720-1812 ?); CMB 1813-34, 1836-37 (DRO)
Cop CMB 1598-1638 from BT (Ptd Granville); B 1813-37 (Ptd DFHS); CMB 1602-1836 (DCRS/WSL, WSL); Extr CMB 1598-1639 (SG); B 1813-37 (SG)
Cop (Mf) Extr C 1598-1836 M 1602-1836 (IGI); C 1598-1836 M 1602-1836 (Mf I SLC)
MI (I, DFHS); Ch cy (Ptd Dwelly 114-132)

BOW St Martin's Chapel, Broad Nymet. United with BOW in 17th century.
OR None. see BOW

BOW (Ind/Cong, later Cong Fed) f 1821; rebuilt *c*.1838 [1851 Religious Census] [1882 Return]
OR ZC 1824-36 (RG 4/578 PRO)
Cop ZC 1825-36 (SG)
Cop (Mf) ZC 1825-36 (Mf DCRS/WSL, SG); Extr C 1825-36 (IGI); C 1825-36 (Mf I SLC)
MI Burial ground (Ptd Dwelly 132-34)

BOW (Presb/Unit) f 1753 Closed 1816. members joined CREDITON
OR *see* CREDITON

BOW (S of F) fl *c*.1743. Part of EXETER MM

BOW (Brethren) Higher Chapel, Coleford Row [1882 Return]
MI Burial ground (Ptd Dwelly 133-34)

BOYTON [Part Stratton Hundred (Cornwall); part Black Torrington Hundred (Devon)]; civil parish in Devon 1866. *see* NIPR vol.8 part 4 Cornwall

BRADFORD All Saints [Black Torrington Hundred; Holsworthy Union] [487]
Now with BLACK TORRINGTON, COOKBURY, THORNBURY, HIGHAMPTON
OR C 1558-1927 M 1558-1979 B 1558-1991 (DRO)
BT CMB 1609, 1614-15, 1624, 1630, 1634, 1663-64, 1666, 1668-71, 1673-74, 1676-82, 1690, 1695-97, 1699, 1808 (1809-12 ?); CB 1813-23, 1825-38 M 1813-23, 1825-37 (DRO)
Cop CMB 1609 from BT (Ptd Granville); CMB 1558-1837 with index to 1927 (DCRS/WSL); CMB 1558-1837 (SG); CMB 1558-1739 (C of A); C 1837-1927 (I, SG); M 1558-1754 (Boyd)
Cop (Mf) Extr CM 1559-1837 (IGI); CM 1559-1837 (Mf I SLC)
MI Extr (Whitmore MS, SG); Incledon 1055 (NDA)

BRADFORD (Wes) Brandis Corner. Erected 1854, closed 1983

BRADFORD (Bible Christian) Rehoboth, Allemare. Erected 1839 [1882 Return]
fl *c*.1970

BRADNINCH St Disen [Hayridge Hundred; Tiverton Union 1835-1901] [1524]
Now with CLYST HYDON
OR C 1559-1912 M 1559-1954 B 1559-1978 (DRO)
BT CMB 1606, 1608-09, 1614, 1620, 1625-26, 1632, 1668-69, 1675, 1678, 1679?, 1683, 1685, 1690?, 1695 (1696-1812 ?); CMB 1815, 1819-21, 1823, 1827, 1831 CB 1837-56 M 1837 (DRO)
Cop B 1813-37 (Ptd DFHS); CB 1559-1840 M 1557-1840 (WSL, SG); B 1813-37 (SG)
MI Ch: Sainthill family (Ptd *Gent.Mag.*: 1825 II: 499-501)

BRADNINCH (Bapt) Tower Dock, Millway f 1824. Destroyed by fire ? Rebuilt 1832 [1851 Religious Census] [1882 Return]
OR M 1966+ (Ch Sec)

BRADNINCH (Presb) fl *c*.1672-90

BRADNINCH (Wes)
OR for *c*.1806-37 *see* CULLOMMPTON, TIVERTON (RG 4/958,342 PRO)

BRADNINCH (Bible Christian) Erected 1839 [1851 Religious Census]

BRADNINCH (S of F) f 1657; existed 1696. Part of CULLOMPTON MM

BRADSTONE St Nonna [Lifton Hundred; Tavistock Union] [162] United 1923 with KELLY. Redundant. Churches Conservation Trust.
OR C 1654-1812 M 1654-1752, 1766-1922 B 1657-1812 (DRO)
BT CMB 1614, 1616-17, 1623, 1626, 1664, 1666, 1668-72, 1676-77, 1679-80, 1684, 1686, 1695, 1697, 1699-1700 (1701-1812 ?); C 1813-14, 1816, 1820, 1825-26, 1828, 1830, 1832, 1834 M 1814, 1816, 1820, 1825-26, 1828, 1830, 1832, 1834 B 1813, 1816, 1820, 1825-26, 1830, 1832, 1834 (DRO)
Cop M 1813-37 (Ptd DFHS); CMB 1611-26 from BT (Ptd Granville); Extr CMB 1611-27 (SG); M 1611-26 from BT (Boyd); B 1754-1996 (I, PWDRO); Extr C 1658-1709 M 1666-1745 B 1657-1780 (Vol 17, BG/PCL)
Cop (Mf) (Tavistock SP)

BRADSTONE (Bible Christian) Bradstone Mill [1851 Religious Census]

BRADWELL MILLS   see WEST DOWN

BRADWORTHY St John the Baptist [Black Torrington Hundred; Bideford Union 1835-pre-1850; Holsworthy Union pre-1850-1930]   [1027] see also chapelry of PANCRASWEEK
OR C 1596-1909 M 1548-1837 B 1548-1935 (DRO)
BT CMB 1612, 1614, 1618, 1629-30, 1634, 1639, 1663-64, 1669-74, 1676-78, 1680-82, 1694-97, 1699 (1700-1812 ?); CB 1813-41 M 1813-37 (DRO)
Cop M 1813-37 (Ptd DFHS); B 1813-37 (Ptd DFHS); CMB 1548-1860 (DCRS/WSL, SG); B 1813-37 (SG); M 1750-1812 (DFHS)
Cop (Mf) CMB 1592-1860 (Mf SG); Extr C 1592-1860 M 1548-1860 (IGI); C 1592-1860 M 1548-1860 (Mf I SLC)
MI (Ptd C.Collacott 'Bradworthy soldiers and centenarians'; DCNQ 30: 1965-67: 169); Extr (Whitmore MS, SG)

BRADWORTHY Baptisms of Bradworthy persons extracted from non-parochial registers
Cop C 1816-1909 (Bible Christian, Kilkhampton Circuit); C 1818-37 (Bible Christian, Shebbear Circuit); C 1817-37 (Wes, Holsworthy Circuit); C 1838-61 (Wes, Kilkhampton Circuit) (Ts DCRS/WSL, SG)

BRADWORTHY (Wes) Erected 1823 [1851 Religious Census] Rebuilt 1899. fl c.1970
OR for c.1817-37 see HOLSWORTHY (RG 4/1210 PRO)

BRADWORTHY (Wes) Bradworthy Cross. Erected 1842 [1851 Religious Census] fl c.1970

BRADWORTHY (Bible Christian) Erected 1836 [1851 Religious Census] [1882 Return] Closed 1987
OR see Kilkhampton [Cornwall] Bible Christian Circuit C 1838-95 (CRO)

BRADWORTHY (Bible Christian) Attworthy. Erected 1836 [1851 Religious Census] [1882 Return]
OR see Kilkhampton [Cornwall] Bible Christian Circuit C 1838-95 (CRO)

BRAMPFORD SPEKE St Peter [Wonford Hundred; St Thomas Union]   [374] Now with RADDON
OR C 1739-1881 M 1739-1837 B 1739-1939 (DRO) No earlier registers noted in 1831
BT CMB 1608-28, 1630-31, 1636, 1638, 1641, 1644, 1663-64, 1666-72, 1675, 1677?, 1678, 1683, 1687, 1696-97 (1698-1812 ?); CB 1814-50 M 1814-37 (DRO)
Cop CMB 1608-44 from BT (Ptd Granville); CMB 1600-1737 from BT, 1739-1837 (DCRS/WSL); Extr CMB 1608-45 (SG); M 1608-44 from BT (Boyd)

BRAMPFORD SPEKE cont.
Cop **(Mf)** Extr C 1608-1837 M 1608-09, 1620-44, 1663-87, 1713-1837 (IGI);
   C 1608-1837 M 1608-09, 1620-44, 1663-87, 1713-1837 (Mf I SLC)
MI   (I, DFHS)

BRAMPFORD SPEKE St Antony, Cowley, Chapelry in Brampford Speke. Erected
1866, separate parish 1867; later rejoined Brampford Speke. Now with RADDON

BRAMPFORD SPEKE (Bapt)
OR   see THORVERTON

BRANDIS CORNER   see BRADFORD

BRANSCOMBE St Winifred [Colyton Hundred; Honiton Union]   [829]
Peculiar of the Dean and Chapter of Exeter until 1848. Now with BEER
OR   C 1539-1954 M 1545-1989 B 1578-1622, 1653-1933 (DRO)   Noted in 1831:
   C 1539-43, 1560-1613, 1633-53 M 1545-1641,1652-1812 B 1573-93,1617-22,
   1653-1812
BT   CMB 1607, 1614, 1624, 1630, 1634, 1669-71, 1678-79, 1686, 1736, 1756,
   1800 (1801-12 ?); CB 1813-40, 1842-59, 1862-66 M 1813-37 (DRO)
Cop CMB 1539-1812 (Ptd DCRS 1913); CMB 1607, 1614 from BT (Ptd Granville);
   B 1813-37 (Ptd DFHS); B 1813-37 (SG); CMB 1545-1812 (DFHS); M 1545-1812
   (Boyd); M 1790-1812 (Pallot)
Cop **(Mf)** (Colyton SP); Extr C 1539-1812 M 1545-1812 (IGI); C 1539-1812
   M 1545-1812 (Mf I SLC)
MI   Ptd in DCRS vol, above; Extr (Whitmore MS, SG); Incledon 406 (NDA)

BRANSCOMBE (Wes) The Street. Rebuilt 1831 [1851 Religious Census]
New chapel 1900 (old chapel now cottages); closed 1982
OR   for c.1809-37 see AXMINSTER (RG 4/512 PRO)

BRATTON CLOVELLY St Mary the Virgin [Lifton Hundred; Okehampton Union]
[787] Now with OKEHAMPTON
OR   C 1555-1854 M 1555-1972 B 1555-1884 (DRO)
BT   CMB 1609-11, 1614, 1616-17, 1619, 1624, 1631, 1633, 1641, 1663, 1666,
   1668, 1670-72, 1674-77, 1680-81, 1684, 1686-88, 1695-97, 1699
   (1700-1812 ?); C 1813-38, 1841-42 M 1813-23, 1827-37 B 1813-16, 1818-38,
   1841-43 (DRO)
Cop B 1813-37 (Ptd DFHS); B 1813-37 (SG); B 1800-84 (I, PWDRO);
   Extr C 1559-1731 M 1555-1746 B 1555-1745 (Vol 17, BG/PCL)
Cop **(Mf)** (Okehampton SP)

BRATTON CLOVELLY (Bapt) Barton Court. Erected 1843 [1851 Religious Census]

BRATTON CLOVELLY (Bible Christian) Salem, Boasley Cross. Erected 1838
[1851 Religious Census] [1882 Return] Rebuilt 1904

BRATTON CLOVELLY (Bible Christian) Providence. Erected 1859; closed 1982

BRATTON CLOVELLY (Bible Christian) Gilgall. Erected 1834 [1851 Religious
Census] [1882 Return]

BRATTON FLEMING St Peter [Braunton Hundred; Barnstaple Union] [534]
Now with SHIRWELL
OR C 1673-1861 M 1673-1837 B 1673-1913 (NDRO) Noted in 1831: vol.1
CMB 1559-1670. Now missing. *see* copies below
BT CMB 1597-1601, 1607-08, 1610-11, 1620, 1624, 1629, 1641, 1670, 1674,
1678-79, 1682-83, 1690-91, 1694-97, 1700, 1702-04, 1712, 1714-15, 1767
(1768-1812 ?); CMB 1813-16, 1818-19, 1821-22, 1824 C 1826, 1828,
1830-31, 1838-52 M 1828, 1830, 1838 B 1828, 1830-31, 1838-52 (DRO)
Cop CMB 1560-94, 1602, 1621, 1623, 1625-26, 1644-56 from 'lost volume made
1776 by B.Incledon but...related only to gentle families' (Ptd
Granville); B 1800-37 (Ptd DFHS); C 1673-1850 MB 1673-1837 (NDA);
CMB 1673-1850 (DCRS/WSL); M 1754-1812 (DFHS); CMB 1560-1629, 1641-56
(SG); B 1800-37 (SG); M 1562-1644 from BT (Boyd)
Cop (Mf) Extr C 1673-1850 M 1673-1837 (IGI); C 1673-1850 M 1673-1837
(Mf I SLC)
MI (Ptd C.Payne *Monumental Inscriptions, St Peter's*: 1993); Incledon 708
(NDA)

BRATTON FLEMING (Bapt) f *c.*1799. erected 1850 [1851 Religious Census]
[1882 Return]

BRATTON FLEMING (Wes)
OR for *c.*1807-37 *see* BARNSTAPLE CIRCUIT (RG 4/954 PRO)

BRATTON FLEMING (Bible Christian) Erected 1854 [1882 Return] fl *c.*1970

BRAUNTON St Brannock [Braunton Hundred; Barnstaple Union] [2047]
Peculiar of the Dean of Exeter until 1848. Now with SAUNTON
OR C 1538-1842 M 1538-1944 B 1538-1914 (NDRO)
BT CMB 1597-1602, 1607, 1610, 1620, 1623, 1631, 1634-35, 1638, 1640
(1641-1812 ?); CMB 1814-25, 1827 CB 1829-56 M 1829-37 (DRO)
Cop ZMD 1850-99 Ptd B. & A.Brock *From cradle to grave...Braunton births
marriages and deaths from the North Devon Journal*: 2 vols: 1997);
B 1813-37 (Ptd DFHS); C 1538-1900 MB 1538-1837 (NDA); CMB 1538-1812
(DCRS/WSL); CMB 1538-1837 (SG); M 1763-1809 B 1932-75 (DFHS);
M 1538-1812 (Boyd)
Cop (Mf) (Appledore SP); Extr CM 1538-1812 (IGI); CM 1538-1812 (Mf I SLC)
MI Extr 1849-52 (Ptd M.Palmer *'A diarist in Devon'*: TDA 77: 1945: 199-223)

BRAUNTON St Anne, Saunton. Mission church in parish of Braunton

BRAUNTON (RC) St Brannoc, Frog Lane 1958

BRAUNTON (Cong, later URC) f 1662. East Street [1851 Religious Census]
[1882 Return]; united with Meth 1985 as Christ Church, Chaloners Road
OR ZC 1816-37 (RG 4/2402 PRO); C 1807-1846 B 1833-1837 (NDRO)
Cop ZC 1818-37 (SG)
Cop (Mf) ZC 1818-37 (Mf DCRS/WSL); ZC 1818-37, B 1833-37 (Mf SG);
Extr C 1818-37 (IGI); C 1818-37 (Mf I SLC)
MI (I, DFHS)

BRAUNTON (Wes) Hill's View. Erected 1833 [1851 Religious Census] Closed 1985
OR for *c.*1807-37 *see* BARNSTAPLE CIRCUIT (RG 4/954 PRO); C 1911-85 M 1930-85
B 1911-90 (NDRO)

BRAUNTON (Wes) Knowle. Erected 1892. fl *c.*1970

BRAUNTON (Brethren) Erected 1845 [1851 Religious Census]

BRAY, HIGH All Saints [Shirwell Hundred; Barnstaple Union] [280]
Now with SOUTH MOLTON
OR   C 1605-1967 M 1605-1989 B 1605-1716, 1735-1991 (NDRO)
BT   CMB 1597-1602, 1607, 1610-11, 1620, 1623-24, 1629, 1633, 1636, 1638,
     1671, 1673-74, 1679-80, 1682, 1688-90, 1692, 1695-97, 1700, 1702-05,
     1710, 1712, 1714-15, 1718, 1720-23, 1725-28, 1732-41, 1745-56, 1762-84,
     1786-1812; C 1813-65, 1867-72 M 1813-20, 1822, 1824-26, 1828, 1831-36,
     1839-40 B 1813-15, 1818-28, 1830-72 (DRO)
Cop (Mf) Extr CB 1605-1792 M 1605-1837 (Mfc SG)
MI   (I, NDA); Incledon 710 (NDA)

BRAY, HIGH (Wes)
OR   for c.1807-37 see BARNSTAPLE CIRCUIT (RG 4/954 PRO)

BRAYFORD   see CHARLES

BRENDON St Brendon [Shirwell Hundred; Barnstaple Union] [259]
Now with NORTH DEVON COAST
OR   C 1610-1647, 1683-1812 M 1610-1647, 1683-1753, 1838-1992 B 1610-1647,
     1683-1812 (NDRO)
BT   CMB 1598-1602, 1607-08, 1610, 1613, 1668, 1670, 1672, 1674, 1678-79,
     1682-83, 1688, 1690-91, 1694-95, 1697, 1703-04, 1712, 1714, 1715
     (1716-1812 ?); C 1813, 1827-29, 1833, 1838-39 M 1813, 1827-29, 1833
     B 1813, 1827, 1829, 1833, 1838-39 (DRO)
Cop B 1813-37 (Ptd DFHS); B 1813-37 (SG); CMB 1610-1850 (DCRS/WSL, NDA);
     M 1763-1809 (DFHS)
Cop (Mf) Extr C 1610-1850 M 1612-46, 1683-1850 (IGI); C 1610-1850 M 1612-46,
     1683-1850 (Mf I SLC)
MI   (I, DFHS); Ch cy (Ptd Dwelly 14-23); Incledon 645 (NDA)

BRENT, NORTH   see BRENTOR

BRENT, SOUTH St Petroc [Stanborough Hundred; Totnes Union] [1248]
Now with RATTERY
OR   C 1677-1961 M 1677-1945 B 1677-1918 (DRO)
BT   CMB 1597-1602, 1614-15, 1619, 1624, 1626, 1630-31, 1633, 1635, 1666,
     1669-74, 1678-77, 1679, 1681, 1684, 1686-87, 1697, 1699, 1750-95
     (1796-1812 ?); CMB 1813-36 (DRO)
Cop B 1813-37 (Ptd DFHS); Extr C 1679-95 M 1688-1725 B 1678-1702 (Vol 15,
     BG/PCL)
Cop (Mf) (Totnes SP); C 1677-1918 M 1677-1921 B 1677-1883 (Mfc SG)
MI   (Ptd DRMI 16: 1998)

BRENT, SOUTH (RC) St Dunstan, New Park 1937

BRENT, SOUTH (RC) St Saviour, Our Blessed Lady and St Bridget of Syon, Syon
Abbey, Marley Head 1926. Bridgettine Nuns

BRENT, SOUTH (Bapt) Wills Room [1882 Return]

BRENT, SOUTH (Cong, later Cong Fed) Zion f 1819 [1851 Religious Census]
= ? Independent Chapel, South Brent [1882 Return]

BRENT, SOUTH (Presb) fl c.1672-90

BRENT, SOUTH (Ind) Charford Cross. Erected 1845 [1851 Religious Census]
[1882 Return]

BRENT, SOUTH (URC) South Brent Congregational Church
OR M 1909-67 (DRO)

BRENT, SOUTH (Wes)
OR for *c.*1801-37 *see* ASHBURTON CIRCUIT, TEIGNMOUTH (RG 4/1763,840,1220 PRO)

BRENT, SOUTH (Wes) Erected 1842 [1851 Religious Census] [1882 Return]
Rebuilt 1887. fl *c.*1970

BRENTOR or BRENT TOR or NORTH BRENT St Michael [Tavistock Hundred;
Tavistock Union] [147] Now with PETER TAVY, MARY TAVY, LYDFORD
OR   C 1720-1887 M 1720-1834 B 1720-1812 (PWDRO) No earlier registers noted
   in 1831
BT   CMB 1606, 1610, 1618, 1620, 1624, 1627-28, 1634, 1663, 1666, 1668-69,
   1671-72, 1674-76, 1678-81, 1686, 1690, 1694-96 (1697-1812 ?); C 1813-28,
   1830-33, 1836 M 1813-34, 1816-20, 1822-23, 1826-27, 1834 B 1816-19,
   1821-25, 1830, 1832, 1834 (DRO)
Cop M 1720-1754 (I, Ptd, edit M.Brown, Dartmoor Press 1999); B 1772-1897
   (I, PWDRO)
Cop (Mf) (Tavistock SP)
MI (Ptd DRMI 8: 1998); Cy (Ptd *Western Antiquary* 9: 1890: 159)

BRENTOR Christchurch. Erected 1854. Chapel-of-ease in parish of Brentor
MI (Ptd DRMI 8: 1998)

BRENTOR (Wes) Heathfield, near Tavistock [1882 Return]

BRENTOR (Bible Christian) Circuit
OR   C 1839-59 (DRO)

BRENTOR (Bible Christian) North Brentor. Erected 1847. fl *c.*1970

BRENTOR (Bible Christian) Providence, Broadpark. Erected 1868; closed 1987
MI (Ptd DRMI 8: 1998)

BRENTOR, NORTH   *see* LAMERTON

BRIDESTOWE St Bridget [Lifton Hundred; Okehampton Union]   [907]
see also chapelry of SOURTON. Now with OKEHAMPTON
OR   C 1696-1927 M 1696-1928 B 1696-1970 (DRO)
BT   CMB 1609-11, 1614, 1619, 1623-24, 1626, 1628-31, 1641, 1663-64, 1666,
   1668-70, 1672, 1674, 1676, 1678-81, 1686, 1690, 1694-96, 1699, 1811;
   CB 1838-43 (DRO)
Cop B 1813-37 (Ptd DFHS); M 1695-1754 (I, Ptd, edit M.Brown, Dartmoor Press
   1999); B 1800-1900 (I, PWDRO); B 1813-37 (SG)
Cop (Mf) (Okehampton SP)
MI (Ptd G.Oliver 'Bridestowe in the Deanery of Tavistock' *Notes and
   Gleanings, Devon and Cornwall* 4: 1891: 159-63)

BRIDESTOWE (Bapt) Ebenezer. Erected 1833 [1851 Religious Census]
[*Baptist Handbook* 1861]

BRIDESTOWE (Wes) Union Chapel, rented by Richard Crocker [1882 Return]

BRIDESTOWE (Wes) n.d. [1851 Religious Census]

BRIDESTOWE (Bible Christian) Zion, Chapel Street Erected 1844
[1851 Religious Census]

BRIDFORD St Thomas à Becket [Wonford Hundred; St Thomas Union] [529]
Now with CHRISTOW, ASHTON, TRUSHAM
OR C 1538-1991 M 1589-1990 B 1538-1993 (DRO)
BT CMB 1609, 1611, 1610, 1629, 1631, 1634, 1662-64?, 1667, 1669-71, 1675,
    1678-79, 1683, 1687, 1690, 1696-97?, 1699, 1701 (1702-1812 ?);
    C 1813-18, 1820-24, 1826-29, 1831-34, 1836, 1838-56 M 1813-19, 1821-23,
    1825, 1827-29, 1831-34 B 1813-19, 1821-24, 1826-29, 1831-34, 1836,
    1838-56 (DRO)
Cop CMB 1538-1837 (DCRS/WSL); Extr CMB 1547-1682 (Vol 6, BG/PCL)
Cop (Mf) Extr C 1538-1837 M 1589-1837 (IGI); C 1538-1837 M 1589-1837
    (Mf I SLC)
MI (I, DFHS); Ch extr (Ptd Cresswell 42); Ch cy (Ptd Dwelly 150-60)

BRIDFORD (Brethren) Bridford Mill [Kelly 1889]

BRIDGERULE St Bridget [Part Stratton Hundred (Cornwall) part Black
Torrington Hundred until 1844, entirely Black Torrington Hundred 1844-66);
Holsworthy Union] [467] Now with PYWORTHY, PANCRASWEEK
OR C 1702-1977 M 1702-1976 B 1702-1927 (DRO) Noted in 1831: vol.1
    CMB 1561-1701, described as imperfect. Now lost but see extracts, below
BT CMB 1608, 1614, 1618?, 1644, 1664, 1666, 1669-81, 1688, 1692, 1695,
    1697, 1699 (1700-1812 ?); C 1813-15, 1818, 1820, 1822-26, 1828, 1830-34
    M 1813-16, 1818, 1820, 1822-26, 1828, 1830, 1832-34 B 1813-14, 1816,
    1818, 1820, 1822-26, 1828, 1830-34 (DRO)
Cop B 1813-37 (Ptd DFHS); C 1692 CMB 1702-1812 (SG); M 1702-55 (DFHS);
    M 1702-55 (Boyd); Extr CMB 1561-1798 M 1703-49 B 1702-1808 (Vol 4,
    BG/PCL)
Cop (Mf) Extr M 1702-53 (IGI)
MI Extr (Whitmore MS, SG)

BRIDGERULE (Presb) Lupton. Licensed 1672, fl c.1690; closed by 1715

BRIDGERULE (Wes) Ebenezer. Erected 1835 [1851 Religious Census]
[1882 Return]
OR for c.1817-37 see HOLSWORTHY (RG 4/1210

BRIDGERULE (Bible Christian) Erected 1907. fl c.1970

BRIDGERULE (Bible Christian) Siloam, East Bridgerule. Erected 1838 [1851
Religious Census] [1882 Return]

BRIDGETOWN   see BERRY POMEROY, TOTNES

BRIXHAM United benefice including BRIXHAM, LOWER BRIXHAM, CHURSTON FERRERS,
GALMPTON, KINGSWEAR

BRIXHAM St Mary, Upper Brixham [Haytor Hundred; Totnes Union] [5015]
see also chapelry of CHURSTON FERRERS. Now with BRIXHAM united benefice
OR C 1587-1963 M 1556-1984 B 1560-1976 (DRO)
BT CMB 1602, 1606, 1608, 1611, 1614, 1616, 1622-24, 1629, 1633, 1635,
    1663-64, 1666, 1668-72, 1677, 1686-87, 1689-90, 1695, 1698-99
    (1700-1812 ?); C 1813, 1817-18, 1820-228, 1830, 1832, 1837-38, 1840-74
    M 1813, 1815, 1818, 1820-28, 1830 B 1813, 1817-18, 1820-28, 1830,
    1837-74 (DRO)
Cop M 1813-37 (Ptd DFHS); B 1813-37 (Ptd DFHS); B 1813-37 (SG); C 1587-1837
    MB 1556-1837 (DCRS/WSL); M 1556-1837 (Boyd)

BRIXHAM cont.
Cop (Mf) (Torquay SP); Extr C 1587-1646, 1653-1837 M 1556-1837 (IGI);
  C 1587-1646, 1653-1837 M 1556-1837 (Mf I SLC)
MI Ch (Ptd *Gent.Mag.*: 1830 II: 114-5); Cy n.d. (Ts SG); Extr (Whitmore MS,
  SG)

BRIXHAM All Saints, Church Street, Lower Brixham Erected 1820-24. Parish
created 1852 from Brixham. Now with BRIXHAM
OR C 1826-1901 M 1826-1909 B 1831-32 (DRO)
BT C 1827-28, 1830-37, 1839-41 M 1826-27, 1831-39 B 1831-32 (DRO)
Cop M 1826-37 (Ptd DFHS)
MI Extr (Whitmore MS, SG)

BRIXHAM St. Peter, Lower Brixham. Opened 1874; closed 1977
OR C 1909-76 (DRO)

BRIXHAM (RC) Our Lady Star of the Sea, Cavern Road 1967

BRIXHAM (Bapt) Market Street f 1797 from DARTMOUTH; erected 1800
[1851 Religious Census]
OR M 1928+ (Ch Sec)

BRIXHAM (Cong/Evangelical Federation) Galmpton f 1831 [1851 Religious
Census] [1882 Return]

BRIXHAM (Ind/Cong/URC) Bolton Street. f 1841. Erected 1842-43
[1851 Religious Census]
OR M 1849 (DRO)

BRIXHAM (Ind) Spring Gardens [1882 Return]

BRIXHAM (Wes) Circuit
OR C 1811-37 (RG 4/842 PRO); C 1838-1933 (DRO)
Cop ZC 1811-37 (SG)
Cop (Mf) ZC 1811-37 (Mf DCRS/WSL, SG); C 1838-1933 (Mfc Torquay SP);
  Extr C 1811-37 (IGI); C 1811-37 (Mf I SLC)

BRIXHAM (Wes) Fore Street. Erected 1816 [1851 Religious Census] fl *c.*1970
OR M 1907-17 (DRO); *see also* DARTMOUTH. For *c.*1801-37 *see also* ASHBURTON,
  KINGSBRIDGE, PLYMOUTH Ebenezer (RG 4/840,1763,1088,1092 PRO)

BRIXHAM (Wes) Milton Street, Higher Brixham. Erected 1889. fl *c.*1970

BRIXHAM (Wes) Lower Brixham [1882 Return]

BRIXHAM (Christian Brethren) Mount Pleasant Chapel
OR M 1984 (DRO)

BRIXTON St Mary [Plympton Hundred; Plympton St Mary Union] [796]
Chapelry in PLYMPTON ST MAURICE. Separate parish 1814. Now with YEALMPTON
OR C 1668-1950 M 1668-1973 B 1668-1979 (PWDRO)
BT CMB 1609-10, 1613-14, 1617-18, 1623-24, 1630, 1633, 1639, 1676-77, 1679,
  1681-82, 1684, 1686, 1688-90, 1695, 1697, 1699, 1750-51, 1753-61,
  1763-65, 1767-70, 1773-80 (1781-1812 ?); C 1813-50, 1855-59 M 1813-27
  B 1813-50, 1855-56, 1858-59 (DRO)
Cop M 1754-1812 (DFHS); Extr C 1668-1728 M 1669-1754 B 1668-1780 (Vol 19,
  BG/PCL)
MI (I, DFHS); (Ptd A.Jewers 'Brixton church': *Western Antiquary* 10 (3-4)
  1890)

BRIXTON (Ind) n.d.; not a separate building [1851 Religious Census]

BRIXTON (U Meth)
OR C 1926-28, 1946-89 M 1992 (PWDRO)
Cop C 1946-89 M 1992 with index (PWDRO)

BRIXTON (Bible Christian/Meth) Erected 1958; fl c.1970

BRIXTON (Calv) n.d.; not a separate building [1851 Religious Census]

BROAD CLYST   see BROADCLYST

BROAD NYMET   see BOW

BROADCLYST St John the Baptist [Cliston Hundred; St Thomas Union]   [2085]
Now with PINHOE
OR C 1653-1929 M 1653-62, 1685-1989 B 1653-63, 1678-1952 (DRO)
BT B 1606 CMB 1611, 1613-14, 1616, 1622, 1625, 1636, 1663, 1669-72, 1675,
    1678-79, 1687, 1689-90, 1695-97 (1698-1812 ?); CMB 1817-20, 1825
    C 1828-29, 1832-33, 1835-68, 1870-71, 1874-76 M 1828-29, 1832-33,
    1835-37 B 1829, 1832-33, 1835-68, 1870-71, 1874-76 (DRO)
Cop CMB 1653-1850 (DCRS/WSL)
Cop (Mf) Extr C 1653-1850 M 1653-62, 1685-1850 (IGI); C 1653-1850 M 1653-62,
    1685-1850 (Mf I SLC)
MI (I, DFHS); Extr (Whitmore MS, SG)

BROADCLYST St Paul, Westwood. Daughter church of Broad Clyst St John.
Erected 1874

BROADCLYST Killerton Chapel. Proprietary chapel of Killerton Park, home of
Acland family. Chapel erected 1842. National Trust.

BROADCLYST Columbjohn. Earlier home of Acland family. Chapel erected 1608.
Rebuilt
MI (I, DFHS)

BROADCLYST (Bapt) Dog Village f 1880

BROADCLYST (Bapt and Wes) Queen Square [1851 Religious Census]

BROADCLYST (Wes)
OR for c.1818-37 see EXETER Mint (RG 4/1207,1208 PRO)

BROADHEMBURY St Andrew, Apostle and Martyr [Hayridge Hundred; Honiton Union]
[849] Now with PAYHEMBURY, PLYMTREE
OR C 1540-1991 M 1538-1984 B 1538-1954 (DRO)
BT CMB 1607, 1612, 1614, 1626, 1636, 1664, 1668-72, 1675-76, 1678-79, 1683,
    1685, 1690, 1695-96, 1699, 1701 (1702-1812 ?); CB 1813-68 M 1813-37
    (DRO)
Cop (Mf) (Colyton SP)
MI Extr (Whitmore MS, SG); Incledon 236 (NDA)

BROADHEMBURY (Ind/Cong) Hope Chapel, Kerswell f 1815 [1851 Religious Census]
Closed
OR ZC 1816-32 (RG 4/2278 PRO); M 1943-48 (DRO)
Cop (Mf) ZC 1816-32 (Mf DCRS/WSL, SG); 'Kerswell by Honiton' Extr C 1816-32
    (IGI); C 1816-32 (Mf I SLC)

BROADHEMBURY (Presb) fl c.1672-90

BROADHEMPSTON or HEMPSTON MAGNA or HEMPSTON CANTELOW St Peter and St Paul
[Haytor Hundred; Newton Abbot Union] [748] United 1938 with WOODLAND.
Now with WOODLAND, STAVERTON, LANDSCOVE, LITTLEHEMPSTON
OR C 1681-1848 M 1681-1920 B 1678-1874 (DRO)
BT CMB 1597-1601, 1613-14, 1616, 1629, 1632-33, 1638, 1640, 1644, 1664,
1666, 1669, 1671, 1695, 1750-51, 1753-55, 1757-75, 1777-80
(1781-1812 ?); CMB 1813, 1815-16 C 1822-33, 1835-36, 1838-55 M 1819,
1822-30, 1832-33, 1835-36, B 1822, 1824-30, 1832-33, 1835-36, 1838-55
(DRO)
Cop B 1813-37 (Ptd DFHS); CMB 1678-1822 (DCRS/WSL); M 1681-1837 (DFHS)
Cop (Mf) (Totnes SP); Extr C 1681-1822 M 1681-1736 (IGI); C 1681-1822
M 1681-1736 (Mf I SLC)
MI Cy 1975-76 (Ts SG); Extr (Whitmore MS, SG)

BROADHEMPSTON (RC) Beeston. Domestic chapel of Rowe and Hussey families:
1726+ and 1780s
OR none known

BROADHEMPSTON (Part Bapt) Salem. Erected 1834 [1882 Return]

BROADHEMPSTON (Gen Bapt) Building belonging to Jenkin Pearse, Main Street
[1882 Return]

BROADHEMPSTON (Ind) Salem. Erected 1845 [1851 Religious Census]

BROADHEMPSTON (Wes) Erected 1822 [1851 Religious Census] [1882 Return]
Closed; now a house
OR for c.1801-36 see ASHBURTON CIRCUIT (RG 4/840,1763 PRO)

BROADLEY see THRUSHELTON

BROADPARK see BRENTOR

BROADWOODKELLY All Saints [Black Torrington Hundred; Okehampton Union]
[388]
OR C 1609-1941 M 1616-1977 B 1637-1992 (NDRO)
BT CMB 1614, 1663-64, 1666-67, 1669-72, 1674-79, 1681-82, 1684, 1687,
1696-97, 1699?, (1700-1812 ?); C 1813-22, 1825-38 M 1813-19, 1822-36,
1838 B 1813-15, 1817-38 (DRO)
Cop M 1708-90 (DFHS)
Cop (Mf) (Okehampton SP)

BROADWOODKELLY (Bible Christian) Splatt. Erected 1870 [1882 Return]
fl c.1970

BROADWOODWIDGER St Nicholas [Lifton Hundred; Holsworthy Union 1837-52;
Launceston Union (Cornwall) 1852-1930] [879] In Diocese of Truro from 1875
to c.1919
OR C 1654-1845 M 1654-1837 B 1654-1874 (DRO)
BT CMB 1606, 1609-10, 1612, 1614, 1617, 1633, 1663, 1666, 1668-72. 1675-76,
1679, 1686, 1689, 1694-95, 1697, 1699 (1700-1812); C 1814-31, 1833-35
M 1814-20, 1822-35 B 1814-23, 1825-35, 1849 (DRO)
Cop B 1813-37 (Ptd DFHS); CMB 1654-97 (WSL); B 1800-74 (I, PWDRO);
Extr C 1662-1793 M 1658-1793 B 1655-92 (Vol 20, BG/PCL)
Cop (Mf) (Okehampton and Tavistock SPs)

BROADWOODWIDGER (Wes) Downicary. Erected 1861. fl c.1970
OR see LAUNCESTON Circuit

BROADWOODWIDGER (Bible Christian) Broadwood. Erected 1844 [1851 Religious Census] fl c.1970
OR see LAUNCESTON Circuit

BROADWOODWIDGER (Bible Christian) Rexon Cross. Erected 1866. fl c.1970
OR see LAUNCESTON Circuit

BROOKING   see DARTINGTON

BROWNSTON   see MODBURY

BRUSHFORD St Mary the Virgin [North Tawton and Winkleigh Hundred; Crediton Union] [136]
OR C 1695-1812 M 1697-1838 B 1694-1812 (NDRO)
BT CMB 1607-08, 1610, 1619, 1623, 1633, 1635, 1663 [irregular marriages], 1669-70, 1672, 1678-79, 1682, 1684, 1708, 1712, 1714-15 (1716-1812 ?); C 1814-42, 1844-45 M 1814-20, 1822-23, 1827-30, 1832, 1835-37 B 1814-30, 1832-33, 1835-40, 1842, 1844-45 (DRO)
Cop M 1662-63 (Ptd J.F.Chanter 'Irregular Marriages at Brushford' DCNQ 10 1918-19)

BUCKERELL St Mary and St Giles [Hemyock Hundred; Honiton Union] [304]
Now with FENITON, ESCOT
OR C 1650-1950 M 1654-1837 B 1653-1812 (DRO)
BT CMB 1607, 1609, 1631, 1635-36, 1668?, 1672, 1675, 1678, 1683, 1685, 1690, 1695-97, 1699 (1700-1812 ?) None listed after 1812
Cop CMB 1650-1850 (DCRS/WSL); CB 1650-1812 M 1650-1776 (C of A)
Cop (Mf) (Colyton SP); Extr C 1650-1850 M 1654-1837 (IGI); C 1650-1850 M 1654-1837 (Mf I SLC)
MI Incledon 220 (NDA)

BUCKERELL (RC) Deer Park. Private chapel of Hon. Colin Lindsay [Kelly 1889]

BUCKERELL (Presb) f by 1672; closed by 1772

BUCKFAST   see BUCKFASTLEIGH

BUCKFASTLEIGH Holy Trinity [Stanborough Hundred; Totnes Union 1836-94] [2445] Now with DEAN PRIOR
OR C 1602-1948 M 1602-1753, 1780-1966 B 1602-1951 (DRO) Noted in 1831: C 1602-42, 1653-58, 1672-1812 M 1602-41, 1653-57, 1672-53 B 1602-41, 1653-1812
BT CMB 1597-1602, 1613-14, 1620?, 1668, 1671, 1674-76, 1678-81, 1684, 1686-90, 1695-96, 1699-1700 (1701-1812 ?); CMB 1813-43, 1845, 1847-51 M 1813-37 B 1813-43, 1845, 1847-51 (DRO)
Cop CMB 1597-1601 from BT, 1602-1812 (DCRS/WSL); M 1602-1812 (Boyd); Extr C 1602-41, 1673-1743 M 1602-58, 1672-1747 B 1602-1702 (Vol 5, BG/PCL)
Cop (Mf) (Totnes SP); Extr CM 1597-1812 (IGI); CM 1597-1812 (Mf I SLC)
MI (Ptd DRMI 18: 1998);Extr (Whitmore MS, SG)

BUCKFASTLEIGH St Luke. Chapel-of-ease erected 1894

BUCKFASTLEIGH (RC) Buckfast Abbey, St Mary f 1882; church erected 1907-32

BUCKFASTLEIGH (RC) St Benedict, Chapel Street 1939

BUCKFASTLEIGH (Ind/Cong, later URC) Higher Chapel f 1787 [1851 Religious Census] [1882 Return]
OR ZC 1787-1837 (RG 4/1105 PRO); C 1787-1969 B 1947-65 (DRO)
Cop ZC 1787-1837 (SG)
Cop (Mf) ZC 1787-1837 (Mf DCRS/WSL); ZC 1787-1837 (Mf SG); Extr ZC 1787-1837
          (IGI); ZC 1787-1837 (Mf I SLC)

BUCKFASTLEIGH (Wes) Circuit and section
OR C 1857-1935 M 1863-1864 (DRO)
Cop (Mf) C 1857-1935 (Mf Totnes Museum)

BUCKFASTLEIGH (Wes) Chapel Street. Erected pre-1800; rebuilt 1835
[1851 Religious Census] [1882 Return] fl c.1970
OR for c.1801-36 see ASHBURTON CIRCUIT (RG 4/840,1763 PRO)

BUCKFASTLEIGH (Wes) Buckfast. Erected 1881. fl c.1970

BUCKFASTLEIGH (Wes) Scorriton. Erected 1833 [1851 Religious Census]
[1882 Return] Rebuilt 1904. fl c.1970
MI (Ptd DRMI 18: 1998)

BUCKFASTLEIGH (Bible Christian) Circuit
OR ZC 1820-37 (RG 4/332 PRO)
Cop ZC 1820-37 (SG)
Cop (Mf) ZC 1820-37 (Mf DCRS/WSL, SG); Extr ZC 1820-37 (IGI); ZC 1820-37
          (Mf I SLC)

BUCKHORN   see ASHWATER

BUCKLAND   see THURLESTONE

BUCKLAND BREWER St Mary and St Benedict [Shebbear Hundred; Bideford Union]
[1096] see also chapelry of EAST PUTFORD. Now with HARTLAND COAST
OR C 1605-1970 M 1606-1754, 1837-1979 B 1603-1812 (NDRO)
BT CMB 1602, 1605, 1607, 1608, 1610-11, 1614, 1617, 1629, 1635, 1641, 1668,
      1672, 1678-80, 1682-83, 1685, 1689-90, 1694-97, 1700, 1702-03, 1709-11,
      1714-15 (1716-1812 ?); C 1813, 1817-18, 1821-25, 1827-38 M 1813, 1817,
      1821-25, 1827-36 B 1813, 1817-18, 1821-25, 1827-38 (DRO)
Cop B 1813-37 (Ptd DFHS); CMB 1603-1980 (DLS); B 1813-37 (SG); M 1603-1812
      (Boyd)
Cop (Mf) (Appledore SP); CMB 1607-1837 (MF, DCRS/WSL); Extr C 1604-1836
      M 1606-1837 (IGI); C 1604-1836 M 1606-1837 (Mf I SLC)
MI (Ptd J.Benson 'Arms in Buckland Brewer church': DCNQ 23: 1947-49: 88-90)

BUCKLAND BREWER (Bapt) Zion. Erected 1847 [1851 Religious Census]

BUCKLAND BREWER (Wes) Erected 1838 [1851 Religious Census] [1882 Return]
OR M 1923-33 (NDRO); for c.1807-37 see BARNSTAPLE CIRCUIT, BIDEFORD
      (RG 4/954,955 PRO)

BUCKLAND BREWER (Bible Christian) William Reed Memorial. Erected 1903.
fl c.1970

BUCKLAND BREWER (Bible Christian) Salem, Thornhillhead. Erected 1830
[1851 Religious Census] Rebuilt 1863 [1882 Return] fl c.1970

BUCKLAND BREWER (Bible Christian) Twitchen or Twitching. Erected 1842
[1851 Religious Census] [1882 Return]

BUCKLAND FILLEIGH St Mary and Holy Trinity [Shebbear Hundred; Torrington Union] [317] Now with TORRIDGE
OR C 1619-1979 M 1626-1976 B 1626-1979 (NDRO)
BT CMB 1602-03, 1606-07, 1610, 1612, 1629, 1668, 1670, 1672, 1674, 1678-79, 1682-83, 1685, 1690, 1694-97, 1699-1700, 1702, 1704-05, 1707-12, 1714-15, 1717-23, 1725-30, 1732-42, 1743-56, 1762, 1764-84, 1786-1801, 1803-12; C 1821, 1823, 1830, 1833-38, 1840-45 M 1815, 1821, 1823, 1830, 1833-36 B 1815, 1821, 1823, 1830, 1833-38, 1840-45 (DRO)
Cop CMB 1603-12 from BT, 1626-1837 (DCRS/WSL, SG); C 1619-1837 A-B ? (DFHS); C 1813-1979 (NDRO)
Cop (Mf) Extr C 1603-1837 M 1603-12, 1626-1837 (IGI); C 1603-1837 M 1603-12, 1626-1837 (Mf I SLC)
MI Ch cy 1951 (Ts SG)

BUCKLAND IN THE MOOR St Peter [Haytor Hundred;Newton Abbot Union] [139] Chapelry in ASHBURTON. Separate parish between 1878-1910 ? Now with ASHBURTON, BICKINGTON
OR C 1692-1860 M 1694-1837, 1850 B 1728-1860 (DRO)
BT CMB 1624, 1634, 1636, 1664, 1750, 1754-80 (1781-1812 ?); C 1860-65 (DRO)
Cop CMB 1756-1850 (DCRS/WSL); B 1813-37 (Ptd DFHS); M 1624-1754 (I, Ptd, edit M.Brown, Dartmoor Press 1999); C 1803-41 B 1803-46 (I, DFHS); C 1624-1840 MB 1624-1811 (DRO); C 1624, 1636, 1644, 1706, 1711-1860 M 1624, 1636, 1644, 1699, 1703-1837 B 1624, 1634-36, 1644, 1706, 1711-1860 (WSL, DLS, SG)
Cop (Mf) (Totnes SP)
MI (Ptd (Ptd DRMI 19: 1998)

BUCKLAND IN THE MOOR (S of F) fl c.1708; closed by 1731

BUCKLAND MONACHORUM St Andrew [Roborough Hundred; Tavistock Union] [1274] see also HORRABRIDGE
OR C 1552-1961 M 1540-1977 B 1538-1925 (PWDRO)
BT CMB 1611, 1614, 1618, 1626, 1631-32, 1666, 1669-72, 1674 B only, 1675-81, 1684, 1688-90, 1694-97, 1699-1700 (1701-1812 ?); CMB 1813-16, 1818-20, 1822, 1829 CB 1833-38 M 1833-37 (DRO)
Cop M 1813-37 (Ptd DFHS); B 1813-37 (Ptd DFHS); C 1552-1628 M 1540-1703 B 1538-1703, 1800-1900 (I, PWDRO); B 1813-37 (SG); CMB 1538-1778 (DCRS/WSL); M 1542-1898 (I, DFHS); Extr CMB 1538-1837 (Ptd, edit. M.Brown: Dartmoor Press: 2 vols 1998, 1999)
Cop (Mf) (Tavistock SP); C 1552-1853 M 1540-1837 B 1538-1892 (Mfc SG)
MI Ch, cy (Ptd DRMI 3: 1998); graveyard survey, epitaphs etc (Tavistock Lib); Extr (Whitmore MS, SG)

BUCKLAND MONACHORUM St John the Baptist, Horrabridge. Chapelry f 1438 in Buckland Monachorum. Building ruined by 17th cent ? Bible Christian chapel Station Road, purchased 1833 as chapel-of-ease to Buckland. In use by 1835. Consecrated 1866 as St John the Evangelist, and new parish created from Buckland Monachorum, SAMPFORD SPINEY, WHITCHURCH, WALKHAMPTON, PETER TAVY. New church of St John the Baptist erected 1892-93. St John the Evangelist now a civil parish hall. Parish united 1921 with SAMPFORD SPINEY
OR C 1867-1977 M 1869-1988 B 1891-1996 (PWDRO)
BT None
Cop C 1867-1931 with index (PWDRO); B 1891-1900 (I, PWDRO)
MI (Ptd DRMI 1: 1998)

BUCKLAND MONACHORUM St Paul, Yelverton. Erected 1913-14. Parish created 1935 from Buckland Monachorum. Now with MEAVY, SHEEPSTOR, WALKHAMPTON
OR M 1935-80 (PWDRO)
Cop (Mf) Extr C 1552-1778 M 1540-1753 (IGI); C 1552-1778 M 1540-1753 (Mf I SLC)

BUCKLAND MONACHORUM Holy Spirit, Milton Combe. Chapel-of-ease erected 1878

BUCKLAND MONACHORUM (RC) Holy Cross, Dousland Road, Yelverton 1917; 1928

BUCKLAND MONACHORUM (Bapt) Erected 1850 [1851 Religious Census] [1882 Return] Closed; later a hostel

BUCKLAND MONACHORUM (Wes)
OR for *c*.1808-37 *see* TAVISTOCK (RG 4/341 PRO)

BUCKLAND MONACHORUM (Wes) Station Road, Horrabridge [1882 Return] Rebuilt 1910. fl *c*.1970
OR C 1832-1899 B 1832-1929 (DRO); *see also* TAVISTOCK Circuit
Cop B index (PWDRO)

BUCKLAND MONACHORUM (Wes) Milton Combe. Erected 1845 [1851 Religious Census] Closed 1976

BUCKLAND MONACHORUM (Bible Christian) Horrabridge [1882 Return] An earlier chapel sold to Church of England 1833

BUCKLAND MONACHORUM (Bible Christian) Rock, Yelverton. Erected 1907. fl *c*.1970
OR C 1839-97 (PWDRO)

BUCKLAND TOUT SAINTS   *see* LODDISWELL

BUCKLAND, EAST St Michael [Braunton Hundred; South Molton Union] [173] Rebuilt 1860. Now with SOUTH MOLTON
OR C 1684-1812 M 1684-1836 B 1684-1812 (NDRO)
BT CMB 1597-1602, 1605, 1607-08, 1610, 1624, 1631, 1670-71, 1674, 1678-79, 1682-83, 1688-89, 1691, 1700, 1702-04, 1712, 1714-15 (1716-1812 ?); C 1813-46, 1848-65 M 1814-15, 1819-21, 1823, 1825-29, 1832-36 B 1813-17, 1819-56, 1858-62 (DRO)
Cop (Mf) C 1684-1812 M 1684-1836 Banns 1755-1872 B 1684-1794 (Mfc SG)
MI (I, NDA); (I, DFHS)

BUCKLAND, EAST (Wes)
OR for *c*.1807-37 see BARNSTAPLE CIRCUIT, BIDEFORD (RG 4/954,955 PRO)

BUCKLAND, EAST (Bible Christian) A house. f 1840 [1851 Religious Census]

BUCKLAND, EGG   *see* PLYMOUTH

BUCKLAND, WEST St Peter [Braunton Hundred; South Molton Union] [273] Now with SWIMBRIDGE, LANDKEY
OR C 1654-1904 M 1625-1837 B 1686-1812 (NDRO)
BT CMB 1597-1601, 1607-08, 1610-11, 1614, 1617, 1624, 1670, 1674, 1678-79, 1682-83, 1689-90, 1692, 1694-97, 1700, 1702-04, 1709, 1711, 1713-15 (1716-1812 ?); C 1813, 1816-24, 1826-38, 1840 M 1813, 1816-22, 1824, 1826, 1828-36, 1838 B 1813, 1816-38, 1840 (DRO)

NUCKLAND, WEST cont.
Cop CMB 1598-1793 (SG)
Cop (Mf) C 1654-1904 M 1625-1837 B 1686-1812 (Mfc SG)
MI Incledon 851 (NDA)

BUCKLAND, WEST ((Wes) Erected 1829 [1851 Religious Census] [1882 Return]
fl *c*.1970
OR for *c*.1807-37 *see* BARNSTAPLE CIRCUIT (RG 4/954 PRO)

BUCKS MILLS   *see* WOOLFARDISWORTHY WEST

BUDLEIGH SALTERTON   *see* BUDLEIGH, EAST

BUDLEIGH, EAST All Saints [East Budleigh Hundred; St Thomas Union] [2044]
see also chapelry of WITHYCOMBE RALEIGH, United 1926 with BICTON. Now also
with OTTERTON
OR C 1555-1653, 1686-1942 M 1556-1651, 1688-1948 B 1562-1650, 1687-1954
     (DRO)
BT CMB 1606, 1610, 1616, 1620, 1625, 1630, 1633-36, 1638, 1662, 1664,
     1666-67, 1673, 1675, 1678, 1683, 1685, 1688, 1690, 1696, 1698
     (1699-1812 ?); C 1813-47 M 1813-42, 1846-47 B 1814-47 (DRO)
Cop B 1813-37 (Ptd DFHS); C 1555-1812 M 1556-1812 B 1563-1812 (DRO,
     DCRS/WSL)
Cop (Mf) C 1555-1645 M 1556-1837 B 1562-1863 (Mfc SG)

BUDLEIGH, EAST St Peter, Budleigh Salterton. Chapelry in East Budleigh.
Erected 1893. Separate parish 1900
OR C 1856-88 M 1900-79 B 1900-63 (DRO)
MI Cy 1918 (MS, SG)

BUDLEIGH, EAST St John, Knowle. Mission church, now in parish of Budleigh
Salterton

BUDLEIGH, EAST (RC) St Peter, Prince of Apostles, Clinton Terrace, Budleigh
Salterton 1923; 1927

BUDLEIGH, EAST (Bapt) Ebenezer, Little Knowle, Budleigh Salterton f 1843;
erected 1844 [*Baptist Handbook* 1861] [1882 Return]
OR C 1843-1946 (DRO)

BUDLEIGH, EAST (Presb/Cong) Salem f 1717; erected 1719 [1851 Religious
Census] Closed *c*.1975. Later Church of the Assemblies of God
OR C 1762-1807 B 1808-37 (RG 4/2275,2532 PRO)
Cop C 1762-1837 B 1832-27 (SG)
Cop (Mf) C 1762-1837 B 1832-27 (Mf DCRS/WSL, SG); Extr C 1762-1837 (IGI);
        C 1762-1837 (Mf I SLC)

BUDLEIGH, EAST (Wes) Budleigh Salterton Circuit
OR C 1841-1900 (DRO)
Cop (Mf) C 1841-1901 (Mfc Colyton SP)

BUDLEIGH, EAST (Wes) The Temple, Fore Street, Budleigh Salterton. Erected
*c.*1812 [1851 Religious Census] [1882 Return] Rebuilt 1905. fl *c.*1970
OR ZC 1820-37 (RG 4/517 PRO); for *c.*1831-37 *see also* EXETER Mint (RG 4/1208
PRO)
Cop ZC 1820-37 (SG)
Cop (Mf) ZC 1820-37 (Mf DCRS/WSL, SG); Extr ZC 1820-37 (IGI); ZC 1820-37
(Mf I SLC)

BUDLEIGH, EAST (No denomination given) Ebenezer [1851 Religious Census]

BULKWORTHY St Michael [Shebbear Hundred; Bideford Union] [198] Chapelry in
ABBOTS BICKINGTON, with which it is now united
OR C 1709-1812 M 1829-36 B 1724-1812 (DRO)
Noted in 1831: Vol.2 MB 1724-1812. Early marriages may have taken place
at Buckland Brewer, for which no M registers survive for 1754-1837.
BT CMB 1675, 1682-83, 1692, 1695-96, 1707, 1709-10, 1711-12, 1714-16
(1717-1812 ?); C 1813-14, 1816-37, 1840-42 M 1829, 1831-32, 1835-36
B 1813-14, 1816-17, 1819-20, 1823-26, 1828, 1831, 1835-37, 1840-42 (DRO)
Cop CB 1605-1812 from BT, and two M in 1641 copied from BTs for Buckland
Brewer; M 1829-36; C 1709-1837 B 1724-1836 copied from registers in
Buckland Brewer (Ts, DCRS/WSL, SG)
Cop (Mf) (Appledore SP); Extr C 1605-1837 M 1608-41,1806-07, 1829-36 (IGI);
C 1605-1837 (Mf I SLC)
MI Extr (Whitmore MS, SG); Incledon 1054 (NDA)

BULKWORTHY (Bible Christian) Bethel, Haytown. Erected 1841 [1851 Religious
Census] [1882 Return] Closed 1971. Later a workshop

BUNDLEY, BUNDLEIGH   *see* BONDLEIGH

BURLESCOMBE St Mary [Part Bampton Hundred, part Halberton Hundred;
Wellington Union (Somerset)] [999] Now with SAMPFORD PEVERELL
OR C 1579-1871 M 1580-1660, 1682-1989 B 1579-1962 (DRO)
BT CMB 1608, 1610, 1613-15, 1620, 1625, 1631, 1634, 1667-70, 1675, 1678,
1682-83, 1685, 1687, 1693, 1696-97, 1699 (1700-1812 ?); CMB 1814-19,
1821-28, 1830-35 CB 1838-61 M 1837-60 (DRO)
Cop B 1813-37 (Ptd DFHS); B 1813-37 (SG)
Cop (Mf) (Tiverton SP); Extr C 1579-1736, 1779-1871 M 1580-1841 (IGI)
MI Extr (Whitmore MS, SG)

BURLESCOMBE Ayshford House. 15th cent. private chapel of Ayshford family

BURLESCOMBE (Cong, later URC) Westleigh f 1824

BURLESCOMBE (Wes) Westleigh. Erected 1820 [1851 Religious Census]
OR for *c.*1812-37 *see* TIVERTON (RG 4/342 PRO)

BURLESCOMBE (S of F) f by 1655; part of CULLOMPTON MM. Closed post-1818.
Burial ground to 1917
OR Z 1676-1804 M 1676-1790 B 1676-1827 including SPICELAND (RG 6/1545 PRO)

BURLESCOMBE (Brethren) Appledore. Mission room erected 1820, used by
Brethren from *c.*1900 as Blackdown Hills Mission

BURRINGTON Holy Trinity [North Tawton and Winkleigh Hundred; South Molton Union] [987] Now with CHULMLEIGH, CHAWLEIGH, CHELDON, WEMBWORTHY, EGGESFORD
OR C 1601-22, 1637-1886 M 1601-1612, 1637-1975 B 1592-1610, 1637-1960 (NDRO)
BT CMB 1602, 1607, 1610, 1612, 1621, 1627, 1635-36, 1668, 1670, 1672, 1674, 1676, 1680, 1683-86, 1688, 1690-91, 1694-96, 1698, 1700, 1704-06, 1710, 1712, 1715 (1716-1812 ?); C 1813-26, 1829, 1831, 1836-48 M 1813-26, 1828-29, 1832, 1836-37 B 1813-25, 1828-32, 1826-48 (DRO)
Cop B 1813-37 (Ptd DFHS); B 1813-37 (SG); CMB 1592-1867 (DCRS/WSL); M 1601-1837 (Boyd)
Cop (Mf) Extr C 1601-1812 M 1601-12, 1637-1837 (IGI); C 1601-1812 M 1601-12, 1637-1837 (Mf I SLC)
MI Ch, cy 1917 (MS, SG); Incledon 1020 (NDA)

BURRINGTON (Wes)
OR for c.1807-37 see BARNSTAPLE CIRCUIT (RG 4/954 PRO)

BURRINGTON (Bible Christian/Meth) Bethesda. Erected 1829 [1851 Religious Census] [1882 Return] fl c.1970

BURRINGTON (Brethren) White Oak. Erected 1847 [1851 Religious Census]

BURSDON MOOR *see* WELCOMBE

BUTTERLEIGH St Matthew [Cliston Hundred; Tiverton Union] [142] Now with SILVERTON, BICKLEIGH, CADELEIGH
OR C 1698-1903 M 1698-1976 B 1698-1812 (DRO)
BT CMB 1624?, 1625?, 1631, 1663-64, 1666, 1668-69, 1672, 1675, 1678, 1683, 1685, 1687, 1690, 1699 (1700-1812 ?); C 1813-23, M 1817, 1819 B 1813-14, 1816-23 (DRO)
Cop CMB 1624-95 from BT, 1699-1837 (DCRS/WSL);
Cop (Mf) (Tiverton SP); Extr C 1624-1837 M 1624-31, 1664-72, 1685-1837 (IGI); C 1624-1837 (Mf I SLC)
MI Extr (Whitmore MS, SG)

CADBURY St Michael and All Angels [Hayridge Hundred; Tiverton Union] [256] Now with RADDON
OR C 1762-1935 M 1756-1971 B 1762-1812 (DRO) Noted in 1831: 'The earlier Registers have been accidentally burnt'
BT CMB 1606-07, 1610-11, 1614, 1620, 1624, 1626, 1630, 1669, 1672-73, 1675, 1683, 1687, 1695, 1697 (1698-1812 ?); C 1813-39, 1841-52, 1854 M 1814-22, 1824-29, 1831-32, 1836 B 1813, 1815-39, 1841-54 (DRO)
Cop CMB 1606-1700 from BT, 1762-1837 (DCRS/WSL); M 1756-1837 (Boyd)
Cop (Mf) (Tiverton SP); Extr C 1606-1837 M 1606-1836 (IGI); C 1606-1837 M 1606-1836 (Mf I SLC)
MI (I, DFHS)

CADELEIGH St Bartholomew [Hayridge Hundred; Tiverton Union] [312] Now with SILVERTON, BUTTERLEIGH, BICKLEIGH
OR C 1665-1942 M 1725-1977 B 1725-1992 (DRO) No earlier registers noted in 1831
BT CMB 1606, 1613-16, 1624, 1626, 1629-30, 1664, 1667-73, 1675, 1678-79, 1683, 1690, 1697 (1698-1812 ?); C 1819-21, 1823-25, 1828-29, 1831, 1833, 1837 M 1821, 1824-25, 1828-29, 1831, 1837 B 1819-21, 1824-25, 1828-29, 1831, 1933, 1837 (DRO)
Cop B 1800-37 (Ptd DFHS); B 1800-37 (SG); CMB 1606-1715 from BT, 1665-1837 (DCRS/WSL)

CADELEIGH cont.
Cop (Mf) (Tiverton SP); Extr C 1606-1837 M 1613-30, 1664-97, 1711-13,
        1725-1837 (IGI); C 1606-1837 M 1613-30, 1664-97, 1711-13, 1725-1837
        (Mf I SLC)
MI Extr (Whitmore MS, SG)

CADELEIGH (Ind) Erected 1835 [1851 Religious Census]

CADELEIGH (Ind) Yate. A house. f 1850 [1851 Religious Census]

CADELEIGH (Bible Christian/Meth) Bethel, Little Silver. Erected 1843
[1851 Religious Census] [1882 Return] Closed 1977
Cop Sums paid for grave spaces, with names of deceased 1891-1972 (SG)

CALVERLEIGH or CALWOODLEIGH St Mary the Virgin [Tiverton Hundred; Tiverton
Union 1835-85] [91] Now with EXE VALLEY
OR C 1679-82, 1712-1812 M 1679-1681, 1712-1978, 1981-95 B 1679-81,
    1712-1812 (DRO)
BT CMB 1604, 1610, 1613-15, 1621, 1626, 1630, 1667, 1669-70, 1676, 1678,
    1683, 1690, 1697 (1698-1812 ?); C 1813-27, 1829-36, 1840-54 M 1813-15,
    1822, 1825, 1833-36 B 1813-27, 1829-35, 1840-54 (DRO)

CALVERLEIGH (RC) f 1795. Domestic chapel of Chichester and Nagel families.
Missiion moved to TIVERTON 1836
OR None known. Possible entries at ARLINGTON

CAPTON   see DITTISHAM

CATTLEDOWN   see SUTTON ON PLYM

CHAGFORD St Michael [Wonford Hundred; Okehampton Union] [1868] Now with
GIDLEIGH, THROWLEIGH
OR C 1702-1949 M 1599-1996 B 1598-1981 (DRO) No earlier registers noted in
    1831
BT CMB 1608-09, 1616 B only, CMB 1630-33, 1669-71, 1675, 1677-79, 1683,
    1687, 1690 (1691-1812 ?); CMB 1813-14, 1826, 1832-33 CB 1838-41, 1852-72
    (DRO)
Cop CMB 1598-1850 (DCRS/WSL); B 1800-1900 (I, PWDRO)
Cop (Mf) (Okehampton SP); Extr C 1612-1843 M 1598-1850 (IGI); C 1612-1843
        M 1598-1850 (Mf I SLC)
MI (Ptd DRMI 22: 1998)

CHAGFORD (RC) The Holy Family 1963

CHAGFORD (Bapt) Zion, Southcombe Street. Erected 1823, closed 1834, sold to
Bible Christians 1842; Easton, a building in the occupation of John Rich
[1882 Return]

CHAGFORD (Wes) Mill Street. Erected 1867. fl c.1970. Building owned by John
Breby and others, Mill Street [1882 Return]; Building belonging to Stephen
Nosworthy and others [1882 Return]

CHAGFORD (Wes) Erected 1834 [1851 Religious Census]

CHAGFORD (Wes) see HENNOCK and MORETONHAMPSTEAD

CHAGFORD (Bible Christian) Zion [1882 Return]
OR ZC 1822-37 (RG 4/340 PRO); see also OKEHAMPTON (RG 4/1089 PRO)
Cop (Mf) ZC 1822-37 (Mf DCRS/WSL, SG); Extr ZC 1822-37 (IGI); ZC 1822-37
(Mf I SLC)

CHAGFORD (Bible Christian) Bethel. Erected c.1830 [1851 Religious Census]

CHAGFORD (Brethren) n.d. [1851 Religious Census]; later used former Bible
Christian chapel as Ebenezer Gospel Hall

CHALLABOROUGH   see RINGMORE

CHALLACOMBE Holy Trinity [Shirwell Hundred; Barnstaple Union]   [240]
Now with SHIRWELL
OR C 1673-1955 M 1673-1837 B 1673-1812 (NDRO)
BT CMB 1597-1602, 1607-08, 1610, 1614, 1620-21, 1670, 1672, 1674, 1678-80,
1682-83, 1691-92, 1694, 1696-97, 1700, 1702, 1712, 1714-16, 1718-23,
1726, 1728, 1731-40, 1742, 1745-49, 1752-53, 1755-56, 1762-64, 1766-84,
1786-1812; CMB 1816, 1822, 1828-32 C 1834-36, 1838-48 M 1832, 1834-36
B 1834-35, 1838-43, 1845-48 (DRO)
Cop M 1673-1834 (DFHS, SG); M 1597-1837 (Boyd); M 1597-1621, 1673-1837
(Phil Ms)
Cop (Mf) C 1673-1955 M 1673-1837 Banns 1754-1858 B 1673-1812 (Mfc SG)
MI Incledon 826 (NDA)

CHALLACOMBE (Bapt) A house [1851 Religious Census]

CHALLACOMBE (Bible Christian) Erected 1869 [1882 Return] fl c.1970

CHAPELTON   see TAWSTOCK

CHAPING TAWTON   see TAWTON, NORTH

CHARDSTOCK [Dorset] Transferred 1896 to Devon. see NIPR Dorset

CHARLES   see PLYMOUTH Charles

CHARLES St John the Baptist [Shirwell Hundred; South Molton Union] [343]
Rebuilt 1876. Now with SOUTH MOLTON
OR C 1579-1989 M 1538-1926 B 1531-1996: 7 deaths 1531-37 (NDRO)
BT CMB 1607, 1610-12, 1615, 1621, 1624, 1641, 1644, 1668, 1670, 1674,
1678-80, 1682-83, 1688-91, 1696-97, 1700, 1702, 1712, 1715?, 1719
(1720-1812 ?); CB 1838-63 (DRO)
Cop C 1579-1837 M 1539-1837 DB 1531-1837 (DCRS/WSL, SG); M 1754-1812 (DFHS);
M 1539-1837 (Boyd)
Cop (Mf) Extr C 1579-1837 M 1538-1837 (IGI); C 1579-1837 M 1538-1837
(Mf I SLC)
MI (I, NDA); (I, DFHS); Ch, cy: 1929 (Ts SG)

CHARLES (Bapt) Brayford f 1815. Erected 1820 [1851 Religious Census]
[1882 Return]
OR Z 1831-37 (RG 4/607 PRO)
Cop Z 1831-37 (SG)
Cop (Mf) Z 1831-37 (Mf DCRS/WSL, SG); Extr Z 1831-37 (IGI)
MI (I, NDA); (I, DFHS); (Ptd A.Ruston Brayford Baptist Chapel.. monumental
inscriptions: 1983)

65

CHARLES (Wes) Brayford. Erected 1813 [1851 Religious Census] [1882 Return]
New chapel 1927. fl *c*.1970
OR for *c*.1807-37 *see* BARNSTAPLE CIRCUIT (RG 4/954 PRO)

CHARLES (Bible Christian) A house f 1840 [1851 Religious Census]; Jubilee,
Charles Bottom. Erected 1865 [1882 Return] Closed 1978

CHARLETON St Mary [Coleridge Hundred; Kingsbridge Union] [644] Now with
BUCKLAND TOUT SAINTS, EAST PORTLEMOUTH, SOUTH POOL, CHIVELSTONE
OR C 1561-1861 M 1563-1983 B 1562-1903 (DRO)
BT CMB 1602, 1608-09, 1613-14, 1617-18, 1628, 1638, 1663-64, 1666, 1668-69,
   1671-72, 1674-75, 1677, 1679-80, 1682, 1686, 1688-89, 1695-97, 1699
   (1700-1812 ?); CMB 1813, 1815-18 C 1820-35, 1837-39 M 1820-27, 1829-35,
   1837 B 1820-23, 1825-27, 1829-35, 1837-39 (DRO)
Cop B 1780-1812 (Ptd DFHS); B 1780-1812 (WSL, SG); CMB 1560-1812;
   M 1750-1812 indexed by male spouse (DFHS); Extr C 1585-1717 M 1581-1726
   B 1579-1708 (Vol 8, BG/PCL)
Cop (Mf) C 1561-1861 M 1563-1837 B 1562-1812 (Mfc SG)

CHARLETON (Ind/Cong) House, Gaveton [1851 Religious Census]

CHARLETON (Wes) House f 1839 [1851 Religious Census]

CHARLETON (Brethren) Lidstone Road [1851 Religious Census]

CHAWLEIGH St James [North Tawton and Winkleigh Hundred; Crediton Union]
[865] Now with CHULMLEIGH, CHELDON, WEMBWORTHY, EGGESFORD, BURRINGTON
OR C 1544-1693, 1743-1894 M 1547-1693, 1743-1837 B 1558-1693, 1743-1871;
   transcript only CMB 1694-1742 (DRO)
BT CMB 1602, 1607-08, 1610, 1624, 1635, 1668, 1670, 1674, 1678?, 1680,
   1682-83, 1685, 1688, 1694-97, 1699-1700, 1703-04, 1706, 1708-12, 1714-15
   (1716-1812 ?); C 1814-34, 1838 M 1814-18, 1820-25, 1827-34 B 1814-19,
   1821-25, 1827-34, 1838 (DRO)

CHAWLEIGH (Ind/Cong) Erected 1838 [1851 Religious Census]

CHAWLEIGH (Bible Christian/U Meth) Siloam. Erected 1922. fl *c*.1970

CHAWLEIGH (Bible Christian) Hope [1882 Return]

CHAWLEIGH (Bible Christian) Salem [1882 Return]

CHAWLEIGH (Bible Christian) Hooper's Chapel. Erected 1820 [1851 Religious
Census]

CHELDON St Mary [Witheridge Hundred; South Molton Union] [90]
Now with CHULMLEIGH, CHAWLEIGH, WEMBWORTHY, EGGESFORD, BURRINGTON
OR CB 1673-1812 M 1673-1835 (DRO)
BT CMB 1597-1601, 1607-08, 1610-12, 1614, 1617, 1630, 1633, 1638, 1672,
   1674, 1678-79, 1683, 1688-91, 1694, 1700, 1704, 1706, 1712, 1714-15
   (1716-1812 ?); C 1813-37, 1839-41, 1843 M 1816-21, 1823-24, 1829, 1831,
   1835 B 1813-19, 1821-37, 1840-41, 1843 (DRO)

CHELSON MEADOW [Plympton Hundred from 1858; Plympton St Mary Union 1858-94]
Extra-parochial place, located in PLYMPTON ST MARY

CHELSTON   *see* TORQUAY

CHERITON BISHOP St Mary [Wonford Hundred; Crediton Union] [799]
Now with NORTH KENN
OR C 1538-1846 M 1538-1841 B 1538-1888 (DRO)
BT CMB 1608, 1610-11, 1614 or 1615, 1625-26, 1632, 1635-36, 1663-64,
    1667-73, 1675, 1678, 1683, 1687, 1690, 1697, 1701, 1704, 1706, 1710,
    1712, 1714-15, 1717-20, 1722, 1726-27, 1732, 1734-35, 1737-38, 1742-43,
    1745, 1749-54, 1762-64, 1766, 1768-75, 1777-84, 1787-1812; CB 1813,
    1840-43 M 1813, 1830-37, 1839-42 (DRO)
Cop B 1813-37 (Ptd DFHS); B 1813-37 (SG); Extr C 1763-82 B 1764-91 (Vol 2,
    BG/PCL)
MI Ch extr (Ptd Cresswell 46-7); Extr (Whitmore MS, SG)

CHERITON BISHOP Crockernwell. Chapel-of-ease erected 1880. Closed

CHERITON BISHOP (Wes) Cheriton Cross. Erected 1842 [1851 Religious Census]
Rebuilt 1874. fl c.1970

CHERITON BISHOP (Meth) Crockernwell. Erected 1938/1980

CHERITON FITZPAINE St Matthew [West Budleigh Hundred; Crediton Union]
[1085] Now with NORTH CREADY
OR C 1660-1936 M 1663-1954 B 1662-1678, 1748-1864 (DRO)
BT CMB 1610, 1617, 1625-26, 1638, 1667, 1669-71, 1673, 1675, 1678-79, 1683,
    1696-97 (1698-1812 ?); CB 1813-60 M 1813-37 (DRO)
Cop CMB 1610-1743 from BT, 1660-1837 (DCRS/WSL); CMB 1660-1837 (WSL)
Cop (Mf) (Tiverton SP); Extr C 1610-1837 M 1610-38, 1663-1837 (IGI);
         C 1610-1837 M 1610-38, 1663-1837 (Mf I SLC)
MI (I, DFHS); Extr (Whitmore MS, SG)

CHERITON FITZPAINE (Ind) Cheriton Chapel. Erected 1844 [1851 Religious
Census]

CHERITON FITZPAINE (Bible Christian) [1882 Return] Erected 1887. fl c.1970

CHERITON FITZPAINE (Bible Christian/Meth) Upham. Erected 1895

CHEVITHORNE   see TIVERTON

CHILLA   see TORRINGTON, BLACK

CHILLATON   see MILTON ABBOT

CHILLINGTON   see STOKENHAM

CHILSWORTHY   see HOLSWORTHY

CHITTLEHAMHOLT   see CHITTLEHAMPTON

CHITTLEHAMPTON St Hieritha [South Molton Hundred; South Molton Union]
[1897] Now with SOUTH MOLTON
OR CMB 1575-1812 (NDRO); CMB 1812+ (Inc)
BT CMB 1597-1602, 1608, 1610-12, 1615, 1617, 1627, 1629, 1631-32, 1635,
    1668, 1671, 1674, 1679, 1682, 1688-90, 1694-96, 1699-1700, 1702-10,
    1712, 1714-15, 1785 (1786-1812 ?); CMB 1816-19, 1821-24, 1828-29,
    1833-45, 1848, 1850-51, 1853-64 (DRO)

CHITTLEHAMPTON cont.
Cop B 1813-37 (Ptd DFHS); C 1637-1812 M 1637-1760 B 1658-1812 (NDA);
B 1813-37 (SG, DLS); C 1813-37 (WSL); CMB 1575-1812 (DCRS/WSL);
M 1762-1812 B 1637-52 (C of A); M 1575-1812 (Boyd); Extr CMB 1575-1684
C 1654-1785 M 1654-1759 B 1653-1802 (Vol 12, BG/PCL)
Cop (Mf) Extr C 1575-1812 M 1576-78, 1597-1812 (IGI); C 1575-1812 M 1576-78,
1597-1812 (Mf I SLC)
MI (I, NDA); Extr (Whitmore MS, SG); Incledon 856 (NDA)

CHITTLEHAMPTON St John, Chittlehamholt. Chapelry in Chittlehampton, Erected
1838. Separate parish 1839. Now with SOUTH MOLTON
OR C 1843-1992 (NDRO)
MI (I, NDA)

CHITTLEHAMPTON Church of the Good Shepherd, Umberleigh. Mission church in
parish of Chittlehampton

CHITTLEHAMPTON Brightley. Domestic chapel of Giffard family

CHITTLEHAMPTON (Bapt) Erected 1834 [1851 Religious Census]

CHITTLEHAMPTON (Presb) fl c.1672-90

CHITTLEHAMPTON (Wes) Erected 1849 [1851 Religious Census] [1882 Return]
fl c.1970
OR for c.1807-37 see BARNSTAPLE CIRCUIT (RG 4/954 PRO)

CHITTLEHAMPTON (Bible Christian) Salem. Erected 1837 [1851 Religious Census]

CHITTLEHAMPTON (Protestants) Meeting Room, being part of a cottage occupied
by William Ford [1882 Return]

CHITTLEHAMPTON (Brethren) Erected 1850 [1851 Religious Census]

CHITTLEHAMPTON (Brethren) Chittlehamholt. Erected 1838 [1851 Religious
Census]

CHIVELSTONE St Sylvester [Coleridge Hundred; Kingsbridge Union] [601]
Chapelry in STOKENHAM. United 1932 with SOUTH POOL Now with CHARLETON,
BUCKLAND TOUT SAINTS, EAST PORTLEMOUTH, SOUTH POOL
OR C 1630-1873 M 1630-1953 B 1630-1920 (DRO)
BT CMB 1606, 1614, 1617, 1624, 1634, 1638, 1663-64, 1666, 1668-72, 1674-76,
1678, 1680-81, 1684, 1686, 1688, 1697, 1699-1700 (1701-1812 ?); CB 1834
M 1829, 1834 (DRO)
Cop CMB 1684-1812 (DCRS/WSL); M 1754-1812 indexed by male spouse (DFHS);
M 1684-1812 (Boyd)
Cop (Mf) C 1530-1873 M 1630-1836 B 1630-1929 (Mfc SG); Extr CM 1684-1812
(IGI); CM 1684-1812 (Mf I SLC)
MI (I, DFHS)

CHIVELSTONE (Cong) Stokenham and Chivelstone, Ford Chapel f 1662; rebuilt
late 18th cent. [1851 Religious Census] [1882 Return] Closed
OR ZCB 1772-1837 (RG 4/834 PRO)

CHIVELSTONE (Bible Christian) East Prawle. Erected 1848 [1851 Religious
Census] fl c.1970

CHIVENOR   see HEANTON PUNCHARDON

CHRISTOW St James [Wonford Hundred; St Thomas Union] [601]
Now with ASHTON, TRUSHAM, BRIDFORD
OR C 1557-1922 M 1555-1963 B 1557-1883 (DRO)
BT CMB 1609-10, 1620, 1628, 1632, 1638, 1666, 1669-72, 1675, 1678, 1683,
1687, 1690, 1695-97 (1698-1812 ?); C 1813-24, 1838-48 M 1814-22, 1824,
1838-40, 1843 B 1813-22, 1838-48 (DRO)
Cop Extr C 1564-1665 M 1565-1749 B 1559-1775 (Vol 6, BG/PCL)
Cop (Mf) C 1557-1858 M 1557-1812 B 1557-1800 (Mfc SG)
MI (I, DFHS); Ch extr (Ptd Cresswell 50-54); Ch, cy (Ptd Dwelly 171-96);
Extr (Whitmore MS, SG)

CHRISTOW (Bapt) Bethesda f 1835 [1851 Religious Census] Part of East
Dartmoor f 1976

CHRISTOW (Wes) Erected 1861 [1882 Return] Closed 1978
OR M 1907-49 M 1952-78 (DRO); for *c*.1815-37 *see* ASHBURTON CIRCUIT,
OKEHAMPTON (RG 4/840,1089 PRO)

CHRISTOW (S of F) Clampitt f by 1669; moved to BOVEY TRACEY by 1700.
Part of EXETER MM

CHUDLEIGH St Martin and St Mary [Exminster Hundred; Newton Abbot Union]
[2278] Peculiar of the Bishop of Exeter until 1848
OR C 1558-1917 M 1558-1909 B 1558-1912 (DRO)
BT CMB 1597-1602, 1614, 1617, 1620, 1624, 1630, 1634, 1638-39, 1644,
1664-72, 1675-77, 1679-89, 1692-1706, 1730 (1731-1812 ?); CMB 1813-20,
1822-27, 1830, 1833, 1835 CB 1838-56 (DRO)
Cop B 1813-37 (Ptd DFHS); B 1813-37 (SG); CMB 1558-1800 (DCRS/WSL);
Extr C 1559-1737 M 1558-1727 B 1558-1737 (Vol 19, BG/PCL)
Cop (Mf) C 1558-1858 M 1558-1837 B 1558-1853 (Mfc SG)
MI Ch, cy (Ptd M.Jones *The History of Chudleigh*: 2nd edit.: 1875)

CHUDLEIGH (RC) St Cyprian, Ugbrooke 1671. Domestic chapel of Clifford family
[1851 Religious Census] [1882 Return]
OR Register of Rev. Dominic Darbyshire C 1736-55 (Dominican Archives,
Hinkley, Leicestershire); Confirmations 1863, 1869, 1877, 1880, 1887,
1892-1935 (Plymouth Diocesan Archives). Served from Chudleigh
Cop C 1736-55 (Ptd CRS 25: 1925)

CHUDLEIGH (RC) St Alphonsus Ligouri f 1887

CHUDLEIGH (Bapt) Erected 1850 [1851 Religious Census] [1882 Return]
Later became a house

CHUDLEIGH (Presb/Ind/Cong, later URC) Woodway Street. f 1662; lapsed.
Revived 1710. Presb until 1794. Rebuilt 1830 [1851 Religious Census]
[1882 Return]
OR ZC 1711-1837 (RG 4/518,3560 PRO); C 1711-1896, 1942-85 M 1945-79
B 1834-1881, 1945-91 (DRO)
Cop ZCB 1711-1810 (DCRS/WSL); C 1711-1837 (SG)
Cop (Mf) ZC 1711-1837 (Mf DCRS/WSL, SG); Extr ZC 1711-1837 (IGI);
ZC 1711-1837 (Mf I SLC)

CHUDLEIGH (Wes) Erected 1837 [1851 Religious Census]
OR for *c*.1801-36 *see* ASHBURTON CIRCUIT (RG 4/840,1763 PRO)

CHUDLEIGH (S of F) fl *c*.1703-08, associated with BOVEY TRACEY

CHUDLEIGH (Brethren) f *c*.1836 [1851 Religious Census]

CHUDLEIGH KNIGHTON partly in BOVEY TRACEY *q.v.* partly in HENNOCK

CHULMLEIGH St Mary Magdalene [Witheridge Hundred; South Molton Union] [1573] Now with CHAWLEIGH, CHELDON, WEMBWORTHY, EGGESFORD, BURRINGTON
OR C 1653-1953 M 1653-1986 B 1653-1989 (DRO)
BT CMB 1610, 1621, 1624, 1635-36, 1668, 1678-80, 1682-83, 1688-91, 1696-97, 1699-1700, 1702?, 1703, 1705-07, 1709-12, 1714-16, 1718, 1720, 1722, 1726, 1728, 1730, 1732-41, 1743, 1745-56, 1762, 1764-65, 1768-84, 1786-99, (1800-12 ?); CMB 1813-15, 1820, 1822 C 1826, 1829-33, 1835, 1838 M 1829-35 B 1826, 1829-35, 1838-50, 1852-64 (DRO)
Cop CMB 1610-36 from BT, 1651-54, 1682-1726 (DCRS/WSL); Extr CB 1655-1726 M 1655-1747 (SG); M 1610-1812 (Great Card Index, SG); M 1653-1726 (Boyd); Extr C 1655-81 M 1686-1747 B 1688-1726 (Vol 18, BG/PCL)
Cop (Mf) Extr C 1610-1726 M 1610-21, 1635-36, 1653-1726 (IGI); C 1610-1726 M 1610-21, 1635-36, 1653-1726 (Mf I SLC)
MI Incledon 163 (NDA)

CHULMLEIGH (RC) Our Lady and St Bernard 1955

CHULMLEIGH (Ind/Cong, later Cong Fed) East Street f 1662. Licensed 1672. Rebuilt 1710 [1851 Religious Census]
OR ZC 1812-37 (RG 4/579 PRO); C 1848-1972 M 1848-1976 B 1848-1964; unfit for production (DRO)
Cop ZC 1812-37 (SG)
Cop (Mf) ZC 1812-37 (Mf DCRS/WSL, SG); Extr ZC 1812-37 (IGI); ZC 1812-37 (Mf I SLC)

CHULMLEIGH (Wes) New Street. Erected 1810 [1851 Religious Census]
OR for *c.*1806-37 *see* BARNSTAPLE CIRCUIT, BIDEFORD, CULLOMPTON (RG 4/954,955,958 PRO)

CHULMLEIGH (Bible Christian) Bethlehem, South Molton Street. Erected 1836 [1851 Religious Census] [1882 Return] fl *c.*1970

CHULMLEIGH (S of F) Meeting house 1743

CHURCHSTANTON [Hemyock Hundred; Taunton Union] see NIPR Vol 8 Part 3 Somerset

CHURCHSTOW St Mary [Stanborough Hundred; Kingsbridge Union] [326] see also chapelry of KINGSBRIDGE. Now with MALBOROUGH, SOUTH HUISH, WEST ALVINGTON
OR C 1542-1652, 1695-1876 M 1539-1653, 1695-1993 B 1539-1641, 1695-1959 (DRO)
BT CMB 1602, 1606, 1610, 1614-17, 1633, 1666, 1668-69, 1677, 1689, 1696-97, 1699 (1700-1812 ?); C 1813-36, 1838-39 M 1813-19, 1821-23, 1825-34, 1836-37, 1839 B 1813-39 (DRO)
Cop CMB 1542-1812; M 1754-1812 indexed by male spouse (DFHS); Extr C 1696-1756 M 1698-1725 B 1696-1802 (Vol 8, BG/PCL); Extr C 1544-1644 M 1541-1773 B 1543-1640 (Vol 17, BG/PCL)
Cop (Mf) C 1542-1652, 1695-1876 M 1539-1653, 1695-1837 B 1539-1641, 1695-1812 (Mfc SG)

CHURCHSTOW (Bapt) Burial Ground, Venn. 18th and 19th century monuments. Served Loddiswell and Kingsbridge

CHURSTON FERRERS St Mary the Virgin [Haytor Hundred; Totnes Union] [763]
Chapelry in BRIXHAM; separate parish by 1850. United with GOODRINGTON 1954.
Now with BRIXHAM
OR C 1590-1906 MB 1590-1936 (DRO)
BT CMB 1597-1601, 1606, 1610, 1614, 1616, 1623, 1632, 1635, 1663-64,
1666-67, 1671?, 1678, 1684, 1695 (1696-1812 ?); C 1813, 1815, 1820-32,
1833-44, 1846-49, 1851-60, 1863 M 1813, 1815, 1818, 1820-32, 1834-36
B 1813 (DRO)
Cop C 1589-1653 MB 1590-1653 (Ptd *New York Genealogical Record* 63, 64:
1932-33); B 1800-37 (Ptd DFHS); CMB 1589-1837 (DCRS/WSL); B 1800-37
(WSL, SG); M 1590-1836 (Boyd)
Cop (Mf) (Torquay SP); Extr C 1589-1837 M 1590-1836 (IGI); C 1589-1837
M 1590-1836 (Mf I SLC)
MI (Ptd M.Adams 'Some notes on the church and parish of Churston Ferrers':
TDA 36: 1904: 506-16); Extr (Whitmore MS, SG)

CHURSTON FERRERS Chapel of the Good Shepherd, Galmpton. Chapel-of-ease to
St Mary, Churston Ferrers. Converted from a barn 1961. Now with BRIXHAM
OR *see* St Mary

CHURSTON FERRERS (Wes)
OR for *c*.1811-37 *see* BRIXHAM CIRCUIT, TEIGNMOUTH (RG 4/842,1220 PRO)

CLANNABOROUGH St Petrock [North Tawton and Winkleigh Hundred; Crediton
Union] [58] Now with NORTH CREADY
OR C 1697-1812 M 1696-1913 B 1697-1809 (DRO)
BT CMB 1606, 1610, 1625, 1627, 1635, 1672, 1675, 1678, 1682, 1694, 1715,
1741, 1751, 1793 (1794-1812 ?); C 1813-30, 1833-38, 1840, 1843-46
M 1816, 1818, 1821-23, 1825-26, 1828, 1834 B 1814, 1816, 1818, 1820-22,
1824-26, 1828-30, 1833-36, 1839, 1843, 1846 (DRO)
Cop CMB 1696-1850 (DCRS/WSL)
Cop (Mf) Extr C 1696-1849 M 1696-1844 (IGI); C 1696-1849 M 1696-1844
(Mf I SLC)
MI (I, DFHS)

CLAWTON St Leonard [Black Torrington Hundred; Holsworthy Union] [570]
Now with ASHWATER, HALWILL, BEAWORTHY, TETCOTT, LUFFINCOTT
OR C 1694-1917 M 1697-1977 B 1693-1920 (DRO)
BT CMB 1604, 1612, 1614, 1618, 1625-26, 1629, 1636, 1638, 1664, 1666,
1669-74, 1676-82, 1697 (1698-1812 ?); CMB 1813-15 CM 1821-25 B 1821-24
CMB 1827, 1829, 1831, 1833-36 (DRO)
Cop M 1813-37 (Ptd DFHS); CMB 1604-80 from BT, 1692-1837 (DCRS/WSL);
M 1604-1837 (Boyd)
Cop (Mf) Extr C 1612-1837 M 1612-38, 1664-82, 1697-1837 (IGI); C 1612-1837
M 1612-38, 1664-82, 1697-1837 (Mf I SLC)
MI Ch extr (Ptd H.Harvey *History of Clawton*: 1979: 38-40); Extr (Whitmore
MS, SG)

CLAWTON (Wes) Erected 1825 [1851 Religious Census]
OR for *c*.1817-37 *see* HOLSWORTHY (RG 4/1210 PRO)

CLAWTON (Wes) Clawton Bridge. Erected 1870. Building belonging to
Mr P.Stacey and others [1882 Return] fl *c*.1970

CLAWTON (Bible Christian) Bethesda. Erected 1831 [1851 Religious Census]
[1882 Return]

CLAWTON (Bible Christian) Affaland Cross, West Clawton. Erected 1880.
fl *c*.1970

CLAYHANGER St Peter [Bampton Hundred; Tiverton Union] [272] Now with
BAMPTON, MOREBATH, PETTON
OR C 1538-1961 M 1538-1833 B 1538-1812
BT CMB 1609, 1611-12, 1615, 1625, 1631, 1634, 1664, 1666-68, 1670, 1675,
   1677-78, 1683, 1685, 1687, 1690, 1696-97 (1698-1812 ?); C 1819-20,
   1828-29 B 1819-21, 1828-29 (DRO)
Cop CMB 1538-1837 (DCRS/WSL, WSL, Museum of Dartmoor Life, Okehampton);
   M 1754-1812 (DFHS); M 1538-1770 (Boyd)
Cop (Mf) (Tiverton SP); Extr C 1538-1837 M 1538-1662, 1684-1833 (IGI);
   C 1538-1837 (Mf I SLC)

CLAYHANGER (Wes) Clayhanger Wood. Erected 1840 [1851 Religious Census]

CLAYHANGER (Bible Christian) Erected 1892. Closed 1971. Now a house

CLAYHIDON St Andrew [Hemyock Hundred; Wellington Union (Somerset)] [767]
see also DUNKESWELL Abbey. Now with HEMYOCK, CULM DAVY, CULMSTOCK
OR C 1637-1848 M 1637-1788, 1803-37, 1940-48 B 1637-1870 (DRO) Noted in
   1831: 'The Marriage Register 1789-1802 was accidentally destroyed by a
   fire at the Glebe House'
BT CMB 1617, 1620, 1624-25, 1663, 1667, 1669-70, 1672, 1675, 1678, 1683,
   1685, 1687, 1690, 1695-96, 1700 (1701-1812 ?); CMB 1813-22, 1831-35
   (DRO)
Cop M 1813-37 (Ptd DFHS)
Cop (Mf) (Tiverton SP)
MI (Ptd I.Wakeling edit. The Monumental Inscriptions of the church and
   churchyard of...Clayhidon: Clayhidon Local History Group: 1986);
   Incledon 298 (NDA)

CLAYHIDON (Bapt) Bolham Chapel, Bolham Hill [1882 Return]

CLAYHIDON (Wes)
OR for c.1806-31 see CULLOMPTON (RG 4/958 PRO)

CLAYHIDON (Brethren) Black Down mission room, Rosemary Lane [1882 Return]

CLOVELLY All Saints [Hartland Hundred; Bideford Union] [907] Now with
HARTLAND COAST
OR C 1686-1838 M 1695-1989 B 1686-1863 (NDRO)
BT CMB 1610, 1621, 1623-24, 1627, 1634, 1644, 1668-70, 1674, 1678-79,
   1682-83, 1685?, 1688-91, 1694-95, 1699-1700, 1710, 1713-14, 1716
   (1717-1812 ?) None post-1812 listed
Cop B 1813-37 (Ptd DFHS); B 1813-37 (SG); M 1620-1837 (NDA)
Cop (Mf) (Appledore SP); C 1686-1838 M 1695-1837 Banns 1858-1946 B 1686-1863
   (Mfc SG)
MI (I, NDA)

CLOVELLY St Peter, Lower Clovelly. Chapel-of-ease licensed 1846; dedicated
1948 as daughter church to Clovelly All Saints
OR None. see All Saints

CLOVELLY (Wes) Erected 1816 [1851 Religious Census] [1882 Return] Rebuilt
1898. fl c.1970
OR for c.1807-37 see BARNSTAPLE CIRCUIT, BIDEFORD (RG 4/954,955 PRO)

CLOVELLY (Bible Christian) Dyke. Erected 1835 [1851 Religious Census]
[1882 Return]

CLYST FOMISON see SOWTON

CLYST HONITON St Michael and All Angels [East Budleigh Hundred; St Thomas Union] [426] Peculiar of the Dean and Chapter of Exeter until 1848, Now with AYLESBEARE, ROCKBEARE, FARRINGDON, SOWTON
OR C 1683-1875 M 1683-1840 B 1683-1915 (DRO)
BT CMB 1608, 1610, 1614, 1616, 1625, 1630-31, 1635, 1670, 1673 (1674-1812 ?); C 1819, 1825-27, 1834-35, 1838, 1840-41, 1843-48, 1851-72 M 1818, 1826, 1834, 1840 B 1819, 1824-27, 1832, 1835, 1838, 1841, 1843-48, 1851-72 (DRO)
Cop CMB 1683-1860 (WSL); CM 1683-1923 B 1683-1812 (DCRS/WSL); M 1683-1837 (Boyd)
Cop (Mf) Extr C 1683-1875 M 1683-1874 (IGI); C 1683-1875 M 1683-1874 (Mf I SLC)
MI (I, DFHS); Incledon 566 (NDA)

CLYST HYDON St Andrew [Cliston Hundred; St Thomas Union] [331]
Now with BRADNINCH
OR C 1552-1988 M 1548-1979 B 1548-1986 (DRO)
BT CMB 1611, 1668-69, 1672, 1675, 1678, 1683, 1685, 1687, 1690, 1697 (1698-1812 ?); CB 1813-36 M 1813, 1815-21, 1823-24, 1826-32, 1834-36 (DRO)
Cop B 1790-1837 (Ptd DFHS); B 1790-1837 (SG); CMB 1548-1837 (DCRS/WSL, WSL)
Cop (Mf) Extr C 1552-1837 M 1548-1837 (IGI); C 1552-1837 M 1548-1837 (Mf I SLC)
MI Incledon 247 (NDA)

CLYST ST FOUNSON   see SOWTON

CLYST ST GEORGE or CLYST WICK St George [East Budleigh Hundred; St Thomas Union] [359] Rebuilt 1851-59. Destroyed by bombing 1940. Rebuilt 1952. Now with CLYST ST MARY, WOODBURY SALTERTON
OR C 1813-93 M 1754-1993 B 1813,1834 (DRO) Noted in 1831: vol.1 CB 1567-1812 M 1567-1753. All other registers destroyed by bombing; see printed copy below
BT CMB 1615, 1620, 1628, 1633, 1639, 1641, 1662-64, 1670-72, 1675, 1677-78, 1680, 1683, 1691, 1695-97, 1701 (1702-1812 ?); C 1813-52, 1868-71 M 1813-20, 1822-17, 1830-32, 1834-37 B 1813-34, 1836-52, 1868-71 (DRO)
Cop CMB 1565-1812 (Ptd PRS vol 25: 1899); M 1813-37 (DCRS/WSL, SG); M 1565-1837 (Boyd); M 1790-1812 (Pallot); B 1813-37 (Ptd DFHS); Extr CMB 1583-1700 (Vol 19, BG/PCL)
Cop (Mf) Extr C 1568-1812 M 1567-1837 (IGI); C 1568-1812 M 1567-1837 (Mf I SLC)
MI (I, DFHS); Extr (Ptd H.Ellacombe 'The parish of Clyst St George, Devon' *Trans. Exeter Dioc. Archit. and Archaeo.Soc* 2nd ser 1: 1867: 89-158)

CLYST ST LAWRENCE St Lawrence [Cliston Hundred; St Thomas Union] [185]
Now with WHIMPLE, TALATON
OR C 1539-1995 M 1540-1971 B 1541-1811 (DRO) Noted in 1831: 'The early entries are very defective, and some nearly illegible'
BT CMB 1611, 1626, 1629, 1663, 1665, 1668-69, 1672, 1675, 1686-87, 1691, 1696-97 (1698-1812 ?); C 1813-35 M 1813-14, 1816, 1818-21, 1823-24, 1826-28, 1830-34 B 1814, 1816-21, 1823-29, 1831-35 (DRO)
MI Extr (Whitmore MS, SG)

CLYST ST MARY St Mary [East Budleigh Hundred; St Thomas Union] [137]
Now with CLYST ST GEORGE, WOODBURY SALTERTON
OR C 1662-1901 M 1662-1971 B 1662-1958 (DRO)
BT CMB 1610, 1613, 1621, 1625-26, 1630, 1637, 1664, 1667, 1669-70, 1672-73, 1675, 1679, 1683, 1696-97 (1698-1812 ?); CB 1813-18, 1820-29, 1832, 1834, 1838-57 M 1814-15, 1818, 1820, 1823-24, 1827-29 (DRO)

CLYST ST MARY cont.
Cop B 1813-37 (Ptd DFHS)
Cop (Mf) C 1662-1901 M 1676-1836 B 1662-1958 (Mfc SG)
MI (I, DFHS)

CLYST ST MARY (Who object to be designated) The Chapel [1882 Return]

CLYST ST MICHAEL   see SOWTON

CLYST WICK   see CLYST ST GEORGE

CLYST, BROAD   see BROADCLYST

COBBATON   see SWIMBRIDGE

COCKINGTON   see TORQUAY

COFFINSWELL St Bartholomew [Haytor Hundred; Newton Abbot Union]   [265]
Chapelry in ST MARYCHURCH. Separate parish 1913. Now with KINGSKERSWELL
OR C 1560-1812 M 1560-1837 B 1561-1811 (DRO)
BT CMB 1606, 1614, 1616, 1624, 1629, 1632-36, 1641, 1690 (1691-1812 ?);
    C 1813-36 M 1813-17, 1819-26, 1830-32, 1835, 1837 B 1813-15, 1817-28,
    1830-36 (DRO)
Cop M 1601-25 (SG); CMB 1560-1837 (DCRS/WSL); M 1601-25 (Boyd);
    Extr CMB 1571-1707 (Vol 16, BG/PCL)
Cop (Mf) (Torquay SP); Extr CM 1560-1837 (IGI); CM 1560-1837 (Mf I SLC)
MI Incledon 128 (NDA)

COFTON   see DAWLISH

COLATON RALEIGH St John the Baptist [East Budleigh Hundred; St Thomas Union]
[857] Now with NEWTON POPPLEFORD, HARPFORD. see also SALTERTON
OR C 1673-1981 M 1673-1932 B 1673-1982 (DRO)
BT CMB 1607, 1614, 1618, 1634-35, 1637, 1639, 1663-64, 1667-68, 1670-72,
    1675, 1678, 1683, 1685, 1687, 1690, 1693, 1695-97, 1699 (1700-1812 ?);
    none listed after 1812
Cop B 1813-37 (Ptd DFHS); B 1813-37 (SG)
Cop (Mf) C 1673-1842 M 1673-1837 B 1673-1871 (Mfc SG)
MI Incledon 715 (NDA)

COLATON RALEIGH Hawkerland mission chapel, erected 1889

COLATON RALEIGH Place Court, St Michael. Domestic chapel

COLATON RALEIGH (Wes) Chapel Lane. Erected 1894. fl c.1970

COLATON RALEIGH (S of F) Grindle burial ground 1658-1759. No meeting house.
Part of TOPSHAM MM

COLD EAST   see ILSINGTON

COLDRIDGE or COLERIDGE St Matthew [North Tawton and Winkleigh Hundred;
Crediton Union] [644] Now with LAPFORD, NYMET ROWLAND
OR C 1556-1854 M 1556-1978 B 1556-1961 (DRO)
BT CMB 1597, 1607, 1610, 1620, 1629, 1633, 1635, 1640, 1664, 1668, 1670,
    1674, 1678-79, 1683, 1688, 1690-91, 1694-97, 1699, 1700, 1703-04,
    1706-12, 1714, 1727-56, 1762, 1764 (1765-1812 ?); CMB 1813-17, 1818-29,
    1832 CB 1835-36, 1838-39, 1844-45 M 1835-37 (DRO)

COLDRIDGE cont.
Cop CMB 1556-1837 (DCRS/WSL, WSL); M 1556-1750 (Boyd)
Cop (Mf) Extr C 1558-1837 M 1556-1837 (IGI); C 1558-1837 M 1556-1837
(Mf I SLC)

COLDRIDGE (Who object to be designated) Allerbridge Chapel [1882 Return]

COLEBROOKE   see PLYMPTON ST MARY

COLEBROOKE St Andrew [Crediton Hundred; Crediton Union]   [880]
Peculiar of the Dean and Chapter of Exeter until 1848
OR C 1558-1939 M 1558-1605, 1623-1976 B 1558-1947 (DRO)
BT CMB 1610-11, 1613, 1626, 1631-32, 1669-70, 1678, 1690, 1696, 1701,
    1703-05, 1713-15, 1719-23, 1725-31, 1733-35, 1737-45, 1750, 1752,
    1754-66, 1768-76, 1778-99, 1801-12; CMB 1813-28 CB 1830-40 M 1830-38
    (DRO)
Cop Extr C 1558-1793 M 1563-1740 B 1564-1739 (Vol 10, BG/PCL)
Cop (Mf) C 1558-1845 M 1558-1838 B 1558-1865 (Mfc SG)
MI (I, DFHS)

COLEBROOKE (Brethren) Erected 1842 [1851 Religious Census]; Coleford [Kelly
1889]

COLERIDGE   see COLDRIDGE

COLLATON ST MARY   see PAIGNTON

COLLUMPTON   see CULLOMPTON

COLUMBJOHN   see BROADCLYST

COLYFORD   see COLYTON

COLYTON United benefice including COLYTON, SOUTHLEIGH, OFFWELL, WIDWORTHY,
FARWAY, NORTHLEIGH, MUSBURY

COLYTON St Andrew [Colyton Hundred; Axminster Union]   [2182] Peculiar of the
Dean and Chapter of Exeter until 1848. Included the Borough of Colyford.
see also the chapelries of SHUTE and MONKTON
OR C 1538-1934 M 1538-1930 B 1538-1940 (DRO)
BT CMB 1609, 1617, 1621, 1625-26, 1635 (1636-1812 ?); CMB 1813-35 C 1838,
    1840-42, 1845, 1847-56 B 1838, 1840-45, 1847-56 (DRO)
Cop CMB 1538-1837 (Ptd DCRS: 2 vols 1928); B 1813-37 (Ptd DFHS);
    CMB 1538-1837 (WSL); M 1813-37 (Ptd DFHS); M 1538-1837 (Boyd);
    M 1790-1837 (Pallot); M 1538-1837 indexed by grooms' names
    (Colyton SP)
Cop (Mf) (Colyton SP); Extr CM 1538-1837 (IGI); C 1538-1837 (Mf I SLC)
MI Ch (Ptd Pulman Book of the Axe: 1875; reprint 1969)(I, DFHS); Cy 1909
    (A.W.Matthews Ye Olde Mortality vol.8: MS SG); Incledon 371 (NDA); cy
    (Colyton SP)

COLYTON St Michael, Colyford. Chapel-of-ease erected 1889

COLYTON (Bapt) Harcombe Bottom. Erected 1843 [1851 Religious Census]
[Baptist Handbook 1861]

COLYTON (Presb/Unit) f 1662 Old Meeting or George's Meeting fl 1745-1939.
Rebuilt 1746 [1851 Religious Census]
OR C 1773-1836 (RG 4/2276 PRO); ZC 1824-62 B 1832-62 (RG 8/6 PRO)
Cop C 1773-1826 ZC 1823-36 DB 1832-36 (SG); C 1773-1836 (DFHS)
Cop (Mf) ZC 1823-62 (Mf DCRS/WSL); ZC 1823-62 B 1832-62 (Mf SG); C 1773-1826
        ZC 1823-36 DB 1832-36 (Mf DCRS/WSL, SG); Extr C 1773-1862 (IGI);
        C 1773-1862 (Mf I SLC)
MI Ch, cy (Ptd G.Evans *Colytonia: being some account of the Old and
        George's Meetings, Colyton, 1662-1898*: 1898: 56-64)

COLYTON (Ind/Cong) King Street. f 1814 [1851 Religious Census] Closed 1952.
Sold to Meth 1964
OR C 1815-57 (RG 4/521,3559 PRO)
Cop ZC 1815-37 (SG)
Cop (Mf) C 1815-57 (Mf DCRS/WSL); ZC 1815-37; Extr C 1815-57 (IGI);
        C 1815-57 (Mf I SLC)

COLYTON (Wes) Colyford. Erected 1833. Closed 1981. Now a house. New church
at Seaton
OR for *c.*1809-37 *see* AXMINSTER (RG 4/512 PRO)

COLYTON (Meth) King Street. Cong. chapel erected 1814; purchased 1964

COLYTON (Wes) Centenary. Erected 1839 [1851 Religious Census]

COLYTON (Brethren) Gospel Hall
OR M 1979 (DRO)

COLYTON Burial Board
OR B 1865-1921 (DRO)
Cop (Mf) B 1859-1979 (DRO)

COMBE MARTIN St Peter [Braunton Hundred; Barnstaple Union] [1031] Now with
NORTH DEVON COAST
OR C 1671-1894 M 1680-1904 B 1679-1980 (NDRO)
BT CMB 1597-1601, 1607-08, 1610, 1621, 1627, 1630-31, 1634, 1636, 1668,
        1670, 1671?, 1679, 1682, 1690-91, 1695-96, 1700, 1703-04, 1712, 1714-15,
        1776, 1778 (1779-1812 ?); C 1825, 1827, 1834, 1836-49 M 1825, 1827-28,
        1834, 1836 B 1825, 1834, 1836-49 (DRO)
Cop M 1754-1812 (DFHS); CMB 1597-1800 (I, NDRO)
MI Incledon 518 (NDA)

COMBE MARTIN (RC) The Assumption of Our Lady, Castle Street 1946

COMBE MARTIN (Bapt) Ebenezer, High Street f 1850 [1851 Religious Census]
[1882 Return]

COMBE MARTIN (Cong) f 1819. Erected 1823 [1851 Religious Census] Closed
OR ZC 1829-37 (RG 4/3874 PRO)
Cop ZC 1829-37 (SG)
Cop (Mf) ZC 1829-37 (Mf DCRS/WSL, SG); Extr ZC 1829-37 (IGI); ZC 1829-37
        (Mf I SLC)

COMBE MARTIN (Wes) Preaching room f 1847 [1851 Religious Census];
Castle Street [1882 Return] Erected 1884. fl *c.*1970
OR for *c.*1807-37 *see* BARNSTAPLE CIRCUIT (RG 4/954 PRO)

COMBE PYNE St Mary the Virgin [Axminster Hundred; Axminster Union] [142]
United 1972 with ROUSDON. Now with AXMINSTER
OR C 1685-1988 M 1690-1986 B 1690-1988 (DRO) Noted in 1831: gaps B 1781-95
   M 1749-56
BT CMB 1610, 1614, 1616-17, 1619-20, 1626, 1629, 1631, 1633, 1636, 1669-70,
   1672, 1675, 1678, 1683, 1685, 1687, 1690, 1697, 1700 (1701-1812 ?);
   C 1820, 1824-35, 1841-49, 1870-71 M 1824, 1827-32, 1835 B 1823-24,
   1827-31, 1833-36, 1843-44, 1846-49, 1870-71 (DRO)
Cop M 1813-37 (Ptd DFHS); CMB 1685-1837 (DCRS/WSL); C 1610-1812 M 1611-1956
   B 1610-1963 (Colyton SP)
Cop (Mf) (Colyton SP); Extr C 1685-1837 M 1690-1837 (IGI); C 1685-1837
     M 1690-1837 (Mf I SLC)
MI Cy 1909 (A.W.Matthews *Ye Olde Mortality* vol.8: MS SG); Incledon 355
   (NDA)

COMBE RALEIGH or COMBE RAWLEIGH St Nicholas [Axminster Hundred; Honiton
Union] [296] Now with HONITON
OR C 1653-1914 M 1654-1837 B 1653-1812 (DRO)
BT CMB 1608, 1616, 1619-20, 1625-26, 1633, 1666, 1668?, 1669, 1672, 1675,
   1678-79, 1682-85, 1687, 1690, 1698-1700, 1704, 1707, 1711 (1712-1812 ?);
   CMB 1817, 1819, 1821-24, 1826-27, 1830, 1833; 1817-33 unfit for
   production (DRO)
Cop (Mf) (Colyton SP); C 1653-1914 M 1654-1837 B 1653-1812 (Mfc SG)
MI Incledon 263 (NDA)

COMBEINTEIGNHEAD All Saints [Wonford Hundred until 1885; Newton Abbot Union
1836-85] [460] Now with STOKEINTEIGNHEAD, HACCOMBE
OR C 1669-1880 M 1653-1837 B 1653-1913 (DRO)
BT CMB 1602, 1606, 1611, 1617, 1624, 1626, 1630, 1635, 1638, 1641, 1663,
   1667, 1669-70, 1673, 1675, 1678-79, 1683, 1687, 1690, 1696, 1699, 1701,
   1750-54, 1757-58; CB 1759-62, 1765-70, 1772-80, 1796 (1797-1812 ?);
   CB 1813-38 M 1813-21, 1824-36, 1838 (DRO)
Cop B 1800-37 (Ptd DFHS); CMB 1606-70 from BT, 1669-1913 (WSL); C 1669-1913
   M 1653-1837, 1880-1913 B 1653-1913 (SG); B 1800-37 (SG)
Cop (Mf) (Torquay SP)
MI Ch, cy 1979 (Ts SG); Incledon 120 (NDA)

COMBEINTEIGNHEAD (Wes) A house [1851 Religious Census]

COMPTON GIFFORD *see* PLYMOUTH

COOKBURY St John the Baptist and the Seven Maccabees [Black Torrington
Hundred; Holsworthy Union] [290] Chapelry in MILTON DAMEREL. United 1954
with HOLSWORTHY. Now with BLACK TORRINGTON, BRADFORD, THORNBURY, HIGHAMPTON
OR C 1746-1980 M 1750-63, 1813-1974 B 1746-1990 (DRO) Noted in 1831: 'also
   Bapt Bur of Milton Damarel until 1791'
BT CMB 1609, 1613, 1616-17, 1624, 1631, 1633-34, 1663-64, 1666, 1668-72,
   1674, 1676-81, 1689, 1695-96, 1699 (1700-1812 ?); C 1818, 1826-27,
   1830-32, 1839 MB 1826-27, 1831, 1839 (DRO)
Cop CMB 1609-1812 from BT, 1746-1837 (DCRS/WSL); CMB 1609-34, 1663-1837 (SG)
Cop (Mf) Extr C 1609-1837 M 1609-34, 1663-98, 1721-37, 1750-64, 1779-98,
     1811-37 (IGI); C 1609-1837 M 1609-34, 1663-98, 1721-37, 1750-64,
     1779-98, 1811-37 (Mf I SLC)

COOKBURY (Wes)
OR for *c.*1817-37 *see* HOLSWORTHY (RG 4/1210 PRO)

COOKBURY (Bible Christian) Zion. Erected 1840 [1851 Religious Census]
[1882 Return] fl *c.*1970

COOKBURY (Bible Christian) Providence. Erected *c*.1836 [1851 Religious Census] [1882 Return]

COPPLESTONE   *see* DOWN ST MARY

CORNWOOD St Michael and All Angels [Ermington Hundred; Plympton St Mary Union] [1056] *see also* IVYBRIDGE
OR   C 1669, 1685-1925 M 1685-1957 B 1685-1897 (PWDRO)
BT   CMB 1610, 1613-15, 1623, 1633, 1677, 1682, 1686, 1688-90, 1695 (1696-1812 ?); CB 1838, 1840-44 (DRO)
Cop CMB 1685-1782 (DCRS/WSL); B 1813-37 (Ptd DFHS); Extr n.d. (DFHS); Extr CMB 1685-1834 (SG); Extr C 1686-1800 M 1685-1811 B 1685-1782, 1785-1810 (Vol 7, BG/PCL)
Cop (Mf) Extr C 1665-1783 M 1685-1783, 1806-11 (IGI); C 1665-1783 M 1685-1783, 1806-11 (Mf I SLC)
MI   (Ptd DRMI 12,13,14: 1998); (I, DFHS)

CORNWOOD Fardel. 15th cent. domestic chapel of Raleigh family

CORNWOOD (Ind/Cong now Cong Fed) John Poynter's house, Lutton [1882 Return] A cottage belonging to Richard Peake, Lutton [1882 Return] Underwood Memorial, New Road f 1853

CORNWORTHY St Peter [Coleridge Hundred; Totnes Union] [567]
Now with ASHPRINGTON, DITTISHAM
OR   C 1565-1859 M 1568-1837 B 1562-1889 (DRO)
BT   CMB 1602, 1609-11, 1615, 1618-20, 1623, 1633, 1639, 1663, 1666, 1668-69, 1671-72, 1674-77, 1679-82, 1684, 1686-87, 1689, 1695-96, 1699; CM 1750-59; CMB 1762-69; CM 1771-80 (1781-1812 ?); CB 1838-45 (DRO)
Cop Extr C 1562-1744 M 1578-1746 B 1562-1776 (Vol 5, BG/PCL)
Cop (Mf) (Totnes SP); C 1565-1859 M 1568-1837 B 1562-1889 (Mfc SG)

CORNWORTHY (Wes) f by 1848. 2 buildings [1851 Religious Census] Rebuilt 1896. fl *c*.1970

CORNWORTHY (Wes) West Cornworthy [1882 Return]

CORYTON St Andrew [Lifton Hundred; Tavistock Union] [314]
Now with MARYSTOW, STOWFORD, LEWTRENCHARD, THRUSHELTON
OR   C 1655-1991 M 1654-1992 B 1655-1992 (PWDRO)
BT   CMB 1609-11, 1614, 1616, 1619, 1624, 1631, 1641, 1664, 1666, 1668-71, 1674-76, 1678, 1688-90, 1695, 1699 (1700-1812 ?); C 1814-50 M 1814-15, 1817, 1820, 1822-23, 1825-27, 1829, 1831-32, 1834, 1836-37 B 1814-20, 1822-50 (DRO)
Cop B 1775-1900 (I, PWDRO)
Cop (Mf) (Tavistock SP)

CORYTON (Bible Christian) A house. 1813 [1851 Religious Census]

CORYTON (Bible Christian) Coryton Mill [1851 Religious Census]

COTLEIGH St Michael [Colyton Hundred; Honiton Union] [240]
Now with YARCOMBE, MEMBURY, UPOTTERY
OR   C 1653-1926 M 1664-1837 B 1653-1678, 1763-1812 (DRO)
     No earlier registers found in 1831
BT   CMB 1609, 1612, 1620, 1626, 1663-64, 1666-72, 1675, 1678, 1683, 1685, 1687, 1690, 1696, 1699 (1700-1812 ?); C 1813-14, 1816-19, 1821-26, 1828-33, 1835-41 M 1813-14, 1816-18, 1821-25, 1827, 1829-33, 1835, 1839-40 B 1813-14, 1816-19, 1821-26, 1828-33, 1835-41 (DRO)

COTLEIGH cont.
Cop CMB 1608-36 from BT, 1653-1837 (DCRS/WSL)
Cop (Mf) (Colyton SP); Extr C 1608-31, 1653-1837 M 1609-25, 1663-1837 (IGI);
    C 1608-31, 1653-1837 M 1609-25, 1663-1837 (Mf I SLC)
MI Incledon 492 (NDA)

COUNTESS WEAR   see TOPSHAM

COUNTISBURY St John the Evangelist [Shirwell Hundred; Barnstaple Union]
[187] Chapelry in LYNTON. Separate parish 1747. Now with NORTH DEVON COAST
OR C 1676-1955 M 1676-1973 B 1676-1812 (NDRO)
BT CMB 1601, 1608, 1610, 1614, 1624, 1633, 1638, 1668, 1670, 1672-73, 1678,
    1680, 1682-83, 1689-90, 1692, 1694-97, 1702-23, 1725-28, 1732-34,
    1736-37, 1739-42, 1745-56, 1762-81, 1783-84, 1786-87, 1789-1803,
    1805-12; CB 1813-20, 1823-25, 1827 C 1829-57 M 1814-20, 1823-25, 1827,
    1829-33, 1835-36 B 1829-38, 1840-46, 1848-57 (DRO)
Cop M 1676-1757 (Ptd Phil 112: 1909); B 1813-37 (Ptd DFHS); CMB 1676-1850
    (DCRS/WSL, NDA); CMB 1676-1757 (WSL); M 1754-1812 (DFHS); M 1676-1837
    (Great Card Index, SG); B 1813-37 (SG); M 1676-1837 (Boyd); M 1790-1836
    (Pallot)
Cop (Mf) Extr CM 1676-1850 (IGI); CM 1676-1850 (Mf I SLC)
MI (I, DFHS); Ch, cy (Ptd Dwelly 1-13); Incledon 648 (NDA)

COUNTISBURY St John the Baptist, Lynmouth. Chapel-of-ease in Countisbury.
Opened 1871. Now with NORTH DEVON COAST
OR None

COUNTISBURY (Free Church of England) A loft belonging to Robert Roe
[1882 Return]

COVE St John the Baptist [Tiverton Hundred; Tiverton Union] Chapelry in
TIVERTON. Rebuilt 1846. Parish created 1886 from Tiverton St Peter. United
with Chevithorne. Redundant. Now an artist's studio
OR C 1680-1987 M 1682-1982 B 1680-1939 (DRO)
BT None; see TIVERTON

COWLEY   see BRAMPFORD SPEKE

CRAB TREE   see PLYMOUTH

CREACOMBE   hamlet in HOLBETON

CREACOMBE St Michael [Witheridge Hundred; South Molton Union] [43] Rebuilt
1857. Redundant. Now with WITHERIDGE, THELBRIDGE, MESHAW, EAST WORLINGTON,
WEST WORLINGTON.
OR C 1696-1990 M 1759-1984 B 1695-1974 (NDRO)
BT CMB 1607-08, 1617, 1620, 1630, 1635, 1641, 1668, 1674, 1678, 1683,
    1688-91, 1694-95, 1699-1700, 1704, 1708-09, 1712, 1714-15 (1716-1812 ?);
    C 1813-17, 1819, 1821-22, 1834-41, 1843-45 M 1813-13, 1817, 1819, 1824,
    1826-29, 1831-35 B 1813-14, 1816-17, 1821, 1826, 1829, 1832-35, 1842-45
    (DRO)
Cop CB 1694-1837 M 1759-1837 (DCRS/WSL); M 1759-1835 (Boyd)
Cop (Mf) Extr C 1694, 1704-1837 M 1759, 1770-1835 (IGI); C 1704-1837
    (Mf I SLC)
MI (I, NDA); (I, DFHS); Incledon 169 (NDA)

CREDITON Collegiate Church of the Holy Cross [Crediton Hundred;
Crediton Union 1836-94] [5922] Peculiar of the Bishop of Exeter until 1848.
see also chapelries of KENNERLEIGH and SANDFORD. Now with SHOBROOKE
OR C 1558-1965 M 1558-80, 1597-1947, 1964-86 B 1557-1929 (DRO)
BT CMB 1606, 1611, 1613, 1617, 1628, 1630, 1636, 1668-71, 1673-86, 1688,
  1690-91, 1693-95, 1697-1720, 1730 (1731-1812 ?); CB 1813-47 M 1813-16,
  1818-39 (DRO)
Cop M 1813-37 (Ptd DFHS); B 1813-37 (Ptd DFHS); B 1813-37 (SG);
  CMB 1557-1837 (DCRS/WSL); Extr C: selected names (DFHS); Extr 'several
  sequences' of CMB 1557-1780 (Vol 10, BG/PCL)
Cop (Mf) Extr C 1558-1843 M 1558-80, 1597-1837 (IGI); C 1558-1843 (Mf I SLC)
MI (I, DFHS); Cy 1967 (Ts SG); Extr (Whitmore MS, SG)

CREDITON Holy Trinity, Yeoford. Chapel-of-ease to Crediton Holy Cross
[PO Directory 1856]
MI (I, DFHS)

CREDITON St Lawrence. Chapel erected 1220-25. Restored 1920-21. Later used
as chapel by Queen Elizabeth Grammar School and Crediton High School.

CREDITON St Luke, Posbury. Proprietary chapel. Erected as chapel-of-ease to
Crediton Holy Cross [PO Directory 1856]

CREDITON St Francis, Posbury. Proprietary chapel erected 1835
OR None
MI (I, DFHS)

CREDITON (RC) St Boniface, Bowden Hill 1948. Park Road 1969

CREDITON (Bapt) Erected 1822 [1851 Religious Census]

CREDITON (Presb/Unit) Bowden Hill. f 1668. Rebuilt 1729
[1851 Religious Census] [1882 Return] Closed 1965. Demolished 1970s ?
OR ZC 1735-84, ZCB 1785-1837 (RG 4/3558,843 PRO)
Cop ZC 1735-1837 B 1785-1837 (SG)
Cop (Mf) ZC 1735-1837 B 1785-1837 (Mf DCRS/WSL, SG); Extr C 1735-1837 (IGI);
  C 1735-1837 (Mf I SLC)

CREDITON (Ind/Cong, later Cong Fed) Broad Street Chapel, High Street.
Erected 1757 [1851 Religious Census]; rebuilt 1865
OR ZCB 1804-37 (RG 4/522 PRO)
Cop ZC 1805-37 (SG)
Cop (Mf) ZCB 1805-37 (DCRS/WSL, SG); Extr ZC 1805-37 (IGI); ZC 1805-37
  (Mf I SLC)

CREDITON (Wes) Erected 1816 [1851 Religious Census]; Union Road, erected
1892. fl *c.*1970
OR for *c.*1806-37 *see* CULLOMPTON, EXETER Mint (RG 4/958,1207,1208 PRO)

CREDITON (Wes) Bowden Hill [1882 Return]

CREDITON (Bible Christian) High Street [1882 Return]

CREDITON (Wes) Uton [1851 Religious Census]

CREDITON (S of F) Crediton MM f 1691; joined EXETER MM 1696

CREDITON (S of F) f *c.*1691. fl *c.*1732

CREDITON (Brethren) High Street [1882 Return]

CREDITON (Salvation Army) Temperance Hall, Searle Street [1882 Return]

CREDITON (Brethren) A room. 1840 [1851 Religious Census]

CREEDY, NORTH United benefice including CHERITON FITZPAINE, PUDDINGTON,
WOOLFARDISWORTHY EAST, KENNERLIEGH, WEASHFORD PYNE, POUGHILL, STOCKLEIGH
ENGLISH, MORCHARD BISHOP, STOCKLEIGH POMEROY, DOWN ST MARY, CLANNABOROUGH

CROCKERNWELL   see CHERITON BISHOP

CROWDEN   see LEW, NORTH

CROWNHILL   see PLYMOUTH

CROYDE   see GEORGEHAM

CRUWYS MORCHARD Holy Cross [Witheridge Hundred; Tiverton Union]   [634]
Destroyed by fire 1688. Rebuilt. Now with EXE VALLEY
OR C 1572-1960 M 1572-1978 B 1572-1901 (DRO)
BT CMB 1602-03, 1608, 1610, 1612-13, 1615, 1629, 1644, 1668, 1670, 1672,
    1674, 1678, 1682-83, 1688-91, 1694, 1696-97, 1699?, 1700, 1704, 1707-08,
    1712, 1714-15 (1716-1812 ?); CB 1813-36 M 1814-20, 1822-36 (DRO)
Cop CB 1572-1812 M 1572-1790 (DCRS/WSL)
Cop (Mf) (Tiverton SP); Extr C 1572-1812 M 1572-1620, 1638-1790 (IGI);
    C 1572-1812 (Mf I SLC)

CRUWYS MORCHARD (Presb) fl c.1672-90

CRUWYS MORCHARD (Ind/Cong, now Cong Fed) Way Village. Erected 1847
[1851 Religious Census] [1882 Return]

CRUWYS MORCHARD (Ind) Penny Moor. n.d. [1851 Religious Census] [1882 Return]

CULLOMPTON St Andrew [Hayridge Hundred; Tiverton Union]   [3813]
OR C 1601-1884 M 1601-43, 1678-1906 B 1601-45, 1678-1879 (DRO)
BT CMB 1609, 1612, 1615, 1617, 1620, 1638, 1675, 1677, 1683, 1685, 1687,
    1696, 1714-15, 1718-35, 1737, 1739-41, 1743-48, 1750, 1753-54, 1756-77,
    1779-1802, 1804-13; CMB 1813-21, 1824-29 CB 1831, 1833-34, 1861-63
    M 1833-34 (DRO)
Cop CMB 1609-1812 from BT (DCRS/WSL); B 1813-37 (Ptd DFHS)
Cop (Mf) (Tiverton SP); C 1601-1844 M 1601-43, 1678-1837 B 1601-45,
    1678-1837 (Mfc SG)
MI Ch extr (Ptd TDA 42: 1910: 187-203)

CULLOMPTON Langford Chapel. Erected by Corpus Christi College, Oxford.
Now with Cullompton
OR None

CULLOMPTON (RC) St Boniface, Shortlands 1929

CULLOMPTON (Bapt) High Street. Erected 1743 [1851 Religious Census]
Fore Street [1882 Return]
OR C 1803-1959 (DRO)

CULLOMPTON (Cong) Tiverton Lane f 1831 [1851 Religious Census]
OR ZC 1831-37 (RG 4/333, 520 PRO)
Cop ZC 1831-36 (SG)
Cop (Mf) ZC 1831-36 DCRS/WSL, (Mf SG); Extr ZC 1831-36 (IGI); ZC 1831-36
      (Mf I SLC)

CULLOMPTON (Presb/Unit) Pound Square f 1662 erected 1695, rebuilt 1814,
1912 [1851 Religious Census]
OR ZC 1693-1823 ZCB 1823-37 (RG 4/13,2097,519 (PRO); CMB 1756-1923 (DRO)
Cop ZC 1694-1823 CB 1823-37 (SG)
Cop (Mf) ZC 1694-1823 ZCB 1823-37 (Mf DCRS/WSL, SG); Extr ZC 1694-1836
      (IGI); ZC 1694-1836 (Mf I SLC)

CULLOMPTON (Wes) New Cut. Erected 1806 [1851 Religious Census] Rebuilt 1872
[1882 Return]
OR ZC 1806-31 (RG 4/958 PRO); C 1905-90 M 1934-44 (DRO); for c.1812-37 see
      also EXETER Mint, TIVERTON (RG 4/1207,1208,342 PRO)
Cop ZC 1806-31 (SG)
Cop (Mf) ZC 1806-31 (Mf DCRS/WSL, SG); Extr ZC 1806-31 (IGI); ZC 1806-31
      (Mf I SLC)

CULLOMPTON (S of F) Cullompton and Spiceland MM f 1668; united with MEMBURY
MM 1742; with EXETER MM 1785
OR C 1778-90 B 1779-92 (RG 6/270, 271 PRO)

CULLOMPTON (S of F) f 1655. Meeting house 1676; burial ground 1708;
closed 1819
OR Z 1650-1783 M 1664-1790 B 1658-1797 including Cullompton and other
   places (RG 6/1033 PRO)

CULLOMPTON Burial Board
OR B 1898-1902 (DRO)

CULM DAVY   see HEMYOCK

CULMSTOCK All Saints [Hemyock Hundred; Wellington Union (Somerset)]   [1519]
Peculiar of the Dean and Chapter of Exeter until 1848. Now with HEMYOCK,
CULM DAVY, CLAYHIDON
OR C 1645-1911 M 1646-1718, 1740-1941 B 1645-1884 (DRO)
BT CMB 1608-10, 1614?, 1615, 1626, 1630-31, 1635, 1673, 1675, 1678, 1690
   (1691-1812 ?); CB 1813-35, 1841-76 M 1813-35 (DRO)
Cop M 1813-37 (Ptd DFHS); B 1813-37 (Ptd DFHS); B 1813-37 (SG); CMB 1608-35
      from BT, 1645-1837 (DCRS/WSL); C 1802-10 (DFHS); M 1646-1837 (Boyd)
Cop (Mf) (Tiverton SP); Extr C 1608-1837 M 1608-35, 1646-1837 (IGI);
         C 1608-1837 (Mf I SLC)

CULMSTOCK (Bapt) Prescott Chapel f 1715; rebuilt 1785 [1851 Religious
Census]
OR Z 1787-1836 B 1790-1836 (RG 4/523 PRO)
Cop Z 1787-1836 (SG)
Cop (Mf) Z 1787-1836 (Mf DCRS/WSL); Z 1787-1836 B 1790-1836 (Mf SG);
         Extr Z 1787-1836 (IGI)

CULMSTOCK (Wes) Small Brook Chapel. Erected 1808 [1851 Religious Census]
[1882 Return] Rebuilt 1888 ? fl c.1970
OR for c.1806-37 see CULLOMPTON, TIVERTON (RG 4/958,342 PRO)

CULMSTOCK (S of F) Spiceland Meeting f 1671; meeting house by 1683; rebuilt 1815; [1851 Religious Census] [1882 Return] Burial ground used to 1917. Now meeting at Uffculme, Cullompton
OR B 1784-87, 1837 (RG 6/1171 PRO); Z 1839-1846 M 1765-94 B 1839-84 (DRO); *see also* BURLESCOMBE and DEVON Eastern Division
BT B 1869 (DRO)
Cop (Mf) Z 1839-46 M 1765-94 D 1839-84 (Mfc Colyton SP)

DAINTON *see* IPPLEPEN

DALWOOD hamlet in Stockland (Dorset) transferred to Devon 1866.
see NIPR *Dorset*

DARTINGTON St Mary [Stanborough Hundred; Totnes Union] [618] Rebuilt 1878-80 on new site. Now with TOTNES, BRIDGETOWN, BERRY POMEROY, BROOKING
OR C 1542-1630, 1654-1862 M 1538-1635, 1554-1852 B 1539-1618, 1654-1890 (DRO)
BT CMB 1608 or 1609, 1614-15, 1624, 1626, 1633, 1663-64, 1666, 1668-69, 1671-76, 1680-81, 1684, 1685-86, 1689-90, 1695, 1700, 1750-56, 1758-60 (1761-1812 ?); CB 1813-14, 1816-28, 1837-43 M 1813-14, 1816-20, 1822-28, 1838-43 (DRO)
Cop CMB 1538-1850 (DCRS/WSL); Extr C 1558-1629 Z 1654-1712 M 1549-1743 B 1553-1724 (Vol 6, BG/PCL)
Cop (Mf) (Totnes SP); Extr C 1542-1727 M 1538-55, 1569-1635, 1653-1727, 1810-52 (IGI); C 1542-1727 M 1538-55, 1569-1635, 1653-1727, 1810-52 (Mf I SLC)

DARTINGTON St Barnabas, Tigley Cross, Brooking. Erected 1851-55. Rebuilt 1885. Chapel-of-ease to Dartington. Now with TOTNES, BRIDGETOWN, BERRY POMEROY, DARTINGTON
OR *see* DARTINGTON St Mary

DARTINGTON (Christians) Venton. A building [1882 Return]

DARTINGTON (Presb) fl *c.*1672-90

DARTINGTON (Wes)
OR for *c.*1820-36 *see* ASHBURTON CIRCUIT (RG 4/840 PRO)

DARTMOOR FOREST township in LYDFORD [353]

DARTMOOR, EAST (Bapt)
OR Z 1778-1837 (DRO)

DARTMOUTH Borough of Clifton Dartmouth Hardness, consisting of parishes of Townstall,St Saviour and St Clement [4597]

DARTMOUTH St Clement, Townstal [Coleridge Hundred; Totnes Union 1836-91] [1246] Now with Dartmouth St Saviour, St Petrox
OR C 1653-1840 M 1653-1894 B 1653-1876 (DRO)
BT CMB 1597-1602, 1608, 1611, 1613-15, 1619, 1625-26, 1630-31, 1633, 1664, 1666, 1669, 1671-72, 1674-76, 1678, 1679, 1680-81, 1684, 1686-88, 1697, 1699-1700 (1701-1812 ?); CMB 1813-36 (DRO)
Cop B 1813-37 (Ptd DFHS); B 1813-37 (SG); CMB 1597-1633 from BT, 1653-1837 (DCRS/WSL)
Cop (Mf) (Torquay and Totnes SPs); Extr C 1597-1837 M 1597-1633, 1653-1837 (IGI); C 1597-1837 M 1597-1633, 1653-1837 (Mf I SLC)
MI Extr (Whitmore MS, SG)

DARTMOUTH St Saviour. Chapelry in Townstal [2316] Now with St Clement
Townstal, St Petrox
OR   C 1586-1876 M 1586-1883 B 1586-1854, 1881 including some Huguenot
     entries (DRO)
BT   CMB 1609, 1610 or 1616, 1614-15, 1618, 1624-26, 1629, 1633, 1666,
     1668-72, 1676-77, 1679-81, 1684, 1686, 1689-90, 1695, 1697, 1699
     (1700-1812 ?); CMB 1813-35 (DRO)
Cop B 1813-37 (Ptd DFHS); B 1813-37 (SG); CMB 1586-1837 (DCRS/WSL);
     M 1586-1756 (Boyd); 'Townstall and Dartmouth' Extr C 1587-1781
     M 1586-1750 B 1586-1774; St Saviour Extr C 1605-1761 B 1678-1749
     (Vol 6, BG/PCL)
Cop (Mf) (Torquay and Totnes SPs); ; Extr CM 1586-1837 (IGI); CM 1586-1837
     (Mf I SLC)
MI   (Ptd W.H.Rogers *The monumental brasses found in the churches of Stoke
     Fleming, St Saviour's and St Petrock's Dartmouth*: 1906)

DARTMOUTH St Petrox. Chapelry in Townstal. Separate parish 1748 [1035]
Now with St Clement Townstal, St Saviour
OR   C 1652-1901 M 1653-1837 B 1652-1877 (DRO)
BT   CMB 1610, 1614-20, 1629, 1634-35, 1641, 1663, 1666, 1669-72, 1674,
     1677-80, 1682, 1684, 1686-87, 1689-90, 1695-97, 1699 (1700-1812 ?);
     CB 1813-11, 1824-43 M 1813-22, 1824-36 (DRO)
Cop B 1813-37 (Ptd DFHS); B 1813-37 (SG); CMB 1610-42 from BT, 1652-1837
     (DCRS/WSL); Extr C 1652 Z 1656-1730 M 1657-1754 BD 1652-1777 (Vol 6,
     BG/PCL)
Cop (Mf) (Torquay and Totnes SPs); Extr C 1610-1837 M 1610-41, 1653-1837
     (IGI); C 1610-1837 M 1610-41, 1653-1837 (Mf I SLC)
MI   (I, DFHS); (Ptd W.H.Rogers *The monumental brasses found in the churches
     of Stoke Fleming, St Saviour's and St Petrock's Dartmouth*: 1906)

DARTMOUTH St Barnabas. Chapel-of-ease to St Petrox. Closed. Later a workshop

DARTMOUTH Mariners' Chapel fl c.1836. Interdenominational

DARTMOUTH Britannia Royal Naval College
OR   C 1952+ M 1935+; no burials (Chaplain)

DARTMOUTH Dartmouth Training Squadron R.N.
OR   C 1956-63 (MoD)

DARTMOUTH (RC) Served at an early date from Lulworth Castle, Dorset. f 1782,
closed 1814. St John the Baptist, Newcomen Road 1868 [1882 Return]
OR   C 1782-1814 M 1792, 1814 Confirmations 1784, 1793 (Plymouth Diocesan
     Archives); C 1864+ M 1875+ B 1865+ Confirmations 1866+ (Inc)
     see also TORQUAY for 1859-63. Possible earlier entries at Lulworth
     Castle, Dorset C 1755-1840 B 1755-1840 (RG 4/303 PRO)
Cop Lulworth Castle (Ptd CRS 6: 1909)
Cop (Mf) C 1782-1814 (Mfc DRO)

DARTMOUTH (RC) St Philip Howard, Royal Naval College

DARTMOUTH (Bapt) Zion, Chapel Lane, Townstal f by 1640; rebuilt 1783, 1846
[1851 Religious Census]
OR   C 1786-1968 (DRO)

DARTMOUTH (Presb/Ind/Cong, later URC Flavel Memorial, South Parade f 1662.
Rebuilt 1841, 1895 [1851 Religious Census]
OR C 1726-1837 (RG 4/959 PRO)
Cop ZC 1726-1837 (SG)
Cop (Mf) ZC 1726-1837 (Mf DCRS/WSL, SG); Extr C 1726-1837 (IGI); C 1726-1837
     (Mf I SLC)

DARTMOUTH (Wes) (sometimes DARTMOUTH and BRIXHAM) Circuit
OR C 1840-1906 (DRO); for c.1811-37 see BRIXHAM CIRCUIT, KINGSBRIDGE
     (RG 4/842,1088 PRO)
Cop (Mf) C 1840-1906 (Mf Totnes SP); C 1840-67 (Torquay SP)

DARTMOUTH (Wes) Northford Lane. Erected 1816 [1851 Religious Census]
Market Square, Townstal [1882 Return] Closed 1983
OR M 1847-1877, 1912-80 (DRO); for c.1811-37 see also BRIXHAM CIRCUIT
(RG 4/842 PRO)

DARTMOUTH (Prim Meth) Circuit
OR C 1882-1933 (DRO)
Cop (Mf) C 1882-1933 (Mfc Torquay and Totnes SPs)

DARTMOUTH (Prim Meth) Townstal
OR C 1862-1870 (DRO)
Cop (Mf) C 1862-70 (Mf Totnes Museum)

DARTMOUTH (Prim Meth) Crowther's Hill [1882 Return]

DARTMOUTH (Brethren) [1851 Religious Census]

DAWLISH St Gregory [Exminster Hundred; Newton Abbot Union 1836-94] [3151]
Peculiar of the Dean and Chapter of Exeter until 1848. see also chapelry of
EAST TEIGNMOUTH
OR C 1651-1974 MB 1627-1975 (DRO)
BT CMB 1609, 1613, 1633-35, 1638, 1697 (1698-1812 ?); C 1813, 1816,
     1819-23, 1825-27, 1829-30, 1832-34, 1837-39 M 1813, 1816, 1818-23,
     1826-27, 1829-30, 1832-34 B 1813, 1816, 1819-27, 1829-30, 1832-34,
     1837-39 (DRO)
Cop B 1813-37 (Ptd DFHS); B 1813-37 (WSL, SG); M 1754-1812 (DFHS)
MI Ch extr (Ptd Cresswell 62-7); Incledon 89 (NDA)

DAWLISH St George, Holcombe. Mission church erected 1867
OR M 1945-83 (DRO)

DAWLISH St Paul, Starcross. Parish created 1829 from DAWLISH, KENTON.
Now with KENTON, MAMHEAD, POWDERHAM, COFTON
OR C 1828-1992 M 1828-1991 B 1828-1916 (DRO)
BT CB 1831-49 M 1831-37 (DRO)
Cop B 1828-37 (Ptd DFHS); CMB 1828-43 (DCRS/WSL); CMB 1828-37 (SG);
     M 1828-37 (Boyd)
Cop (Mf) Extr C 1828-43 M 1828-37 (IGI); C 1828-43 (Mf I SLC)
MI (I, DFHS); Ch, cy extr (Ptd Cresswell 146-7); 1930 (Ts SG)

DAWLISH St Mary, Cofton. Ancient chapel-of-ease, rebuilt 1839. Parish
created 1864 from Starcross. Now with KENTON, MAMHEAD, POWDERHAM, STARCROSS
OR C 1864-1951 (DRO)
MI (I, DFHS); Ch extr (Ptd Cresswell 57-9)

DAWLISH St. Alban, Luscombe Castle. Oratory of Hoare family, erected 1862
OR C 1872-73 (DRO)

DAWLISH St. Mark. Chapel erected 1849-50. Demolished
OR C 1885-1972 (DRO)

DAWLISH West Counties Idiot Asylum, Starcross

DAWLISH (RC) St Agatha, Exeter Road 1907

DAWLISH (Bapt) Dawlish Baptist Church, Park Road FIEC

DAWLISH (Ind/Cong later URC) The Strand f 1814 [1851 Religious Census]
Rebuilt 1871 [1882 Return]
OR C 1814-37 (RG 4/2277 PRO)
Cop C 1814-37 (SG)
Cop (Mf) C 1814-37 (Mf DCRS/WSL, SG); Extr C 1814-37 (IGI); C 1814-37
        (Mf I SLC)

DAWLISH (Presb) Cofton or Cockwood licensed 1672, closed after 1772

DAWLISH (Wes) Brunswick Place. Erected 1841 [1851 Religious Census] Rebuilt
1860 [1882 Return] fl c.1970
OR for c.1813-37 see TEIGNMOUTH (RG 4/1220 PRO); C 1863-1957 (DRO)

DAWLISH (Prim Meth)
OR C 1879-1914 (DRO)

DAWLISH (Wes) Starcross. f 1869 in old pumping station [1882 Return] Closed
1958 ?

DAWLISH (Wes) Starcross. Erected 1822 [1851 Religious Census]

DEAN PRIOR St George [Stanborough Hundred; Totnes Union] [553]
Now with BUCKFASTLEIGH
OR C 1557-1812 M 1561-1754 B 1561-1812 (DRO)
BT CMB 1612, 1615, 1619, 1626, 1630, 1632, 1634, 1662-64, 1666, 1668-69,
    1671-76, 1679-82, 1684, 1686-88, 1690, 1697, 1699 (1700-1812 ?);
    CM 1817-22, 1825-26 C 1828, 1830-35, 1838, 1841-48 M 1828-35, 1841
    B 1817-21, 1825-26, 1829-35, 1838, 1841-48 (DRO)
Cop M 1561-1754 (I, Ptd, edit M.Brown, Dartmoor Press 1999); CMB 1557-1837
    (DCRS/WSL, WSL)
Cop (Mf) (Totnes SP); Extr C 1557-1837 M 1561-1837 (IGI); M 1561-1837
        (Mf I SLC)
MI (Ptd DRMI 15: 1998); Extr (Whitmore MS, SG)

DENBURY St Mary the Virgin [Haytor Hundred; Newton Abbot Union 1836-94]
[464] Now with OGWELL
OR C 1559-1996 M 1559-1996 B 1559-1681, 1739-1997 (DRO)
BT CMB 1610, 1614, 1619, 1629, 1669-70, 1674, 1676-81, 1686, 1689, 1696,
    1750-80 (1781-1812 ?); CMB 1814-18, 1820-21, 1826, 1828 CB 1830-37,
    1839-45 M 1830-36, 1839-40 (DRO)
Cop C 1559-1746 M 1559-1743 B 1559-1681 (SG); M 1601-25 (Boyd)
Cop (Mf) C 1559-1874 M 1559-1837 B 1559-1691, 1739-1924 (Mfc SG)
MI Ch, cy extr 1971 (Ts SG); Extr (Whitmore MS, SG)

DENBURY (Bapt) Erected 1842 [1851 Religious Census]

DENBURY (Presb) fl c.1672-90

DENBURY (Wes) Building in the occupation of Mr J.Bowden, Main Street [1882
Return]

DERRIL   see PYWORTHY

DEVON (S of F) Quarterly Meeting, f.1668. United 1870 with CORNWALL QM
OR Z 1776-1837 M 1783-91, 1795-1836 B 1777-1837 (RG 6/192, 466-8, 481-2,
    492, 622 PRO); Z notes 1659-1794 M certs 1784-91 B notes 1682-1794
    (RG 6/941, 1580, 942 PRO)

DEVON (S of F) Eastern Division (including Exeter, Culmstock, Cullompton,
Newton Tracey, Spiceland, Topsham)
OR Z 1785-1837 M 1786-94, 1798-1836 B 1785-1837 (RG 6/1424, 193, 392, 393
    PRO); Z 1824-1867, 1888-1896, 1945-58 M 1942-61 B 1824-1884, 1896-1944;
    1942-61 (DRO); see also CULMSTOCK and EXETER
Cop (Mf) Z 1860-67 (Mfc Colyton SP)

DEVON (S of F) Western Division (Plymouth, Kingsbridge etc.)
OR Z 1795-1837 M 1798-1836 B 1795-1837 (RG 6/194, 394-5 PRO)

DEVON COUNTY ASYLUM   see EXMINSTER

DEVONPORT   see PLYMOUTH

DIPPERTOWN   see LIFTON

DIPTFORD St Mary the Virgin [Stanborough Hundred; Totnes Union] [735]
Now with NORTH HUISH, HARBERTON, HARBERTONFORD
OR C 1653-1908 M 1653-1837 B 1653-1886 (DRO)
BT CMB 1596-1601, 1614-16, 1633-34, 1639, 1663, 1666, 1668-71, 1673, 1676,
    1678-80, 1686-90, 1695, 1699, 1750-70, 1772-83, 1785-95 (1796-1812 ?);
    CM 1813-35 M 1842 B 1813, 1829-35 (DRO)
Cop (Mf) (Totnes SP)

DIPTFORD St James, Avonwick. Proprietary chapel. Erected 1878. Licensed
building in parish of Diptford.

DIPTFORD (Christians) Stert [1882 Return]

DITTISHAM St George [Coleridge Hundred; Totnes Union] [816] Now with
ASHPRINGTON, CORNWORTHY
OR C 1651-1884 M 1654-1988 B 1650-1979 (DRO) Early registers said to have
    been burned by Cromwellian troops
BT CMB 1603, 1610, 1614, 1617, 1619, 1624, 1631, 1641, 1663, 1666, 1669,
    1671-72, 1674-75, 1677-82, 1684, 1686-90, 1695, 1697, 1699
    (1700-1812 ?); CMB 1813, 1815-23, 1825-36 (DRO)
Cop CMB 1603-41 from BT, 1651-1837 (DCRS/WSL); Extr C 1653-1710, 1712-24
    M 1654-1753 B 1651-1710, 1714-74 (Vol 5, BG/PCL)
Cop (Mf) (Torquay and Totnes SPs); C 1651-1884 M 1654-1837 B 1650-1711
        (Mfc SG); Extr C 1603-1837 M 1603, 1614-41, 1654-1837 (IGI);
        C 1603-1837 M 1603, 1614-41, 1654-1837 (Mf I SLC)

DITTISHAM (Cong) f 1832 [1851 Religious Census] Closed 1967 = ? Thornwell
[1882 Return]
OR CM 1838-1923 B 1844-1923 (DRO)

DITTISHAM (Wes) Capton. Erected 1830 [1851 Religious Census] [1882 Return]
OR for c.1811-37 see BRIXHAM CIRCUIT, KINGSBRIDGE (RG 4/842,1088 PRO)

DOCCOMBE   see MORETONHAMPSTEAD

DODBROOKE St Thomas of Canterbury [Coleridge Hundred; Kingsbridge Union
1836-93] [1038] Now with KINGSBRIDGE
OR C 1725-1974 M 1727-1966 B 1727-1956 (DRO) No earlier registers noted in
1831
BT CMB 1597-1601, 1608, 1614-17, 1624, 1635, 1663-64, 1666, 1668-72, 1674,
1676, 1678-79, 1684, 1686-90, 1696-97, 1699 (1700-1812 ?); C 1813-23,
1834, 1838, 1840-42, 1850-71 M 1813-22, 1834 B 1813-14, 1816-222, 1834,
1838-42, 1850-71 (DRO)
Cop M 1754-1912 indexed by male spouse (DFHS)
Cop (Mf) C 1725-1881 M 1727-1837 B 1727-1881 (Mfc SG)
MI (I, DFHS)

DODBROOKE (Bapt) The Refuge Chapel f 1819
OR Z 1824-36 (RG 4/2533 PRO)
Cop (Mf) Z 1824-36 (Mf DCRS/WSL, SG); Extr Z 1824-36 (IGI)

DODBROOKE (Wes)
OR for *c*.1813-37 *see* KINGSBRIDGE (RG 4/1088 PRO)

DODBROOKE (Brethren) [1851 Religious Census]

DODDISCOMBSLEIGH St Michael [Exminster Hundred; St Thomas Union] [392]
Now with NORTH KENN
OR C 1681-1920 M 1682-1836 B 1678-1995 (DRO)
BT CMB 1606, 1608, 1613-14, 1617, 1624, 1629-30, 1634, 1662-64, 1667,
1669-70, 1672?, 1673?, 1675, 1678, 1683, 1687, 1690, 1696-97, 1699
(1700-1812 ?); C 1813-41, 1843-49, 1851-52, 1854-55 M 1813-20, 1822-23,
1826-27 B 1813-16, 1818-41, 1843-49, 1851-52, 1854-55 (DRO)
Cop CM 1681-1755 (DRO); Extr CM 1684-1772 B 1683-1773 (Vol 6, BG/PCL)
MI (I, DFHS); Ch extr (Ptd Cresswell 73-4); Ch, cy (Ptd Dwelly 161-70)

DOLTON St Edmund [North Tawton and Winkleigh Hundred; Torrington Union]
[870]
OR C 1608-1921 M 1610-1989 B 1608-1954 (NDRO)
BT CMB 1602, 1607-08, 1610-11, 1617, 1629, 1635, 1668, 1670, 1674, 1679,
1682, 1688, 1690-91, 1695-97, 1699-1700, 1702-03, 1705, 1707-12, 1714-15
(1716-1812 ?); C 1813, 1825-27, 1831-46, 1848-51, 1858-60 M 1813,
1826-27, 1831-37 B 1813, 1823, 1825-27, 1831-46, 1848-49, 1851, 1856-60
(DRO)
Cop CMB 1602-07 from BT, 1608-1837 (DCRS/WSL, WSL); B 1813-37 (Ptd DFHS);
CMB 1597-1742 (DFHS); M 1610-1812 (Great Card Index, SG); M 1608-1812
(Boyd)
Cop (Mf) Extr CM 1602-1837 (IGI); CM 1602-1837 (Mf I SLC)

DOLTON (Bapt) Zion, Chapel Street f 1837 [1851 Religious Census]

DOLTON (Wes)
OR for *c*.1820-36 *see* ASHBURTON CIRCUIT (RG 4/840 PRO)

DOLTON (Bible Christian) Erected 1857/1889 fl *c*.1970 = ? Langham Cross [1882
Return]

DOLTON (Who object to be designated)) The Room [1882 Return]

DOTTON [East Budleigh Hundred from 1858; St Thomas Union 1858-94] [20]
Extra-parochial place, between COLATON RALEIGH, OTTERTON, NEWTON POPPLEFORD.
United 1894 with COLATON RALEIGH

DOWLAND St Peter [North Tawton and Winkleigh Hundred; Torrington Union]
[195] Now with IDDESLEIGH
OR C 1743-1812 M 1742-1984 B 1742-1812 (NDRO) No earlier register noted in
    1831
BT CMB 1597-1602, 1605-08, 1610, 1615, 1621, 1625, 1633, 1641, 1668, 1670,
    1674, 1679-80, 1682, 1685, 1692, 1694-97, 1699, 1702, 1709-12, 1714-15
    (1716-1812 ?); C 1813-37, 1839-52 M 1813-14, 1817-20, 1823, 1825, 1827,
    1831-33, 1835-37 B 1813, 1815-16, 1819-37, 1839-48, 1850-52 (DRO)
Cop CMB 1743-1840 (DCRS/WSL); CMB 1743-1840 (DFHS)
Cop (Mf) Extr C 1743-1840 M 1742-1840 (IGI); C 1743-1840 (Mf I SLC)
MI Ch (Ptd *The Genealogist* 7: 1883: 265-6); Incledon 891 (NDA)

DOWN ST MARY St Mary the Virgin [North Tawton and Winkleigh Hundred;
Crediton Union] [407] Now with NORTH CREADY
OR C 1696-1880 M 1696-1837 B 1696-1947 (DRO) Noted in 1831: CMB 1688+
BT CMB 1608, 1613-14, 1624, 1629-30, 1670-72, 1675, 1677-78, 1680, 1683,
    1687, 1690, 1695-97, 1699 (1700-1812 ?); C 1813-40 M 1813-22, 1824-26,
    1828-34, 1836-39 B 1813-22, 1824-39 (DRO)
Cop CMB 1608-1850 (DCRS/WSL); B 1813-37 (Ptd DFHS); Extr CMB 1702-31
    M '1597'-1778 B '1558-77' (Vol 10, BG/PCL)
Cop (Mf) Extr C 1696-1850 M 1696-1756, 1813-49 (IGI); C 1696-1850
    M 1696-1756, 1813-49 (Mf I SLC)
MI (I, DFHS)

DOWN ST MARY St Boniface, Knowle. Proprietary chapel

DOWN ST MARY (Bible Christian) Ebenezer, Copplestone. Erected 1831
[1851 Religious Census] [1882 Return] Rebuilt 1888. fl *c.*1970

DOWN ST MARY (Who object to be designated) School House, Copplestone
[1882 Return]

DOWN ST PANCRAS   *see* AXMOUTH, Rousdon

DOWN THOMAS   *see* WEMBURY

DOWN, EAST St John the Baptist [Braunton Hundred; Barnstaple Union] [446]
United 1944 with ARLINGTON. Now with SHIRWELL
OR C 1538-1987 M 1538-1978 B 1538-1955 (NDRO)
BT CMB 1597-1601, 1607-08, 1610, 1619 or 1629, 1623-24, 1641, 1644, 1668,
    1670, 1674, 1678-79, 1682-83, 1688-89, 1691, 1694-97, 1702-05, 1707,
    1712, 1714-15 (1716-1812 ?); CM 1815-40 B 1815-17, 1819-40 (DRO)
Cop B 1813-37 (Ptd DFHS); CMB 1538-1837 (DCRS/WSL); M 1539-1837 (SG);
    M 1538-1811 (NDA); B 1813-37 (SG)
Cop (Mf) Extr C 1538-1837 M 1539-1837 (IGI); C 1538-1837 M 1539-1837
    (Mf I SLC)
MI Incledon 666 (NDA)

DOWN, EAST (Bapt) East Down Mill [1851 Religious Census]

DOWN, EAST (Presb) fl *c.*1672-90

DOWN, EAST (Wes) A house, Churchill [1851 Religious Census]; chapel erected
1902. Closed 1984
OR C 1954-79 (NDRO); for *c.*1807-37 *see* BARNSTAPLE (RG 4/454 PRO)

DOWN, WEST St Calixtus [Braunton Hundred; Barnstaple Union] [628]
Now with ILFRACOMBE St Philip and St James
OR C 1582-1913 M 1584-1989 B 1583-1944 (NDRO)
BT CMB 1596-1601, 1607-08, 1610, 1614, 1620, 1628-29, 1631, 1670, 1674,
1678-79, 1682-83, 1690-91, 1694-97, 1700, 1702, 1705, 1714-15
(1716-1812 ?); CB 1813-43 M 1813-37 (DRO)
Cop CMB 1583-1812 (DCRS/WSL); M 1583-1812 (Boyd)
Cop (Mf) Extr C 1583-1812 M 1584-1812 (IGI); C 1583-1812 M 1584-1812
(Mf I SLC)
MI Incledon 838 (NDA)

DOWN, WEST (Ind/Cong) Erected *c.*1830 [1851 Religious Census] [1882 Return]

DOWN, WEST (Wes) Bradwell Mills. Building occupied by Mr Thomas [1882
Return]

DOWNICARY *see* BROADWOODWIDGER

DREWSTEIGNTON or TEIGNTON DREW Holy Trinity [Wonford Hundred; Okehampton
Union] [1313]
OR C 1557-62, 1599-1941 M 1599-1990 B 1599-1855 (DRO)
BT CMB 1610, 1613, 1616-17, 1630, 1632, 1634, 1664, 1667, 1669-72, 1675,
1677-79, 1681, 1683, 1687, 1690, 1695-97, 1699, 1703-05, 1708, 1713-17,
1719-22, 1724-35, 1737-54, 1757-63, 1765, 1767, 1770, 1772, 1774-1812;
CB 1813-46 M 1813-37 (DRO)
Cop B 1813-37 (Ptd DFHS); M 1599-1754 (I, Ptd, edit M.Brown, Dartmoor Press
1999); Extr CMB 1557-1837 (Ptd, *ibid.* 1998); M 1599-1812 (SG); M 1599-
1812 (Boyd); Extr C 1599-1635 M 1602-1730 B 1600-1703 (Vol 2 BG/PCL)
Cop (Mf) (Okehampton SP)
MI (Ptd DRMI 23: 1998)

DREWSTEIGNTON Castle Drogo. House of Drewe family. Chapel early 20th cent.
National Trust

DUNCHIDEOCK St Michael and All Angels [Exminster Hundred; St Thomas Union]
[182] Now with SHILLINGFORD, IDE
OR C 1538-55, 1590-1960 M 1539-1986 B 1540-1682, 1701-1812 (DRO)
BT CMB 1614, 1617, 1624, 1631, 1635, 1673, 1675, 1678, 1683, 1690, 1697
(1698-1812 ?); C 1814, 1816-26, 1828-57 M 1817, 1820-21, 1827, 1829-30,
1832-36 B 1814, 1816-57 (DRO)
Cop CMB 1539-1837 (SG); CMB 1538-1837 (DCRS/WSL, WSL); M 1539-1836 (Boyd)
Cop (Mf) Extr C 1538-1837 M 1539-1783, 1798-1836 (IGI); C 1538-1837
(Mf I SLC)
MI (I, DFHS); Ch extr (Ptd Cresswell 77-9); Ch, cy 1929 (Ts SG)

DUNKESWELL St Nicholas [Hemyock Hundred; Honiton Union] [414] Rebuilt 1817,
1868. United 1929 with Dunkeswell Abbey. Now with SHELDON, LUPPITT
OR C 1750-1993 M 1743-1973 B 1740-1993 (DRO) No earlier registers noted in
1831.'One leaf appears to have been cut out'
BT CMB 1610-11, 1625-26, 1630, 1633-34, 1663-64, 1667-70, 1675, 1683, 1685,
1687, 1690, 1695-96, 1699, 1701, 1703-05, 1713-16, 1718-37, 1739-50,
1752-54, 1757-69, 1771-77, 1779-1812; CMB 1813, 1815 CB 1818-20, 1823,
1829, 1838 M 1818-19, 1823, 1829 (DRO)
Cop (Mf) (Colyton SP); C 1750-1876 M 1743-1838 B 1740-1812 (Mfc SG)
MI Incledon 713 (NDA)

DUNKESWELL Holy Trinity, Dunkeswell Abbey. Erected 1842. Parish created 1844
from Dunkeswell, CLAYHIDON, HEMYOCK. United 1929 with Dunkeswell
OR C 1842-1992 M 1874-1926 B 1842-1990 (DRO)

DUNKESWELL (Presb) fl *c*.1672-90

DUNKESWELL (Wes) Erected 1845 [1851 Religious Census] Rebuilt 1887.
fl *c*.1970

DUNSFORD St Mary [Wonford Hundred; St Thomas Union] [903] Now with NORTH
KENN
OR C 1597-1929 M 1594-1986 B 1594-1867 (DRO)
BT CMB 1614, 1626, 1632, 1638, 1672-74, 1675?, 1677?, 1678-79, 1683, 1687,
    1690, 1695-96, 1699 (1700-1812 ?); CMB 1815-25, 1828 CB 1839-56 (DRO)
Cop Extr C 1598-1807 B 1605-1791 (Vol 10, BG/PCL)
MI Ch extr (Ptd Cresswell 82-6)

DUNSFORD Fulford. Domestic chapel of Fulford family. Licensed 1402; in use
to 19th cent

DUNSFORD (Bapt) f 1868

DUNSFORD (Wes) Halstow [1851 Religious Census] [1882 Return]
OR for *c*.1820-36 *see* ASHBURTON CIRCUIT (RG 4/840 PRO)

DUNSTONE   *see* WIDECOMBE

DUNSTONE   *see* YEALMPTON

DUNTERTON All Saints [Lifton Hundred; Tavistock Union] [207] United 1921
with MILTON ABBOT. Now also with LAMERTON, SYDENHAM DAMEREL
OR C 1639-1994 M 1677-1754, 1813-1922 B 1580-1995 (PWDRO)
BT CMB 1609, 1616-18, 1629-30, 1635, 1663-65, 1668-72, 1674-76, 1678-81,
    1684, 1686, 1690, 1697, 1699-1700 (1701-1812 ?); C 1813-19, 1821-30,
    1833-34, 1838, 1867-71 M 1813, 1815-16, 1819, 1821-23, 1825, 1827-28,
    1830 B 1813-17, 1819, 1821-25, 1827-28, 1830, 1833-34, 1838, 1867-70
    (DRO)
Cop M 1813-37 (Ptd DFHS); M 1677-1754 (I, Ptd, edit M.Brown, Dartmoor Press
    1999); Extr C 1746-1801 M 1677-1729 B 1591-1792 (Vol 11, BG/PCL)
Cop (Mf) (Tavistock SP)

EAST ALLINGTON   *see* ALLINGTON, EAST

EAST ANSTEY   *see* ANSTEY, EAST

EAST BUCKLAND   *see* BUCKLAND, EAST

EAST BUDLEIGH   *see* BUDLEIGH, EAST

EAST DARTMOOR (Bapt) *see* DARTMOOR, EAST

EAST DOWN   *see* DOWN, EAST

EAST LEIGH   *see* HARBERTON

EAST OGWELL   *see* OGWELL, EAST

EAST PILTON   *see* PILTON, EAST

EAST PORTLEMOUTH   *see* PORTLEMOUTH, EAST

EAST PUTFORD   *see* BUCKLAND BREWER and WEST PUTFORD

EAST STONEHOUSE   see PLYMOUTH

EAST TEIGNMOUTH   see TEIGNMOUTH, EAST

EAST VILLAGE   see SANDFORD

EAST WORLINGTON   see WORLINGTON, EAST

EASTACOMBE   see TAWSTOCK

EASTLEIGH   see WESTLEIGH

EDISTONE   see HARTLAND

EFFORD   see PLYMOUTH or SHOBROOKE

EGG BUCKLAND   see PLYMOUTH

EGGESFORD All Saints [North Tawton and Winkleigh Hundred; Crediton Union]
[168] Now with CHULMLEIGH, CHAWLEIGH, CHELDON, WEMBWORTHY, BURRINGTON
OR C 1594-1812 M 1664-1948 B 1594-1710, 1731-1812 (DRO)
    Noted in 1831: M 1586+; now missing but see extracts below
BT CMB 1607-08, 1610, 1621, 1634, 1668, 1674, 1678-79, 1683, 1688-89, 1691,
    1694-97, 1699-1700, 1703-04, 1706-07, 1709, 1711-12, 1714-15
    (1716-1812 ?); C 1814-1511, 1817-29, 1831-33, 1838 M 1814, 1819-23,
    1826, 1828-29, 1831-33 B 1814-29, 1831-33, 1838 (DRO)
Cop Extr C 1596, 1611, 1629-30, 1638-40/41, 1644, 1653, 1664-65,
    1680/81-81/82, 1702/03 M 1580/81, 1618/19, 1624, 1629, 1664-65, 1678-80,
    1689-90/91, 1696 B 1596, 1601, 1603-04, 1606, 1608, 1643-45, 1648,
    1656-57/58, 1663, 1667, 1671: source unknown (Ts SG); Extr C 1596-1703
    M 1580-1696 B 1596-1671 (Vol 18, BG/PCL)

ELBURTON see PLYMSTOCK

ELLACOMBE see TORQUAY

ELMORE see TIVERTON

ERMINGTON St Peter and St Paul [Ermington Hundred; Plympton St Mary Union]
[1471] see also IVYBRIDGE, and chapelry of KINGSTON. Now with UGBOROUGH
OR C 1603-1901 M 1605-1959 B 1603-1914 (PWDRO)
BT CMB 1606, 1612-14, 1618-19, 1623, 1629, 1633, 1664, 1666, 1670-71, 1677,
    1681, 1688, 1695, 1699 (1700-1812 ?); CMB 1813-35 (DRO)
Cop CMB 1603-1850 (DCRS/WSL); B 1813-37 (Ptd DFHS); Extr C 1603-1753
    M 1607-1749 B 1603-1782 (Vol 7, BG/PCL)
Cop (Mf) Extr C 1603-1850 M 1606-1838 (IGI); C 1603-1850 M 1606-1838
    (Mf I SLC)
MI (I, DFHS); Extr (Ptd A.Jewers 'Ermington': WA 2: 1891-92, passim);
    Extr (Whitmore MS, SG)

ERMINGTON (Presb) fl c.1672-90

ERMINGTON (Wes) Ermington village. Erected 1834 [1851 Religious Census]
[1882 Return] Erected 1887. Closed 1981
OR C 1941-68 M 1937-74 (PWDRO); for c.1801-37 see ASHBURTON CIRCUIT,
    KINGSBRIDGE (RG 4/840,1763,1088 PRO)
Cop C 1941-68 M 1937-74 with index (PWDRO)

ERNESETTLE   see PLYMOUTH

ESCOT   see OTTERY ST MARY

ESTOVER   see PLYMOUTH

EXBOURNE St Mary Blessed Virgin [Black Torrington Hundred; Okehampton Union]
[509] Now with HATHERLEIGH, MEETH, JACOBSTOWE
OR C 1769-1870 M 1755-1837 B 1769-1812 (DRO) Noted in 1831: 4 other volumes
    containing C 1540-1769 M 1541-1768 B 1654-1769
BT CMB 1608, 1611, 1614, 1630, 1663-64, 1666, 1668-72, 1674, 1676-77, 1679,
    1684, 1686-88, 1690, 1695-97 (1698-1812 ?); CMB 1813-28 CB 1830-37
    M 1830-31, 1833-37 (DRO)
Cop (Mf) (Okehampton SP)
MI Extr (Whitmore MS, SG)

EXBOURNE (Bible Christian/Meth) A building in the occupation of H.Higman
[1882 Return]; a mid-19th cent building later a house; new chapel 1938
fl c.1970

EXE VALLEY United benefice including WASHFIELD, STOODLEY, WITHLEIGH,
CALVERLEIGH, OAKFORD, TEMPLETON, LOXBEARE, CRUWYS MORCHARD, RACKENFORD

EXE, NETHER or NETHEREXE see THORVERTON

EXE, WEST   see TIVERTON

EXETER Cathedral of St Peter [Wonford Hundred; Exeter Incorporation for the
Poor 1697-1930] [Cathedral Close 675; City of Exeter 28201]
OR C 1594-1967 M 1597-1977 B 1593-1887 (DRO)
BT CM 1813-15, 1817-24, 1829, 1835-36 C 1838 B 1813-24, 1829, 1835-36, 1838
    (DRO)
Cop CMB 1593-1813 (Ptd DCRS 1910-33); B 1813-37 (Ptd DFHS); CMB 1813-37
    (DCRS/WSL, SG); M 1593-1812 (Boyd); M 1790-1812 (Pallot)
Cop (Mf) Extr C 1594-1837 M 1597-1837 (IGI); C 1594-1837 (Mf I SLC)
MI (Ptd V.Hope 'The Exeter Cathedral monumentarium 1956': DCNQ 27: 1956-58:
    149-53); (Ptd J.Hewett 'Remarks on the monumental brasses and certain
    decorative remains in the Cathedral...Exeter, to which is appended a
    complete monumentarium': Trans. Exeter Dioc. Archit. and Archaeo.Soc
    1st ser 3: 1849: 90-138)

EXETER Bishop's Palace. Chapel of St Faith

EXETER All Hallows on the Walls, Bartholomew Street West [889] Demolished
1770; rebuilt 1843. United 1939 with Exeter St Olave. Redundant. Used as a
factory. Demolished 1950.
OR C 1694-1938 M 1695-1699, 1805-1811, 1836-1938 B 1695-1931 (DRO)
    Noted in 1831: 'Marriages were not solemnized in this Church from 1699
    to 1805' No services 1811-24.
BT CMB 1614, 1616, 1620, 1623, 1629, 1635-36, 1638, 1675 (1676-1812 ?);
    CB 1825-26, 1830-33 (DRO)
Cop B 1824-37 (Ptd DFHS); CMB 1614-1837 from BT, 1694-1837 (DCRS/WSL)
Cop (Mf) Extr C 1614-1837 M 1614-38, 1695-99, 1785-1837 (IGI); C 1614-1837
         M 1614-38, 1695-99, 1785-1837 (Mf I SLC)

EXETER Allhallows, Goldsmith Street [420] Church demolished 1906. Parish
united 1934 with Exeter St Lawrence, St Martin, St Paul, St Stephen; 1974
with Central Exeter parish
OR C 1813-1901 M 1809-1902 B 1813-1898 (DRO) Noted in 1831: C 1566+
    M 1561+ B 1568+; M 1754-1809 at Exeter St Stephen. Some (1561-1814)
    unfit for production. see copies below

EXETER Allhallows, Goldsmith Street, cont.
BT CMB 1607, 1614-15, 1617-18, 1620, 1629, 1636, 1638, 1697, 1699
(1700-1812 ?); C 1813, 1816-17, 1819, 1822, 1830, 1835, 1839-57,
1859-60 M 1816-17, 1819, 1822, 1830, 1835 B 1816-17, 1819, 1830, 1835,
1839-60 (DRO)
Cop CMB 1561-1753, 1813-37 Banns 1809-36 (Ptd DCRS 1933); CB 1561-1837
M 1561-1753, 1813-37 (I, SG); M 1561-1837 (Boyd); M 1809-37 (Pallot);
Extr C 1566-1646, 1660-1756 M 1561-1644, 1684-1750 B 1561-1647,
1667-1806 (Vol 11, BG/PCL)
Cop (Mf) Extr C 1566-1837 M 1561-1753, 1809-37 (IGI); C 1566-1837 (Mf I SLC)
MI (Ptd DCRS, as above)

EXETER Holy Trinity, South Street [2806] Former chapelry in Heavitree.
Rebuilt 1820. United 1969 with Exeter St Leonard
OR C 1564-1968 M 1564-1967 B 1564-1960 (DRO)
BT CMB 1608, 1614, 1617, 1632, 1634-35, 1667, 1669-70, 1672, 1675, 1678,
1680, 1683, 1687, 1690, 1696 (1697-1812 ?); CMB 1813, 1815-16, 1819-23,
1827, 1829-34 CB 1836-57 M 1836-37 (DRO)
Cop M 1813-37 (Ptd DFHS); B 1813-37 (Ptd DFHS); B 1813-37 (SG);
CMB 1563-1837 (DCRS/WSL)
Cop (Mf) Extr C 1563-1837 M 1573-1837 (IGI); C 1563-1837 M 1573-1837
(Mf I SLC)
MI (I, DFHS); Headstones removed to Higher Cemetery (DFHS)

EXETER St David, St David's Hill [3078] Chapelry in Heavitree; separate
parish 1826. Rebuilt 1816, 1897-1900
OR CM 1559-1948 B 1559-1983 (DRO)
BT CMB 1614, 1629-30, 1635, 1663, 1677?, 1678-79, 1683, 1699 (1700-1812 ?);
CB 1813-67 M 1813-37 (DRO)
Cop M 1813-37 (Ptd DFHS); CMB 1559-1837 (DCRS/WSL); M 1780-1806 (Pallot);
Extr C 1560-1710 M 1564-1714 B 1561-1719 (Vol 11, BG/PCL)
Cop (Mf) Extr CM 1559-1837 (IGI); C 1559-1837 (Mf I SLC)
MI (I, DFHS)

EXETER St Michael and All Angels, Dinham Road, Mount Dinham. Chapel-of-ease
to Exeter St David, erected 1867-68

EXETER St Edmund, Edmund Street [1523] Rebuilt 1834. Abolished 1956, part
joining Exeter St Mary Steps, part to Exeter St Thomas. Demolished 1970s
OR CM 1572-1956 B 1571-1956 (DRO)
BT CMB 1607, 1615, 1620, 1632, 1634-35, 1638, 1675, 1683, 1696-97,
1699-1700 (1701-1812 ?); CB 1813-36, 1840, 1842-43, 1848 M 1813-36 (DRO)
Cop B 1813-37 (Ptd DFHS); CMB 1571-1837 (DCRS/WSL); Extr C 1573-1700
M 1572-1749 B 1571-1686 (Vol 14, BG/PCL)
Cop (Mf) Extr C 1571-1837 M 1572-1621, 1647-1837 (IGI); C 1571-1837
M 1572-1621, 1647-1837 (Mf I SLC)

EXETER St George, South Street [908] Demolished and united with Exeter
St John, c.1843 but registration continued. United 1935 with Exeter St Mary
Major, St John, St Petrock. Parish renamed 1970 St Petrock with St Mary
Major. United 1974 with Central Exeter parish
OR C 1682-1908 M 1683-1860 B 1682-1925; C 1903-34 catalogued with Exeter
St John (DRO)
BT CMB 1609, 1614, 1619 or 1620, 1629-30, 1675, 1678-79, 1697,
(1698-1812 ?); CMB 1820-28, 1830 CB 1839-43 (DRO)

EXETER St George, cont.
Cop M 1813-37 (Ptd DFHS); B 1813-37 (Ptd DFHS); CMB 1609-1812 from BT,
    1681-1837 (DCRS/WSL)
Cop (Mf) Extr C 1609-1837 M 1609-32, 1675-1837 (IGI); C 1609-1837 (Mf I SLC)
MI (I, DFHS); (Ptd A.Everett 'Gravestones in St George's Church, Exeter':
    DCNQ 23: 1947-9: 243)

EXETER St John [586] United 1935 with Exeter St Mary Major, St George,
St Petrock (Parish re-named 1974 St Petrock with St Mary Major. United 1974
with Central Exeter Parish)
OR C 1682-1934 M 1683-1931 B 1682-1913 (DRO) B 1908-25 catalogued with
    Exeter St George
BT CMB 1608, 1611, 1614, 1620, 1629, 1631, 1635, 1673, 1675, 1678, 1683
    (1684-1812 ?); CMB 1813-23, 1825-37 (DRO); St John and St George
    CB 1841-52 (DRO)
Cop M 1813-37 (Ptd DFHS); B 1813-37 (Ptd DFHS); B 1813-37 (SG);
    CMB 1609-1812 from BT, 1682-1837 (DCRS/WSL)
Cop (Mf) Extr C 1609-1812 M 1609-14, 1626-35, 1673-83, 1695-1745, 1776-1812
    (IGI); C 1609-1812 (Mf I SLC)

EXETER St Kerrian [470] United with St Petrock. United 1934 with Exeter
St Mary Arches, St Pancras
OR C 1559-1933 M 1559-1753, 1810-1837 B 1558-1930; M 1847-58, 1882
    catalogued with Exeter St Petrock (DRO)
BT CMB 1607, 1610, 1614, 1616, 1626?, 1629, 1632, 1635, 1695, 1697
    (1698-1812 ?); CB 1813-14, 1816-23, 1825-49, 1856 M 1816, 1818-23,
    1825-28, 1830-37 (DRO)
Cop CMB 1559-1837 (DCRS/WSL); M 1558-1837 (Boyd); Extr C 1566-1703
    M 1566-1694 B 1558-1701 (Vol 17, BG/PCL)
Cop (Mf) Extr C 1559-1837 M 1558-1659, 1671-1753, 1810-37 (IGI); C 1559-1837
    M 1558-1659, 1671-1753, 1810-37 (Mf I SLC)

EXETER St Lawrence, High Street [620] United 1930 with Exeter St Stephen,
St Martin, and joined 1934 by All Hallows Goldsmith Street, St Paul.
Bomb-damaged 1942. Demolished
OR C 1873-1979 M 1754-1912 (DRO) From 1931 registers contain entries for
    united parishes. Noted in 1831: CMB 1604-73, 1703-47 CB 1750-1812
    M 1754-1812. Registers 1604-19th cent now unfit for production.
BT CMB 1614-15, 1620, 1630, 1632, 1634-35, 1638, 1672 (1673-1812 ?);
    CMB 1813-16, 1818-19, 1821, 1825, 1828, 1830-31, 1835 CB 1847-52 M 1837
    (DRO)
Cop CMB 1604-1837 (DCRS/WSL); M 1604-1837 (Boyd)
Cop (Mf) Extr C 1604-1837 M 1604-1836 (IGI); C 1604-1837 M 1604-1836
    (Mf I SLC)
MI (I, DFHS); (DFHS)

EXETER St Leonard, Topsham Road [467] United 1969 with Exeter Holy Trinity
OR C 1704-1915 M 1708-1949 B 1710-1922 (DRO) B 1610+ existed 1831
BT CMB 1769-71 (1772-1812 ?); C 1814-35, 1839-40, 1844, 1856-57, 1859,
    1861-62 M 1814-35 B 1814-24, 1826-35, 1839-40, 1844, 1856-61 (DRO)
Cop Extr (Ptd R.Dymond History of the suburban parish of St Leonard, Exeter:
    1873); CMB 1704-1837 (DCRS/WSL); M 1708-1837 (Boyd)
Cop (Mf) Extr C 1704-1837 M 1708-1837 (IGI); C 1704-1837 M 1708-1837
    (Mf I SLC)
MI (I, DFHS)

EXETER St Martin, Cathedral Close [298] United 1930 with Exeter St Lawrence,
St Stephen. Joined 1934 by All Hallows Goldsmith Street, St Paul. Entered
Central Exeter parish 1974
OR   C 1784-1796, 1813-1927 M 1754-1906, 1973 B 1783-1795, 1813-1916, 1950-62
     (DRO) M 1944-67 catalogued with Exeter St Lawrence, Noted in 1831:
     CMB 1572-1812, now unfit for production. Others lost in air-raids 1942.
     see copies below
BT   CMB 1608, 1610, 1614, 1620, 1626, 1629, 1634-36, 1696, 1698
     (1699-1812 ?) (DRO)
Cop B 1813-37 (Ptd DFHS); CMB 1572-1837 (DCRS/WSL); M 1572-1837 (Boyd);
     Extr C 1572-1713 M 1572-1729 B 1572-1804 (Vol 11, BG/PCL)
Cop (Mf) Extr C 1572-1836 M 1572-1645, 1669-1836 (IGI); C 1572-1836
     M 1572-1645, 1669-1836 (Mf I SLC)

EXETER St Mary Arches, Mary Arches Street [708] United 1934 with Exeter
St Kerrian, St Pancras. Now part of Central Exeter parish. Redundant
OR   C 1538-1906 M 1538-1964 B 1538-1935 (DRO)
BT   CMB 1614, 1616, 1620, 1635, 1675, 1677?, 1678, 1683, 1687 (1688-1812 ?);
     CMB 1813-37 CB 1839-44 (DRO)
Cop B 1813-37 (Ptd DFHS); B 1813-37 (SG); CMB 1538-1837 (DCRS/WSL);
     M 1538-1837 (Boyd)
Cop (Mf) Extr CM 1538-1837 (IGI); CM 1538-1837 (Mf I SLC)

EXETER St Mary Major [3516] Rebuilt 1865-68. United 1935 with Exeter
St George, St John, St Petrock. Demolished 1970
OR   C 1561-1965 M 1562-1965 B 1562-1927 (DRO)
BT   CMB 1629, 1632, 1664, 1674-75, 1696, 1699 (1700-1812 ?); CB 1813-28,
     1830-55 M 1813-28, 1830-37 (DRO)
Cop M 1813-37 (Ptd DFHS); CMB 1561-1837 (DCRS/WSL)
Cop (Mf) Extr CM 1561-1837 (IGI); CM 1561-1837 (Mf I SLC)

EXETER St Mary Magdalene, Rack Street. Chapel-of-ease to St Mary Major,
erected 1861

EXETER St Mary Steps, West Street [1258]
OR   C 1655-1890 M 1655-1870 B 1655-1885 (DRO)
BT   CMB 1610-11, 1614, 1616, 1618, 1620, 1624, 1629, 1631, 1675, 1696-97,
     1699, 1701 (1702-1812 ?); CMB 1814, 1816-17, 1819, 1822-23, 1828
     CB 1830-50 M 1830-36, 1838 (DRO)
Cop M 1813-37 (Ptd DFHS); B 1813-24, 1825-37 (Ptd DFHS); CMB 1610-1837
     (DCRS/WSL)
Cop (Mf) Extr C 1558-1837 M 1559, 1610-34, 1655-1837 (IGI); C 1558-1837
     M 1559, 1610-34, 1655-1837 (Mf I SLC)

EXETER St Michael and All Angels, Heavitree [Wonford Hundred; St Thomas
Union] [1932] Peculiar of the Dean and Chapter of Exeter until 1848.
Rebuilt 1845
OR   C 1556-1891 M 1654-1885 B 1653-1678, 1695-1935 (DRO)
BT   CMB 1610, 1613-14, 1618, 1625, 1639? (1640-1812 ?); CB 1813-57 M 1813-37
     (DRO)
Cop CMB 1555-1837 (DCRS/WSL); Extr C 1653-1756 M 1654-1751 B 1654-1771
     (Vol 9, BG/PCL)
Cop (Mf) Extr C 1555-1837 M 1653-1837 (IGI); C 1555-1837 M 1653-1837
     (Mf I SLC)
MI   (I, DFHS); (Ptd I.Dallas 'The heraldry of Devonshire churches: St
     Michael's, Heavitree': *Notes and Gleanings, Devon and Cornwall* 3: 1890:
     49-54); Extr (Ptd D.Gander 'Heavitree MIs...and others': DFH 38: 1986:
     4-6)

EXETER Livery Dole St Clare. Medieval proprietary chapel. Now with Heavitree
Team Ministry
OR None

EXETER St Mark, Pinhoe Road. Erected Manston Road 1910 as chapel-of-ease to
St Michael Heavitree. Rebuilt Pinhoe Road, and parish created 1930. Now with
Exeter St Matthew, St Sidwell
OR C 1931-78 M 1931-90 B 1931-79 (DRO)

EXETER St Lawrence, Lower Hill Barton Road. Erected 1956-57 as chapel-of-
ease to St Michael, Heavitree. Now district church with Heavitree Team
Ministry
OR C 1957-60 in St Michael register; C 1960-83 (Inc, St Michael); C 1983+
M 1986+ (Inc, St Lawrence)

EXETER St Paul, Burnthouse Lane. Erected 1931; new church 1950. Now with
Heavitree Team Ministry
OR CM 1931+ (Inc)

EXETER All Saints, Whipton. Chapel-of-ease to Heavitree. Parish created
1938. Redundant 1983. Now Whipton Community Hall
OR C 1939-72 M 1926-75 B 1939-73 (DRO)
MI (I, DFHS)

EXETER St Boniface, Lloyds Crescent, Whipton. Erected 1957-58. Now parish
church of Whipton
OR C 1958+ (Inc); M 1959-78 (DRO)

EXETER Holy Trinity, Beacon Heath. Erected 1993 in parish of Whipton
St Boniface
OR see St Boniface

EXETER St Olave, Fore Street [964] Used also by Huguenots 1685-1758. United
1939 with Exeter All Hallows on the Wall. Entered Central Exeter parish 1974
OR C 1602-1981 M 1601-1753, 1815-1973 B 1601-1970 (DRO) Noted in 1831 that
    M from 1753 took place at Exeter St Mary Arches
BT CMB 1614-15, 1617, 1630, 1632, 1679, 1690, 1697 (1698-1812 ?);
    CB 1813-37, 1839-48 M 1815-37 (DRO)
Cop B 1813-37 (Ptd DFHS); CMB 1601-1837 (DCRS/WSL)
Cop (Mf) Extr C 1601-1838 M 1601-1754, 1815-37 (IGI); C 1601-1838
    M 1601-1754, 1815-37 (Mf I SLC)

EXETER St Pancras, Guildhall Centre [379] Disused 1780s-1830. United 1934
with Exeter St Mary Arches, St Kerrian. Now part of Central Exeter parish
OR C 1664-1896 M 1676-1795, 1813-1932 B 1666-1933 (DRO) M 1942-49
    catalogued with Exeter St Mary Arches
BT CMB 1609, 1617 (1618-1812 ?); C 1813-15, 1826, 1828-30, 1838-59 M 1815,
    1826-30 B 1815, 1826-30, 1838-59 (DRO)
Cop CB 1664-1837 M 1664-1774, 1784-96, 1813-37 Banns 1754-1837 (Ptd DCRS
    1933); CB 1664-1837, M 1664-1774, 1784-96, 1813-27 (I, SG); M 1664-1796
    (Boyd); M 1790-96 (Pallot)
Cop (Mf) Extr C 1664-1837 M 1670-1837 (IGI); C 1664-1837 M 1670-1837
    (Mf I SLC)
MI (Ptd DCRS, as above)

EXETER St Paul, Goldsmith Street/Paul Street [1638] Rebuilt 1860. Demolished
1936
OR C 1813-1934 M 1754-1934 B 1813-1934 (DRO) Noted in 1831:
  CMB 1562-1812; now unfit for production, but see printed copy below
BT CMB 1609-11, 1614, 1617-18, 1625-26, 1628-30, 1634, 1672, 1676, 1697
   (1698-1812 ?); CB 1813-15, 1817-19, 1821-24, 1826-55 M 1813, 1815,
   1817-19, 1821-24, 1826-29, 1831-37 (DRO)
Cop CMB 1562-1837 Banns 1754-1834 (Ptd DCRS 1933); B 1813-37 (Ptd DFHS);
   CB 1562-1837 M 1561-1837 (I, SG); B 1813-37 (SG): M 1562-1821 (Boyd);
   M 1790-1837 (Pallot)
Cop (Mf) Extr CM 1562-1837 (IGI); CM 1562-1837 (Mf I SLC)
MI (I, DFHS); (Ptd DCRS, as above)

EXETER St Petrock, High Street [267] United with St Kerrian. United 1935
with Exeter St Mary Major, St George, St John. Entered Central Exeter parish
1974
OR C 1539-1974 M 1538-1964 B 1539-1931 (DRO)
BT CMB 1608, 1614, 1632-33, 1635, 1638?, 1674 (1675-1812 ?); C 1813-37,
   1839-44, 1846-49, 1856 M 1813-22, 1824-29, 1831-33, 1835-36 B 1813-32,
   1834-37, 1840-44, 1846-49, 1856 (DRO)
Cop CMB 1538-1837 (DCRS/WSL); M 1538-1910 (Boyd); Extr C 1538-1708
   M 1538-1698 B 1538-1726 (Vol 14, BG/PCL)
Cop (Mf) Extr C 1538-1837 M 1538-1836 (IGI); C 1538-1837 M 1538-1836
   (Mf I SLC)
MI (I, DFHS); Ch, cy (Ptd R.Dymond *History of the Parish of St Petrock,
   Exeter*: 1882: 81-92); (Ptd E.Shorto *Some notes on the church of St
   Petrock, Exeter*: 1878)

EXETER St Sidwell, Sidwell Street [6602] Chapelry in Heavitree,
Rebuilt 1812. Separate parish 1825. Now with Exeter St Mark, St Matthew
OR C 1569-1933, 1962-96 Banns 1948-96 M 1569-1992 B 1569-1996 (DRO)
BT CMB 1609, 1611, 1616, 1638, 1640, 1674-75, 1677?, 1679, 1688-91, 1695-97
   (1698-1812 ?); CB 1813-42, 1845-47, 1849-55, 1857-58 M 1813-37 (DRO)
Cop M 1813-37 (Ptd DFHS); CMB 1569-1837 (DCRS/WSL); DB 1577-1802
   (Ptd H Tapley-Soper 'Executions recorded in St Sidwell's parish
   register' DCNQ 15: 1928-29); M 1569-1837 (Boyd)
Cop (Mf) Extr CM 1569-1837 (IGI); CM 1569-1837 (Mf I SLC)
MI (I, DFHS)

EXETER St James, Mount Pleasant Road. Erected 1838. Parish created 1842 from
Exeter St Sidwell
OR C 1842-1876 M 1842-1891,1942 B 1842-1917 (DRO)
BT CB 1842-64 (DRO)

EXETER St Matthew, Clifton Road, Newtown. Parish created 1883 from Exeter
St Sidwell, St James. Now with St Sidwell, St Mark
OR C 1883-1974 M 1883-1961 (DRO)

EXETER St Catherine. Summerland Crescent. Iron church, chapel-of-ease to
St Sidwell [Kelly 1889]

EXETER St Anne's Almshouses f 1418. Used as a chapel-of-ease to St Sidwell.
Served from St James [Kelly 1930]

EXETER St Stephen. High Street [482] United 1930 with St Lawrence,
St Martin; joined 1934 by All Hallows Goldsmith Street, St Paul. Entered
Central Exeter parish 1974
OR C 1813-1928 M 1754-1923 B 1813-1925; 8 vols 1668-20th cent unfit for
    production (DRO) Noted in 1831: CMB 1668+
BT CMB 1609, 1611, 1614, 1621, 1626, 1628-29, 1632, 1635, 1638, 1667,
    1674-75, 1696 (1697-1812 ?); C 1829-30, 1833, 1835-36, 1839-42 M 1829,
    1831, 1833, 1835 B 1829, 1831, 1833, 1835-36, 1839-41 (DRO)
Cop B 1813-37 (Ptd DFHS); CMB 1669-1837 (DCRS/WSL)
Cop (Mf) Extr C 1668-1837 M 1668-1796, 1813-37 (IGI); C 1668-1837 (Mf I SLC)

EXETER Bedford Chapel. Extra-parochial place [114] Proprietary chapel
erected 1832. Bomb-damaged 1942. Demolished
OR C 1833-1960 M 1833-1956 B 1840-1918, 1945 (DRO) Noted in 1831:
    'the Registers are incorporated with those of St Stephen'.
BT C 1827, 1833-36 M 1833-35 (DRO)
Cop CMB 1833-50 (DCRS/WSL)
Cop (Mf) Extr CM 1833-50 (IGI)

EXETER St Thomas the Apostle, Cowick Street [4203] Rebuilt 1656-57. Now with
Emmanuel, St Andrew, St Philip
OR C 1541-1899 M 1577-1887 B 1554-1893 (DRO)
BT CMB 1608, 1611, 1614, 1620, 1626, 1634, 1636, 1669-70, 1695-96, 1699
    (1700-1812 ?); CB 1813-54 M 1813-37 (DRO)
Cop M 1813-37 (Ptd DFHS); B 1813-37 (Ptd DFHS); C 1541-1837 M 1577-1837
    B 1554-1837 with index (DCRS/WSL, SG); Extr C 1554-1698 M 1576-1684
    B 1565-1726 (Vol 16, BG/PCL)
Cop (Mf) Extr C 1541-1837 M 1576-1837 (IGI); C 1541-1837 M 1576-1837
        (Mf I SLC)
MI (I, DFHS); Ch, cy 1935 (Ts SG)

EXETER St Thomas, Oldridge. Chapelry in Exeter St Thomas. Disused after
Commonwealth. Rebuilt 1789. Separate parish 1793. Now with NORTH KENN
OR C 1961+ M 1949+ (Inc); any early registers lost. see Exeter St Thomas
BT M 1620 only (DRO)

EXETER St Andrew, Station Road, Exwick. Parish created 1872 from Exeter
St Thomas
OR C 1842-1872 M 1873-1954 (DRO)

EXETER Emmanuel, Okehampton Road. Parish created 1910 from Exeter St Thomas
and Exwick. Now with Exeter St Thomas
OR (Inc)

EXETER St Philip, Buddle Lane. Licensed building in the parish of Exeter St
Thomas and Emmanuel

EXETER St Andrew, Alphington Road. Licensed building in the parish of Exeter
St Thomas and Emmanuel

EXETER Central Exeter. United benefice created 1974, including St Stephen,
St Mary Arches, St Olave, St Pancras, St Petrock

EXETER Wynard's Hospital and Almshouses, Magdalen Street Chapel erected
1346; Wynard's episcopal chapel [Kelly 1889]

EXETER Exeter University Chaplaincy

EXETER Prison, New North Road

EXETER Bradninch Precinct. Extra-parochial place [41 in 1811]
see Exeter St Lawrence, St Paul, St Stephen

EXETER Castle Yard. Extra-parochial place. see Exeter St Lawrence, St Paul,
St Stephen
MI Castle Precinct (I, DFHS)

EXETER Cathedral Precincts, Extra-parochial place

EXETER (Free Church of England) Christ Church, Grosvenor Place, Southernhay.
Erected 1846 [1851 Religious Census] [1882 Return]

EXETER (RC) St Nicholas Chapel, The Mint. Served by Jesuit priests
1762-1871. Erected 1791 [1851 Religious Census] [1882 Return]
OR C 1774-1808 M 1790-1805 B 1790-1807 Confirmations 1793, 1800 (DRO);
    C 1774+ M 1790+ B 1789+ (Inc, Sacred Heart, Exeter); Confirmations 1862,
    1864, 1867, 1869, 1872, 1875, 1877, 1880, 1887, 1889, 1893+ (Plymouth
    Diocesan Archives)
Cop C 1768+ MB 1790+ copied into registers of ARLINGTON (Inc,Sacred Heart,
    Exeter)

EXETER (RC) Sacred Heart, South Street 1790; 1884

EXETER (RC) The Blessed Sacrament, Fore Street, Heavitree 1930; 1932

EXETER (RC) St Thomas of Canterbury, Dunsford Hill 1938

EXETER (RC) St Bernadette, Galsworthy Road 1960

EXETER (Bapt) f 1656. Gandy Street, South Street erected 1725; rebuilt
1822-23 [1851 Religious Census] Burial ground in Paris Street [1882 Return]
OR ZC 1786-1837 B 1785-1837 (RG 4/964 PRO); C 1742-1906, 1936-64 (DRO)
Cop (Mf) Z 1786-1837 B 1785-1837 (Mf DCRS/WSL, SG); Extr Z 1786-1837 (IGI)

EXETER (Bapt) Bartholomew Street. Erected 1817-18, by seceders from South
Street [1851 Religious Census] [1882 Return] Sold 1953; from 1978 used by
Evangelical church. Bapt moved to Dorset Avenue
OR Z 1817-37 (RG 4/335 PRO); C 1823-1953 (DRO)
Cop (Mf) Z 1817-37 (Mf DCRS/WSL, SG); Extr Z 1817-37 (IGI)

EXETER (Bapt) St Thomas, Dorset Avenue f 1817 Exwick Christian Fellowship

EXETER (Bapt) The Pavilion, Magdalen Street f 1835. Later at Zoar, Longbrook
Street. Erected 1841 [1851 Religious Census]

EXETER (Bapt) Sunday School, Exe Island [1882 Return]

EXETER (Bapt) Wonford, Wonford Street f 1903

EXETER (Bapt) Pinhoe Road f 1933

EXETER (Bapt) Free Evangelical Church
OR C 1936-68 (DRO)

EXETER (Presb/Unit) f 1660. James's Meeting, James Street 1687, George's
Meeting, South Street 1760 [1851 Religious Census] [1882 Return] Closed 1984
OR C 1788-1804 private register of Timothy Kenrick, minister of George's
    Meeting (Dr Williams's Library, Gordon Square, London); ZCB 1824-37
    B 1818-22 (RG 4/1085,47 PRO); B 1837-1882 (DRO)
Cop (Mf) CB 1818-37 (Mf DCRS/WSL, SG)
MI George's Meeting (I, DFHS)

EXETER (Presb/Ind) Bow Meeting
OR ZCB 1687-1823 (RG 4/965 (PRO)
Cop (Mf) C 1687-1823 B 1748-1824 (Mf DCRS/WSL, SG); Bow Meeting now Mint
    Meeting: Extr C 1687-1823 (IGI); C 1687-1823 (Mf I SLC)

EXETER (Presb/Unit) Mint Meeting f 1719. United 1810 with George's Meeting,
Sold to Wes 1811
OR ZC 1719-1810 B 1773-1810 (RG 4/336 PRO)
Cop (Mf) C 1719-1810 B 1773-1810 (Mf SG)

EXETER (Ind/Cong, later URC) f 1795 Castle Street Lane; joined Bow meeting,
separated 1795 [1851 Religious Census] Closed 1870. Later used by British
Legion. New chapel Southernhay 1868, bombed 1942, rebuilt 1956
OR ZC 1798-1836 B 1824-36 (RG 4/1205,582,1206 PRO) M 1927-41 (DRO) Other
    records destroyed by bombing 1942
Cop (Mf) ZC 1798-1816 C 1817-36 B 1824-36 (Mf DCRS/WSL, SG);
    Extr C 1798-1836 (IGI); C 1798-1836 (Mf I SLC)

EXETER (Ind/Cong) High Street f 1816; moved 1835 to Grosvenor Place; erected
1837 [1851 Religious Census]
OR ZC 1820-36 (RG 4/1086 PRO)
Cop (Mf) ZC 1820-36 (Mf DCRS/WSL, SG); Extr ZC 1820-36 (IGI); ZC 1820-36
    (Mf I SLC)

EXETER (Ind/Cong later URC) Stafford Villa, Heavitree [1882 Return];
Fore Street Heavitree f 1867

EXETER (URC) St Thomas, Church Roade f 1901

EXETER (Wes) Circuit
OR C 1838-1911 (DRO)

EXETER (Wes/Lady Hunt Conn/Ind) Tabernacle, Combe Street f 1770. Wes until
1837; Calvinist [Kelly 1889]
OR C 1775-1836 (RG 4/527, 1882 PRO)
Cop (Mf) C 1775-1836 (Mf DCRS/WSL, SG); Extr C 1775-1836 (IGI); C 1775-1836
    (Mf I SLC)

EXETER (Wes) The Mint, Mint Lane. Erected 1812 [1851 Religious Census]
[1882 Return] rebuilt 1970
OR C 1801-19 ZCB 1818-31 ZC 1831-37 (RG 4/528,1207,1208 PRO)
Cop (Mf) ZC 1801-37 B 1818-31 (Mf DCRS/WSL, SG); Extr C 1801-37 (IGI);
    C 1801-37 (Mf I SLC)
MI (I, DFHS)

EXETER (Wes) Heavitree. Erected 1830 [1851 Religious Census]

EXETER (Wes) St Sidwell's Chapel, Sidwell Street. Erected 1834
[1851 Religious Census] [1882 Return] Rebuilt 1896. fl c.1970
OR C 1841-1865 (DRO)

101

EXETER (Wes) A house, Exwick [1851 Religious Census]

EXETER (Wes) Christ Church Chapel, Southernhay. Erected as proprietary
chapel 1846-47 [1882 Return]
OR M 1899-1946 (DRO)

EXETER (Wes) St. Thomas Chapel
OR C 1912-57 (DRO)

EXETER (Bible Christian) Circuit
OR C 1889-1938 (DRO)

EXETER (Bible Christian/UMFC/Meth) Providence, Northernhay Street. Erected
1840; purchased 1851 from Brethren [1851 Religious Census] [1882 Return].
Meth to 1956, then Elim Pentecostal church
OR M 1940-54 (DRO)

EXETER (UMFC) Church Road, St Thomas [1882 Return]
OR C 1886-1935 (DRO)

EXETER (U Meth) Mount Pleasant Chapel
OR M 1917-69 (DRO)

EXETER (Meth) Cowick Street, St Thomas. Erected 1935. fl *c.*1970

EXETER (Meth) Brookway, Whipton. Erected 1956. fl *c.*1970

EXETER (Meth) Burnthouse Lane, Wonford. Erected 1973

EXETER (Second Advent Chapel, later Wes Reform) [1851 Religious Census]

EXETER (S of F) Exeter Monthly Meeting
OR Z 1776-86 M 1779-94 B 1776-83 (RG 6/ 272-3, 356 PRO)

EXETER (S of F) Exeter f 1656; new meeting house Magdalen Street 1691.
Rebuilt 1834 [1851 Religious Census] [Kelly 1889] Now at Wynards Lane
OR Z 1694-1823 M 1697-1725 B 1693-1794 (RG 6/1399, 1445 PRO); B 1864-1879
    (DRO); *and see* DEVON Eastern Division
BT B 1865-66, 1868, 1870-71 (DRO)
Cop (Mf) Z 1824-37 B 1825-69 (Mfc Colyton SP)
MI (I, DFHS)

EXETER (Brethren) Paul Street [1851 Religious Census]

EXETER (Brethren) Blackboy Road
OR M 1974-81 (DRO)

EXETER (Brethren) Sidwell Street [Kelly 1889]

EXETER (Brethren) Gospel Hall, Lower Market [Kelly 1889]

EXETER (Brethren) Victoria Hall, Heyman Wreford [Kelly 1889]

EXETER (Brethren) Friernhay Street [Kelly 1889]

EXETER (Brethren) Providence, Northernhay Street. Erected 1839; sold 1851 to
Bible Christians

EXETER (Christians) The Priory, The Mint [1882 Return]

EXETER (Salvation Army) Temperance Hall, The Friars [1882 Return]

EXETER (Jews) Synagogue Place, St Mary Arches Street, erected 1763, rebuilt 1835 [1851 Religious Census] [1882 Return] Cemetery, Magdalen Road f 1757
OR D 1858-1911 in Exeter Memorbuch (Jewish Museum, Camden, London)
Cop List of burials 1880+ (Ts Mocatta Library, University College, London)
MI (I, DFHS); inscriptions 1807-1958, plan and history of burial ground (on synagogue web-site: see p.19)

EXETER St. Bartholomew's Yard. Burial ground from 1637. All Hallows on the Walls church erected on site 1843
OR B 1834-37 (DRO)

EXETER St. Bartholomew's New Cemetery. Opened 1837, closed 1866
OR B 1837-1946 (DRO)
BT B 1864-68, 1870 (DRO)

EXETER Exeter Cemetery, Bath Road, Heavitree. Opened 1866
OR B 1866-1915 (DRO)
BT B 1866-70 (DRO)

EXETER St. Thomas (Cowick Street)
OR B 1857-1957 (DRO)

EXETER St. Thomas (Exwick Road)
OR B 1877-1918; War graves B 1940-47 (DRO)

EXETER St. Leonard's Burial Board
OR B 1873-1879 (DRO)

EXMINSTER St Martin [Exminster Hundred; St Thomas Union] [1113]
Now with KENN
OR C 1562-1984 Banns 1932-97 M 1562-1957, 1966-71 Confirmations 1905-77
    B 1562-1936 (DRO)
BT CMB 1613, 1615-16, 1636, 1666, 1669-72, 1675, 1678-79, 1691, 1699
    (1700-1812 ?); C 1813-36, 1838-49 M 1813-36, 1838 B 1813-14, 1816-36,
    1838-48 (DRO)
Cop B 1813-37 (Ptd DFHS); CMB 1562-1837 with index (DCRS/WSL, SG); B 1813-37
    (SG); M 1562-1836 (Boyd)
Cop (Mf) Extr C 1562-1812 M 1562-1836 (IGI); C 1562-1812 M 1562-1836
        (Mf I SLC)
MI (I, DFHS); Ch, cy extr (Ptd Cresswell 89-93); Ch, cy 1938 (Ts SG);
    Extr (Whitmore MS, SG)

EXMINSTER County Asylum Cemetery
OR B 1900-64 (DRO)
Cop B 1900-14 (DFHS)

EXMINSTER (Wes) Erected 1893. fl c.1970

EXMOUTH   Seaside resort developed in the 18th century out of the ancient parishes of Littleham and Withycombe Raleigh

EXMOUTH St Margaret, Littleham [East Budleigh Hundred; St Thomas Union]
[3189] Peculiar of the Dean and Chapter of Exeter until 1848. United with Exmouth Holy Trinity
OR C 1612-1705, 1744-1913 M 1603-1705, 1744-1951 B 1603-1678, 1744-1952
    (DRO) Noted in 1831: 'no other registers can be found'

EXMOUTH St Margaret, Littleham   cont.
BT CMB 1607, 1609, 1617, 1620, 1625-26, 1629-31, 1699, 1711, 1714-15,
1718-35, 1737-38, 1741, 1743, 1745-46, 1750, 1752, 1754-66, 1768-69,
1771-72, 1774-85, 1787-90, 1792-93, 1796-99, 1802-13; CB 1813, 1816-30,
1832, 1834-67 M 1813, 1816-29, 1832, 1834-37 (DRO)
Cop M 1813-37 (Ptd DFHS); B 1813-37 (Ptd DFHS); B 1813-37 (SG);
Extr C 1612-1811 M 1603-1793 B 1603-1811 (Vol 11, BG/PCL)

EXMOUTH St John in the Wilderness, Withycombe Raleigh [East Budleigh
Hundred; St Thomas Union] [1063] Chapelry in EAST BUDLEIGH. Separate parish
1850 as Withycombe Raleigh with Exmouth All Saints. Ruined by 18th cent but
rebuilt 1926-37. Now daughter church of Withycombe Raleigh St John the
Evangelist
OR C 1562-1913 M 1562-1947 B 1562-1876 (DRO)
BT CMB 1608-1812 with gaps; CB 1813-47 M 1813-38 (DRO)
Cop B 1813-37 (Ptd DFHS); C 1562-1709, 1768-1812 M 1562-1708 B 1562-1709,
1768-1812 (DCRS/WSL); M 1562-1600 B 1813-37 (SG); B 1813-37 (WSL);
Extr CMB 1574-1729 (Vol 11, BG/PCL)
Cop (Mf) Extr C 1562-1709, 1768-1812 M 1562-1708 B 1562-1709, 1768-1812
(IGI); C 1562-1709, 1768-1812 M 1562-1708 B 1562-1709, 1768-1812
(Mf I SLC)
MI Cy 1917 (MS, SG)

EXMOUTH St John the Evangelist, Withycombe Raleigh. Erected 1722, demolished
1865. New church 1864. Now parish church. *see above*

EXMOUTH All Saints. Chapel-of-ease to Withycombe Raleigh

EXMOUTH Holy Trinity, Chapel Hill. Medieval chapel, rebuilt 1779. Rebuilt on
new site 1823-25, and 1905-07. United with St Margaret, Littleham
OR M 1878-1895 (DRO) catalogued with Littleham

EXMOUTH (Free Church) Christ Church, North Street. Erected 1896

EXMOUTH (RC) Marley Lodge 1862-66. The Holy Ghost, Radden Stile Lane f 1885
OR C 1887+ M 1895+ B 1888+ Confirmations 1888+ (Inc)

EXMOUTH (RC) St Anne, Withycombe 1968

EXMOUTH (Bapt) Brixington, Churchill Road n.d.

EXMOUTH (Bapt) Victoria Road f 1891

EXMOUTH (Lady Glenorchy's Connexion, Ind/Cong, later URC) Glenorchy,
Withycombe Raleigh. Erected 1777 [1851 Religious Census] Rebuilt 1866-69
[1882 Return]
OR ZC 1751-1837 B 1784-1818 (RG 4/1209 PRO); C 1779+ M 1837-87, 1908+
B 1812-81 (Ch Sec)
Cop (Mf) ZC 1751-1837 B 1784-1818 (Mf DCRS/WSL, SG); Extr ZC 1751-1837
(IGI); ZC 1751-1837 (Mf I SLC)

EXMOUTH (Cong) Beacon. f 1806 by secession from Glenorchy; closed 1953
OR C 1891-1932 with Minute Books (Ch Sec, Glenorchy); M 1904-50 (DRO)

EXMOUTH (Ind/Cong) Ebenezer. Erected 1807 [1851 Religious Census] Closed
1965
OR C 1809-37 (RG 4/2905 PRO)
Cop (Mf) ZC 1809-37 (Mf DCRS/WSL, SG); Extr C 1809-37 (IGI); C 1809-37
(Mf I SLC)

EXMOUTH (Ind/Cong) Point in View, Withycombe Raleigh. f 1826 [1851 Religious
Census] Associated with TOPSHAM. Closed
OR C 1829-37 (RG 4/2032 PRO)
Cop (Mf) C 1829-37 (Mf DCRS/WSL, SG); Extr C 1829-37 (IGI); C 1829-37
        (Mf I SLC)

EXMOUTH (Wes) Erected c.1843 [1851 Religious Census]; Tower Street, erected
1896. fl c.1970
OR for c.1831-37 see EXETER Mint (RG 4/1208 PRO)

EXMOUTH (Wes) Brunswick Square [1882 Return]

EXMOUTH (Wes) Withycombe Raleigh. Erected 1907; fl c.1970

EXMOUTH (Bible Christian) York House n.d. [1851 Religious Census]

EXMOUTH (Prim Meth) Parade Chapel [1882 Return]
OR M 1945-57 (DRO)

EXMOUTH (Meth) Littlemead, Roundhouse Lane. Erected 1968

EXMOUTH (Evangelical) Exmouth Independent Evangelical Church, Scott Drive
FIEC

EXMOUTH (S of F) Reading room, Globe Inn 1815. Part of TOPSHAM MM

EXMOUTH (Brethren) Withycombe Raleigh. Erected 1843 [1851 Religious Census]
Cop B 1843-1953 (SG)
MI Burial ground 1980-81 (Ts SG); (I, DFHS)

EXMOUTH (Christian Association) Zion. Erected 1851 [1851 Religious Census]

EXMOUTH (Baptised Believers) Bethesda, Little Albion Street, Withycombe
Raleigh [1851 Religious Census]

EXTON   see WOODBURY WITH EXTON

EXWICK   see EXETER

FARRINGDON or BISHOP'S CLYST St Petrock and St Barnabas [East Budleigh
Hundred; St Thomas Union] [377] Rebuilt 1871. Now with AYLESBEARE,
ROCKBEARE, CLYST HONITON, SOWTON
OR C 1678-1897 M 1679-1836 B 1678-1812 (DRO)
BT CMB 1610, 1614, 1617, 1626, 1631, 1633, 1635, 1639, 1671-72, 1678,
    1682-83, 1687, 1690 (1691-1812 ?); C 1813-36, 1838-67 M 1813, 1815-23,
    1825, 1827-30, 1832-33, 1835-36 B 1813-25, 1827-36, 1838-67 (DRO)
Cop CMB 1678-1850 (DCRS/WSL); M 1620-33, 1670-1788 (Phil Ms); M 1620-1788
    (DFHS, SG); M 1620-1788 (Boyd)
Cop (Mf) Extr C 1610-1812 M 1610-39, 1679-1788, 1840-50 (IGI); C 1610-1812
         M 1610-39, 1679-1788, 1840-50 (Mf I SLC)
MI (I, DFHS)

FARWAY St Michael and All Angels [Colyton Hundred; Honiton Union] [360]
Now with COLYTON
OR C 1567-1993 M 1574-1977 B 1573-1994 (DRO)
BT CMB 1617, 1624, 1629, 1633, 1664, 1668, 1669 or 1670, 1672, 1675, 1677?,
    1678, 1683, 1685, 1687, 1691, 1695-97 (1698-1812 ?); CMB 1815-19,
    1821-37 CB 1838-47 M 1839, 1841-47 (DRO)

FARWAY cont.
Cop C 1567-1884 M 1574-1837 B 1573-1938 (DCRS/WSL)
Cop (Mf) (Colyton SP); Extr C 1567-1875 M 1574-1842 (IGI); C 1567-1875
M 1574-1842 (Mf I SLC)
MI (I, DFHS); Extr (Whitmore MS, SG); Incledon 500 (NDA)

FARWAY (Wes) Erected 1895. fl c.1970

FEN OTTERY see VENN OTTERY

FENITON St Andrew [Hayridge Hundred; Honiton Union] [343]
Now with BUCKERELL, ESCOT
OR C 1549-1884 M 1550-1959 B 1549-1957 (DRO)
BT CMB 1606-07, 1613, 1620, 1638, 1664, 1668-70, 1675, 1678, 1683, 1685,
1687, 1690, 1695 (1696-1812 ?); CMB 1813-15 MB 1817-18 C 1818, 1820,
1822, 1824-26, 1830-34, 1838-39 M 1820, 1822, 1824-26, 1830, 1833-34
B 1822, 1824-26, 1832-34, 1836, 1838-39 (DRO)
Cop CMB 1549-1837 (DCRS/WSL); M 1550-1837 (Boyd)
Cop (Mf) (Colyton SP); Extr C 1549-1837 M 1550-1837 (IGI); C 1549-1837
M 1550-1837 (Mf I SLC)
MI Incledon 528 (NDA)

FENITON (Bapt) f 1832

FENITON (Wes) Fenny Bridges. erected 1839. Closed. Later farm building

FILLEIGH St Paul [Braunton Hundred; South Molton Union] [329] Rebuilt 1732,
1877. Now with SOUTH MOLTON
OR C 1685-1876 M 1685-1837 B 1685-1946 (NDRO)
BT CMB 1608, 1610-11, 1613-14, 1668, 1670, 1679, 1681-83, 1688-90, 1695-97,
1699?, 1700, 1704-10, 1714-15 (1716-1812 ?); CB 1820, 1826-71 M 1820,
1826-35 (DRO)
Cop (Mf) Extr C 1597-1601 M 1601 (IGI); C 1597-1601 (Mf I SLC)
MI (I, NDA); (I, DFHS); Incledon 64 (NDA)

FILLEIGH (Wes)
OR for c.1807-37 see BARNSTAPLE CIRCUIT (RG 4/954 PRO)

FILLEIGH (Bible Christian) Heddon. Erected 1862. Closed 1966. Later a garage

FOLLY GATE see INWARDLEIGH

FORD see ALWINGTON, or PLYMOUTH, or STOKENHAM, or CHIVELSTONE

FOXHOLE see PAIGNTON

FREMINGTON St Peter [Fremington Hundred; Barnstaple Union] [1180]
OR C 1602-1896 M 1602-1927 B 1602-1948 (NDRO)
BT CMB 1607, 1610-11, 1614, 1619, 1623-24, 1631, 1672, 1674, 1678-79, 1682,
1689, 1691, 1697-98, 1704-07, 1709, 1712, 1714-15 (1716-1812 ?);
CB 1813-14, 1817, 1821, 1823, 1826 C 1830, 1832-34, 1836, 1838-54,
1856-64 M 1813, 1817, 1821, 1823, 1826, 1830-34, 1836 B 1830-34, 1836,
1838-39, 1842-55, 1857-64 (DRO)
Cop B 1813-37 (Ptd DFHS); B 1813-37 (SG); C 1602-1943 M 1602-1927
B 1602-1948 (WSL); CMB 1602-1837 (DCRS/WSL); M 1602-1837 (Boyd)
Cop (Mf) C 1602-1896 M 1602-1927 B 1602-1948 (Mfc SG); Extr C 1602-1812
M 1602-1730, 1758-1837 (IGI); C 1602-1812 M 1602-1730, 1758-1837
(Mf I SLC)
MI (I, DFHS); Incledon 805 (NDA)

FREMINGTON St Andrew, Bickington. Mission church erected 1910; rebuilt 1956 after fire

FREMINGTON (Bapt) Lovacott Chapel n.d. [1851 Religious Census] [1882 Return]

FREMINGTON (Cong, later URC) Bickington Hill f 1838 [1882 Return]
OR C 1956+ (Ch Sec)

FREMINGTON (Wes) Erected 1816 [1851 Religious Census] rebuilt 1862
[1882 Return] fl c.1970
OR for c.1807-37 see BARNSTAPLE CIRCUIT (RG 4/954 PRO)

FREMINGTON (Bible Christian) Hope Chapel, Holmacott. Erected 1843
[1851 Religious Census] [1882 Return] closed 1979. Later a house

FRITHELSTOCK St Mary and St Gregory [Shebbear Hundred; Torrington Union]
[696] Now with GREAT TORRINGTON, LITTLE TORRINGTON
OR C 1556-1895 M 1573-1837 B 1571-1911 (NDRO)
BT CMB 1607-08, 1611, 1620, 1624, 1629-30, 1631?, 1633, 1668, 1670, 1674,
   1678-80, 1682-83, 1685, 1689, 1691, 1694, 1696-97, 1699-1700, 1702,
   1709-12, 1714-15, 1717-21, 1725-30, 1732-37, 1739-43, 1745-56, 1762,
   1764-84, 1786-1812; CB 1830-31, 1835, 1837-39 C 1840-45 M 1830, 1835,
   1837-39 B 1841, 1843-45 (DRO)
Cop CMB 1556-1873 (DCRS/WSL)
Cop (Mf) (Appledore SP); Extr C 1556-1873 M 1575-1859 (IGI); C 1556-1873
       M 1575-1859 (Mf I SLC)
MI (I, DFHS); Incledon 604 (NDA)

FRITHELSTOCK (Bapt) Frithelstockstone f 1833 [1851 Religious Census]
[Baptist Handbook 1861]

FRITHELSTOCK (Cong) Licensed 1672; closed by 1715

FRITHELSTOCK (Wes) Peacleave n.d. [1851 Religious Census]
OR for c.1819-37 see BIDEFORD (RG 4/955 PRO)

FRITHELSTOCK (Bible Christian/Meth) Bethesda, Frithelstockstone. Erected
1833 [1851 Religious Census] [1882 Return] fl c.1970

FULFORD   see DUNSFORD

GALMPTON   see BRIXHAM All Saints, Churston Ferrers

GALMPTON   see SOUTH HUISH

GAMMATON   see WEARE GIFFARD

GEORGE NYMPTON   see NYMET ST GEORGE

GEORGEHAM or HAM ST GEORGE St George [Braunton Hundred; Barnstaple Union]
[925]
OR C 1540-1843 M 1538-1986 B 1538-1954 (NDRO)
BT CMB 1597-1605, 1607-08, 1610, 1614, 1631, 1638, 1641, 1670, 1674,
   1678-79, 1682-83, 1690-91, 1694-97, 1699-1700, 1702, 1712, 1714-15, 1731
   (1732-1812 ?); CMB 1813-37 CB 1839-40 (DRO)

GEORGEHAM cont.
Cop B 1813-37 (Ptd DFHS); B 1813-37 (WSL, DLS, SG); C 1540-1840 M 1538-1860
    B 1538-1850 (NDA); CMB 1538-1850 from BT, 1559-1812 (DCRS/WSL)
Cop (Mf) Extr C 1540-1850 M 1538-1850 (IGI); C 1540-1850 M 1538-1850
    (Mf I SLC)
MI (I, NDA); (Ptd H.Balfour 'An armory of Georgeham church': TDA 101: 1969:
    107-13); Incledon 454 (NDA)

GEORGEHAM St Mary Magdalene, Croyde. Erected 1874

GEORGEHAM (Bapt) St Mary's Road, Croyde f 1816 [1851 Religious Census]
OR Z 1821-35 (RG 4/944 PRO); M 1984+ (Ch Sec)
Cop Z 1821-35 (SG)
Cop (Mf) Z 1821-35 (Mf DCRS/WSL); Extr Z 1821-35 (IGI)

GEORGEHAM (Bapt) f 1884

GEORGEHAM (Wes) [1882 Return]

GEORGEHAM (Bible Christian) Erected 1833 [1851 Religious Census]

GERMANSWEEK or WEEK ST GERMANS, St German [Lifton Hundred; Okehampton Union]
[370] Now with OKEHAMPTON
OR C 1652-1892 M 1654-1837 B 1654-1812 (DRO)
BT CMB 1608, 1613, 1615, 1639, 1663-64, 1666, 1668-72, 1674-78, 1680-81,
    1686-88, 1694-96, 1699-1700 (1701-1812 ?); C 1814, 1816-18, 1822,
    1833-34 M 1814, 1816-18, 1833-34 B 1816-18, 1822, 1833-34 (DRO)
Cop (Mf) (Okehampton SP)

GERMANSWEEK (Bapt) Erected 1842 [1851 Religious Census] [1882 Return]

GERMANSWEEK (Bible Christian) Zion, Eworthy. Erected 1863 [1882 Return]
fl c.1970

GIDLEIGH Holy Trinity [Wonford Hundred; Okehampton Union] [155]
Now with CHAGFORD, THROWLEIGH
OR C 1613-1987 M 1599-1753, 1814-1978 B 1599-1735, 1768-1989 (DRO)
BT CMB 1609, 1625, 1630, 1633, 1666-69, 1671-73, 1675, 1677, 1679, 1683,
    1687, 1690, 1695-97, 1699, 1701 (1702-1812 ?); C 1813-35 M 1814,
    1818-21, 1824-25, 1828-35 B 1813, 1815-16, 1820-21, 1823, 1826, 1830-32,
    1834-35 (DRO)
Cop CMB 1599-1812 (DCRS/WSL); Extr CMB 1599-1837 (Ptd, edit. M.Brown:
    Dartmoor Press: 1998)
Cop (Mf) (Okehampton SP); Extr C 1613-1812 M 1599-1753 (IGI); C 1613-1812
    M 1599-1753 (Mf I SLC)
MI (Ptd DRMI 22: 1998)

GITTISHAM St Michael [East Budleigh Hundred; Honiton Union] [370]
Now with HONITON
OR C 1559-1888 M 1571-1990 B 1559-1952 (DRO)
BT CMB 1614, 1620, 1630-31, 1635, 1662, 1668-72, 1675, 1678, 1682-83, 1687,
    1690, 1695, 1699, 1701 (1702-1812 ?); CMB 1836 (DRO)
Cop Extr CMB 1572-1687: a few families (Ptd W.C.Trevelyan 'Extracts from the
    registers of Gittisham' Miscellanea Genealogica et Heraldica NS 1:
    1874); B 1800-37 (Ptd DFHS); B 1800-37 (WSL, SG)
Cop (Mf) (Colyton SP); Extr C 1559-1888 M 1571-1838 B 1559-1952 (Mfc SG)

GITTISHAM (Presb) fl c.1672-90

GITTISHAM (Wes)
OR for c.1809-37 see AXMINSTER (RG 4/512 PRO)

GLENHOLT   see BICKLEIGH near Plymouth

GOLDSWORTHY see PARKHAM

GOODLEIGH St Gregory [Braunton Hundred; Barnstaple Union] [442]
Rebuilt 1882. Now with BARNSTAPLE
OR C 1538-1927 M 1538-1981 B 1538-1978 (NDRO)
BT CMB 1596-1602, 1607-08, 1610, 1614, 1631, 1638, 1641, 1643-44, 1670,
    1674, 1678-79, 1683, 1688, 1690-91, 1694, 1696-97, 1702-05, 1710, 1712,
    1714-15 (1716-1812 ?); C 1819, 1839-59 M 1819 B 1819, 1839-50, 1852-59
    (DRO)
Cop CMB 1538-1850 (DCRS/WSL, NDA)
MI Incledon 52 (NDA)

GOODLEIGH (Cong) f 1830 [1851 Religious Census] [1882 Return] Closed 1967

GOODLEIGH (Cong) f 1821 [1851 Religious Census]

GOODLEIGH (Wes) Brithambottom. Erected 1844 [1851 Religious Census]

GOODLEIGH (Bible Christian) Erected 1880. fl c.1970

GOODRINGTON   see PAIGNTON

GREAT TORRINGTON see TORRINGTON, GREAT

GULLIFORD   see WOODBURY

GULWORTHY   see TAVISTOCK ST PAUL

GUNN   see SWIMBRIDGE

HACCOMBE St Blaise [Wonford Hundred; Newton Abbot Union] [13] Chapel of
house of Carew family. Now with STOKEINTEIGNHEAD, COMBEINTEIGNHEAD
OR Z 1687-1757 C 1711-14, 1755-57, 1779+ M 1779-1821, 1989+ B 1819+ (Inc)
    M 1859-1991 (DRO) Noted in 1831: 'No Registers can be found prior to
    1813; there are only two houses in the parish of Haccombe'
BT None
Cop Z 1687-1757 C 1711-14, 1779-1821 M 1773-1801 (WSL)
MI Extr (Ptd W.Crabbe 'An account of Haccombe church': TDA: 2nd ser. 1:
    1867: 61-71); Incledon 148 (NDA)

HACCOMBE St Luke, Milber Area in Haccombe, Separate parish 1963

HALBERTON St Andrew [Halberton Hundred; Tiverton Union] [1636]
Now with SAMPFORD PEVERELL
OR C 1620-1674, 1700-1850 M 1612-1672, 1699-1989 B 1605-1672, 1699-1865
    (DRO) Some early events registered at WILLAND
BT CMB 1612, 1614, 1616, 1625, 1630, 1633-34, 1636, 1664, 1667-69, 1672,
    1678, 1683, 1685, 1699 (1700-1812 ?); CMB 1813-15, 1818-22 C 1825-48
    M 1826-49 B 1826-49 (DRO)
Cop CM 1612-1837 B 1605-1837 M licences 1568-1837 (Ptd DCRS 1930-31);
    CMB 1605-1837 (DCRS/WSL); M 1790-1837 (Pallot)
Cop (Mf) (Tiverton SP); Extr C 1605-1837 M 1612-1837 (IGI); C 1605-1837
        M 1612-1837 (Mf I SLC)
MI 1843 (Ptd DCRS, as above); Incledon 278 (NDA)

HALBERTON Ash Thomas Chapel. Mission church erected 1877. Now with SAMPFORD PEVERELL

HALBERTON (Presb) fl *c.*1672-90

HALBERTON (Wes) High Street. Erected 1816 [1851 Religious Census] fl *c.*1970 **OR** for *c.*1812-37 *see* TIVERTON (RG 4/342 PRO)

HALBERTON (Bible Christian) A house n.d. [1851 Religious Census]; Halberton Church [1882 Return]

HALDON United benefice including TEIGNMOUTH EAST. TEIGNMOUTH WEST, IDEFORD, LUTON, ASHCOMBE, BISHOPSTEIGNTON

HALSTOW *see* DUNSFORD

HALWELL St Leonard [Coleridge Hundred; Totnes Union] [474] Now with MORELEIGH
OR C 1584-1951 M 1560-1837 B 1561-1952 (DRO)
BT CMB 1597-1601, 1611, 1615, 1620, 1622-23, 1663-64, 1666, 1668, 1670?, 1671-76, 1679-80, 1684, 1686-87, 1690, 1695-96, 1697?, 1699, 1719-30, 1732-44, 1746-83, 1785-1812; CMB 1813-15, 1817, 1819-22, 1824-25 CB 1827-45 M 1827-29, 1831-37, 1839 (DRO)
Cop (Mf) (Totnes SP)

HALWELL (Ind/Cong) Morley or Moreleigh Chapel. Rebuilt 1842 [1851 Religious Census] [1882 Return] Closed

HALWILL St Peter and St James [Black Torrington Hundred; Holsworthy Union] [230] Rebuilt 1879. Now with ASHWATER, BEAWORTHY, CLAWTON, TETCOTT, LUFFINCOTT
OR C 1695-1925 M 1695-1965 B 1695-1812 (DRO)
BT CMB 1602, 1609, 1612-14, 1639, 1630?, 1641, 1663-64, 1668-71, 1674-82, 1686, 1696, 1697?, 1699-1700 (1701-1812 ?); C 1813-44 M 1813-39, 1822-23, 1825-35 B 1813-39, 1842-44 (DRO)
Cop CMB 1695-1837 (DCRS/WSL)
Cop (Mf) Extr C 1695-1812 M 1695-1837 (IGI); C 1695-1812 M 1695-1837 (Mf I SLC)

HALWILL (Bapt) Refuge. Erected 1831 [1851 Religious Census]; [1851 Religious Census]; Halwill Group

HAM *see* PLYMOUTH

HAM ST GEORGE *see* GEORGEHAM

HARBERTON St Andrew [Coleridge Hundred; Totnes Union] [1584] Now with DIPTFORD, NORTH HUISH, HARBERTONFORD
OR C 1624-1943 M 1626, 1648-1837, 1941-78 B 1624-1975 (DRO)
BT CMB 1597-1602, 1608, 1611, 1614-15, 1620, 1633, 1635-36, 1639, 1641, 1663, 1668-77, 1679-80, 1682?, 1683-84, 1686-88, 1690, 1695-97, 1699, 1701-02, 1709, 1712, 1714-15, 1719-21, 1723-30, 1732-37, 1743-62, 1764-65, 1767-68, 1770, 1773-75, 1777-83, 1785-98 (1799-1812 ?); CM 1813-37 B 1813-14, 1816, 1818-24, 1826-37 (DRO)
Cop (Mf) (Totnes SP)

HARBERTON St Peter, Harbertonford, Erected 1859. Parish created 1860 from Harberton. Now with DIPTFORD, NORTH HUISH, HARBERTON
OR B 1859-1954 (DRO)

HARBERTON East Leigh. Mission chapel erected 1894

HARBERTON (RC) Domestic chapel of Risdon family, 18th century
OR None known

HARBERTON (Bapt) Zion, Harbertonford f 1799. Rebuilt c.1830 [1851 Religious
Census] [1882 Return] Later used by Brethren

HARBERTON (Presb) fl 1715; closed by 1772

HARBERTON (Ind) Harbertonford [1882 Return]

HARBERTON (Wes) [1882 Return]
OR for c.1813-37 see ASHBURTON CIRCUIT, KINGSBRIDGE (RG 4/840,1088 PRO)

HARBERTON (Prim Meth) Bow Road, Harbertonford. Erected 1900. fl c.1970

HARBERTON (No distinctive religious appleation) Ebenezer [1882 Return]

HARBERTON (Brethren) Harbertonford

HARFORD St Petroc [Ermington Hundred; Plympton St Mary Union]   [210]
Now with IVYBRIDGE
OR C 1725-1993 M 1724-1978 B 1724-1986 (PWDRO) No earlier registers noted
   in 1831
BT CMB 1613-14, 1616-19, 1621, 1623, 1625, 1633, 1635, 1639, 1664, 1670,
   1672, 1674, 1676-77, 1682, 1690, 1695-96, 1699, 1750-51, 1753-54, 1756,
   1758-1800 (1801-1812 ?); CB 1813-40, 1854 M 1813, 1816-18, 1821-24,
   1826-29, 1831, 1833, 1835-37 (DRO)
Cop M 1724-54 (I, Ptd, edit M.Brown, Dartmoor Press 1999); Extr C 1780
   M 1734-39 B 1732-87 (Vol 7, BG/PCL)
MI (Ptd DRMI 15: 1998); Extr (Whitmore MS, SG)

HARFORD (Wes)
OR for c.1813-37 see ASHBURTON CIRCUIT (RG 4/840 PRO)

HARPFORD St Gregory the Great [East Budleigh Hundred; Honiton Union]   [307]
Renamed 1968 Newton Poppleford with Harpford. Now with NEWTON POPPLEFORD,
COLATON RALEIGH. see also VENN OTTERY
OR C 1638-1996 M 1638-1837 B 1638-1995 (DRO) M 1839+ (Inc)
Noted in 1831: C 1569, CMB 1638+
BT CMB 1610-11, 1613, 1617-18, 1626, 1631, 1636-37, 1667, 1669-70, 1672,
   1675, 1678, 1683, 1685, 1687, 1690, 1695-97, 1699 (1700-1812 ?);
   CB 1813-39, 1845-51 M 1813-19, 1823, 1825-31, 1834-37, 1839 (DRO)
Cop CMB 1638-1837 (DCRS/WSL)
Cop (Mf) Extr CM 1638-1837 (IGI); CM 1638-1837 (Mf I SLC)
MI Incledon 676 (NDA)

HARPFORD (Presb) fl c.1672-90

HARRACOTT   see TAWSTOCK

HARTLAND St Nectan, Stoke [Hartland Hundred; Bideford Union]   [2143]
Now with HARTLAND COAST
OR C 1559-1894 M 1559-1949 B 1559-1890 (NDRO)
BT CMB 1602, 1607, 1610, 1612, 1614, 1617, 1621, 1629, 1634, 1636, 1640,
   1668, 1671, 1673-74, 1678-79, 1682-83, 1685, 1688-91, 1694-97,
   1699-1700, 1702, 1704-05, 1707, 1709-11, 1714-15 (1716-1812 ?);
   C 1813-43, 1847 M 1813-37 B 1813-20, 1822-43, 1847 (DRO)

HARTLAND cont.
Cop CMB 1558-1837 (Ptd DCRS 1930-34); M 1813-37 (Ptd DFHS); B 1813-37
    (Ptd DFHS); CMB 1558-1837 (WSL); B 1813-37 (SG); M 1558-1837 (Boyd);
    M 1790-1837 (Pallot)
Cop (Mf) (Appledore SP); Extr CM 1558-1837 (IGI); C 1558-1837 (Mf I SLC)
MI Ch, cy (Ptd DCRS, as above); (I, NDA); Ch extr (Ptd R.Pearse Chope *The
    Book of Hartland*: 1940)

HARTLAND St John, Hartland Square. Former market hall converted 1837 as
chapel-of-ease to HARTLAND St Nectan.

HARTLAND St Martin, Bursdon Moor. Mission church opened 1910. Now with
HARTLAND COAST

HARTLAND (RC) Our Lady and St Nectan, Well Lane 1964

HARTLAND (Presb) fl *c*.1672-90

HARTLAND (Ind/Cong) Erected 1819 [1851 Religious Census] Closed 1886 ?
OR C 1821-37 (RG 4/529 PRO)
Cop ZC 1821-37 (SG)
Cop (Mf) ZC 1821-37 (Mf DCRS/WSL, SG); Extr C 1821-37 (IGI); C 1821-37
    (Mf I SLC)

HARTLAND (Ind/Cong) South Hole. Erected 1835 [1851 Religious Census]

HARTLAND (Wes) Rimscott. Erected 1821 [1851 Religious Census]; Meadow New
Chapel [1882 Return]

HARTLAND (Bible Christian/U Meth) Edistone. Erected 1821 [1851 Religious
Census] Rebuilt 1878 [1882 Return] fl *c*.1970

HARTLAND (Bible Christian) Erected 1835 [1851 Religious Census]

HARTLAND (Bible Christian/U Meth) Providence. Erected 1860. Closed 1982

HARTLAND (Bible Christian) A building in the possession of Thomas Trick,
Hartland Town [1882 Return]

HARTLAND (Bible Christian/U Meth) Fore Street. Erected 1915. fl *c*.1970

HARTLAND COAST United benefice including PARKHAM, CLOVELLY, HARTLAND,
WELCOMBE, ALWINGTON, BUCKLAND BREWER, ABBOTSHAM, WOOLFARDISWORTHY WEST,
BUCKS MILLS

HATHERLEIGH St John the Baptist [Black Torrington Hundred; Okehampton Union]
[1606] Now with MEETH, EXBOURNE, JACOBSTOWE
OR C 1558-1883 M 1558-1975 B 1558-1955 (DRO)
BT CMB 1610, 1614, 1618, 1624, 1634, 1663-64, 1666, 1668-72, 1674-82, 1684,
    1686-89, 1694, 1699 (1700-1812 ?); CMB 1813-16, 1831 CB 1833-60, 1862-65
    M 1833-37 (DRO)
Cop CMB 1610-1812 from BT, 1558-1837 (DCRS/WSL); CB 1558-1837 M 1559-1837
    (SG); CMB 1558-1836 (WSL); C 1838-43 B 1838-72 (I,SG); M 1558-1823
    (Boyd); B 1800-1900 (I, PWDRO)
Cop (Mf) (Okehampton SP); Extr CM 1558-1837 (IGI); CM 1558-1837 (Mf I SLC)

HATHERLEIGH (Bapt) Conduit Street. Erected 1833 [1851 Religious Census]
[*Baptist Handbook* 1861]

HATHERLEIGH (Presb) Licensed 1672. Closed *c.*1790
OR C 1729-89 (RG 8/7 PRO)
Cop (Mf) C 1729-89 (Mf DCRS/WSL, SG); Extr C 1729-89 (IGI); C 1729-89
    (Mf I SLC)

HATHERLEIGH (Bible Christian) Bridge Street. Erected 1880 [1882 Return]
Rebuilt 1983

HATHERLEIGH (S of F) fl *c.*1743. Part of EXETER MM

HAWKCHURCH [Dorset] Transferred 1896 to Devon. see NIPR *Dorset*

HEANTON PUNCHARDON St Augustine [Braunton Hundred; Barnstaple Union] [586]
Now with MARWOOD
OR C 1657-1923 M 1559-1990 B 1559-1882 (NDRO) Noted in 1831: vol.1 to 1700
    'quite illegible'
BT CMB 1597-1602, 1607, 1610, 1614, 1620, 1623-24, 1627, 1629, 1631, 1668,
    1670, 1674, 1678-79, 1682-83, 1690-91, 1694-97, 1699-1700, 1702-03,
    1711-12, 1714-15 (1716-1812 ?); CB 1813-34, 1838-57, 1859-76 M 1813-25,
    1827-34 (DRO)
Cop B 1800-37 (Ptd DFHS); B 1813-37 (SG); CMB 1597-1631 from BT, 1559-1812
    (DCRS/WSL); M 1559-1812 (Boyd)
Cop (Mf) Extr C 1597-1835 M 1560-1812, 1823-77 (IGI); C 1597-1835
        M 1560-1812, 1823-77 (Mf I SLC)
MI (I, DFHS); Incledon 187 (NDA)

HEANTON PUNCHARDON Royal Air Force, Chivenor. Chaplaincy
OR C 1941-69, 1980-94 Confirmations 1982-94 (AFCC)

HEANTON PUNCHARDON (RC) Royal Air Force, Chivenor

HEANTON PUNCHARDON (Ind/Cong) Erected 1839 [1851 Religious Census]; Chivenor
Independent Chapel [1882 Return]

HEANTON PUNCHARDON (Wes)
OR for *c.*1807-37 *see* BARNSTAPLE CIRCUIT (RG 4/954 PRO)

HEASLEY MILL   *see* MOLTON, NORTH

HEATHFIELD   *see* BOVEY TRACEY

HEATHFIELD   *see* BRENTOR

HEATHFIELD   *see* LAMERTON

HEAVITREE   *see* EXETER

HEMPSTON ARUNDEL   *see* LITTLHEMPSTON

HEMPSTON MAGNA   *see* BROADHEMPSTON

HEMPSTON, LITTLE or **PARVA** *see* LITTLEHEMPSTON

HEMYOCK St Mary [Hemyock Hundred; Wellington Union (Somerset)] [1228]
Rebuilt 1847. Now with CULM DAVY, CLAYHIDON, CULMSTOCK
OR C 1635-1856 M 1635-1837 B 1635-1923 (DRO)
BT CMB 1602, 1606, 1609-11, 1617, 1625-26, 1633, 1636, 1664, 1667-69,
    1671-72, 1675, 1677-78, 1683, 1685, 1687, 1690, 1695-96 (1697-1812 ?);
    CB 1813-50 M 1813-37, 1839, 1841-42 (DRO)

HEMYOCK cont.
Cop CMB 1602-36 from BT, 1635-1837 (Ptd DCRS 1923); CMB 1602-1837 from BT
(WSL); M 1813-37 (Ptd DFHS); M 1602-1837 (Boyd); M 1790-1837 (Pallot)
Cop (Mf) (Tiverton SP); Extr CM 1602-1837 (IGI); C 1602-1837 (Mf I SLC)
MI (I, DFHS); Ch, cy 1980 (Ts SG); Incledon 306 (NDA)

HEMYOCK St Mary's Chapel, Culm Davy. Ancient chapelry in Hemyock. Now with
HEMYOCK, CLAYHIDON, CULMSTOCK
OR None

HEMYOCK (RC) St Joseph, Station Road

HEMYOCK (Bapt) Erected 1838 [1851 Religious Census] [1882 Return]
OR None at church
MI 1980 (Ts SG)

HEMYOCK (Presb) fl *c.*1672-90

HEMYOCK (Wes) High Street. Erected 1838 [1851 Religious Census]
[1882 Return] Rebuilt 1938. Closed 1988
OR for *c.*1812-37 *see* TIVERTON (RG 4/342 PRO)

HEMYOCK (Brethren) A building the property of Joseph Gregory, Symonsborough
[1882 Return]

HENNOCK St Mary [Teignbridge Hundred; Newton Abbot Union]   [747]
Now with BOVEY TRACEY St John
OR C 1541-1973 M 1541-1622, 1653-1837 B 1541-1880 (DRO)
BT CMB 1602, 1614, 1616, 1622, 1633-34, 1641, 1663-64, 1668-71, 1674-81,
1683, 1687-88, 1690, 1695-96, 1703?, 1712-15, 1719-30, 1732-37, 1742-72,
1774-1801, 1803-11; CMB 1813-24 CB 1826-45 M 1826-27 (DRO)
Cop B 1813-37 (Ptd DFHS); B 1813-37 (SG); CMB 1541-1756 (DCRS/WSL);
M 1544-1753 (Boyd); Extr CMB 1544-1750 C 1678-1756 B 1677-1756 (Vol 14,
BG/PCL)
Cop (Mf) C 1552-1600, 1756-1850 M 1552-1600, 1754-1837 B 1552-1600,
1756-1812 (Mfc SG); Extr C 1541-1748 M 1541-1752 (IGI); C 1541-1748
(Mf I SLC)

HENNOCK (Ind) Chudleigh Knighton. Building owned and occupied by William
Harris [1882 Return]

HENNOCK (Wes) Erected 1835 [1882 Return] Closed 1975. Later a house
OR C 1833-1942 (DRO); for *c.*1801-36 *see* ASHBURTON CIRCUIT (RG 4/840,1763
PRO)
Cop (Mf) C 1833-1942 (Torquay SP)

HERNER   *see* BISHOP'S TAWTON

HIGH BICKINGTON   *see* BICKINGTON, HIGH

HIGH BRAY   *see* BRAY, HIGH

HIGHAMPTON Holy Cross [Black Torrington Hundred; Okehampton Union]   [364]
Now with BLACK TORRINGTON, BRADFORD, COOKBURY, THORNBURY
OR C 1653-1703, 1734-1916 M 1653-1703, 1735-1976 B 1653-1703, 1735-1992
(DRO)
BT CMB 1609, 1629, 1663, 1665, 1667, 1670-72, 1674-79, 1681-82, 1684,
1686-88, 1690, 1694-95, 1697, 1699 (1700-1812 ?); C 1813-46, 1848
M 1813, 1815, 1818-23, 1826-29, 1831-37 B 1813-37, 1839-46, 1848 (DRO)

HIGHAMPTON cont.
Cop CMB 1609-1810 from BT, 1654-1837, with index to 1916 (DCRS/WSL);
    CMB 1653-1703, 1734-1837 (SG)
Cop (Mf) (Okehampton SP); Extr C 1609-1837 M 1633, 1657-1714, 1735-1837
    (IGI); C 1609-1837 M 1633, 1657-1714, 1735-1837 (Mf I SLC)

HIGHAMPTON (Bible Christian) Bethesda, Lydacott. Erected 1836
[1851 Religious Census] [1882 Return] fl c.1970

HIGHLEY ST MARY Extra-parochial place [Witheridge Hundred; Tiverton Union]
with STOODLEY

HIGHWEEK   see NEWTON ABBOT

HILL, WEST   see OTTERY ST MARY

HISCOTT   see TAWSTOCK

HITTISLEIGH St Andrew [Wonford Hundred; Crediton Union] [168]
OR C 1677-1813 M 1678-1979 B 1676-1813 (DRO)
BT CMB 1610-12, 1616, 1620, 1624, 1631-33, 1635, 1663-64, 1667, 1668?,
    1669-73, 1675, 1678-79, 1687, 1690, 1695-96, 1699 (1700-1812 ?);
    C 1813-14, 1816-17, 1819-40, 1847 M 1813-17, 1819-24, 1827, 1829-34,
    1836 B 1813-15, 1817, 1820-23, 1825, 1827-35, 1837-40, 1847 (DRO)
Cop CMB 1676-1837 (DCRS/WSL); M 1678-1837 (Boyd)
Cop (Mf) (Okehampton SP); Extr C 1676-1837 M 1678-1837 (IGI); C 1676-1837
    M 1678-1837 (Mf I SLC)

HITTISLEIGH (Ind) Merrymeet. Erected 1816 [1851 Religious Census];
Mercy Meet Chapel, adjoining the Turnpike [1882 Return]

HITTISLEIGH (Bible Christian) Erected 1904. fl c.1970

HITTISLEIGH (Bible Christian) Hittisleigh Mill [1882 Return]

HOCKWORTHY St Simon and St Jude [Bampton Hundred; Tiverton Union] [335]
Now with SAMPFORD PEVERELL
OR C 1577-1995 M 1577-1978 B 1578-1899 (DRO)
BT CMB 1610, 1613-15, 1619, 1635, 1638, 1663-64, 1667-71, 1675, 1679, 1683,
    1685, 1687, 1690, 1697, 1699 (1700-1812 ?); C 1813-18, 1820-39, 1842
    M 1813, 1815-20, 1823-29, 1831, 1834, 1837, 1839, 1842 B 1813-24, 1827,
    1829-39, 1842 (DRO)
Cop (Mf) (Tiverton SP)
MI Incledon 692 (NDA)

HOLBETON All Saints [Ermington Hundred; Plympton St Mary Union] [1107]
OR C 1619-1869 M 1620-1974 B 1619-1913 (PWDRO)
BT CMB 1609-10, 1613-14, 1616-19, 1623, 1627, 1629-30, 1633-34, 1666, 1669,
    1686, 1688-89, 1696-97, 1699 (1700-1812 ?); C 1813-35, 1838-40
    M 1817-31, 1833, 1835, 1838-40 B 1817-23, 1825-35, 1838-40 (DRO)
Cop CMB 1620-1850 (DCRS/WSL)
Cop (Mf) Extr C 1620-1850 M 1620-1837 (IGI); C 1620-1850 M 1620-1837
    (Mf I SLC)
MI (Ptd A.Jewers 'The church of Holbeton and its monumental remains': TDA
    32: 1900: 552-70); (Ptd J.Beckerlegge 'Holbeton church reviewed': TDA
    64: 1932: 485-96)' Extr (Whitmore MS, SG)

HOLBETON (Wes) Reading room 1841 [1851 Religious Census] [1882 Return]
Battisborough Cross. Erected 1897. Closed 1988

HOLBETON (Prim Meth) [1882 Return] Erected 1904. fl c.1970

HOLBETON (S of F) fl 18th cent. Part of PLYMOUTH MM

HOLBETON (Calv) Rehoboth. Erected 1833 [1851 Religious Census]

HOLCOMBE   see DAWLISH

HOLCOMBE BURNELL St John the Baptist [Wonford Hundred; St Thomas Union]
[264] Now with NORTH KENN
OR C 1657-1927 M 1657-1976 B 1657-1812 (DRO)
BT CMB 1609-10, 1618-19, 1626, 1629, 1633, 1635, 1667?, 1668-70, 1672,
    1675, 1677-79, 1683, 1690 (1691-1812 ?); C 1813-14, 1816-45 M 1814,
    1816, 1818-28, 1832-34, 1836 B 1814, 1816-23, 1825-45 (DRO)
Cop B 1753-1812 (Ptd DFHS); B 1753-1812 (WSL, SG)
MI (I, DFHS); Ch extr (Ptd Cresswell 97-8)

HOLCOMBE ROGUS All Saints [Bampton Hundred; Tiverton Union 1835-pre-1850;
Wellington Union (Somerset) pre-1850-1930] [915] Now with SAMPFORD PEVERELL
OR C 1540-1888 M 1540-1979 B 1540-1961 (DRO)
BT CMB 1610, 1615-16, 1620, 1630, 1632, 1635, 1667, 1668?, 1669-70, 1672,
    1675, 1678, 1683, 1695, 1786 (1787-1812 ?); CMB 1813-36, 1838 C 1842-43,
    1847, 1850, 1855, 1857-71 M 1845, 1847, 1850, 1855, 1857-59, 1861-71
    B 1843, 1845, 1847, 1850, 1855, 1867-71 (DRO)
Cop (Mf) (Tiverton SP)
MI Extr (Whitmore MS, SG)

HOLCOMBE ROGUS (Bapt) Four Elms. Erected 1850 [1851 Religious Census]
[1882 Return]

HOLLACOMBE   see WINKLEIGH

HOLLACOMBE St Petrock [Black Torrington Hundred; Holsworthy Union] [100]
Now with HOLSWORTHY, MILTON DAMEREL
OR C 1638-1732 M 1640-1738, 1816-1979 B 1638-1738 (DRO) Noted in 1831:
    volumes 2, 3: CMB 1739-1811
BT CMB 1608-09, 1616, 1624-25, 1636, 1666, 1669-72, 1674-80, 1694-97, 1699
    (1700-1812 ?); C 1813-42 M 1816, 1818-19, 1821-26, 1828-30, 1832,
    1835-36 B 1813-14, 1816-36, 1838-42 (DRO)
Cop CMB 1608-1812 from BT, 1638-1950 with index (DCRS/WSL); CMB 1638-1738,
    1813-37 (SG); M 1628-1739 (Boyd)
Cop (Mf) Extr C 1608-1855 M 1608-25, 1640-1715, 1729-93, 1838-71 (IGI);
        C 1608-1855 M 1608-25, 1640-1715, 1729-93 (Mf I SLC)
MI Extr (Whitmore MS, SG)

HOLLACOMBE (Ind/Cong) Hayes and Hollacombe fl 1836-91
OR C 1868-1883 B 1870-1883 (NDRO)

HOLMACOTT   see FREMINGTON

HOLNE St Mary the Virgin [Stanborough Hundred; Totnes Union] [369] Now with
MOORLAND
OR C 1603-1877 M 1653-1837 B 1618-1812 (DRO)
BT CMB 1596-1602, 1610, 1614, 1616-17, 1620, 1625, 1627, 1632, 1635,
    1663-64, 1666, 1668-69, 1671-72, 1674-76, 1680, 1686, 1690, 1695-96,
    1700, 1750-72, 1774-76, 1780-95 (1796-1812 ?); CMB 1813-36 (DRO)
Cop Extr C 1610-80, 1698-1747 M 1658-1749 B 1621-1803 (Vol 16, BG/PCL)
Cop (Mf) (Totnes SP)
MI (Ptd DRMI 18: 1998)

HOLNE (Wes)
OR for c.1801-36 see ASHBURTON CIRCUIT (RG 4/840,1763 PRO)

HOLNE (Wes) Michelcombe
OR for c.1820-36 see ASHBURTON CIRCUIT (RG 4/840 PRO)

HOLSWORTHY St Peter and St Paul [Black Torrington Hundred; Holsworthy Union]
[1628] United with COOKBURY 1954. Now with HOLLACOMBE, MILTON DAMEREL
OR C 1563-1941 M 1563-1988 B 1563-1955 (DRO)
BT CMB 1612, 1617, 1619, 162?, 1626, 1634, 1663-64, 1668-72, 1674-82, 1688,
    1690, 1694-97 (1698-1812 ?); CMB 1813-34 (DRO)
Cop CMB 1563-1837 (DCRS/WSL, SG)
Cop (Mf) Extr CM 1563-1837 (IGI); CM 1563-1837 (Mf I SLC)

HOLSWORTHY (RC) St Cuthbert Mayne 1958

HOLSWORTHY (Cong) fl 1828-30. Closed 1831 ?
OR ZC 1828-30 (RG 4/2098 PRO)
Cop (Mf) ZC 1828-30 (Mf DCRS/WSL, SG); Extr C 1828-30 (IGI)

HOLSWORTHY (Presb/Ind) Licensed 1672. fl.1715; closed by 1772

HOLSWORTHY (Wes) Erected 1830 [1851 Religious Census]
OR Circuit ZC 1817-37 (RG 4/1210 PRO); C 1839-1974 (NDRO)
Cop (Mf) ZC 1817-37 (Mf DCRS/WSL); ZC 1817-37 (Mf SG); Extr ZC 1817-37
    (IGI); ZC 1817-37 (Mf I SLC)

HOLSWORTHY (Wes) Chilsworthy. Erected 1820 [1851 Religious Census]
[1882 Return] Rebuilt 1886/1907. fl c.1970

HOLSWORTHY (Wes) Soldon Cross. Erected 1886. fl c.1970

HOLSWORTHY (Bible Christian) Anvil Corner. Erected 1854 [1882 Return]
Closed 1988

HOLSWORTHY (Bible Christian) Simpson Moore Chapel [1882 Return]

HOLSWORTHY (Bible Christian/U Meth) Circuit
OR C 1837-1939 (NDRO)

HOLSWORTHY (Bible Christian/U Meth) Bodmin Street [1882 Return]
Erected 1910. fl c.1970

HOLSWORTHY (Meth)
OR M 1936-57 (NDRO)

HOLSWORTHY (S of F) fl c.1743-73

HOLSWORTHY BEACON   see THORNBURY

HOLSWORTHY BEACON   see FREMINGTON

HOLWELL   see PARKHAM

HONEYCHURCH St Mary [Black Torrington Hundred; Okehampton Union] [72]
Now with NORTH TAWTON, BONDLEIGH, SAMPFORD COURTENAY
OR C 1728-1822 M 1757-1837 B 1730-1813 (DRO); C 1813+ M 1848+ B 1812+
    (Inc) Noted in 1831: 'One register Bap 1728-1812 Bur 1730-1811, no Marr
    entered'

HONEYCHURCH cont.
BT CMB 1610, 1613?, 1615, 1618, 1667, 1669, 1672, 1674-75, 1677-81, 1684, 1686-87, 1695, 1697-99 (1700-1812 ?); C 1813-18, 1820-27, 1841-46 M 1813, 1821, 1831-34, 1837 B 1813, 1815-16, 1828-29, 1831-34, 1836-37, 1842, 1845-46 (DRO)
Cop (Mf) (Okehampton SP); C 1728-1812 M 1757-1837 B 1730-1813 (Mfc SG)

HONEYWILL   see ILSINGTON

HONICKNOWLE   see PLYMOUTH

HONITON United benefice including HONITON, GITTISHAM, COMBE RALEIGH, MONKTON, AWLISCOMBE

HONITON St Michael [Axminster Hundred; Honiton Union] [3509] Damaged by fire 1911. Now a chapel-of-ease to St Paul, below
OR C 1562-1946 M 1598-1967 B 1562-1961 (DRO)
BT CMB 1609, 1611, 1620, 1624, 1629-31, 1633-34, 1638, 1663?, 1664, 1667-70, 1672, 1675, 1678, 1685-86, 1690, 1695-99 (1700-1812 ?); none listed after 1812
Cop M 1813-37 (Ptd DFHS); CB 1562-1837 M 1598-1837 with indexes (DCRS/WSL); M 1598-1837 (Boyd)
Cop (Mf) (Colyton SP); Extr C 1598-1850 MB 1598-1837 (Mfc SG); 'Honiton on Otter' Extr C 1562-1837 M 1598-1837 (IGI); C 1562-1837 M 1598-1837 (Mf I SLC)
MI (Ptd A.Skinner 'St Michael's Church, Honiton: memorial inscriptions destroyed in the fire': DCNQ 9: 1917: 253); Incledon 265 (NDA)

HONITON St Paul. Erected 1837-38. Now parish church

HONITON St Margaret's Hospital Almshouse f 14th cent. Chapel

HONITON All Hallows Grammar School Chapel

HONITON (RC) f at Deer Park. The Holy Family, Exeter Road 1877; 1935; 1937
OR C 1879+ M 1899+ B 1895+ Confirmations 1915+ (Inc)

HONITON (Bapt) High Street f by 1655. Licensed 1672. New church 1737. Silver Street erected 1821 [1851 Religious Census] [1882 Return]
OR Z 1829-37 (RG 4/2027 PRO); C 1879-1970 (DRO)
Cop (Mf) Z 1829-37 (Mf DCRS/WSL, SG); Extr Z 1829-37 (IGI)

HONITON (Presb/Ind/Cong, later Evang.Fed) High Street. Licensed 1672. New Meeting House 1774 [1851 Religious Census] [1882 Return]
OR ZC 1697-1711, 1725-52, 1772-1837 B 1774-1837 (RG 4/2028,4463,4464,4485, 441 PRO)
Cop (Mf) ZC 1697-1711, 1725-52, 1772-1837 B 1774-1837 (Mf DCRS/WSL, SG); Extr C 1697-1711, 1725-52, 1772-1837 (IGI); C 1697-1711, 1725-52, 1772-1837 (Mf I SLC)

HONITON (Bapt/Presb/Unit) f 18th cent. Bridge Meeting House [1851 Religious Census] High Street 1860

HONITON (Wes) New Street. Erected 1842 [1882 Return] Closed 1971. Then in former school
OR C 1876-1961 (DRO); for c.1809-37 see AXMINSTER, CULLOMPTON, TIVERTON (RG 4/512,958,342 PRO)
Cop (Mf) C 1876-1958 (Mfc Colyton SP)

HONITON (Wes) Queen Street. Erected 1830 [1851 Religious Census]

HONITON (S of F) fl c.1654-96 part of MEMBURY MM

HONITON CLYST   see CLYST HONITON

HOO MEAVY   see MEAVY

HOOE   see PLYMSTOCK

HOPE COVE   see SOUTH HUISH

HORNDON   see MARY TAVY

HORRABRIDGE   see BUCKLAND MONACHORUM

HORWOOD St Michael [Fremington Hundred; Barnstaple Union]   [130]
Now with TWO RIVERS
OR C 1653-1812 M 1654-1978 B 1654-1992 (NDRO)
BT CMB 1607-08, 1610, 1629, 1632, 1668, 1670, 1674, 1678, 1680, 1682-83,
    1685, 1687, 1689-91, 1694-97, 1699-1700, 1702, 1704-09, 1712, 1714,
    1718-23, 1725-28, 1732-35 (1736-1812 ?); C 1822-24, 1826-27, 1836,
    1838-43, 1845-51, 1855 M 1826, 1836 B 1822-27, 1836, 1838-43, 1845-51,
    1855 (DRO)
Cop C 1653-1837 MB 1654-1837 (DCRS/WSL, NDA, SG); CB 1653-1812 M 1654-1837
    (DFHS)
Cop (Mf) C 1653-1812 M 1654-1837 B 1654-1812 (Mfc SG)
MI (I, NDA); Ch (Ptd Gent.Mag. 1879 I: 398-400)

HUCCABY   see LYDFORD

HUISH St James the Less [Shebbear Hundred; Torrington Union]   [131]
Rebuilt 1873. Now with TORRIDGE
OR C 1595-1812 M 1600-1981 B 1595-1812 (NDRO)
BT CMB 1602, 1608, 1610, 1623, 1629, 1634, 1644, 1669, 1670, 1673-74,
    1678-79, 1682-83, 1685, 1688, 1690-91, 1694, 1696-97, 1699-1700, 1702,
    1704-05, 1707-16 (1717-1812 ?); C 1813-33, 1835-44 M 1813, 1816, 1819,
    1822-25, 1828-32 B 1813, 1815-16, 1818, 1823, 1826, 1829, 1831, 1833,
    1835-44 (DRO)
Cop CB 1593-1812 M 1600-1789 (DCRS/WSL)
Cop (Mf) C 1595-1812 M 1600-1981 B 1595-1812, with gaps (Mfc SG); 'Huish by
    Hatherleigh' Extr C 1595-1812 M 1600-1789 (IGI); C 1595-1812
    M 1600-1789 (Mf I SLC)
MI Incledon 1077 (NDA)

HUISH, NORTH dedication unknown [Stanborough Hundred; Totnes Union]   [457]
Redundant. Now with DIPTFORD, HARBERTON, HARBERTONFORD
OR C 1656-1992 M 1656-1992 B 1656-1707, 1772-1812 (DRO)
BT CMB 1602, 1608, 1610-14, 1617, 1624, 1627, 1663, 1668-71, 1677, 1686,
    1689, 1695, 1697, 1699, 1713-15, 1719-30, 1732-37, 1743-51, 1753-98,
    1800, 1802-04, 1806-12; CMB 1816-24, 1829, 1832; 1816-32 returns unfit
    for production (DRO)
Cop (Mf) (Totnes SP)

HUISH, NORTH (Bapt) f 1851 [Baptist Handbook 1861]

HUISH, NORTH (Christians) Erected 1850 [1851 Religious Census]

HUISH, SOUTH St Andrew, South Huish [Stanborough Hundred; Kingsbridge Union]
[357] Chapelry in WEST ALVINGTON. Church abandoned 1866 and replaced by Holy
Trinity, below. Separate parish 1877. Ruins leased to Friends of Friendless
Churches. Now with MALBOROUGH, WEST ALVINGTON, CHURCHSTOW
OR C 1576-1918 M 1566-1941 B 1564-1986 (DRO)
BT CMB 1610, 1613-15, 1617, 1620, 1663, 1668, 1671, 1677, 1679, 1681, 1686,
1688-90, 1695-97, 1699-1700 (1701-1812 ?); C 1815-21, 1823-28, 1830-31,
1838, 1840-41 M 1815-21, 1824-26, 1828, 1830-31 B 1815, 1818-21,
1823-28, 1830-31, 1836, 1840-41 (DRO)
Cop C 1576-1837 MB 1564-1837 (DCRS/WSL); M 1754-1812 indexed by male spouse
(DFHS)
Cop (Mf) Extr C 1576-1837 M 1566-1664, 1676-1837 (IGI); C 1576-1837
(Mf I SLC)
MI (I, DFHS)

HUISH, SOUTH Holy Trinity, Galmpton Erected 1867. Replaced St Andrew, South
Huish as parish church
OR see St Andrew, above

HUISH, SOUTH St Clement, Hope Cove Erected 1862, chapel-of-ease to South
Huish. Now with WEST ALVINGTON, MALBOROUGH, SOUTH HUISH, CHURCHSTOW
OR see St Andrew, above

HUISH, SOUTH (Wes)
OR for c.1813-37 see KINGSBRIDGE (RG 4/1088 PRO)

HUISH, SOUTH (Prot Diss) Tupperidge Chapel [1882 Return]

HUISH, SOUTH (Brethren) Galmpton. Erected 1847 [1851 Religious Census]

HUNTSHAM All Saints [Tiverton Hundred; Tiverton Union] [170]
Now with SAMPFORD PEVERELL
OR C 1558-1937 M 1597-1836 B 1560-1812 (DRO)
BT CMB 1615, 1619-20, 1632, 1635, 1664, 1666?, 1667-69, 1672, 1675, 1678,
1683, 1687, 1690, 1695?, 1696-97 (1698-1812 ?); C 1813-19, 1821-27,
1829-36, 1838 M 1815-18, 1820-27, 1830, 1834-35, 1837 B 1813-15,
1817-19, 1821-27, 1829-36, 1838 (DRO)
Cop CMB 1559-1900 (Ptd C.Luxmoore *Registers of the Parish of Huntsham*: 1905.
3 copies printed: one at DCRS/WSL, one at SG); M 1597-1837 (Boyd)
Cop (Mf) (Tiverton SP); Extr C 1559-1875 M 1597-1675, 1690-1875 (IGI);
C 1559-1875 M 1597-1675, 1690-1875 (Mf I SLC)

HUNTSHAW St Nary Magdalene [Fremington Hundred; Torrington Union] [312]
Now with TWO RIVERS
OR C 1746-1907 M 1746-1977 B 1747-1992 (NDRO) No earlier registers noted in
1831
BT CMB 1607-08, 1610-11, 1614, 1618, 1631, 1636, 1638, 1668, 1670, 1678-79,
1682-83, 1688-91, 1695-97, 1699-1700, 1702, 1704-05, 1708-10, 1712,
1714-15 (1716-1812 ?); CB 1813-37 C 1839-42 M 1813-25, 1827-37 B 1839-41
(DRO)
Cop CMB 1607-1754 from BT, 1746-1812 (DCRS/WSL); M 1755-1812 (Boyd)
Cop (Mf) Extr C 1607-1812 M 1607-18, 1632-38, 1668-1812 from OR and BT
(IGI); C 1607-1812 M 1607-18, 1632-38, 1668-1812 from OR and BT
(Mf I SLC)
MI (I, NDA)

HUNTSHAW (Wes)
OR for c.1819-37 see BIDEFORD (RG 4/955 PRO)

HUXHAM St Mary the Virgin [Wonford Hundred; St Thomas Union]   [153]
Now with STOKE CANON, POLTIMORE, REWE, NETHEREXE
OR   C 1667-1812 M 1682-1976 B 1678-1812 (DRO)
BT   CMB 1629-30, 1635-36, 1675, 1679, 1687, 1690 (1691-1812 ?); CB 1838-45
         (DRO)
Cop CMB 1614-1812 from BT, 1667-1837 (DCRS/WSL); Extr C 1667-1812
         M 1682-1753 B 1678-1806 (Vol 3, BG/PCL)
Cop (Mf) Extr C 1614-36, 1667-1837 M 1614-36, 1679-1836 (IGI)

HUXHAM (Wes)
OR   for c.1818-31 see EXETER Mint (RG 4/1207 PRO)

IDDESLEIGH St James [Shebbear Hundred; Okehampton Union]   [574]
Now with DOWLAND
OR   C 1541-1611, 1632-1857 M 1566-1613, 1632-1837 B 1555-1598, 1632-1903
         (NDRO)
BT   CMB 1597, 1602, 1607, 1610, 1612, 1668, 1670, 1672, 1674, 1678-80,
         1682-83, 1688, 1690-91, 1694-97, 1699-1702, 1704, 1707-12, 1714-15
         (1716-1812 ?); CMB 1822-23 CB 1825-35, 1838-40 M 1825-30, 1832-35 (DRO)
Cop B 1813-37 (Ptd DFHS); CMB 1566-1837 with index (DCRS/WSL); CMB 1541-1840
         (WSL); Extr CMB 1542-1801 (SG); B 1813-37 (SG)
Cop (Mf) (Okehampton SP); Extr C 1540-1840 M 1566-1613, 1632-1837 (IGI);
         C 1540-1840 (Mf I SLC)
MI   Ch (Ptd *The Genealogist* 7: 1883: 262-64); Extr (Whitmore MS, SG)

IDDESLEIGH (Bible Christian) Eastpark Chapel. Erected 1840
[1851 Religious Census] [1882 Return] New chapel 1890. fl c.1970

IDE St Ida [Exminster Hundred; St Thomas Union]   [757] Peculiar of the Dean
and Chapter of Exeter until 1848. Rebuilt 1834. Now with DUNCHIDEOCK,
SHILLINGFORD
OR   C 1591-1608, 1653-1843 M 1591-1608, 1653-1837 B 1591-1608, 1655-1716,
         1736-1855 (DRO)
BT   CMB 1606, 1607?, 1611, 1617, 1619, 1621, 1624, 1633, 1636, 1670, 1697
         (1698-1812 ?); CMB 1813-14 C 1816-21, 1823-25, 1827-33, 1835, 1837-52,
         1873-76 M 1816-19, 1821, 1824-25, 1827-33, 1835 B 1816-19, 1821,
         1823-25, 1827-33, 1838-52, 1873-76 (DRO)
Cop B 1813-37 (Ptd DFHS); CMB 1590-1811 (DCRS/WSL); M 1653-1736 (Boyd);
         B 1813-37 (SG)
Cop (Mf) Extr CM 1590-1609, 1653-1736, 1810-11 (IGI); CM 1590-1609,
         1653-1736, 1810-11 (Mf I SLC)
MI   (I, DFHS); Ch extr (Ptd Cresswell 102)

IDE (Ind) Building in the occupation of James Joint [1882 Return]

IDE (Cong. now Cong Fed) High Street f 1833

IDE (Wes) n.d. [1851 Religious Census]
OR   for c.1818-37 see EXETER Mint (RG 4/1207 PRO)

IDEFORD St Mary the Virgin [Teignbridge Hundred; Newton Abbot Union]   [381]
Now with HALDON
OR   C 1598-1993 MB 1598-1992 (DRO)
BT   CMB 1606, 1608, 1614, 1617-18, 1629, 1636, 1641, 1644?, 1663-64, 1666,
         1669, 1671-72, 1674-79, 1681, 1684, 1686, 1688, 1690, 1695, 1697, 1699
         (1700-1812 ?); C 1813-32 M 1813-15, 1817-21, 1823, 1825-32 B 1813-22,
         1824-29, 1831-32 (DRO)
Cop B 1800-37 (Ptd DFHS); B 1800-37 (SG); CMB 1598-1840 (DCRS/WSL)
Cop (Mf) Extr CM 1598-1837 (IGI); CM 1598-1837 (Mf I SLC)

ILFRACOMBE United benefice including ILFRACOMBE Holy Trinity, St Peter, LEE, WOOLACOMBE, BITTADON, MORTHOE

ILFRACOMBE Holy Trinity, Church Hill [Braunton Hundred; Barnstaple Union] [3201] Now with ILFRACOMBE united benefice
OR C 1567-1907 MB 1567-1899 (NDRO)
BT CMB 1607-08, 1610, 1616, 1619, 1624, 1630-31, 1633-35, 1638, 1670, 1674, 1678-79, 1682-83, 1689-91, 1694-97, 1700, 1702-06, 1712, 1714-15 (1716-1812 ?); CMB 1813-20, 1823-26 CB 1835-37 M 1833, 1835-36 (DRO)
Cop M 1813-37 (Ptd DFHS); C 1567-1854 M 1567-1837 B 1567-1843 (NDA); CMB 1567-1837; described as 'inaccurate' (DCRS/WSL)
Cop (Mf) Extr CM 1567-1837 (IGI); CM 1567-1837 (Mf I SLC)
MI Ch, cy extr (Ptd F.Nesbitt *Ilfracombe Parish*: 1901: 54-61); Extr 1849-52 (Ptd M.Palmer 'A diarist in Devon': TDA 77: 1945: 199-223); Incledon 736 (NDA)

ILFRACOMBE St Peter, Highfield Road. Erected 1902-03. Chapel-of-ease to Ilfracombe Holy Trinity. Now with ILFRACOMBE united benefice
OR *see* Holy Trinity

ILFRACOMBE St Philip and St James, St James's Place. Erected 1856. Parish created 1857 from Ilfracombe. Now with WEST DOWN
OR C 1857-1932 M 1859-1930 (NDRO)

ILFRACOMBE St Matthew and St Wardrede, Lee. Erected 1835. Parish created 1869 from Ilfracombe and MORTEHOE. Now with ILFRACOMBE united benefice
OR C 1869+ M 1878+ (Inc)

ILFRACOMBE (Free Church of England) Christ Church, Portland Street. Erected 1844 [1851 Religious Census]

ILFRACOMBE (RC) Our Lady Star of the Sea, Runnacleave Crescent 1874 [1882 Return] 1929
OR (Inc) Confirmations 1875+ (Plymouth Diocesan Archives)

ILFRACOMBE (Bapt) High Street. Erected pre-1800 [1851 Religious Census] Rebuilt 1851 ? [1882 Return]

ILFRACOMBE (Presb/Ind/Cong, later URC) Higher Chapel f 1687. Erected 1728-29; rebuilt 1819 [1882 Return] Wilder Road
OR ZB 1729-1837 B 1821-37 (RG 4/1211,1087 PRO); C 1858-1911 M 1838-1911 B 1859-1881 (NDRO)
Cop (Mf) ZC 1729-1837 B 1821-37 (Mf DCRS/WSL); Extr C 1729-71, 1785-1837 (IGI); C 1729-71, 1785-1837 (Mf I SLC)

ILFRACOMBE (Ind) Workmen's Club Room, High Street [1882 Return]

ILFRACOMBE (Ind) Heal Chapel. Erected 1846 [1851 Religious Census]

ILFRACOMBE (Wes) Erected 1832 [1851 Religious Census]
OR for *c.*1807-37 *see* BARNSTAPLE CIRCUIT, BIDEFORD (RG 4/954,955 PRO)

ILFRACOMBE (Wes) Circuit
OR C 1878-1913 (NDRO); *see also* BARNSTAPLE and ILFRACOMBE Circuit 1850-77.

ILFRACOMBE (Wes) Wilder Road. Erected 1898. fl *c.*1970

ILFRACOMBE (Wes) Lee-on-Sea. Erected 1889. fl *c.*1970

ILFRACOMBE (S of F) Meeting house 1773

ILFRACOMBE (Evangelical) Brookdale Avenue FIEC
OR M 1977-87 (NDRO)

ILFRACOMBE (Christians) Cemetery Church [1882 Return]

ILFRACOMBE (Union of Protestant Nonconformists) Bethel. A room [1851
Religious Census]

ILFRACOMBE (Orthodox Christians) Room in the house of Mr Turner near the
Quay [1851 Religious Census]

ILFRACOMBE War Graves
OR B 1939-47 (NDRO)

ILSHAM   see TORQUAY

ILSINGTON St Michael [Teignbridge Hundred; Newton Abbot Union] [1298]
OR C 1558-1845 M 1559-1837 B 1558-1868 (DRO)
BT CMB 1614, 1616, 1623-24, 1629, 1636, 1638 M 1642, 1664, 1668-72,
   1674-81, 1686-89, 1695, 1697, 1699 (1700-1812 ?); CMB 1813, 1815 C 1819,
   1826-29, 1834-35 M 1819, 1826-29, 1835 B 1826-29, 1835 (DRO)
Cop CMB 1558-1837 with index (DCRS/WSL, Exeter Univ Lib); M 1837-87 (DFHS);
   M 1539-1837 (Boyd); Extr 'several sequences' of CMB 1558-1796 (Vol 14,
   BG/PCL)
Cop (Mf) (Totnes SP); Extr CM 1558-1837 (IGI); CM 1558-1837 (Mf I SLC)
MI (Ptd DRMI 20: 1998); (Ptd P and W Ransom St Michael's Church, Ilsington:
   monumental inscriptions and memorials: 1984); (I, DFHS)

ILSINGTON (Bapt) Ebenezer Room, Leverton [1882 Return]

ILSINGTON (Ind) Cold East Chapel [1882 Return]

ILSINGTON (Wes) f c.1847; two houses [1851 Religious Census] Erected 1852
[1882 Return] fl c.1970
OR for c.1801-36 see ASHBURTON CIRCUIT (RG 4/1763,840 PRO)

ILSINGTON (Wes) Honeywill, Ilsington [1882 Return]

ILSINGTON (Wes) Knighton
OR for c.1815-37 see ASHBURTON CIRCUIT, OKEHAMPTON (RG 4/840,1089 PRO)

ILSINGTON (Prot Diss) Building in the occupation of Francis Richards, Hayter
Vale [1882 Return]

INSTOW St John the Baptist [Fremington Hundred; Barnstaple Union] [369]
OR C 1717-1962 M 1717-1988 B 1717-1917 (NDRO) No earlier registers noted in
   1831
BT CMB 1607-08, 1610-12, 1614, 1617, 1629, 1638, 1670-71, 1674, 1678-79,
   1682, 1684, 1688-91, 1694-96, 1699-1700, 1702, 1704-09, 1712, 1714-15
   (1716-1812 ?); C 1814-24, 1827-28, 1838-58, 1861, 1865-66 M 1814-21,
   1823-24, 1838-40, 1842-44 B 1814, 1816-20, 1822-24, 1839, 1841-58, 1861,
   1866 (DRO)
Cop B 1813-37 (Ptd DFHS); B 1813-37 (WSL, DLS, SG)
Cop (Mf) (Appledore SP)
MI (I, NDA)

INSTOW All Saints Erected 1936. Chapel-of-ease in parish of Instow
OR none

INSTOW (Bapt) f 1854 [Baptist Handbook 1861]; Day Peep, Worlington, Instow [1882 Return]

INSTOW (Wes) Erected 1838 [1882 Return] fl *c.*1970
OR for *c.*1807-37 *see* BARNSTAPLE CIRCUIT, BIDEFORD (RG 4/954,955 PRO)

INWARDLEIGH St Petrock [Black Torrington Hundred; Okehampton Union] [638]
Now with OKEHAMPTON
OR CM 1699-1978 B 1699-1924 (DRO) Noted in 1831: 'one general register
Bap.Bur,1699-1812. Marr 1699-1754. No marriages after that date'
BT CMB 1608-09, 1612-14, 1616, 1618, 1630, 1632, 1663, 1666-67, 1669-72,
1674-79, 1681, 1684, 1686-88, 1694-95, 1697, 1699 (1700-1812 ?);
CMB 1813, 1826 CB 1838-47 (DRO)
Cop CMB 1608-1811 from BT, 1699-1838 (DCRS/WSL); CM 1608-18, 1663-1838
B 1608-18, 1663-1842 (SG); Extr CMB 1692-1774 (Vol 9, BG/PCL)
Cop (Mf) (Okehampton SP)
MI Extr (Whitmore MS, SG)

INWARDLEIGH (Bapt) Oak. Erected 1841 [1851 Religious Census]; Way Park n.d.

INWARDLEIGH (Ind) Providence [1882 Return]

INWARDLEIGH (Wes) Chapel Lane, Folly Gate. Erected 1842 [1851 Religious
Census] [1882 Return] New chapel 1905. fl *c.*1970

INWARDLEIGH (Bible Christian) Bethany, Waytown. Erected 1840 [1851 Religious
Census] [1882 Return] Closed 1983. Later a craft workshop

IPPLEPEN St Andrew [Haytor Hundred; Newton Abbot Union] [927]
see also the chapelries of KINGSWEAR and WOODLAND. Now with TORBRYAN
OR C 1558-1645, 1671-1947 M 1612-1619, 1634-1653, 1671-1754, 1813-1958
B 1671-1973 (DRO)
BT CMB 1610, 1623-25, 1629, 1632, 1664, 1669-71, 1674, 1676, 1678, 1680-81,
1695, 1699 (1700-1812 ?); CM 1813-26, 1828-29, 1831-38, 1841
C 1844, 1848-54, 1856 M 1846-54, 1856 B 1813-17, 1819-26, 1828-29,
1831-38, 1841, 1844, 1846-54, 1856 (DRO)
Cop M 1612-1813 (Ptd Phil 1: 1909); CMB 1558-1794 (DCRS/WSL); CMB 1612-1913
(WSL); M 1612-1813 (Great Card Index, SG); M 1612-1837 (Boyd);
M 1790-1837 (Pallot); Extr C 1578-1633 M 1586-1702 (Vol 16, BG/PCL)
Cop (Mf) (Torquay SP)

IPPLEPEN (RC) St Mary 1974

IPPLEPEN (Bapt) Erected 1836 [1851 Religious Census] Building in the higher
part of Ipplepen, adjacent to the Wellington Inn [1882 Return]

IPPLEPEN (Wes) East Street. Erected 1812 [1851 Religious Census]
Rebuilt 1866 = ? corner of Doonafield Lane [1882 Return] fl *c.*1970
OR M 1869-1872 (DRO); *see also* HENNOCK; for *c.*1811-37 *see* BRIXHAM,
TEIGNMOUTH (RG 4/842,1220 PRO)

IPPLEPEN (Wes) Dainton
OR for *c.*1813-37 *see* TEIGNMOUTH (RG 4/1220 PRO)

IVYBRIDGE St John the Evangelist. District in CORNWOOD, ERMINGTON, UGBOROUGH. Separate parish 1835. Now with HARFORD
OR C 1835-1989 M 1835-1990 B 1836-1978 (PWDRO)
BT CB 1838-39 (DRO)
Cop M 1938-66 (DFHS)
MI (Ptd DRMI 14: 1998); (I, DFHS)

IVYBRIDGE (RC) St Austin's Priory 1910

IVYBRIDGE (Ind/Cong now Cong Fed) Erected 1843-44 [1851 Religious Census] [1882 Return] Exeter Road f 1842
OR C 1861-1949 M 1892-1970 (PWDRO)
Cop C 1861-1950 M 1892-1970 (DFHS, PWDRO)

IVYBRIDGE (Wes) Fore Street. Erected 1812 [1851 Religious Census] Rebuilt 1875 [1882 Return] fl c.1970
OR for c.1801-37 see ASHBURTON CIRCUIT, AXMINSTER (RG 4/1763,840,512 PRO)

JACOBSTOWE or STOW ST JAMES St James [Black Torrington Hundred; Okehampton Union] [293] Now with HATHERLEIGH, MEETH, EXBOURNE
OR C 1587-1812 M 1587-1837 B 1586-1812 (DRO)
BT CMB 1624, 1635, 1639, 1664, 1666, 1668, 1671-72, 1674-82, 1684, 1686-87, 1695-96, 1700 (1701-1812 ?); C 1813-36 M 1813-18, 1821-27, 1829-30, 1832-33, 1835-36 B 1813-20, 1822-36 (DRO)
Cop Extr C 1596-1757 M 1587-1713 B 1595-1804 (Vol 9, BG/PCL)
Cop (Mf) (Okehampton SP)

KELLY St Mary the Virgin [Lifton Hundred; Tavistock Union] [250]
United 1823 with BRADSTONE
OR CB 1653-1812 M 1653-1837 (DRO)
BT CMB 1609-10, 1612, 1614, 1617, 1623, 1627, 1632, 1663-64, 1666, 1668, 1670-72, 1676-77, 1681-82, 1686, 1689-90, 1694-96 (1697-1812 ?); C 1815-34, 1836 M 1815-20, 1822-25, 1827, 1829, 1832, 1834, 1836 B 1815-24, 1827-30, 1832-34, 1836 (DRO)
Cop B 1778-1996 (I, PWDRO); Extr CMB 1654-1829 C 1830-61 B 1819-80 (Vol 17, BG/PCL)
Cop (Mf) (Tavistock SP)

KENN St Andrew [Exminster Hundred; St Thomas Union] [982]
Now with EXMINSTER
OR C 1538-1866 M 1538-1669, 1695-1979 B 1538-1671, 1688-1960 (DRO)
BT CMB 1615-17, 1633-34, 1635?, 1636, 1639, 1664, 1668?, 1669-70, 1672, 1673?, 1675, 1678, 1679?, 1695-96, 1699 (1700-1812 ?); CMB 1813-20, 1822-23, 1825-28, CB 1830-34, 1837-57 M 1830-32, 1834 (DRO)
Cop B 1813-37 (Ptd DFHS); CMB 1538-1837 (DCRS/WSL, SG); B 1813-37 (SG); M 1538-1669 (Boyd)
Cop (Mf) Extr C 1538-1837 M 1538-1667, 1695-1836 (IGI); C 1538-1837 M 1538-1667, 1695-1836 (Mf I SLC)
MI (I, DFHS); Ch extr (Ptd Cresswell 109-10); Ch, cy (Ts SG)

KENN (Presb) fl c.1672-90

KENN (Wes) Zion. Erected 1825 [1851 Religious Census]
OR for c.1810-37 see EXETER Mint (RG 4/1207,1208 PRO)

KENN (Wes) Kennford [1882 Return] Erected 1901. Closed 1985

KENN, NORTH United benefice including TEDBURN, WHITESTONE, OLDRIDGE, HOLCOMBE BURNELL, DUNSFORD, DODDISCOMBELEIGH, CHERITON BISHOP

KENNERLEIGH St John the Baptist [Crediton Hundred; Crediton Union] [110]
Chapelry in CREDITON. Peculiar of the Bishop of Exeter 1752-1848. Separate
parish 1752. Now with NORTH CREADY
OR C 1645-1812 M 1648-1835 B 1648-1810 (DRO)
BT CMB 1608, 1611, 1614, 1621, 1624, 1629, 1631, 1666-67, 1669-70, 1674-79,
    1681, 1683-85, 1687-88, 1690, 1693, 1695-1704, 1707-08, 1710, 1712-15,
    1717-18, 1720, 1722, 1724-25, 1728-58, 1771, 1779-1812; C 1813-38
    M 1813-16, 1818, 1823-24, 1827-28, 1831-32, 1834-36 B 1815, 1817,
    1819-21, 1824-29, 1832-38 (DRO)
MI Incledon 706 (NDA)

KENNFORD   see KENN

KENTISBEARE St Mary [Hayridge Hundred; Tiverton Union] [1336 including
Blackborough] Now with BLACKBOROUGH
OR C 1695-1903 M 1695-1839 B 1695-1925 (DRO) Noted in 1831: 'including the
    Blackborough registry'
BT CMB 1608, 1615, 1617-19, 1626, 1635, 1668?, 1669, 1670, 1672, 1675,
    1678, 1685, 1687-88, 1690-91, 1696-97, 1699, 1725-34, 1736-48, 1750,
    1753-54, 1756-74 (1775-1812 ?); CMB 1813-38 (DRO)
Cop B 1813-37 (Ptd DFHS); B 1813-37 (WSL, DLS, SG)
Cop (Mf) (Tiverton SP); C 1695-1865 M 1695-1839 B 1695-1825 (Mfc SG)
MI Ch (Ptd *TDA: Parochial Histories* 3: 1934: 64-70)

KENTISBEARE All Saints, Blackborough. Long ruined church, rebuilt 1838,
Now with KENTISBEARE
OR M 1840-1973 (DRO) Noted in 1831 that Blackborough events were registered
    at KENTISBEARE
Cop (Mf) (Tiverton SP); M 1840-1973 (Mfc SG)
MI Ch (Ptd *TDA Parochial Histories* 4: 1934: 16)

KENTISBEARE (Bapt) Sainthill Meeting f 1803; rebuilt 1830 [1851 Religious
Census] [1882 Return]
OR Z 1806-36 (RG 4/337 PRO)
Cop (Mf) Z 1806-36 (Mf DCRS/WSL, SG); Extr Z 1806-36 (IGI)

KENTISBEARE (Presb) fl *c.*1672-90

KENTISBEARE (Wes)
OR for *c.*1812-37 *see* TIVERTON (RG 4/342 PRO)

KENTISBURY St Thomas [Braunton Hundred; Barnstaple Union] [340]
Now with SHIRWELL
OR C 1674-1896 M 1676-1975 B 1675-1990 (NDRO)
BT CMB 1597-1602, 1605, 1607, 1610, 1614, 1620, 1623-24, 1626, 1638, 1670,
    1674, 1678-79, 1682-83, 1690-91, 1694, 1696-97, 1700, 1703-05, 1712,
    1714-16, 1718-23, 1726-28, 1732-43, 1745-50, 1752-56, 1762-66,
    1768-1812; CMB 1838-39 CB 1841-53 (DRO)
Cop B 1813-37 (Ptd DFHS); C 1675-1850 M 1675-1798 (NDA); M 1675-1841
    (DCRS/WSL); B 1813-37 (SG)
Cop (Mf) Extr M 1675-1841 (IGI)
MI Incledon 445 (NDA)

KENTISBURY (Bapt) Long Lane f 1850 [1851 Religious Census] Building occupied
by Mr Thos. Lerwith, near Way Town Farm [1882 Return]

KENTISBURY (Wes) Kentisbury Ford. Erected 1883. Closed 1975

KENTON All Saints [Exminster Hundred; St Thomas Union] [2050]
Now with MAMHEAD, POWDERHAM, COFTON, STARCROSS
OR C 1694-1914 M 1694-1990 B 1694-1933 (DRO)
BT CMB 1609, 1611, 1613, 1616, 1624-26, 1634-36, 1668?, 1672, 1673?, 1675,
    1678-79, 1683, 1687 (1688-1812 ?); CB 1813-42, 1844-45, 1847-53, 1855-63
    M 1813-37 (DRO)
Cop B 1813-37 (Ptd DFHS); CMB 1694-1837 (DCRS/WSL, WSL, SG); B 1813-37 (SG);
    Extr C 1694-1753 M 1705-52 B 1695-1753 (Vol 17, BG/PCL)
Cop (Mf) Extr CM 1694-1837 (IGI); CM 1694-1837 (Mf I SLC)
MI (I, DFHS); Ch extr (Ptd Cresswell 119-21); Ch, cy (Ts SG)

KENTON (Bapt) f 1831 ? Erected 1850-51 [1851 Religious Census]
[*Baptist Handbook* 1861]

KENTON (Wes) Erected 1831 [1851 Religious Census] Rebuilt 1870. Mamhead Road
[1882 Return] fl *c*.1970
OR C 1917-54 (DRO); *for* c.1813-37 *see* TEIGNMOUTH (RG 4/1220 PRO)

KERSWELL REGIS   *see* KINGSKERSWELL

KEYHAM, NORTH   *see* DEVONPORT St Mark, Ford

KIGBEAR   hamlet in OKEHAMPTON [116 in 1821]

KILLERTON   *see* BROADCLYST

KILMINGTON St Giles [Axminster Hundred; Axminster Union] [540] Chapelry in
AXMINSTER. Separate parish 1911. Now with STOCKLAND, DALWOOD, SHUTE
OR C 1577-1600, 1723-1875 M 1577-89, 1727-1994 B 1577-98, 1723-1982 (DRO)
BT CMB 1606, 1609, 1614, 1620, 1634, 1636, 1667, 1669, 1675, 1677-78, 1683,
    1685, 1688?, 1690, 1693, 1695, 1697-99, 1717 (1718-1812 ?); C 1813-16,
    1818-35, 1862 M 1813, 1815-25, 1827-35 B 1813-35, 1862 (DRO)
Cop B 1813-37 (Ptd DFHS); B 1813-37 (SG); CMB 1577-1837 (DCRS/WSL);
    CMB 1577-1891 (WSL)
Cop (Mf) (Colyton SP); C 1577-1600, 1723-1875 M 1577-89, 1727-1837
        B 1577-98, 1723-1891; with gaps (Mfc SG); Extr C 1577-1837
        M 1577-89, 1727-1837 (IGI); C 1577-1837 M 1577-89, 1727-1837
        (Mf I SLC)
MI Ch, cy (Ptd Pulman *Book of the Axe* 1875; reprint 1969); (I, DFHS);
    Incledon 321 (NDA)

KILMINGTON (Bapt) with Loughwood, DALWOOD, Shute Road f 1650. Rebuilt 1832
[1851 Religious Census]
OR C 1778-1904 (DRO)

KINGSBRIDGE St Edmund King and Martyr [Stanborough Hundred; Kingsbridge
Union 1836-93] [1586] Chapelry in CHURCHSTOW. Now with DODBROOKE
OR C 1613-1941 M 1612-1980 B 1631-1912 (DRO)
BT CMB 1606, 1609, 1613-17, 1624, 1626, 1628, 1633, 1636?, 1666, 1669,
    1671-72, 1674, 1679-80, 1681?, 1682, 1684?, 1687, 1689-90, 1695, 1696?,
    1699 (1700-1812 ?); CMB 1813-39 (DRO)
Cop B 1813-37 (Ptd DFHS); B 1813-37 (SG); C 1613-1797 M 1616-1837
    B 1631-1797; M 1754-1812 indexed by male spouse (DFHS); Extr C 1614-30
    M 1675-85 B 1635-89 (Vol 8, BG/PCL)
Cop (Mf) Extr C 1613-1797 M 1612-1837 (IGI); C 1613-1797 M 1612-1837
        (Mf I SLC)
MI (I, DFHS); (Ptd L.Collins 'Heraldry in the Kingsbridge parish churches':
    Kingsbridge Hist.Soc.Recorder 2: 1989: 9-11); L.Collins 'Walking the
    churchyards' ibid.1: 1989: 7-11)

KINGSBRIDGE (RC) Sacred Heart and Our Lady of Compassion, Fore Street 1902

KINGSBRIDGE (Bapt) Baptist Lane, off Fore Street. f 17th cent. Erected 1705, rebuilt 1798 on new site [1851 Religious Census] [*Baptist Handbook* 1861]; Phoenix Place [1882 Return]
OR ZB 1785-1831 B 1835-57 (RG 4/2099,442 PRO); later M records (Ch Sec)
Cop (Mf) ZB 1785-1831 B 1835-57 (Mf DCRS/WSL, SG); Extr Z 1785-1831 (IGI)

KINGSBRIDGE (Presb/Ind/Cong) Ebenezer, Fore Street. Licensed 1672; rebuilt 1791-92, 1826 [1851 Religious Census] [1882 Return] Associated with STOKENHAM, CHIVELSTONE
OR ZC 1775-1837 B 1826-37 (RG 4/1212,443 PRO); C 1774-1931 M 1837-1897, 1906-42 B 1793-1897 (DRO)
Cop (Mf) ZC 1775-1837 B 1826-37 (Mf DCRS/WSL, SG); ZC 1775-1932 M 1837-97
         B 1793-1897 (Mfc Colyton SP); Extr ZC 1775-1837 (IGI); ZC 1775-1837
         (Mf I SLC)

KINGSBRIDGE (Wes) Circuit
OR C 1849-1946 (DRO)

KINGSBRIDGE (Wes) Ebenezer, Fore Street. Erected 1814 [1882 Return]
fl c.1970
OR C 1813-37 (RG 4/1088 PRO)
Cop (Mf) C 1813-37 (Mf DCRS/WSL, SG); Extr C 1813-37 (IGI); C 1813-37
         (Mf I SLC)

KINGSBRIDGE (U Meth) Circuit
OR C 1909-29 (DRO)

KINGSBRIDGE (Brethren) Gospel Hall, Fore Street f 1853. A building belonging to Thomas Adams, Fore Street [1882 Return]
OR M 1900-20 (DRO)

KINGSBRIDGE (Prot Diss) Hazelwood Chapel [1882 Return]

KINGSBRIDGE (Evangelical) Kingsbridge Evangelical Church FIEC

KINGSBRIDGE (S of F) Kingsbridge MM f 1668/69; joined PLYMOUTH MM 1785
[1851 Religious Census]
OR Z 1776-94 (RG 6/275 PRO)

KINGSBRIDGE (S of F) f c.1665; meeting house 1697. Fore Street [1882 Return]
Closed by 1871. Building later used by Salvation Army, then 1917 RC church.
S of F now at Leigham Terrace, Fore Street

KINGSKERSWELL or KERSWELL REGIS St Mary [Haytor Hundred; Newton Abbot Union]
[771] Chapelry in ST MARYCHURCH. Separate parish 1829. Peculiar of the Dean and Chapter of Exeter 1829-48. Now with COFFINSWELL
OR C 1752-1847 M 1752-1837 B 1752-1914 (DRO) Noted in 1831:
vol.1 CB 1702-52 M 1712-38, 1746-52
BT CMB 1606, 1614, 1617, 1628-29, 1632-33, 1635-36, 1702, 1707, 1716-17,
   1750, 1752, 1754-95 (1796-1812 ?); CMB 1814-16, 1819-26, 1828 C 1830-31,
   1833, 1838-41, 1843-44, 1849 M 1830-32 B 1830-33, 1838, 1840, 1842-44
   (DRO)
Cop M 1752-1837 (Ptd Phil 1: 1909); CMB 1752-1837 (WSL); M 1752-1837
    (Great Card Index, SG); M 1752-1837 (Boyd); M 1790-1837 (Pallot)
Cop (Mf) (Torquay SP)
MI Extr (Whitmore MS, SG)

KINGSKERSWELL (RC) St Gregory, Coles Lane 1961

KINGSKERSWELL (Bapt) Zion. Erected 1847 [1851 Religious Census]

KINGSKERSWELL (Presb) f between 1690-1715; closed 1770s

KINGSKERSWELL (Cong ? later URC) Yon Street f 1910

KINGSKERSWELL (Wes) Erected c.1820 [1851 Religious Census] [1882 Return]
Rebuilt 1911. fl c.1970
OR for c.1813-37 see TEIGNMOUTH (RG 4/1220 PRO)

KINGSKERSWELL (Evang Prot Diss) Union Chapel, Yonder Street [1882 Return]

KINGSNYMPTON or NYMET REGIS St James the Apostle [Witheridge Hundred;
South Molton Union] [699] Now with SOUTH MOLTON
OR C 1538-1685, 1700-1860 M 1539-1685, 1700-1958 B 1538-1685, 1700-1897
    (NDRO)
BT CMB 1607-08, 1610-11, 1628, 1630, 163?, 1634, 1641, 1643, 1668, 1674,
    1678?, 1679, 1683, 1688-91, 1694-97, 1699, 1706-07, 1710, 1714-22,
    1725-28, 1730-40, 1744-46, 1748-55, 1762-66, 1768, 1770-84, 1786-1812;
    CMB 1813-33 (DRO)
Cop (Mf) C 1538-1860 M 1539-1837 B 1538-1812 with gaps (Mfc SG)
MI (I, NDA)

KINGSNYMPTON (Bible Christian/Meth) Bethel. Erected 1833 [1851 Religious
Census] [1882 Return] New chapel 1963. fl c.1970

KINGSTEIGNTON or STEIGNTON REGIS St Michael [Teignbridge Hundred;
Newton Abbot Union] [1288] see also chapelry of HIGHWEEK
OR C 1670-1966 M 1670-1987 B 1670-1978 (DRO)
BT CMB 1602-03, 1606, 1619, 1629, 1631, 1636, 1640, 1663-64, 1668-69,
    1671-72, 1674-81, 1686, 1690?, 1695, 1699 (1700-1812 ?); CB 1813-33
    M 1813-21, 1823-33 (DRO)
Cop CMB 1606-70 from BT, 1670-1837 (DCRS/WSL)
Cop (Mf) Extr C 1606-1837 M 1606, 1619-1837 (IGI); C 1606-1837 M 1606,
         1619-1837 (Mf I SLC)
MI Incledon 109 (NDA)

KINGSTEIGNTON (RC) St Columba

KINGSTEIGNTON (Bapt) Community Hall f 1993

KINGSTEIGNTON (Cong, later URC) Zion, Church Street f 1816 [1851 Religious
Census] [1882 Return]
OR C 1808-35 (RG 4/2534 PRO)
Cop (Mf) C 1808-35 (Mf DCRS/WSL, SG); Extr C 1808-35 (IGI); C 1808-35
         (Mf I SLC)

KINGSTEIGNTON (Wes) Erected 1851 [1851 Religious Census] [1882 Return]
OR for c.1801-37 see ASHBURTON CIRCUIT, TEIGNMOUTH (RG 4/1763,1220 PRO)

KINGSTEIGNTON (Wes) Chudleigh Road [1882 Return]

KINGSTON St James the Less [Ermington Hundred; Kingsbridge Union] [504]
Chapelry in ERMINGTON. United with RINGMORE 1934. Now with MODBURY
OR C 1635-1865 M 1631-1836 B 1630-1813 (DRO)
BT CMB 1611, 1614, 1617-18, 1623, 1626, 1629, 1633-34, 1663, 1677, 1690,
    1694-97, 1700 (1701-1812 ?); CMB 1819, 1825-27, 1829, 1834-35, 1838
    CB 1840-46 (DRO)
Cop C 1635-1813 M 1631-1836 B 1630-1729 (DFHS)
Cop (Mf) 'Kingston near Ivy Bridge' Extr C 1635-1814 M 1631-1836 (IGI);
        C 1635-1814 M 1631-1836 (Mf I SLC)

KINGSTON (Wes) Erected c.1806 [1851 Religious Census] Rebuilt 1873
[1882 Return] fl c.1970
OR for c.1813-37 see KINGSBRIDGE (RG 4/1088 PRO)

KINGSWEAR St Thomas of Canterbury [Haytor Hundred; Totnes Union] [275]
Chapelry in IPPLEPEN. Separate parish 1720. Rebuilt 1847. Now with BRIXHAM
OR C 1601-1939 M 1601-1960 B 1601-1925 (DRO)
BT CMB 1608-09, 1611, 1614, 1620, 1629-30, 1663-64. 1669-72, 1675-77, 1679,
    1686, 1688-90, 1699 (1700-1812 ?); CB 1813-36 M 1813-16, 1818-30,
    1832-34, 1836 (DRO)
Cop B 1780-1837 (Ptd DFHS); B 1780-1837 (SG); Extr C 1602-06 M 1603-1730
    B 1602-94, 1615-83 (Vol 6, BG/PCL)
Cop (Mf) (Torquay SP); C 1601-1882 M 1601-1837 B 1601-1925; with gaps
        (Mfc SG)

KINGSWEAR (Wes) [1882 Return]
OR C 1884-1967 (DRO); for c.1811-37 see BRIXHAM (RG 4/842 PRO)

KNACKERSKNOWLE   see PLYMOUTH

KNOWLE   see BUDLEIGH SALTERTON, DOWN ST MARY

KNOWLE   see BRAUNTON

KNOWSTONE St Peter [South Molton Hundred; South Molton Union] [521]
Now with OAKMOOR
OR C 1538-1653, 1690-1712, 1813-1976 M 1539-1653, 1693-1712, 1837-1991
    B 1538-1653, 1695-1713, 1813-1922 (Inc) Missing registers destroyed by
    fire 1890.
BT CMB 1597-1602, 1607-08, 1610, 1613, 1619-20, 1624, 1628-30, 1633, 1668,
    1670, 1674, 1679, 1683, 1690-91, 1694-96, 1699-1700, 1707-07, 1709-10,
    1712, 1714-15, 1719-22, 1725-28, 1732-33, 1735-40 (1741-1812 ?);
    C 1838-39, 1844-47, 1850 B 1813-39, 1844-47, 1850 (DRO)
Cop CMB 1668-1812 M 1538-1653 (DCRS/WSL); C 1813-37 (DRO); M 1693-1712
    (Boyd); Extr C 1538-1651, 1729 M 1539-1642, 1719-44 B 1539-1650, 1720-62
    (Vol 5, BG/PCL)
Cop (Mf) Extr C 1538-1837 M 1539-1836 (IGI); C 1538-1837 (Mf I SLC)
MI (I, NDA)

KNOWSTONE (Wes) n.d. [1851 Religious Census]

KNOWSTONE (Wes) Building occupied by Abraham Cockram junior [1882 Return]

KNOWSTONE (Wes) West Knowstone. Erected 1927. Closed 1981

KNOWSTONE (Bible Christian) n.d. [1851 Religious Census]

LAIRA, LAIRA GREEN see PLYMOUTH

LAKE   *see* SHEBBEAR

LAMERTON St Peter [Lifton Hundred; Tavistock Union]   [1209]   Burnt down 1877; rebuilt. United 1938 with SYDENHAM DAMEREL. Now with MILTON ABBOT, DUNTERTON, SYDENHAM DAMEREL
OR   C 1545-1994 M 1538-1962 B 1549-1994 (PWDRO)
BT   CMB 1606, 1610-12, 1614-16, 1625-26, 1634-35, 1663-64, 1666, 1668-72, 1674-76, 1678-80, 1686, 1688-90 (1691-1812 ?); CMB 1813-36 CB 1838-41 M 1838-39 (DRO)
Cop M 1813-37 (Ptd DFHS); M 1538-1754 (I, Ptd, edit M.Brown, Dartmoor Press 1999); B 1813-37 (Ptd DFHS); B 1800-1900 (I, PWDRO); B 1812-38 (SG); Extr C 1547-1687 M 1548-1770 B 1549-1809 (Vol 20, BG/PCL)
Cop (Mf) (Tavistock SP); C 1545-1841 M 1538-1844 B 1549-1854 (Mfc SG)

LAMERTON Christchurch, North Brentor. Chapel-of-ease in Lamerton. Erected 1857. With BRENTOR from 1883

LAMERTON (Wes) Erected 1849 [1851 Religious Census]
OR   for *c.*1808-37 *see* TAVISTOCK (RG 4/341 PRO)

LAMERTON (Wes) Heathfield. Erected 1890. Closed 1970s

LAMERTON (Bible Christian) North Brentor. Erected 1840 [1851 Religious Census] [1882 Return]

LAMERTON (Wes) Lamerton Chapel, Rushford [1882 Return]

LAMERTON (Wes) Longcross [1882 Return]

LANA   *see* PANCRASWEEK

LANDCROSS Holy Trinity [Shebbear Hundred; Bideford Union]   [96]
Now with TORRIDGE ESTUARY
OR   C 1595-1989 M 1609-1735, 1761-1911 B 1611-1989 (NDRO)
BT   CMB 1607, 1610, 1612, 1616, 1624, 1634-35, 1695, 1700, 1708, 1710, 1713-14, 1718-19, 1721, 1723, 1725-27, 1732-37, 1739, 1741-43, 1745, 1747-51, 1754, 1756, 1762, 1764-65, 1767-75 (1776-1812 ?); CB 1838-44 (DRO)
Cop B 1813-37 (Ptd DFHS); B 1813-37 (SG); M 1607-1837 (NDA)
Cop (Mf) (Appledore SP)

LANDCROSS (Wes) A house [1851 Religious Census]; chapel erected 1854; rebuilt 1880-81 [1882 Return] Closed 1988

LANDKEY St Paul [South Molton Hundred; Barnstaple Union]   [790] Chapelry in BISHOP'S TAWTON. Separate parish 1775. Now with SWIMBRIDGE, WEST BUCKLAND
OR   C 1602-1928 M 1602-1988 B 1602-1974 (NDRO)
BT   CMB 1602, 1607-08, 1613-14, 1624, 1630, 1634-36, 1643, 1663-67, 1669, 1671, 1678-88, 1690-1706, 1730 (1731-1812 ?); CB 1813-39, 1841-54, 1859, 1862-73 B 1813-36 (DRO)
Cop CMB 1602-1850 (DCRS/WSL, NDA)
Cop (Mf) Extr C 1602-1850 M 1602-1837 (IGI); C 1602-1850 M 1602-1837 (Mf I SLC)
MI   Incledon 57 (NDA)

LANDKEY Ackland Barton House. 15th century chapel

LANDKEY (Wes) Erected 1816 [1851 Religious Census] Rebuilt 1869
[1882 Return] fl *c.*1970
OR ZC 1816-37 (RG 4/1213 PRO); C 1816-1869 M 1994 B 1848-1868 (NDRO);
    for 1816-37 *see also* BARNSTAPLE CIRCUIT, BIDEFORD (RG 4/954,955 PRO)
Cop (Mf) ZC 1816-37 (Mf DCRS/WSL, SG); Extr C 1816-37 (IGI); C 1816-37
    (Mf I SLC)

LANDKEY (Bible Christian) Bethel, Newland. Erected 1841 [1851 Religious
Census]; Beulah Chapel, Landkey Newland [1882 Return]

LANDSCOVE   *see* STAVERTON

LANGFORD   *see* CULLOMPTON

LANGHAM CROSS   *see* DOLTON

LANGTREE dedication unknown [Shebbear Hundred; Torrington Union] [888]
Now with TORRIDGE
OR C 1659-1995 M 1659-1988 B 1659-1990 NDRO)
BT CMB 1603, 1607-08, 1612-13, 1616 or 1617, 1627, 1632-34, 1668, 1670,
    1672, 1674, 1678-80, 1682-83, 1688, 1690-91, 1694-97, 1699-1700,
    1706-12, 1714-15, 1797, 1800 (1801-12 ?); C 1813, 1815-41 M 1813,
    1815-37 B 1813, 1815-37, 1841 (DRO)
Cop CMB 1603-34 from BT, 1659-1872 (DCRS/WSL); M 1659-1837 (Boyd)
Cop (Mf) Extr C 1603-1850 M 1603-34, 1659-1837 (IGI); C 1603-1850 M 1603-34,
    1659-1837 (Mf I SLC)
MI Incledon 1036 (NDA)

LANGTREE (Bapt) Erected 1831 [1851 Religious Census]

LANGTREE (Ind)   *see* Bible Christian, below

LANGTREE (Wes) New Inn [1882 Return]

LANGTREE (Bible Christian) Using Independent Chapel [1851 Religious Census]

LANGTREE (Bible Christian) Zion. Erected 1825 [1851 Religious Census]
Rebuilt 1904. fl *c.*1970

LANGTREE (Bible Christian) Stibbs Cross. Erected 1825 [1851 Religious
Census]; rebuilt 1896. fl *c.*1970

LANGTREE (Bible Christian) Siloam, Suddon Cross. Erected 1828
[1851 Religious Census] [1882 Return]

LAPFORD St Thomas of Canterbury [North Tawton and Winkleigh Hundred;
Crediton Union] [700] Now with NYMET ROWLAND, COLDRIDGE
OR C 1586-1949 M 1567-1984 B 1570-1986 (DRO) C 1567+ now missing but see
    printed copy, below
BT CMB 1603, 1607-08, 1610, 1612, 1624, 1635-36, 1663, 1668, 1672,
    1674-75, 1678-79, 1683, 1688, 1690-91, 1694-97, 1708-09?, 1712, 1714,
    1716-22, 1726-27, 1730-32, 1735-36, 1778 (1779-1812 ?); CMB 1813-15,
    1817-18, 1821-37 (DRO)
Cop CMB 1567-1850 (Ptd DCRS 1954); B 1813-37 (Ptd DFHS); B 1813-37 (WSL,SG);
    CMB 1664 (WSL)
Cop (Mf) Extr CM 1567-1850 (IGI); CM 1567-1850 (Mf I SLC)
MI (I, DFHS)

LAPFORD Bury Barton Manor. Chapel licensed 1434. Now ruined

LAPFORD (Cong, later Cong Fed) School Road f 1838; erected 1846
[1882 Return]

LAPFORD (Presb) fl c.1672-90

LAPFORD (Ind/Cong) f 1805; rebuilt 1840 [1851 Religious Census]

LAPFORD (Bible Christian) Siloam, on a part of Northlake Farm [1882 Return]

LAPFORD (Bible Christian) Gilgal [1882 Return]

LAUNCESTON [Cornwall] Methodist Circuits. Some Devon chapels, in
Broadwoodwidger, St Giles in the Heath, Lifton, Stowford and Virginstow,
belonged to these Circuits
OR   [Wes] C 1837-1932 B 1819-1905; [Bible Christian] C 1841-1910; [UMFC]
     C 1909-26; [Meth] ex-Wes C 1932-51, ex-UMFC C 1930-44 (CRO)

LEA   see MILTON ABBOT

LEE   see ILFRACOMBE

LEE MOOR   see SHAUGH PRIOR

LEIGH, EAST   see HARBERTON

LEIGH, NORTH   see NORTHLEIGH

LEIGH, SOUTH   see SOUTHLEIGH

LEIGH, WEST   see WESTLEIGH

LETTAFORD   see BOVEY, NORTH

LEUSDON   see WIDECOMBE IN THE MOOR

LEVERTON   see ILSINGTON

LEW TRENCHARD St Peter [Lifton Hundred; Tavistock Union] [438] Now with
MARYSTOWE, CORYTON, SROWFORD, THRUSHELTON
OR   C 1706-1992 M 1713-1756, 1813-1837 B 1713-1992 (PWDRO) No earlier
     registers noted in 1831
BT   CMB 1610, 1614, 1616-17, 1625-26, 1631, 1633, 1638-39, 1664, 1666,
     1669-72, 1674-77, 1686, 1688, 1695, 1697, 1699-1700 (1701-1812 ?)
Cop M 1713-54 (I, Ptd, edit M.Brown, Dartmoor Press 1999); B 1778-1900
     (I, PWDRO); Extr C 1711-1881 M 1713-1814 B 1721-1881
     (Vol 17, BG/PCL)
Cop (Mf) (Tavistock SP)

LEW, NORTH or NORTHLEW St Thomas of Canterbury [Black Torrington Hundred;
Okehampton Union] Now with OKEHAMPTON
OR   C 1692-1973 M 1692-1837 B 1690-1947 (DRO)
BT   CMB 1610, 1614, 1624, 1631, 1633, 1663-64, 1666, 1669, 1671-72, 1674-80,
     1686-87, 1695, 1699 (1700-1812 ?); CMB 1813, 1816, 1820-21 CM 1823-24,
     1826, 1832 C 1833 B 1824, 1826, 1832-33 (DRO)
Cop (Mf) (Okehampton SP)

LEW, NORTH (Wes) n.d. [1851 Religious Census]; Building owned by Richard Carter and others [1882 Return]
OR for *c.*1815-37 *see* OKEHAMPTON (RG 4/1089 PRO)

LEW, NORTH (Wes) Crowden
OR for *c.*1815-37 *see* OKEHAMPTON (RG 4/1089 PRO)

LEW, NORTH (Bible Christian) Hebron. Erected 1815 [1851 Religious Census] [1882 Return] fl *c.*1970

LEW, NORTH (Bible Christian) Providence, Whiddon. Erected 1839 [1851 Religious Census] fl *c.*1970

LEW, NORTH (Bible Christian/U Meth) Circuit
OR C 1841-1861 (DRO)

LEW, NORTH (Meth) North Lew and Okehampton Circuit
OR C 1934-67 (DRO)

LIDFORD *see* LYDFORD

LIFTON St Mary [Lifton Hundred; Tavistock Union] [1535]
OR C 1653-1851 M 1654-1979 B 1653-1873 (DRO)
BT CMB 1603, 1606, 1614, 1618, 1624, 1633, 1663-64, 1666, 1668-74, 1676-82, 1684, 1686, 1688-90, 1695, 1697 (1698-1812 ?); none listed after 1812 (DRO)
Cop M 1813-37 (Ptd DFHS); M 1654-1754 (I, Ptd, edit M.Brown, Dartmoor Press 1999); CMB 1653-1812 (WSL); B 1800-1993 (I, PWDRO)
Cop (Mf) (Tavistock SP)
MI Ch 1978 (Ts SG)

LIFTON (Bapt) Erected 1850 [1851 Religious Census]; [1882 Return]

LIFTON (Wes) Dippertown Chapel [1882 Return]
OR *see* LAUNCESTON Circuit

LIFTON (Wes) Liftondown. Erected 1839 [1851 Religious Census] [1882 Return] Rebuilt 1889. fl *c.*1970
OR *see* LAUNCESTON Circuit

LIFTON (Bible Christian) Tinney or Tinhay. Erected c.1838 [1851 Religious Census] Rebuilt 1876. fl *c.*1970
OR *see* LAUNCESTON Circuit

LIFTON (Wes) Two houses, at Dippertown and Cholwill [1851 Religious Census]

LIFTON (Bible Christian) Room, Higher Cockworthy. 1851 [1851 Religious Census]

LILLIESFORD   *see* LITTLEHEMPSTEAD

LITTLE BICKINGTON   *see* BICKINGTON, ABBOT'S

LITTLE SILVER   *see* CADELEIGH

LITTLE TORRINGTON   *see* TORRINGTON, LITTLE

LITTLEHAM   *see* EXMOUTH

LITTLEHAM by Bideford St Swithin [Shebbear Hundred; Bideford Union] [424]
Now with TORRIDGE ESTUARY
OR CB 1539-1812 M 1539-1821, 1837-1983 B 1539-1812 (NDRO)
BT CMB 1602, 1607-09, 1614, 1617, 1624, 1632, 1636, 1668-70, 1672, 1674,
    1679, 1682, 1685, 1688, 1690-91, 1694-96, 1699-1700, 1702-04, 1707-12,
    1715 (1716-1812 ?); CB 1813-42 M 1813-22, 1824-37 (DRO)
Cop CMB 1538-1836 (DCRS/WSL); M 1538-1837 (Boyd)
Cop (Mf) (Appledore SP); Extr CM 1538-1836 (IGI); CM 1538-1836 (Mf I SLC)

LITTLEHAM by Bideford (Wes) Erected 1818 [1851 Religious Census]
[1882 Return] Rebuilt 1883. fl c.1970
OR for c.1819-37 see BIDEFORD (RG 4/955 PRO)

LITTLEHEMPSTON or HEMPSTON ARUNDEL St John the Baptist [Haytor Hundred;
Totnes Union] [321] Now with BROADHEMPSTON, WOODLAND, STAVERTON, LANDSCOVE
OR C 1544-1617, 1645-1956 M 1539-1595, 1654-1837 B 1546-1612, 1652-1680,
    1731-1812 (DRO) C 1956+ M 1837+ B 1812+ (Inc)
BT CMB 1606-07, 1614, 1616, 1620, 1629, 1632-35, 1638, 1641, 1668-72,
    1674-81, 1684, 1686-89, 1697, 1699, 1751-80 (1781-1812 ?); CB 1813-36
    M 1813-16, 1818-19, 1821, 1825-28, 1832-36 (DRO)
Cop CMB 1539-1904 (DCRS/WSL); Extr CMB 1546-1785 M 1544-1727 B 1552-1773
    (Vol 14, BG/PCL)
Cop (Mf) (Totnes SP); Extr C 1544-1875 M 1539-95, 1654-1809 (IGI);
        C 1544-1875 M 1539-95, 1654-1809 (Mf I SLC)
MI Extr (Whitmore MS, SG)

LITTLEHEMPSTON (Wes)
OR for c.1811-37 see BRIXHAM (RG 4 842 PRO)

LITTLEHEMPSTON (Wes) Lilliesford
OR for c.1813-37 see TEIGNMOUTH (RG 4/1220 PRO)

LITTLEHEMPSTON (Prot Diss) A room in the dwelling house of Mr H.Brooks
[1882 Return]

LITTLEMEAD see EXMOUTH

LODDISWELL St Michael and All Angels [part Coleridge Hundred; part
Stanborough Hundred; Kingsbridge Union] [826] Now with MODBURY
OR C 1559-1852 M 1560-1906 B 1560-1884 (DRO)
BT CMB 1606, 1608, 1614, 1616-17, 1620, 1622, 1627, 1636, 1663, 1666-74,
    1676, 1679-82, 1687-89, 1695, 1697, 1699 (1700-1812 ?); CB 1814-39,
    1847-60 M 1814-36 (DRO)
Cop C 1559-1798 M 1560-1756 B 1560-1783 (DRO); Extr C 1559-1798 M 1572-1744
    B 1560-1778 (Vol 15, BG/PCL)
Cop (Mf) (Totnes SP)
MI Extr (Whitmore MS, SG)

LODDISWELL St Peter, Buckland Tout Saints. Chapelry in Loddiswell [46]
Rebuilt 1779. Now with CHARLETON, EAST PORTLEMOUTH, SOUTH POOL, CHIVELSTONE
OR C 1815-1987 M 1818-1822, 1848-1988 B 1821-1988 (DRO) Noted in 1831:
    'annexed to Loddiswell; entered in the registers of Loddiswell'
BT C 1816, 1818, 1838-39, 1859 M 1818 (DRO); and see Loddiswell
Cop C 1815-1900 B 1903-81 (DRO)
Cop (Mf) M 1818-22 (Mfc SG)

LODDISWELL (RC) Bearscombe, Buckland Tout Saints. Domstic chapel of Chester
family, pre-1747. Closed 1780
OR None known

LODDISWELL (Ind/Cong, later Cong Fed) Providence, Fore Street. Erected 1808 [1851 Religious Census] Rebuilt 1864 [1882 Return]

LODDISWELL (Wes) House, f 1850 [1851 Religious Census]

LODDISWELL (Bible Christian) Hazelwood. Erected 1845 [1851 Religious Census]

LODDISWELL (Bible Christian) Staunton. Erected 1846 [1851 Religious Census]

LOVACOTT   see FREMINGTON

LOWER BRIXHAM   see BRIXHAM

LOXBEARE St Michael and All Angels [Tiverton Hundred; Tiverton Union]   [157]
United 1924 with TEMPLETON. Now with EXE VALLEY
OR C 1572-1982 M 1563-1652, 1716-1980 B 1560-1688, 1714-1983 (DRO)
BT CMB 1609-11, 1614-15, 1633, 1635, 1663-64, 1667, 1670, 1676, 1679,
    1683?, 1685, 1687, 1690, 1696, 1701, 1703-05, 1711, 1713-15, 1718,
    1720-35, 1737, 1739-48, 1750, 1752-55, 1757-61, 1763-72, 1775-77,
    1779-82, 1784-89, 1791-97, 1799-1812; C 1813-16, 1835, 1838-42, 1844-54
    M 1813, 1815 B 1813-14, 1816, 1838-42, 1844-54 (DRO)
Cop (Mf) (Tiverton SP)
MI Extr (Whitmore MS, SG)

LOXBEARE (Presb) fl c.1672-90

LOXBEARE (Bible Christian/U Meth) Erected 1923. fl c.1970

LOXHORE St Michael and All Angels [Shirwell Hundred; Barnstaple Union]
[248] Now with SHIRWELL
OR CB 1652-1988 M 1652-1839 (NDRO)
BT CMB 1596-1601, 1606-08, 1610, 1619, 1629, 1635, 1638, 1668, 1670, 1674,
    1679, 1683, 1690-91, 1694-97, 1700, 1702-05, 1712, 1714-16, 1718-23,
    1725-28, 1731-42, 1745-56, 1762-66, 1768-84, 1786-1812; C 1813, 1815-17
    M 1813-25, 1828-32, 1834-37 B 1813-37 (DRO)
Cop B 1813-37 (Ptd DFHS); B 1813-37 (SG); C 1597-1638, 1652-1850
    M 1597-1638, 1652-1849 B 1597-1850 (NDA); Extr C 1667-1757 M 1653-1728
    B 1666-1762 (Vol 8, BG/PCL)
MI (I, NDA); (I, DFHS); Ch, cy 1972 (Ts SG); Incledon 182 (NDA)

LOXHORE (Wes) Erected 1840 [1851 Religious Census] [1882 Return]
OR for c.1807-37 see BARNSTAPLE CIRCUIT, BIDEFORD (RG 4/954,955 (PRO)

LOXHORE (Wes) Lower Loxhore. Erected 1926. fl c.1970

LUDBROOK   see MODBURY

LUFFINCOTT St James [Black Torrington Hundred; Holsworthy Union] [92]
Now with ASHWATER, HALWILL, BEAWORTHY, CLAWTON, TETCOTT. Redundant.
Churches Conservation Trust
OR C 1659-1961 M 1654-1837 B 1666-1812 (DRO)
BT CMB 1608, 1610, 1619, 1624, 1631, 1633, 1635, 1663-64, 1666, 1668-72,
    1674-82, 1690, 1694-97, 1699 (1700-1812 ?); C 1813-34, 1836-39 M 1817,
    1819-20, 1823-26, 1832, 1834, 1836-37 B 1814-15, 1817-26, 1830-32,
    1834-40 (DRO)
Cop M 1813-37 (Ptd DFHS); CMB 1608-36 from BT, 1653-1812 (DCRS/WSL);
    M 1610-1753 (Boyd)

LUFFINCOTT cont.
Cop (Mf) (Tavistock SP); Extr C 1698-1812 M 1610, 1633-36, 1650-55,
    1670-1753 (IGI); C 1698-1812 M 1610, 1633-36, 1650-55, 1670-1753
    (Mf I SLC)
MI Extr (Whitmore MS, SG)

LUNDY ISLAND St Helen [Shebbear Hundred; Bideford Union] 12th cent chapel of
St Anne, Beacon Hill, later St Elena. Demolished. Iron hall, High Street,
used from 1860, dismantled 1868. Iron church, Millcombe Valley 1885,
replaced by St Helena or St Helen, erected 1895. Licensed for marriages
1912. Formerly extra-parochial, now in Hartland Deanery and served from the
mainland.
OR C 1901+ M 1916+ B 1905+ (Inc)
BT None
Cop Z 1865-69 C 1901-94 M 1916-86 B 1905-78 (SG)
MI (I, DFHS); (SG)

LUPPITT St Mary [Axminster Hundred; Honiton Union] [702]
Now with DUNKESWELL, SHELDON
OR CB 1711-1993 M 1711-1992 (DRO)
BT CMB 1610, 1613, 1617, 1625-26, 1633-34, 1638, 1663-64, 1666-67, 1683,
    1685, 1689-90, 1696-97, 1699, 1724-27, 1729-32, 1734-35, 1737, 1739-50,
    1752, 1754, 1757, 1759-70 (1771-1812 ?); CB 1813-38 M 1815-37 (DRO)
Cop B 1813-37 (Ptd DFHS); B 1813-37 (SG)
Cop (Mf) (Colyton SP); C 1711-1852 M 1711-1838 B 1711-1884 (Mfc SG)
MI Extr (Whitmore MS, SG); Incledon 511 (NDA)

LUPPITT (Bapt) f 1652; later moved to Upottery ?; house n.d. [1851 Religious
Census]; Beacon Chapel erected 1859; now a house

LUPPITT (Presb) Licensed 1672; fl 1772; closed by 1776. Members joined
HONITON

LUPPITT (Free Church) Union Chapel, Beacon [1882 Return]

LUSCOMBE see DAWLISH

LUSTLEIGH St John the Baptist [Teignbridge Hundred; Newton Abbot Union]
[361] Now with MORETONHAMPSTEAD, MANATON, NORTH BOVEY
OR C 1631-1971 M 1631-1837 B 1631-1949 (DRO) Includes some baptisms of
    BOVEY TRACEY inhabitants
BT CMB 1608, 1611, 1613, 1618, 1620, 1624, 1630, 1634, 1636, 1641, 1663-64,
    1666, 1668-71, 1674-81, 1686-88, 1690, 1695, 1697 (1698-1812 ?);
    post-1812 returns unfit for production (DRO)
Cop CMB 1608-1837 (Ptd DCRS 1927-30); B 1785-1837 (Ptd DFHS); CMB 1609-1837
    (WSL); B 1785-1837 (SG); M 1608-1837 (Boyd); M 1790-1837 (Pallot);
    Extr C 1642-1783 M 1640-1729 B 1631-1757 (Vol 14, BG/PCL)
Cop (Mf) Extr CM 1608-1837 (IGI); CM 1608-1837 (Mf I SLC)
MI (Ptd DRMI 20: 1998)

LUSTLEIGH (RC) Blessed Cuthbert Mayne 1946

LUSTLEIGH (Bapt) A room used 'since time immemorial' [1851 Religious
Census]; chapel mid-19th cent, now a house

LUTON see BISHOPSTEIGNTON

LUTTON see CORNWOOD

LYDFORD or **LIDFORD** St Petrock [Lifton Hundred; Tavistock Union] [477] Now
with PETER TAVY, MARY TAVY, BRENT TOR
OR C 1716-1995 M 1719-1995 B 1716-1955 (PWDRO) No earlier registers noted
in 1831
BT CMB 1608, 1610, 1614, 1617-18, 1620, 1624, 1626, 1635, 1663-64, 1666,
1668-72, 1674, 1676, 1678-80, 1686-89, 1696-97, 1699 (1700-1812 ?);
C 1813-37 M 1813-36 B 1813-16, 1818-37 (DRO)
Cop M 1608-1754 (I, Ptd, edit M.Brown, Dartmoor Press 1999); CMB 1716-1869
(SG); CMB 1716-1839 (WSL); B 1786-1900 (I, PWDRO); Extr C 1720-1811
M 1720-33 B 1726-94 (Vol 20, BG/PCL)
Cop (Mf) (Okehampton and Tavistock SPs)
MI (Ptd DRMI 8: 1998); (I, DFHS); Ch, cy 1973 (Ts SG)

LYDFORD St Michael and All Angels, Princetown. Erected 1813. Parish created
1912 from Lydford. Now with MOORLAND
OR C 1807-1970 M 1866-1992 B 1815-1993 (DRO)
Cop B 1815-1900 (I, PWDRO)
Cop (Mf) (Tavistock SP)
MI (Ptd DRMI 7: 1988)

LYDFORD St Gabriel, Postbridge. Mission church and school erected 1869.
School closed 1931. Consecrated 1934. Now with MOORLAND
OR M 1935+ C 1974+ (Inc) B 1906+: no register; cemetery belongs to Parish
Council. Earlier entries at St Michael, Princetown.
MI (Ptd DRMI 7: 1988)

LYDFORD St Raphael, Huccaby Chapel. Erected 1868. Now with MOORLAND
OR C 1991+ M 1900+; no B (Inc) Earlier entries at St Michael, Princetown

LYDFORD H.M. Prison, Princetown, Dartmoor. Erected 1806. Prisoner-of-war
depot until 1815. Closed 1816; re-opened 1850 as convict prison
OR Deaths of French prisoners of war (ADM 103: PRO)

LYDFORD (RC) H.M.Prison, Princetown. Served from Plymouth until 1863, when
chaplain appointed
OR Confirmations 1856+ (Plymouth Diocesan Archives)

LYDFORD (Wes)
OR for *c.*1820-36 *see* ASHBURTON CIRCUIT (RG 4/840 PRO)

LYDFORD (Wes) Peatcott. Erected 1912. Closed 1985

LYDFORD (Wes) Princetown. Erected 1874 [1882 Return] fl *c.*1970

LYDFORD (Wes) Postbridge. Erected 1837 [1851 Religious Census]
[1882 Return]

LYDFORD (Bible Christian/U Meth) Erected 1839 [1851 Religious Census]
[1882 Return]; Silver Street erected 1908. Closed 1988

LYMPSTONE Nativity of the Blessed Virgin Mary [East Budleigh Hundred;
St Thomas Union] [1066]
OR C 1654-1918 M 1654-1985 B 1654-1915 (DRO)
BT CMB 1608, 1613, 1616, 1625?, 1630, 1635, 1669-72, 1675, 1678, 1683,
1687, 1690, 1695-97 (1698-1812 ?); CB 1813-57 M 1813-26, 1828-36 (DRO)

LYMPSTONE cont.
Cop B 1813-37 (Ptd DFHS); CMB 1654-1906 (DCRS/WSL, WSL); M 1654-1837 (Boyd);
    B 1813-37 (WSL); Extr C 1689 M 1664-77 B 1656-75, 1690-1732 (Vol 11,
    BG/PCL)
Cop (Mf) Extr CM 1654-1875 (IGI); CM 1654-1875 (Mf I SLC)
MI (Ptd D.Lewis and church members Lympstone Monumental Inscriptions: 1997)

LYMPSTONE (RC) St Boniface n.d.

LYMPSTONE (Wes) Erected 1820 [1851 Religious Census]
OR for c.1820-37 see BUDLEIGH Temple, EXETER Mint (RG 4/517, 1208 PRO)

LYMPSTONE (Prim Meth) Chapel Road. Erected 1883. fl c.1970

LYMPSTONE (Prim Meth) School Room, The Marsh [1882 Return]

LYNEHAM   see YEALMPTON

LYNMOUTH   see COUNTISBURY

LYNTON St Mary the Virgin [Shirwell Hundred; Barnstaple Union] [792]
see also chapelry of COUNTISBURY. Now with NORTH DEVON COAST
OR C 1569-1970 M 1591-1992 B 1568-1982 (NDRO)
BT CMB 1606-07, 1610, 1614-15, 1620-21, 1629-31, 1644, 1668, 1670-71, 1679,
    1683, 1688-91, 1694-97, 1699-1700, 1702-03, 1705, 1709, 1711-12, 1714-15
    (1716-1812 ?); CB 1813-14, 1816, 1828, 1836-53, 1855-64 M 1814, 1816,
    1828, 1836-38 (DRO)
Cop CMB 1569-1850 (DCRS/WSL, NDA); M 1568-1837 (SG); M 1591-1837 (Phil Ms);
    M 1568-1837 (DFHS); M 1591-1837 (Boyd)
Cop (Mf) Extr C 1569-1845 M 1591-1850 (IGI); C 1569-1845 M 1591-1850
    (Mf I SLC)
MI (I, DFHS); Ch, cy (Ptd Dwelly 71-113); Incledon 651 (NDA)

LYNTON St Bartholomew, Barbrook Mill. Mission church in parish of Lynton.
Opened 1875. Now with NORTH DEVON COAST
OR None

LYNTON (RC) The Most Holy Saviour, Lee Road f 1904; erected 1910

LYNTON (Ind) Lee Road. Erected 1850 [1851 Religious Census] [1882 Return]

LYNTON (Wes)
OR for c.1807-37 see BARNSTAPLE CIRCUIT (RG 4/954 PRO)

LYNTON (Wes) Barbrook. Erected 1871 [1882 Return] Closed 1974. Reopened 1986

LYNTON (Wes) Lee Road. Erected 1910. fl c.1970

LYNTON (Wes) Wesleyan Methodist School Chapel [1882 Return]

MADWORTHY   see BEAWORTHY

MAKER [Part East Hundred (Cornwall); part Roborough Hundred (Devon)]
[2637] Devon part was tything of Vaultershorne [1092] see NIPR Vol 8 Part 4
Cornwall

MALBOROUGH All Saints [Malborough Borough; Kingsbridge Union] [1604]
Chapelry in WEST ALVINGTON. Separate parish 1877. Now with SOUTH HUISH, WEST
ALVINGTOPN, CHURCHSTOW
OR C 1558-1869 M 1558-1946 B 1558-1866 (DRO)
BT CMB 1608-09, 1613-14, 1618, 1620?, 1638, 1664, 1669-72, 1674, 1677-82,
     1684, 1686, 1690, 1696, 1700 (1701-1812 ?); CMB 1813-32, 1834-35 (DRO)
Cop CMB 1558-1837 (DCRS/WSL); M 1754-1812 indexed by male spouse (DFHS)
Cop (Mf) Extr CM 1558-1837 (IGI); CM 1558-1837 (Mf I SLC)
MI (I, DFHS); Extr (Ptd L.Collins 'Deaths at sea' DFH 61: 1992: 18-19)

MALBOROUGH Holy Trinity, Salcombe. Chapelry in Malborough. Separate parish
1844. Peculiar of the Dean and Chapter of Exeter 1844-48.
OR C 1802-1867 (DRO) Noted in 1831: 'Burials and Marriages do not take
     place at this chapel, but at Malborough, which itself acknowledges West
     Alvington as a Mother Church'
BT C 1813-20, 1823-38 (DRO)
Cop CMB 1750-1814 from BT (DCRS/WSL); M 1845-1907 (DRO)
MI (I, DFHS); Extr (Ptd K,Prideaux *Salcombe church and its builders*: 1913);
     Incledon 423 (NDA)

MALBOROUGH (RC) Our Lady Star of the Sea, Devon Road, Salcombe 1959

MALBOROUGH (Bapt) f 1815 from KINGSBRIDGE [*Baptist Handbook* 1861]

MALBOROUGH (Bapt) Salcombe f 1864 [1882 Return]
OR M 1985-89 (DRO)

MALBOROUGH (Bapt) Courtney Park Chapel, Salcombe [1882 Return]

MALBOROUGH (Wes) Allenhayes Road, Salcombe. Erected 1926. fl *c.*1970

MALBOROUGH (Wes) [1882 Return]
OR for *c.*1813-37 *see* KINGSBRIDGE (RG 4/1088 PRO)

MALBOROUGH (Wes) Hope Cove. Erected *c.*1826 [1851 Religious Census] rebuilt
1861 [1882 Return] fl *c.*1970

MALBOROUGH (Wes) Salcombe. Erected 1824 [1851 Religious Census]
OR for *c.*1813-37 *see* KINGSBRIDGE Ebenezer, PLYMOUTH Ebenezer
     (RG 4/1088,1092 PRO)

MALBOROUGH (S of F) Batson. fl *c.*1696. Part of KINGSBRIDGE MM

MALBOROUGH (Brethren) Salcombe [1851 Religious Census] Building near and
south of the Market Place, occupied by Richard Balkwill [1882 Return]

MALBOROUGH (Who object to be designated) A loft, fitted as a Chapel, being
part of the premises belonging to Miss A.H.Russell, Fore Street, Salcombe
[1882 Return]

MAMHEAD St Thomas the Apostle [Exminster Hundred; St Thomas Union] [330]
Now with KENTON, POWDERHAM, COFTON, STARCROSS
OR C 1556-1942 M 1556-1974 B 1556-1812 (DRO)
BT CMB 1608, 1611, 1614, 1617, 1620, 1633, 1639, 1663-64, 1667, 1669-71,
     1672?, 1673, 1675, 1677?, 1678-79, 1683, 1687, 1690, 1696-97
     (1698-1812 ?); C 1813-80 M 1814, 1817-29, 1831-33, 1835-37 B 1813-69,
     1871-80 (DRO)

MAMHEAD cont.
Cop CMB 1549-1837 (DCRS/WSL); CMB 1556-1837 (SG)
Cop (Mf) Extr C 1549-1837 M 1556-1837 (IGI); C 1549-1837 M 1556-1837
    (Mf I SLC)
MI (I, DFHS); Ch extr (Ptd Cresswell 125-7); Ch, cy 1932 (Ts SG)

MANATON St Winifred [Teignbridge Hundred; Newton Abbot Union] [435]
Now with MORETONHAMPSTEAD, NORTH BOVEY, LUSTLEIGH
OR C 1653-1898 M 1654-1991 B 1653-1974 (DRO)
BT CMB 1602, 1611, 1613-14, 1616, 1623, 1626, 1629, 1663-64, 1666, 1669-72,
    1674, 1676-79, 1682, 1686, 1689-90, 1695, 1697, 1699 (1700-1812 ?);
    CMB 1813-15, 1817 CB 1822, 1827-33, 1835, 1837-63 M 1813-15, 1817,
    1827-33, 1835, 1837 (DRO)
Cop M 1654-1754 (I, Ptd, edit M.Brown, Dartmoor Press 1999); CMB 1653-1840
    (SG); Extr B 1840-61 (SG)
Cop (Mf) (Totnes SP); C 1653-1898 M 1654-1837 B 1653-1813 (Mfc SG)
MI (Ptd DRMI 20: 1998)

MANATON (Wes) Erected 1839 [1851 Religious Census] [1882 Return]
OR see HENNOCK and MORETONHAMPSTEAD. For c.1815-37 see also ASHBURTON
    CIRCUIT, OKEHAMPTON (RG 4/840,1089 PRO)

MARIANSLEIGH St Mary [Witheridge Hundred; South Molton Union] [282]
Rebuilt after fire 1932. Now with OAKMOOR
OR C 1736-1985 M 1757-1982 B 1727-1987 (DRO) No earlier registers noted in
    1831
BT CMB 1597-1602, 1606-07, 1610, 1623, 1627, 1629, 1634, 1668, 1670, 1674,
    1678-79, 1683-84, 1688, 1690, 1692-97, 1699-1700, 1712, 1714-15
    (1716-1812 ?); CB 1813-50, 1856-57 M 1816-37 (DRO)
Cop CMB 1594-1988 (NDRO); CMB 1597-1751 from BT, 1727-1837 (DCRS/WSL);
    M 1598-1837 (Boyd)
Cop (Mf) Extr C 1597-1837 M 1598-1606, 1629-34, 1668-1700, 1712-1837 (IGI);
    C 1597-1837 M 1598-1606, 1629-34, 1668-1700, 1712-1837 (Mf I SLC)
MI (I, NDA)

MARIANSLEIGH (Ind/Cong) Alswear. Erected 1841. Connected with South Molton
[1851 Religious Census] [1882 Return]

MARIANSLEIGH (Wes) Alswear. Erected 1887. Closed 1974

MARISTOW see TAMERTON FOLIOT

MARLDON St John the Baptist [Haytor Hundred; Totnes Union] [438]
Former chapelry in PAIGNTON
OR C 1602-1930 M 1598-1979 B 1598-1904 (DRO)
BT CMB 1612, 1614, 1616, 1620, 1629-30, 1632, 1635, 1641, 1644, 1663-81,
    1682?, 1683-86, 1688, 1690-1706, 1708-36, 1738-59, 1778-1813; CB 1813-39
    M 1813-23, 1825-37 (DRO)
Cop (Mf) (Torquay SP); Extr C 1650-1750 M 1651-1765 (IGI); C 1650-1750
    M 1651-1765 (Mf I SLC)
MI Extr (Whitmore MS, SG)

MARLDON Compton Castle. Home of Gilbert family. Chapel c.1420. National
Trust

MARLDON (Bapt) Compton Chapel [1882 Return]

MARLDON (Presb) fl c.1672-90

MARLDON (Cong) Clapp Hill [1882 Return]

MARLDON (URC) Ipplepen Road f 1841

MARTINHOE St Martin [Shirwell Hundred; Barnstaple Union] [235]
Now with NORTH DEVON COAST
OR C 1656-1980 M 1633-1963 B 1632-1980 (NDRO)
BT CMB 1597-1601, 1607-08, 1610, 1613-14, 1617, 1631, 1638, 1643, 1668,
    1672, 1674, 1678, 1680, 1684-85, 1690-91, 1694-98, 1705, 1707-09, 1712,
    1714-16, 1718-28, 1731-37, 1739-42, 1745-51, 1753-56 (1757-1812 ?);
    C 1813-50, 1852-62, 1867 M 1814-28, 1831-37 B 1813-15, 1817-28, 1831-50,
    1852-58, 1860-62, 1867 (DRO)
Cop M 1633-1812 (Ptd Phil 1: 1909); CMB 1597-1645 from BT; 1632-1733
    (DCRS/WSL); C 1656-1728 M 1633-1729 B 1632-1733 (NDA); CMB 1633-1812
    (WSL); M 1597-1812 (Great Card Index, SG); M 1597-1812 (Boyd);
    M 1790-1812 (Pallot)
Cop (Mf) Extr C 1597-1728 M 1597-1729 (IGI); C 1597-1728 M 1597-1729
    (Mf I SLC)
MI (I, DFHS); Ch, cy (Ptd Dwelly 24-36)

MARTINSTOW *see* TAMERTON FOLIOT

MARWOOD St Michael and all Angels [Braunton Hundred; Barnstaple Union]
[944] Now with HEANTON PUNCHARDON
OR C 1602-1784, 1813-1985 M 1602-1983 B 1602-1986 (NDRO) Noted in 1831:
    vol.3 C 1784-1812
BT CMB 1607, 1610-11, 1623, 1630-31, 1633, 1644, 1668, 1670, 1672, 1674,
    1678-79, 1682-83, 1688, 1690-91, 1702-05, 1707, 1709, 1712, 1714-15
    (1716-1812 ?); C 1813-48, 1850 MB 1813-50 (DRO)
Cop C 1602-1838 M 1602-1853 B 1602-1868 (NDA); CMB 1602-1812 (DCRS/WSL);
    M 1602-1812 (Boyd)
Cop (Mf) Extr C 1602-1784 M 1602-1812 (IGI); C 1602-1784 M 1602-1812
    (Mf I SLC)
MI Incledon 76 (NDA)

MARWOOD (Cong) Muddiford. Erected 1846 [1851 Religious Census] [1882 Return]

MARWOOD (Wes)
OR for c.1807-37 *see* BARNSTAPLE CIRCUIT (RG 4/954 PRO)

MARWOOD (Wes) Prixford. Erected 1829 [1851 Religious Census] Rebuilt 1873.
fl c.1970. Closed. Now a house
Cop B 1924-40 (DFHS)
MI (I, DFHS)

MARWOOD (Bible Christian) Unity Chapel, Middle Marwood. Erected 1841
[1851 Religious Census] [1882 Return]

MARY TAVY or MARYTAVY or TAVY ST MARY St Mary [Lifton Hundred; Tavistock
Union] [1123] Now with PETER TAVY, LYDFORD, BRENT TOR
OR C 1560-1912 M 1560-1966 B 1560-1916 (DRO)
BT CMB 1613-14, 1617-20, 1623-24, 1632, 1638, 1663, 1666, 1669-72, 1674,
    1676-82, 1684, 1686-90, 1695, 1699 (1700-1812 ?); CB 1813-42, 1844,
    1847-74, 1876 M 1813-36 (DRO)

MARY TAVY cont.
Cop M 1560-1754 (I, Ptd, edit M.Brown, Dartmoor Press 1999); CMB 1560-1837
(DCRS/WSL); Extr C 1562-1798 M 1581-1760 B 1563-1809 (SG); M 1682-1827;
fees for coffins: names 1841-53 (DFHS); Extr C 1562-1798 M 1581-1760
B 1563-1809 (Vol 18, BG/PCL)
Cop (Mf) (Tavistock SP); Extr CM 1560-1837 (IGI); CM 1560-1837 (Mf I SLC)
MI (Ptd DRMI 9: 1998); (I, DFHS)

MARY TAVY (Wes) Blackdown. Erected 1821 [1851 Religious Census]
Marytavy Chapel, Blackdown [1882 Return]

MARY TAVY (Wes) Erected 1835; fl c.1970
OR C 1846-1990 (DRO); for c.1808-37 see TAVISTOCK (RG 4/341 PRO)

MARY TAVY (Wes) Horndon. Erected 1837 [1851 Religious Census] [1882 Return]
Closed 1890. Later used as a barn

MARY TAVY (Bible Christian) Zoar, Horndon. Erected 1837 [1851 Religious
Census] [1882 Return] Rebuilt 1904. fl c.1970
MI (Ptd DRMI 9: 1998)

MARYSTOWE St Mary the Virgin [Lifton Hundred; Tavistock Union] [508]
see also the chapelry of THRUSHELTON. Now with CORYTON, STOWFORD, LEW
TRENCHARD, THRUSHELTON
OR C 1651-1873, 1875-1992 M 1654-1837 B 1654-1993 (PWDRO)
BT CMB 1611, 1614, 1617, 1619, 1629, 1634, 1663-64, 1666, 1669-70, 1672-74,
1681, 1684, 1686, 1688-90, 1696-97 (1698-1812 ?); C 1813-39 M 1814-27,
1829-36 B 1813-26, 1829-39 (DRO)
Cop B 1792-1837 (Ptd DFHS); B 1800-37 (WSL, SG); B 1768-1911 (I, PWDRO)
Cop (Mf) (Tavistock SP)

MARYSTOWE (Bapt) Erected 1830 [1851 Religious Census]

MARYSTOWE (Wes) Allerford [1882 Return]
OR for c.1808-37 see TAVISTOCK (RG 4/341 PRO)

MEAVY St Peter [Roborough Hundred; Tavistock Union] [336]
Now with YELVERTON, SHEEPSTOR, WALKHAMPTON
OR C 1653-1992 M 1654-1984 B 1653-1978 (Inc)
BT CMB 1614, 1618 or 1619, 1663-64, 1666-68, 1670-72, 1674-80, 1682, 1684,
1686, 1688-89 (1690-1812 ?); C 1814, 1817-18, 1821, 1824-27, 1830,
1832-36, 1838-39, 1841-46, 1848-71 M 1814-15, 1818, 1821, 1824-27, 1830,
1832, 1834-36 B 1814-15, 1817-18, 1824-27, 1830, 1832-36, 1838-39,
1841-46, 1848-55, 1857-71 (DRO)
Cop M 1614-1754 (I, Ptd, edit M.Brown, Dartmoor Press 1999); CB 1619-1811
(DFHS); C 1653-1992 M 1654-1985 B 1653-1978 (I, PWDRO, Tavistock Lib);
B 1775-1900 (I, PWDRO)
MI (Ptd DRMI 2: 1998); (I, DFHS); Cy 1978 (Ts SG)

MEAVY (Bapt) [Kelly 1889]

MEAVY (Ind) Hoo Meavy Chapel. Erected 1850 [1851 Religious Census]
MI (Ptd DRMI 2: 1998); (Ptd V.Turvey 'Hoo Meavy Chapel MI': DFH 40:1986:
20-21); (I, DFHS);

MEETH   see SATTERLEIGH

MEETH St Michael and All Angels [Shebbear Hundred; Okehampton Union]   [298]
Now with HATHERLEIGH, EXBOURNE, JACOBSTOWE
OR   C 1653-1986 M 1656-1981 B 1653-1812 (DRO)
BT   CMB 1597-1602, 1607-08, 1610, 1615, 1618, 1641, 1668, 1670, 1674,
        1678-79, 1682-83, 1685, 1688-91, 1694-97, 1699-1700, 1704, 1708-09,
        1711-12, 1714-15 (1716-1812 ?); none listed after 1812 (DRO)
Cop CMB 1597-1641 from BT, 1653-1812 (DCRS/WSL); M 1653-1812 (Boyd)
Cop (Mf) (Okehampton SP); CB 1653-1812 M 1653-1981 (Mfc SG);
        Extr C 1597-1812 M 1600-18, 1656-1811 (IGI); C 1597-1812 M 1600-18,
        1656-1811 (Mf I SLC)
MI   Incledon 895 (NDA)

MEETH (Bible Christian) [1882 Return]

MEMBURY St John the Baptist [Axminster Hundred; Axminster Union]   [670]
Chapelry in AXMINSTER. Separate parish 1911. Now with YARCOMBE, UPOTTERY.
COTLEIGH
OR   C 1637-1959 M 1638-1837 B 1637-1868 (DRO)
BT   CMB 1620, 1624, 1629, 1631, 1666, 1669, 1676, 1678, 1693, 1696-97, 1699
        (1700-1812 ?); CB 1813-56, 1858-59, 1862 M 1813-37 (DRO)
Cop CB 1637-86 M 1638-76 (Ptd edit R.Cornish 1903); M 1813-37 (Ptd DFHS);
        B 1813-37 (Ptd DFHS); CMB 1620-31 from BT, 1637-1837 (DCRS/WSL);
        B 1813-37 (SG); M 1637-1837 (Boyd)
Cop (Mf) (Colyton SP); C 1637-1846 M 1638-1837 B 1637-1868 (Mfc SG);
        Extr C 1620-1837 M 1624-1837 (IGI); C 1620-1837 M 1624-1837
        (Mf I SLC)
MI   Incledon 621 (NDA)

MEMBURY (Presb) fl *c.*1672-90

MEMBURY (S of F) Membury MM f 1668-69; united with CULLOMPTON AND SPICELAND
MM 1742

MEMBURY (S of F) f by 1662; closed by late 18th cent. Later became a
cottage. Burial ground
OR   Z 1662-1724 M 1666-1733 B 1660-1788 transcript only (DRO); Burials also
        in MEMBURY and AXMINSTER parish registers. *see also* Hawkchurch Meeting,
        Dorset
Cop ZMB 1662-1775 (DCRS); CMB 1660-1788 (SG)
Cop (Mf) Extr ZC 1662-67, 1682-94, 1711-33, 1781-86 M 1662-1733 (IGI);
        C 1662-67, 1682-94, 1711-33, 1781-86 M 1662-1733 (Mf I SLC)
MI   Extr ('The Quakers' Meeting House and Burial Ground, Membury': *Western
        Antiquary* 2 188 181-2)

MERTON All Saints [Shebbear Hundred; Torrington Union]   [740]
Now with TORRIDGE
OR   C 1687-1997 M 1688-1981 B 1687-1896 (NDRO)
BT   CMB 1597-1601, 1607, 1609-10, 1612, 1619, 1624, 1629, 1634, 1641, 1644,
        1668, 1671, 1674, 1678-79, 1682-85, 1688-91, 1696-97, 1700, 1702, 1704,
        1706-07, 1709-11, 1714-15 (1716-1812 ?); CB 1838-44, 1846 (DRO)
Cop CMB 1597-1685 from BT, 1687-1812 (DCRS/WSL); M 1687-1812 (Boyd)
Cop (Mf) C 1687-1846 M 1688-1981 B 1687-1875 (Mfc SG); Extr C 1597-1812
        M 1598-1644, 1668-1812 (IGI); C 1597-1812 M 1598-1644, 1668-1812
        (Mf I SLC)
MI   Incledon 1088 (NDA)

MERTON (Bible Christian/U Meth) A Building [1882 Return] Erected 1907.
fl *c.*1970

MESHAW St John [Witheridge Hundred; South Molton Union] [166] Rebuilt 1838.
Now with WITHERIDGE, THELBRIDGE, EAST WORLINGTON, WEST WORLINGTON
OR C 1581-1988 M 1581-1989 B 1580-1812 (NDRO)
BT CMB 1607-08, 1610, 1614-15, 1617, 1629-30, 1633?, 1668, 1670, 1672,
    1674, 1680, 1682, 1688-90, 1692, 1694-97, 1699, 1700?, 1704, 1712,
    1714-19, 1721-22, 1726, 1728, 1732-37, 1739-40, 1742, 1745, 1747,
    1749-52, 1754, 1756, 1762-65, 1768-70, 1772-84, 1786-1812; C 1813-50
    M 1813-15, 1817-25, 1828-29, 1831-36 B 1813-14, 1816-17, 1819-20,
    1822-42, 1844-50 (DRO)
Cop CMB 1589-1797 (DCRS/WSL);
Cop (Mf) Extr C 1580-1797 M 1581-1645, 1660-1752 (IGI); C 1580-1797
        M 1581-1645, 1660-1752 (Mf I SLC)
MI (I, NDA); (I, DFHS)

MESHAW (Bible Christian) Prospect. Erected 1839 [1851 Religious Census]
[1882 Return] Rebuilt 1889 ? fl c.1970

MILBER   see HACCOMBE

MILLBRIDGE   see PLYMOUTH

MILTON ABBOT St Constantine [Tavistock Hundred; Tavistock Union] [1205]
United 1921 with DUNTERTON. Now also with LAMERTON, SYDENHAM DAMEREL
OR C 1653-1973 M 1654-1994 B 1653-1994 (PWDRO)
BT CMB 1606, 1610-11, 1613, 1614, 1616, 1617, 1625, 1626, 1628, 1633,
    1668-72, 1676, 1686, 1690, 1697, 1699, 1700 (1701-1812 ?); CMB 1813-37
    (DRO)
Cop M 1813-37 (Ptd DFHS); M 1654-1754 (I, Ptd, edit M.Brown, Dartmoor Press
    1999); CMB 1653-1786 (DCRS/WSL); C 1653-1703 M 1654-1812 B 1653-1723
    (DFHS); M 1654-1767 (Boyd); B 1800-1900 (I, PWDRO);
    Extr C 1655-1799 M 1654-1754 B 1653-1789 (Vol 2, BG/PCL)
Cop (Mf) (Tavistock SP); Extr C 1653-1786 M 1654-1767 (IGI); C 1653-1786
        M 1654-1767 (Mf I SLC)

MILTON ABBOT (Wes) Erected 1835 [1882 Return] fl c.1970
OR for c.1808-37 see TAVISTOCK (RG 4/341 PRO)

MILTON ABBOT (Bible Christian) Zion Chapel, Lea. Erected 1837
[1851 Religious Census] [1882 Return] Closed 1982

MILTON ABBOT (Bible Christian) Milton Abbot Chapel [1882 Return]

MILTON ABBOT (Wes) Milton Buckland Chapel, Milton [1882 Return]

MILTON COMBE   see BUCKLAND MONACHORUM

MILTON DAMEREL Holy Trinity [Black Torrington Hundred; Holsworthy Union]
[761] see also the chapelry of COOKBURY, Now with HOLSWORTHY, HOLLACOMBE
OR C 1683-1886 M 1678-1837 B 1685-1779 (DRO) Noted in 1831: CB 1791-1812.
    Cookbury registers contained Milton Damerel entries CB 1749-91
BT CMB 1606, 1609-11, 1620, 1624, 1626-27, 1633-34, 1636, 1663-64, 1666,
    1668-69, 1671, 1676-77, 1680-82, 1686, 1695-96, 1699 (1700-1812 ?);
    CMB 1813, 1815-33, 1835-36 CB 1838-39 (DRO)
Cop CMB 1606-1812 from BT, 1678-1837 (DCRS/WSL, SG)
Cop (Mf) Extr C 1609-37 M 1606-36, 1666-1837 (IGI); C 1609-37 M 1606-36,
        1666-1837 (Mf I SLC)

MILTON DAMEREL (Wes) Gidcot Cross. Erected 1840 [1851 Religious Census] [1882 Return]
OR for *c.*1813-37 *see* HOLSWORTHY, KINGSBRIDGE (RG 4/1210,1088 PRO)

MILTON DAMEREL (Bible Christian) Erected 1836 [1851 Religious Census]

MILTON DAMEREL (Bible Christian) Erected 1840 [1851 Religious Census]

MILTON DAMEREL (Bible Christian) Milton Chapel [1882 Return] rebuilt 1892 ? fl *c.*1970

MILTON DAMEREL (Bible Christian) Gidcot Cross [1882 Return]

MILTON, SOUTH All Saints [Stanborough Hundred; Kingsbridge Union] [415] Chapelry in WEST ALVINGTON. Separate parish 1886. Now with THURLESTONE
OR C 1686-1879 M 1735-1836 B 1686-1717, 1733-1963 (DRO)
BT CMB 1608-09, 1614, 1616-18, 1626, 1634, 1639, 1666, 1668-71, 1676, 1687-90, 1699 (1700-1812 ?); CB 1837-38, 1840-41 (DRO)
Cop M 1754-1812 indexed by male spouse (DFHS)
Cop (Mf) CMB 1686-1789 M 1735-1836 B 1696-1963 (Mfc SG)
MI (I, DFHS)

MILTON, SOUTH (Ind) Connected to Kingsbridge [1851 Religious Census]

MILTON, SOUTH (Wes) Erected 1847 [1851 Religious Census]
OR for *c.*1813-37 *see* KINGSBRIDGE (RG 4/1088 PRO)

MODBURY United benefice including MODBURY, BIGBURY, RINGMORE, KINGSTON, AVETON GIFFORD, WOODLEIGH, LODDISWELL, EAST ALLINGTON

MODBURY St George [Ermington Hundred; Kingsbridge Union] [2116] Rebuilt 1622. Now with MODBURY united benefice
OR C 1601-1812, 1839-1875 M 1553-1565, 1601-1812 B 1601-1812 (DRO)
BT CMB 1613-14, 1618, 1626, 1632-33, 1677, 1686, 1688, 1690, 1695-96, 1699 (1700-1812 ?); CB 1813-40, 1843-58 M 1813-37 (DRO)
Cop CMB 1553-1837 (DCRS/WSL); M 1553-1812 (Boyd); Extr C 1602-1791 M 1601-1790 B 1601-1787 (Vol 7, BG/PCL)
Cop (Mf) (Totnes SP); Extr C 1599-1837 M 1553-65, 1601-37 (IGI); C 1599-1837 M 1553-65, 1601-37 (Mf I SLC)
MI Extr (Whitmore MS, SG)

MODBURY St John the Baptist, Brownston. Chapel-of-ease erected 1844. Now converted to residence

MODBURY (RC) St Monica, Palm Cross Green 1963

MODBURY (Bapt) Church Street. f 1791 from KINGSBRIDGE. Erected 1807 [1851 Religious Census] Church Street [1882 Return]
OR Destroyed by bombing, Plymouth, 1942

MODBURY (Presb) Little Modbury. Licensed 1672

MODBURY (Wes) Erected 1835 [1851 Religious Census] [1882 Return] Rebuilt 1935. fl *c.*1970
OR for *c.*1801-36 *see* ASHBURTON CIRCUIT (RG 4/1763,840 PRO)

MODBURY (Wes) Little Modbury
OR for *c.*1820-36 *see* ASHBURTON CIRCUIT (RG 4/840 PRO)

MODBURY (Wes) Brownston [1882 Return]

MODBURY (Wes) Ludbrook
OR for c.1801-36 see ASHBURTON CIRCUIT (RG 4/1763,840 PRO)

MODBURY (S of F) f c.1761-85 [1851 Religious Census] Closed 19th cent.
Part of KINGSBRIDGE MM

MOLLAND St Mary [South Molton Hundred; South Molton Union]   [531]
Now with OAKMOOR
OR C 1541-1985 M 1538-1987 B 1541-1987 (NDRO)
BT CMB 1602, 1607-08, 1610, 1613?, 1614, 1619, 1623, 163?, 1668, 1671-72,
    1674, 1679, 1682-83, 1688-89, 1691, 1694-95, 1699-1700, 1708-12,
    1714-16, 1718-21, 1723, 1725-28, 1732-40 (1741-1812 ?); C 1813-39,
    1843-44, 1847-50 M 1814-16, 1818-36 B 1813-39, 1843, 1847-50 (DRO)
Cop CMB 1538-1837 (DCRS/WSL, WSL); Extr 'several sequences' of CMB 1542-1773
    (Vol 5, BG/PCL)
Cop (Mf) Extr C 1541-1837 M 1538-51, 1576-1601, 1646-1712, 1723-1837 (IGI);
        C 1541-1837 M 1538-51, 1576-1601, 1646-1712, 1723-1837 (Mf I SLC)
MI (I, NDA)

MOLLAND (Presb) fl c.1672-90

MOLLAND (Wes) Bottreaux Mill. Erected 1850 [1851 Religious Census]
[1882 Return] Rebuilt 1897. Closed 1982

MOLLAND (Bible Christian/Meth) Erected 1957

MOLLAND CROSS   see MOLTON, NORTH

MOLTON, NORTH All Saints [South Molton Hundred; South Molton Union]   [1937]
see also the chapelry of TWITCHEN. Now with SOUTH MOLTON
OR C 1539-1985 M 1539-1982 B 1539-1858 (NDRO) Noted in 1831: 'almost
    illegible until 1634'
BT CMB 1602, 1605, 1607-08, 1610-12, 1617, 1619, 1633-34, 1668, 1670, 1672,
    1674, 1678-80, 1683, 1688, 1690-91, 1694-95, 1699, 1703-04, 1706,
    1708-12, 1714-15 (1716-1812 ?); CB 1813-63, 1865-75 M 1813-29, 1831-37
    (DRO)
Cop CMB 1539-1850 (DCRS/WSL, NDA)
Cop (Mf) Extr C 1539-1850 M 1539-71, 1606-1850 (IGI); C 1539-1850 M 1539-71,
        1606-1850 (Mf I SLC)
MI (I, NDA)

MOLTON, NORTH (Cong) Erected c.1825 [1851 Religious Census] Closed c.1868

MOLTON, NORTH (Presb) Licensed 1672. fl c.1715; closed by 1772

MOLTON, NORTH (Wes) Erected 1836 [1851 Religious Census] [1882 Return]
Rebuilt 1891 ? fl c.1970
OR for c.1807-37 see BARNSTAPLE CIRCUIT (RG 4/954 PRO)

MOLTON, NORTH (Wes) Heasley Mill. Erected 1867 [1882 Return] fl c.1970

MOLTON, NORTH (Wes) Molland Cross. Erected 1898. Closed 1982

MOLTON, NORTH (Prim Meth) Molland Cross [1882 Return]

MOLTON, NORTH (S of F) fl 1720s, 1730s

MOLTON, SOUTH United benefice including SOUTH MOLTON, NYMET ST GEORGE, HIGH BRAY, CHARLES, FILLEIGH, EAST BUCKLAND, WARKLEIGH WITH SATTERLEIGH, CHITTLEHAMHOLT, KINGSNYMPTON, ROMANSLEIGH, NORTH MOLTON, TWITCHEN, CHITTLEHAMPTON AND UMBERLEIGH.

MOLTON, SOUTH St Mary Magdalene [South Molton Hundred; South Molton Union] [382] United 1945 with NYMET ST GEORGE. Now with SOUTH MOLTON united benefice
OR C 1601-1979 M 1601-1982 B 1601-1913 (NDRO)
BT CMB 1602, 1607, 1610, 1614-15, 1620, 1634, 1667-68, 1670, 1674, 1678-79, 1682-83, 1688, 1690-91, 1694-97, 1699-1700, 1711, 1714-15 (1716-1812 ?); C 1813-19, 1838-55 M 1813-19 B 1813, 1815-18, 1838-55 (DRO)
Cop B 1813-37 (Ptd DFHS); CMB 1601-1812 (DCRS/WSL); M 1601-42 B 1676-1704 (SG); M 1601-1786 (Boyd)
Cop (Mf) Extr C 1601-1812 M 1601-1795 (IGI); C 1601-1812 M 1601-1795 (Mf I SLC)
MI Ts 1990 (SG); Cy 1906 (Ms SG)

MOLTON, SOUTH Holy Trinity, Queen's Nympton. Private chapel of Southcomb family at Honiton Barton. Erected 1790 on site of older chapel. Derelict.
OR None

MOLTON, SOUTH (RC) St Joseph, Cook's Cross 1957

MOLTON, SOUTH (Bapt) New Road. Erected 1843 [1851 Religious Census] [1882 Return]

MOLTON, SOUTH (Presb/Ind/Cong) North Street f 1662; rebuilt 1701, 1834 [1851 Religious Census] [1882 Return] Closed
OR ZC 1758-1837 (RG 4/449 PRO); C 1842-1921 M 1899-1983 (NDRO)
Cop (Mf) ZC 1758-1837 (Mf DCRS/WSL, SG); Extr C 1758-59, 1773-1837 (IGI); C 1758-59, 1773-1837 (Mf I SLC)

MOLTON, SOUTH (Wes) Circuit
OR C 1846-1955 (NDRO)

MOLTON, SOUTH (Wes) North Street. Erected 1821 [1851 Religious Census] [1882 Return]
OR for c.1807-37 see BARNSTAPLE CIRCUIT, BIDEFORD, TEIGNMOUTH (RG 4/954,955,1220 PRO)

MOLTON, SOUTH (Wes) Duke Street. Erected 1883/1906. fl c.1970
OR M 1899-1937 (NDRO)

MOLTON, SOUTH (Bible Christian) Circuit
OR C 1859-1934 (NDRO)

MOLTON, SOUTH (Bible Christian) Erected 1847 [1851 Religious Census]; Ebenezer [1882 Return]

MOLTON, SOUTH (Prim Meth) Circuit
OR C 1858-1888 (MDRO)

MOLTON, SOUTH (Prim Meth) Jubilee, East Street [1882 Return]

MOLTON, SOUTH (S of F) fl c.1702-73

MOLTON, SOUTH (Brethren) Room, Adelaide Place, South Street [1851 Religious Census]

MOLTON, SOUTH (Latter Day Saints) Churchyard. Erected 1830
[1851 Religious Census]

MOLTON, SOUTH Registration district
OR Marriage notices 1837-1894 (NDRO)

MONKLEIGH St George [Shebbear Hundred; Bideford Union]   [562]
OR C 1567-1857 M 1548-1837 B 1558-1901 (NDRO)
BT CMB 1602, 1607, 1614, 1631-33, 1641, 1670?, 1672?, 1674, 1678-79,
    1682-83, 1685, 1688-91, 1694-97, 1699-1700, 1702-03, 1707-12, 1714-15
    (1716-1812 ?); CB 1813-43 M 1814-37 (DRO)
Cop B 1813-37 (Ptd DFHS); B 1813-37 (SG); CMB 1548-1850 (DCRS/WSL, NDA)
Cop (Mf) (Appledore SP); Extr C 1567-1850 M 1548-1850 (IGI); C 1567-1850
        M 1548-1850 (Mf I SLC)
MI Incledon 592 (NDA)

MONKLEIGH (Bapt) Cottage. f c.1844 [1851 Religious Census]

MONKLEIGH (Wes) Erected 1833 [1851 Religious Census] [1882 Return]
Closed 1975. Later used as a garage
OR for c.1819-37 see BIDEFORD (RG 4/955 PRO); (Meth) C 1956-69 (NDRO)

MONKLEIGH (Bible Christian) Bethel Chapel, Annery Cottage [1882 Return]

MONKOKEHAMPTON All Saints [Black Torrington Hundred; Okehampton Union]
[259]
OR CB 1653-1812 M 1654-1754, 1814-1838 (NDRO)
BT CMB 1609, 1611, 1613-14, 1635, 1641, 1663-64, 1666, 1668-72, 1674-76,
    1678-79, 1681-82, 1684, 1686-88, 1694 (1695-1812 ?); C 1813-37, 1839-43,
    1845-50 M 1814-17, 1819-24, 1827-29, 1833, 1835, 1837 B 1813-14,
    1817-19, 1821-28, 1830-37, 1839-43, 1845-50 (DRO)
Cop CMB 1609-1811 from BT (DCRS/WSL); M 1723-90 (DFHS)
Cop (Mf) (Okehampton SP); Extr C 1609-1811 M 1613, 1635-41, 1663-1702,
        1714-32, 1749-1811 (IGI); C 1609-1811 M 1613, 1635-41, 1663-1702,
        1714-32, 1749-1811 (Mf I SLC)

MONKOKEHAMPTON (Bible Christian) Lower Orchard, house [1851 Religious
Census]; chapel erected 1896. fl c.1970

MONKTON St Mary Magdalene [Colyton Hundred; Honiton Union]   [120]
Chapelry in COLYTON. Rebuilt 1863. Separate parish 1867. Now with HONITON
OR C 1737-1992 M 1742-1978 B 1741-1812 (DRO) No earlier registers noted in
    1831
BT CMB 1617, 1620, 1626, 1668-69, 1721-26, 1738, 1742, 1750, 1753, 1755,
    1757-60, 1762-71, 1773-84 (1785-1812 ?); C 1813-19, 1826-28, 1830-32,
    1834-35, 1837-42 M 1813-14, 1817-19, 1826-27, 1830-31, 1835, 1837, 1839-
    40 B 1814-18, 1826-27, 1830-32, 1835, 1837, 1839-42 (DRO)
Cop (Mf) (Colyton SP); C 1737-1812 M 1742-1837 B 1741-1812 (Mfc SG)
MI Incledon 225 (NDA)

MONKTON WYLD Parish created 1850 from WHITCHURCH CANONICORUM (Dorset),
UPLYME. see NIPR Dorset

MOORLAND United benefice including WIDECOMBE IN THE MOOR, LEUSDON,
PRINCETOWN, POSBRIDGE, HUCCABY CHAPEL, HOLNE

MORCHARD BISHOP or **MORCHARD EPISCOPI** or **BISHOP'S MORCHARD** St Mary
[Crediton Hundred; Crediton Union]   [2003] Peculiar of the Bishop of Exeter
until 1848. Now with NORTH CREADY
<u>OR</u>   C 1660-1900 M 1660-1940 B 1660-1940 (DRO)
<u>BT</u>   CMB 1606, 1611, 1621, 1624, 1633, 1638, 1641, 1644, 1664-69, 1671-77,
        1679-80, 1682-83, 1685-88, 1690-93, 1695, 1700-01, 1723, 1730
        (1731-1812 ?); C 1813-38 M 1813-37 B 1813-23, 1825-38 (DRO)
<u>Cop</u> CMB 1606-44 (Ptd J.Cole *Morchard Bishop, Devon, Bishop's Transcripts
        1606-44*: 1995); B 1813-37 (Ptd DFHS); CMB 1606-44, 1660-1850 (DCRS/WSL,
        SG); CMB 1754-1839 (WSL); B 1813-37 (WSL)
<u>Cop (Mf)</u> Extr CM 1660-1850 (IGI); CM 1660-1850 (Mf I SLC)
<u>MI</u> (I, DFHS); Extr (Whitmore MS, SG)

MORCHARD BISHOP (Ind/Cong) Room shared with Wes. 1838 [1851 Religious
Census]; a building [1882 Return]

MORCHARD BISHOP (Wes) n.d. [1851 Religious Census]
<u>OR</u> for *c.*1807-37 *see* BARNSTAPLE CIRCUIT, EXETER Mint (RG 4/954,1207.1208
      PRO)

MORCHARD BISHOP (Bible Christian) Emmanuel. Erected 1846 [1851 Religious
Census] [1882 Return] fl *c.*1970

MORCHARD CRUWYS   *see* CRUWYS MORCHARD

MOREBATH St George [Bampton Hundred; Tiverton Union 1835-56 and 1894-1930;
Dulverton Union (Somerset) 1856-94] [436] Now with BAMPTON, CLAYHANGER,
PETTON
<u>OR</u> C 1558-1876 M 1558-1979 B 1558-1943 (DRO)
<u>BT</u> CMB 1615-17, 1626, 1635, 1664, 1666-70, 1672?, 1675, 1678, 1684-85,
      1687, 1691, 1695-97 (1698-1812 ?); CB 1813-38 M 1813-27, 1829-38 (DRO)
<u>Cop (Mf)</u> (Tiverton SP)

MORELEIGH All Saints [Stanborough Hundred; Totnes Union]   [182]
Now with HALWELL
<u>OR</u> CB 1695-1812 M 1695-1836 (DRO)
<u>BT</u> CMB 1608, 1611, 1614-16, 1620, 1625, 1663-64, 1666, 1668-76, 1679,
      1682-83, 1686-88, 1690, 1695-96, 1700, 1750-95, 1797 (1798-1812 ?);
      post-1812 unfit for production (DRO)
<u>Cop (Mf)</u> (Totnes SP)
<u>MI</u> (I, DFHS)

MORETONHAMPSTEAD St Andrew [Teignbridge Hundred; Newton Abbot Union]   [1864]
Now with MANATON, NORTH BOVEY, LUSTLEIGH
<u>OR</u> C 1603-1898 M 1603-1906 B 1603-1864 (DRO)
<u>BT</u> CMB 1609, 1611, 1614, 1630, 1632, 1634, 1663-64, 1666, 1670-72, 1674-77,
      1679, 1681, 1684, 1686, 1688, 1695-96, 1699 (1700-1812 ?); CB 1813-45,
      1847-64 M 1813-37 (DRO)
<u>Cop</u> CMB 1603-1850 (DCRS/WSL); CMB 1603-1710 (SG)
<u>Cop (Mf)</u> (Okehampton SP); C 1711-1849 M 1711-1837 B 1711-1864 (Mfc SG);
        Extr C 1603-1849 M 1603-1850 (IGI); C 1603-1849 M 1603-1850
        (Mf I SLC)
<u>MI</u> (Ptd DRMI 22: 1998)

MORETONHAMPSTEAD Doccombe Chapel. Mission chapel [Kelly 1889] Now with
Moretonhampstead

MORETONHAMPSTEAD (Bapt) Fore Street. f by 1715. Rebuilt 1786, Burial ground by 1806 [1851 Religious Census] Tabernacle Chapel, Fore Street [1882 Return] later used as a workshop

MORETONHAMPSTEAD (Bapt and Ind: Free Communion of Calvinists) Bethlehem, Lime Street. Erected 1834 [1851 Religious Census]

MORETONHAMPSTEAD (Presb/Unit) Cross Chapel, Cross Street. f 1662. Licensed 1672. Erected 1692, rebuilt 1802 [1851 Religious Census] With burial ground
OR C 1672-1836 (RG 4/444 PRO)
Cop C 1672-1836 (SG)
Cop (Mf) C 1672-1836 (Mf DCRS/WSL, SG); Extr C 1672-1743, 1765-1836 (IGI);
          C 1672-1743, 1765-1836 (Mf I SLC)
MI (Ptd DRMI 22: 1998)

MORETONHAMPSTEAD (Bapt/Presb/Unit) f 1690. Erected Fore Street 1786. United 1818 with Cross Chapel
OR *see* Cross Chapel

MORETONHAMPSTEAD (Cong) Station Road [1882 Return]

MORETONHAMPSTEAD (Wes) Okehampton or Moretonhampstead Circuit
OR C 1815-37 (RG 4/1089 PRO)
Cop ZC 1815-37 (SG)
Cop (Mf) Extr C 1815-37 (IGI); C 1815-37 (Mf I SLC)

MORETONHAMPSTEAD (Wes) Cross Street. Erected 1817 [1851 Religious Census] Rebuilt 1866 [1882 Return] Closed 1976
OR C 1839-1878, 1921-42 M 1877-1932 (DRO); for *c.*1801-37 *see* ASHBURTON
CIRCUIT, OKEHAMPTON (RG 4/1763,840,1089 PRO)
Cop (Mf) C 1839-1921 (Mfc Torquay SP)

MORETONHAMPSTEAD (S of F) fl *c.*1708. Meeting house 1771

MORTEHOE St Mary [Braunton Hundred; Barnstaple Union]   [338]
Now with ILFRACOMBE
OR C 1727-1902 M 1727-1837 B 1727-1944 (NDRO) Noted in 1831: no earlier
      registers. No M entries after 1753
BT CMB 1604, 1607, 1610, 1612, 1634, 1638, 1674, 1678-79, 1682-83, 1688-91,
      1694-95, 1697, 1700, 1703-04, 1712, 1714-15 (1716-1812 ?); CB 1814 (DRO)
Cop B 1750-1837 (Ptd DFHS); B 1750-1837 (SG)
MI Incledon 178 (NDA)

MORTEHOE St Sabinus, Woolacombe. Erected 1911. Parish created 1922 from
Mortehoe. Now with ILFRACOMBE
OR CM 1922+ (Inc) No graveyard: B at Mortehoe

MORTEHOE (Wes) Mr Irwin's Chapel [1882 Return]; Chapel Hill. Erected 1901.
Closed 1988
OR for *c.*1807-37 see BARNSTAPLE CIRCUIT (RG 4/954 PRO)

MORTEHOE (Bible Christian) Erected 1834 [1851 Religious Census]; Beach Road,
Woolacombe. Erected 1892. fl *c.*1970

MORWELLHAM   *see* TAVISTOCK

MUCKWORTHY   *see* ASHWATER

MUDDIFORD   *see* MARWOOD

MUSBURY St Michael [Axminster Hundred; Axminster Union] [418]
Now with COLYTON
OR C 1622-1962 M 1622-1978 B 1622-1916 (DRO)
BT CMB 1619 or 1620, 1625, 1629, 1633, 1635, 1663-64, 1667, 1669-70, 1672,
    1675, 1678, 1683, 1685, 1687-88, 1690, 1695-97, 1717 (1718-1812 ?);
    CMB 1813-35, 1837-38 (DRO)
Cop M 1813-37 (Ptd DFHS); B 1813-37 (Ptd DFHS); CMB 1617-20 from BT,
    1622-1837 (DCRS/WSL); M 1614-1837 (Boyd)
Cop (Mf) (Colyton SP); Extr CM 1614-1837 (IGI); C 1614-1837 (Mf I SLC)
MI Ch, cy (Ptd Pulman *Book of the Axe* 1875; reprint 1969); Cy extr 1909
    (A.W.Matthews *Ye Olde Mortality* vol.8: MS SG); Extr (Whitmore MS, SG);
    Incledon 357 (NDA)

MUSBURY Ashe House Chapel. Rebuilt 17th cent

MUSBURY (Presb) fl *c*.1672-90

MUSBURY (Christians) Musbury Chapel. Road leading to Whitford [1882 Return]

MUTLEY   *see* PLYMOUTH

NETHEREXE St John the Baptist [Hayridge Hundred; St Thomas Union] [99]
Chapelry in THORVERTON, Separate parish 1730. Now with STOKE CANON,
POLTIMORE, HUXHAM, REWE
OR C 1731-1812 M 1773-1807, 1844-1924 B 1743-1812 (DRO) No earlier
    registers noted in 1831. *see* THORVERTON
BT CMB 1609 (1610-1812 ?); C 1814-27, 1838-39, 1861, 1863-67, 1869, 1871-72
    B 1813-17, 1819-25, 1827, 1838-61, 1863-64, 1866-67, 1869, 1871 (DRO)
Cop CMB 1609-1773 from BT, 1731-1837 (DCRS/WSL)
Cop (Mf) Extr C 1714-1837 M 1731-35, 1773-1807 (IGI); C 1714-1837 M 1731-35,
    1773-1807 (Mf I SLC)
MI (I, DFHS); Extr (Whitmore MS, SG)

NETHEREXE (Presb) fl *c*.1672-90

NEW BUILDINGS   *see* UPTON HELLIONS

NEWPORT (Barnstaple)   *see* BISHOP'S TAWTON

NEWTON ABBOT   town in parishes of WOLBOROUGH and HIGHWEEK

NEWTON ABBOT St Mary, Wolborough [Haytor Hundred; Newton Abbot Union]
[2194]
OR C 1558-1859 M 1558-1949 B 1558-1949 (DRO) Some later baptisms recorded
    in St Leonard registers, below
BT CMB 1597-1702 with gaps; CB 1813-40 M 1813-37 (DRO)
Cop CMB 1558-1805 (DCRS/WSL); Extr C 1558-1686; 1607-1775 M 1558-1740;
    1692-1777 B 1558-1759; 1760-76 (Vols 10,19 BG/PCL)
Cop (Mf) (Torquay SP); 'Newton Abbot' Extr CM 1558-1805 (IGI); CM 1558-1805
    (Mf I SLC)
MI Extr (Whitmore MS, SG); Incledon 130 (NDA)

NEWTON ABBOT St. Leonard, Wolborough. Old St Leonard demolished 1836 except
for tower. Church preserved as a monument. New St Leonard erected 1834-35
OR C 1860-1920 M 1858-1981 (DRO) catalogued with Wolborough

NEWTON ABBOT St. Paul, Devon Square. Erected 1861, Chapelry annexed to
St Mary
OR C 1861-1951 M 1866-1968 (DRO) catalogued with Wolborough

NEWTON ABBOT All Saints, Highweek (or Teignweek) [Teignbridge Hundred;
Newton Abbot Union] [1109] Chapelry in KINGSTEIGNTON. Separate parish 1864.
Now with TEIGNGRACE
OR C 1653-1984 M 1653-1980 B 1653-1979 (DRO)
BT CMB 1609, 1614, 1617, 1631, 1638, 1663?, 1664, 1666, 1668, 1670-72,
1675, 1677-79, 1681, 1684, 1686, 1688, 1695, 1697, 1699-1700,
(1701-1812 ?); CMB 1819-20, CB 1830-31 M 1831 B 1837-40 (DRO)
Cop B 1813-37 (Ptd DFHS); B 1813-37 (SG); CMB 1609-38 from BT, 1654-1837
(DCRS/WSL); Extr C 1657-1719 M 1657-1745 B 1654-1759 (Vol 16, BG/PCL)
Cop (Mf) (Torquay SP); 'Highweek or Newton Bushel': Extr C 1609-38
M 1609-17, 1631-38, 1654-1837 (IGI); M 1609-17, 1631-38, 1654-1837
(Mf I SLC)
MI Incledon 136 (NDA)

NEWTON ABBOT St Mary, Newton Bushel, Highweek. Ancient chapelry.
Chapel-of-ease closed by 1900

NEWTON ABBOT Bradley Manor, Highweek. Chapel 1428

NEWTON ABBOT St Mary the Virgin, Abbotsbury. Erected 1904-08 in parish of
Highweek
OR C 1919-63 M 1907-81 catalogued with Highweek (DRO)

NEWTON ABBOT Wolborough Workhouse Chapel [1851 Religious Census]

NEWTON ABBOT (RC) St Augustine's Priory f 1863. Convent chapel, Augustinian
Canoneses of the Lateran. Closed 1983
OR C 1864+ D 1862+ (Inc, St Joseph's, Newton Abbot)
Cop D 1862-1982 (Catholic FHS)
MI (Catholic FHS)

NEWTON ABBOT (RC) Oratory of the Blessed Sacrament 1868-71 then St Joseph,
Queen Street,1871 [1882 Return]
OR C 1883+ M 1879+ D 1857+ Confirmations 1883+ (Inc) Confirmations 1876+
(Plymouth Diocesan Archives)

NEWTON ABBOT (Bapt) East Street, rebuilt 1818, 1860 [1851 Religious Census]
[1882 Return]
OR Church books 1819-71, 1874-1919 (Strict Baptist Historical Society
Library, Dunstable Baptist Chapel, Bedfordshire)

NEWTON ABBOT (Cong,later URC) Salem, Wolborough Street f 1662
[1851 Religious Census]. Erected 1836. Moved to Queen Street 1876
[1882 Return] Building now an office. Now at Avenue Road
OR C 1726-1837 (RG 4/445 PRO); C 1865-1901, 1908 M 1865-1867, 1891-1984
B 1865-1866, 1881-1901 (DRO)
Cop (Mf) C 1726-1837 (Mf DCRS/WSL, SG); Extr C 1726-1837 (IGI); C 1726-1837
(Mf I SLC)

NEWTON ABBOT (Presb/Unit) Newton Bushel. Licensed 1672. fl 1979
OR None known

NEWTON ABBOT (Ind/Cong) Providence, Wolborough f 1814. Closed
OR C 1817-37 (RG 4/1225 PRO)
Cop (Mf) C 1817-37 (Mf DCRS/WSL, SG); Extr C 1817-37 (IGI); C 1817-37
(Mf I SLC)

NEWTON ABBOT (Wes) Newton Abbot Circuit
OR C 1838-1943 (DRO)
Cop (Mf) C 1838-1943 (Mfc Torquay SP)

NEWTON ABBOT (Wes) Wolborough. Erected 1848 [1851 Religious Census]
OR for c.1811-37 see ASHBURTON CIRCUIT, BRIXHAM, TEIGNMOUTH
(RG 4/840,842,1220 PRO)

NEWTON ABBOT (Wes) Highweek
OR for c.1811-37 see BRIXHAM CIRCUIT, TEIGNMOUTH (RG 4/842,1220 PRO)

NEWTON ABBOT (Wes) Newton Bushell
OR for c.1811-37 see BRIXHAM, TEIGNMOUTH (RG 4/842,1220 PRO)

NEWTON ABBOT (Wes) Courtenay Street [1882 Return]
OR M 1868-1954 (DRO)

NEWTON ABBOT ((Wes) Keyberry Park. Erected 1909. fl c.1970

NEWTON ABBOT (Bible Christian) Newton Abbot Circuit
OR C 1865-1907 (DRO)
Cop (Mf) C 1865-1907 (Mfc Torquay SP)

NEWTON ABBOT (Bible Christian) Jubilee Chapel, Queen Street [1882 Return]

NEWTON ABBOT (Free Meth)
OR C 1896-1909 (DRO)
Cop (Mf) C 1896-1909 (Mfc Torquay SP)

NEWTON ABBOT (UMFC/U Meth) Courtenay Street [1882 Return]
OR C 1908-09 (DRO)

NEWTON ABBOT (U Meth) Queen Street
OR C 1911-32 (DRO)
Cop (Mf) C 1911-32 (Mfc Torquay SP)

NEWTON ABBOT (Meth) The Avenue. Erected 1909. fl c.1970

NEWTON ABBOT (Meth) Keybury Park Chapel see HENNOCK

NEWTON ABBOT (S of F) fl c.1761-64. Connected with BOVEY TRACEY

NEWTON ABBOT (Brethren) Building adjoining the British School Rooms, Station
Road [1882 Return]

NEWTON ABBOT Poor Law Union
OR None. ZD 1836-38 in letter book (DRO)

NEWTON BUSHEL   see NEWTON ABBOT

NEWTON FERRERS Holy Cross [Ermington Hundred; Plympton St Mary Union] [767]
Now with REVELSTOKE
OR C 1600-1954 M 1600-1968 B 1600-1960 (PWDRO)
BT CMB 1610, 1614, 1617-18, 1624, 1631?, 1633, 1639, 1677-78, 1686, 1690,
    1694-95, 1699 (1700-1812 ?); CB 1838-46, 1848-58, 1860-64, 1866-71
    C 1872 (DRO)
Cop (Mf) CMB 1600-1850 (DCRS/WSL); Extr CM 1600-1836 (IGI); CM 1600-1836
    (Mf I SLC)

NEWTON FERRERS (Wes) Erected 1849 [1851 Religious Census]
OR for c.1813-37 see PLYMOUTH Ebenezer (RG 4/1325 PRO)

NEWTON FERRERS (Prim Meth) Chapel [1882 Return] Building adjacent to a
cottage occupied by Mr Mannell, about 80 yards from the church [1882 Return]

NEWTON FERRERS (S of F) fl 18th cent. Part of PLYMOUTH MM

NEWTON POPPLEFORD   see AYLESBEARE

NEWTON ST CYRES St Cyr and St Julitta [Crediton Hundred; Crediton Union]
[1311] Now with RADDON
OR C 1554-1946 M 1555-1959 B 1554-1886 (DRO)
BT CMB 1608, 1610, 1624, 1630, 1631?, 1632, 1636, 1663-64, 1667, 1669-70,
    1672, 1675, 1677, 1697 (1698-1812 ?); CMB 1814, 1823-27, 1829, 1833-37
    CB 1839-49 (DRO)
Cop CMB 1554-1837 (DCRS/WSL, WSL); B 1752-1837 (DFHS); Extr C 1555-1789
    M 1557-1735 B 1556-1887 (SG); M 1554-1837 (Boyd); Extr C 1555-1718
    M 1557-1735 B 1556-1887 (Vol 18, BG/PCL)
Cop (Mf) Extr C 1564-1837 M 1555-1837 (IGI); C 1564-1837 M 1555-1837
    (Mf I SLC)
MI (I, DFHS); Extr (Whitmore MS, SG)

NEWTON ST CYRES (RC) Kirkham House, domestic chapel of Kirkham family.
Served by Benedictine monks 1752-55
OR None known

NEWTON ST CYRES (Wes)
OR for c.1818-31 see EXETER Mint (RG 4/1207 PRO)

NEWTON ST CYRES (Bible Christian) Erected 1864. Closed 1988

NEWTON ST PETROCK St Petrock [Shebbear Hundred; Bideford Union] [250]
Now with TORRIDGE
OR C 1578-1994 M 1578-1989 B 1737-1995 (NDRO) No earlier burials noted in
    1831
BT CMB 1607-08, 1611, 1617, 1619, 1621, 1624, 1626, 1638, 1668, 1670, 1674,
    1678-79, 1682-83, 1685?, 1688-91, 1696-97, 1699, 1704, 1707, 1711 or
    1712 (1713-1812 ?); C 1820-24, 1827-29, 1832-35, 1837, 1840-42, 1848-49
    M 1823, 1829-30, 1832-34 B 1821-24, 1827, 1829, 1833-35, 1837, 1841-42,
    1848-49 (DRO)
Cop C 1578-1812 M 1578-1811 B 1723-1812 (Ms DCRS/WSL, C of A); CMB 1607-1812
    from BT, 1578-1837 (Ts DCRS/WSL, SG); M 1578-1812 (Boyd)
Cop (Mf) Extr C 1578-1837 M 1578-1642, 1654-1837 (IGI); C 1578-1837
    M 1578-1642, 1654-1837 (Mf I SLC)
MI Extr 1952 (Ts SG)

NEWTON ST PETROCK (Bapt) f 1825 [1851 Religious Census]; now Torridge
Fellowship

NEWTON ST PETROCK (Bible Christian) Pourches, a house [1851 Religious Census]

NEWTON TRACEY St Thomas à Beckett [Fremington Hundred; Barnstaple Union] [111] Now with TWO RIVERS
<u>OR</u> C 1566-1812 M 1570-1677, 1721-1754, 1786-1978 B 1562-1993 NDRO)
<u>BT</u> CMB 1607-08, 1610-11, 1613-14, 1619, 1630, 1638, 1670, 1674, 1678-79, 1682-83, 1685, 1688, 1690-92, 1694-97, 1699-1700, 1704-09, 1712-15, 1785 (1786-1812 ?); C 1813-18, 1820-43, 1845-50, 1855 M 1813, 1819, 1822-24, 1826-28, 1831-33, 1835, 1838 B 1813-16, 1820, 1822-26, 1828-31, 1833-35, 1837, 1840-43, 1845-50, 1855 (DRO)
<u>Cop</u> B 1725-1837 (Ptd DFHS); C 1569-1837 M 1570-1837 B 1562-1837 (DCRS/WSL, DRO, NDA, WSL, DFHS, SG); B 1725-1837 (DLS, WSL)
<u>MI</u> (I, NDA)

NEWTON TRACEY (S of F) Meeting at Loverings farmhouse by 1782; burial ground given 1782. Closed 1834. see CULLOMPTON AND SPICELAND MM. *see also* M.Oliver 'Notes on Newton Tracey and a forgotten Quaker burying ground' TDA 86: 1955: 161-5)

NEWTOWN   *see* NYMPTON, BISHOP'S

NORTH ALLINGTON   *see* ALLINGTON, EAST

NORTH BOVEY   *see* BOVEY, NORTH

NORTH BRENT   *see* BRENTOR

NORTH CREEDY   *see* CREEDY, NORTH

NORTH DEVON COAST United benefice including COMBE MARTIN, BERRYNARBOR, LYNTON, BARBROOK, BRENDON, COUNTISBURY, LYNMOUTH, PARRACOMBE, MARTINHOE, TRENTISHOE

NORTH HUISH   *see* HUISH, NORTH

NORTH KENN   *see* KENN, NORTH

NORTH KEYHAM   *see* DEVONPORT St Mark, Ford

NORTH MOLTON   *see* MOLTON, NORTH

NORTH PETHERWIN   *see* PETHERWIN, NORTH

NORTH POOL   *see* POOL, SOUTH

NORTH SUTTON   united benefice with PLYMOUTH Emmanuel, St Paul Efford

NORTH TAWTON   *see* TAWTON, NORTH

NORTHAM St Margaret [Shebbear Hundred; Bideford Union] [2727]
Now with TORRIDGE ESTUARY
<u>OR</u> C 1538-1969 M 1606-1965 B 1541-1971 (NDRO) No earlier marriages noted in 1831
<u>BT</u> CMB 1607, 1610, 1612, 1614, 1617, 1621, 1624, 1629, 1634, 1636, 1674, 1678-79, 1682-83, 1685, 1689, 1691, 1694-96, 1699-1700, 1702-03, 1705-07, 1710-12, 1714-15 (1716-1812 ?); CB 1820-21, 1823-26, 1828-30, 1832-51 M 1820-26, 1828-30, 1832-36 (DRO)

NORTHAM cont.
Cop C 1538-1836 M 1606-1836 B 1541-1836 (DCRS/WSL); M 1601-1837 (Boyd)
Cop (Mf) (Appledore SP); Extr C 1538-1836 M 1606-1836 (IGI); C 1538-1836
        M 1606-1836 (Mf I SLC)
MI (I, DFHS)

NORTHAM St Mary, Appledore. Erected 1838. Parish created 1841 from Northam.
Now with TORRIDGE ESTUARY
OR CMB 1844-1920 (NDRO)
Cop M 1844-94 (I, SG)
Cop (Mf) (Appledore SP)

NORTHAM Holy Trinity, Westward Ho ! Chapel-of-ease erected 1867-70. Now with
TORRIDGE ESTUARY
OR M 1939-49 (NDRO)

NORTHAM (Bapt) Ebenezer, Meeting Street, Appledore. f.1833 [1851 Religious
Census] Rebuilt 1858 [1882 Return]
OR Z 1831-37 (RG 4/950 PRO); M 1902-42 (NDRO)
Cop Z 1834-37 (SG); M 1802-90 (DLS)
Cop (Mf) Z 1834-37 (Mf DCRS/WSL, SG); Extr Z 1831-37 (IGI)

NORTHAM (Bapt) Nelson Road, Westward Ho! f 1887

NORTHAM (Bapt) Bethel, Appledore. Erected 1834 [1851 Religious Census]

NORTHAM (Ind/Cong later URC) Great Meeting f 1662; Meeting Street,
Appledore. Rebuilt 1816 [1851 Religious Census] United with Northam and
Bideford
OR C 1755-1994 M 1862-1991 B 1898-1961 (NDRO)
Cop Z 1755-1860 (DLS)

NORTHAM (Cong) Erected 1829 [1851 Religious Census] Closed c.1868

NORTHAM (Cong) The Square, Northam [1882 Return] United with Appledore and
Bideford
OR C 1890-1993 (NDRO)

NORTHAM (Wes) Cross Street. Erected 1835 [1851 Religious Census] Rebuilt
1878 [1882 Return] fl c.1970
OR for c.1819-37 see BIDEFORD (RG 4/955 PRO)

NORTHAM (Wes) Richmond Road, Appledore. Erected 1851 [1882 Return]
fl c.1970

NORTHAM (Bible Christian) Ebenezer, West Appledore, in former Bapt chapel
[1882 Return]

NORTHAM (Wes) Appledore. Erected 1830 [1851 Religious Census] [1882 Return]
OR for c.1819-37 see BIDEFORD (RG 4/955 PRO)

NORTHAM (Wes) Appledore Street, Northam [1882 Return]

NORTHAM (Brethren) A building, the property of John Fishwick, on the Quay,
Appledore [1882 Return]

NORTHAM Cemetery
OR B 1950-82 (NDRO)

NORTHLEIGH St Giles [Colyton Hundred; Honiton Union] [340] Now with COLYTON
OR C 1700-1994 M 1708-1978 B 1697-1993 (DRO) No earlier registers noted in
   1831
BT CMB 1614, 1617, 1620, 1624-26, 1633, 1635-36, 1667, 1668?, 1669-71,
   1673, 1675, 1679, 1683, 1685, 1687, 1690, 1695-97, 1699, 1729-31, 1735,
   1737, 1739, 1740?, 1743-48, 1750-75, 1777, 1779-1802, 1804-09, 1811-12;
   C 1813-40 M 1813-19, 1821-24, 1826-28, 1830-32, 1834, 1838 B 1814-40
   (DRO)
Cop CMB 1700-1812 (DCRS/WSL)
Cop (Mf) (Colyton SP); Extr C 1700-1812 M 1708-1812 (IGI); C 1700-1812
   M 1708-1812 (Mf I SLC)
MI (I, DFHS); Incledon 509 (NDA)

NORTHLEW   see LEW, NORTH

NOSS MAYO   see REVELSTOKE

NYMET BISHOP or **NYMET EPISCOPI** see NYMPTON, BISHOP'S

NYMET REGIS   see KINGSNYMPTON

NYMET ROWLAND St Bartholomew [North Tawton and Winkleigh Hundred;
Crediton Union] [99] Now with LAPFORD, COLDRIDGE
OR C 1719-1981 M 1734-1981 B 1734-1980 (NDRO) No earlier registers noted in
   1831
BT CMB 1602, 1607, 1611, 1615-16, 1633, 1635, 1668, 1670, 1675, 1678, 1683,
   1688-90, 1694, 1700, 1712, 1714-15 (1716-1812 ?); C 1838-43,
   1845-46 B 1840-41, 1843, 1845-46 (DRO)
Cop CMB 1719-1812 (DCRS/WSL); C 1719-1812 M 1734-55 B 1734-1812 (SG)
Cop (Mf) Extr C 1719-1812 M 1724-53 (IGI); C 1719-1812 (Mf I SLC)

NYMET ROWLAND (Brethren) Cottage [1851 Religious Census]

NYMET ST GEORGE or GEORGE NYMPTON St George [South Molton Hundred;
South Molton Union] [268] Now with SOUTH MOLTON
OR C 1599-1958 M 1599-1943 B 1600-1992 (NDRO)
BT CMB 1598-1602, 1607, 1610, 1617, 1621, 1633, 1635, 1670, 1672, 1674,
   1679, 1783, 1688-91, 1694-97, 1704, 1706, 1710-12, 1714-15, 1717-22,
   1726-28, 1732, 1734-35, 1737-38, 1742-43, 1745, 1749-54, 1762-64, 1766,
   1768-75, 1777-84, 1786-1813; C 1838-50, 1852, 1872-74, 1878 B 1838-48,
   1851-52, 1872-74, 1878 (DRO)
Cop CMB 1599-1812 (NDRO)
MI (I, NDA)

NYMET ST GEORGE (Bible Christian) Providence. n.d. [1851 Religious Census];
new chapel 1862 [1882 Return] Closed 1977

NYMET TRACEY   see BOW

NYMPTON, BISHOP'S or BISHOPSNYMPTON or NYMET EPISCOPI, or NYMET BISHOP
St Mary the Virgin [Witheridge Hundred; South Molton Union] [1116]
Peculiar of the Bishop of Exeter until 1848. Now with OAKMOOR
OR C 1556-1662, 1690-1986 M 1558-1660, 1677-1987 B 1557-1987 (NDRO)
BT CMB 1607, 1610, 1613-14, 1632-33, 1641, 1663-64, 1668, 1670-71, 1673-75,
   1677-84, 1686-87, 1689-1705, 1707, 1730 (1731-1812 ?); CB 1814-36,
   1839-66 M 1814-62, 1864-66 (DRO)

NYMPTON, BISHOP'S cont.
Cop CMB 1607-14, 1633 from BT (Ptd Granville); B 1813-37 (Ptd DFHS);
    CMB 1556-1837 (DCRS/WSL); CMB 1607-14, 1633 M 1558-1600 (SG); B 1813-37
    (SG); M 1601-60 (Boyd)
Cop (Mf) Extr C 1556-1837 M 1558-1837 (IGI); C 1556-1837 M 1558-1837
    (Mf I SLC)
MI (I, NDA); (I, DFHS)

NYMPTON, BISHOP'S (Wes) Erected 1837 [1851 Religious Census] Rebuilt 1857 ?
fl c.1970
OR for c.1807-37 see BARNSTAPLE CIRCUIT (RG 4/954 PRO)

NYMPTON, BISHOP'S (Wes) Newtown. Erected 1849 [1851 Religious Census]
[1882 Return] fl c.1970

NYMPTON, BISHOP'S (Prim Meth) South Rock [1882 Return]

NYMPTON, BISHOP'S (S of F) fl c.1707-18

NYMPTON, KING'S see KINGSNYMPTON

OAKFORD St Peter [Witheridge Hundred; Tiverton Union] [497]
Now with EXE VALLEY
OR C 1568-1853 M 1568-1993 B 1568-1892 (DRO)
BT CMB 1597-1602, 1607-08, 1614, 1622, 1630, 1668, 1670, 1672, 1679,
    1682-83, 1689-91, 1695-96, 1708, 1710-12, 1714-15 (1716-1812 ?);
    C 1814-38, 1841-60 M 1814-31, 1834-35, 1841-46 B 1814-38, 1841-56,
    1858-60 (DRO)
Cop CMB 1568-1812 (DCRS/WSL, SG);
Cop (Mf) (Tiverton SP); Extr CM 1568-1812 (IGI); CM 1568-1812 (Mf I SLC)

OAKFORD (Wes)
OR for c.1812-37 see TIVERTON (RG 4/342 PRO)

OAKFORD (Bible Christian) n.d. [1851 Religious Census]; Spurway Mill
[1882 Return]

OAKHAMPTON see OKEHAMPTON

OAKMOOR United benefice including BISHOP'S NYMPTON, ROSE ASH, MARIANSLEIGH,
MOLLAND, KNOWSTONE, EAST ANSTEY, WEST ANSTEY

OFFWELL St Mary [Colyton Hundred; Honiton Union] [385] Now with COLYTON
OR C 1551-1885 M 1554-1954 B 1551-1965 (DRO)
BT CMB 1616-17, 1620, 1626, 1629, 163?, 1663, 1669-70, 1672, 1675, 1678,
    1685, 1687, 1690, 1696-97 (1698-1812 ?); CMB 1813-21, 1823-36 CB 1837-43
    M 1838-42 (DRO)
Cop B 1800-37 (Ptd DFHS); B 1800-37 (WSL, SG); CMB 1551-1840 (DCRS/WSL, WSL)
Cop (Mf) (Colyton SP); B 1943-64 (Mfc SG); Extr C 1551-1840 M 1554-1840
        (IGI); C 1551-1840 M 1554-1840 (Mf I SLC)
MI (I, DFHS); Incledon 480 (NDA)

OFFWELL (Bapt) Wilmington Chapel. Erected 1835 [1851 Religious Census]

OGBEAR see TAVISTOCK

OGWELL, EAST now with WEST OGWELL as St Bartholomew, Ogwell [Wonford
Hundred; Newton Abbot Union]   [318] Now with DENBURY
OR CM 1674-1996 M 1675-1996 (DRO)
BT CMB 1608-09, 1613, 1616-17, 1635, 1663-64, 1667, 1669, 1671-72, 1675,
    1678-79, 1683, 1687, 1690, 1696, 1699, 1750-54, 1757-62, 1765, 1767,
    1770, 1772, 1774-80 (1781-1812 ?); C 1813-40 M 1813-19, 1824-25,
    1827-28, 1830-37 B 1813-20, 1822-25, 1827-40 (DRO)
Cop Extr C 1741-46 M 1732-40 B 1675-1736 (Vol 16, BG/PCL)
Cop (Mf) C 1674-1909 M 1675-1837 B 1674-1812 (Mfc SG)
MI (Ptd M.Adams 'Some notes on the churches and manors of East and West
    Ogwell': TDA 32:1900: 229-48)

OGWELL, EAST (Presb) fl *c.*1672-90

OGWELL, WEST dedication unknown [Wonford Hundred; Newton Abbot Union]   [50]
Formerly united with East Ogwell. Redundant. Churches Conservation Trust
OR C 1684-1979 M 1695-1976 B 1696-1988 (DRO) Noted in 1831: CMB 1681+
BT CMB 1613, 1635, 1639, 1670-72, 1676-78, 1683, 1687, 1690, 1696-97, 1699,
    1701, 1750-54, 1757-58, 1760, 1762, 1765, 1767, 1771, 1774, 1776-77,
    1780 (1781-1812 ?); C 1813-19, 1821-26, 1828-31 M 1815-16, 1820-21,
    1827, 1831-33 B 1815-16, 1818, 1823, 1825-29, 1831-33 (DRO)
Cop Extr CMB 1685-1747 (Vol 16, BG/PCL)
Cop (Mf) C 1684-1811 M 1695-1843 B 1696-1812 (Mfc SG)
MI *see* EAST OGWELL

OKEHAMPTON United benefice including OKEHAMPTON, INWARDLEIGH, BRATTON
CLOVELLY, GERMANSWEEK, NORTHLEW, BRIDESTOWE, SOURTON

OKEHAMPTON All Saints [part Black Torrington Hundred; part Lifton Hundred;
Okehampton Union]   [2055] Now with Okehampton united benefice
OR C 1634-1929 M 1634-1951 B 1634-1949 (DRO)
BT CMB 1609, 1611, 1613-14, 1635, 1641, 1663-64, 1666, 1668-72, 1674-76,
    1678-79, 1681-82, 1684, 1686-88, 1694 (1695-1812 ?); CB 1813-38, 1856-62
    M 1813-37 (DRO)
Cop CMB 1608-26 from BT, 1634-1843 with index (DCRS/WSL); Extr CMB 1685-1785
    C 1720-74 M 1719-93 (Vol 1, BG/PCL)
Cop (Mf) (Okehampton SP); Extr C 1608-1843 M 1608-1706, 1717-1837 (IGI);
        C 1608-1843 M 1608-1706, 1717-1837 (Mf I SLC)

OKEHAMPTON St James, Fore Street. Proprietary chapel. Rebuilt 1862. Now with
OKEHAMPTON
OR C 1911-40 (DRO)

OKEHAMPTON (RC) St Boniface, Station Road 1906

OKEHAMPTON (Bapt) Fore Street f 1882
OR M 1909-86 (DRO)

OKEHAMPTON (Ind/Cong, later URC Ebenezer, North Lane f 1799. Erected 1822
[1851 Religious Census] [1882 Return] Closed 1974; joined Okehampton Meth.
OR ZC 1799-1810, 1821-36 B 1829-37 (RG 4/446,447,1214 PRO). None later.
Cop (Mf) ZC 1799-1810, 1821-36 B 1829-37 (Mf DCRS/WSL, SG);
        Extr ZC 1799-1836 (IGI); ZC 1799-1836 (Mf I SLC)

OKEHAMPTON (Presb) f pre-1690; fl *c.*1772
OR *see* HATHERLEIGH

OKEHAMPTON (Wes) Okehampton or Moretonhampstead Circuit
OR C 1815-37 (RG 4/1089 PRO)
Cop ZC 1815-37 (SG)
Cop (Mf) C 1815-37 (Mf DCRS/WSL, SG); Extr C 1815-37 (IGI); C 1815-37
    (Mf I SLC)

OKEHAMPTON (Wes) [1882 Return]
OR for c.1806-31 see CULLOMPTON (RG 4/958 PRO)

OKEHAMPTON (Wes/Meth) Fairplace. Erected 1904. fl c.1970
OR C 1946+ M 1900+ (Ch Sec)

OKEHAMPTON (Bible Christian) Cruft [1882 Return]

OKEHAMPTON (Bible Christian/Meth) East Street [1882 Return] United with
Fairplace
OR None

OKEHAMPTON (Meth) North Lew and Okehampton Circuit
OR C 1934-67 (DRO)

OKEHAMPTON (Meth) Circuit
OR C 1937-46 (DRO)

OKEHAMPTON (Meth) East Street
OR M 1954-64 (DRO)

OKEHAMPTON (Wes) f c.1691; meeting house rebuilt 1739, 1773. Part of NORTH
TAWTON/CREDITON MM. Joined EXETER MM 1706

OLDRIDGE   see EXETER

ORESTON   see PLYMSTOCK

OTTER VALE United benefice including OTTERY ST MARY, WIGGATON, WEST HILL,
ALFINGTON, TIPTON, VENN OTTERY

OTTERTON St Michael [East Budleigh Hundred; St Thomas Union] [1178]
Now with EAST BUDLEIGH, BICTON
OR C 1559-1984 M 1559-1995 B 1559-1965 (DRO)
BT CMB 1609-10, 1613, 1615-16, 1618, 1624-26, 1629-30, 1635-37, 1663,
    1664?, 1666, 1667?, 1668?, 1669, 1670?, 1672-73, 1675, 1677?, 1678,
    1683, 1685, 1687, 1690, 1695-97, 1699 (1700-1812 ?); CB 1813-38
    M 1813-37 (DRO)
Cop B 1813-37 (Ptd DFHS); CMB 1558-1720 (DCRS/WSL); CMB 1558-1837 (Great
    Card Index, SG); B 1813-37 (WSL, SG); M 1559-1659 (Boyd)
Cop (Mf) Extr C 1558-1700 M 1559-1700 (IGI); C 1558-1700 M 1559-1700
    (Mf I SLC)
MI Incledon 681 (NDA)

OTTERTON (Presb) fl c.1672-90

OTTERTON (Wes)
OR for c.1820-37 see BUDLEIGH (RG 4/517 PRO)

OTTERTON (Brethren) Erected c.1830 [1851 Religious Census]

OTTERY ST MARY St Mary the Virgin [Ottery St Mary Hundred; Honiton Union]
[3849] Now with OTTER VALE
<u>OR</u> C 1601-1885 M 1601-1663, 1679-1973 B 1601-1812, 1865-1923 (DRO)
<u>BT</u> CMB 1608-09, 1613, 1616, 1626, 1630-32, 1636-37, 1675, B 1683, 1685,
    1687, 1690, 1696-97, 1699, CMB 1717 (1718-1812 ?); CB 1813-74 M 1813-37
    (DRO)
<u>Cop</u> CMB 1601-1837 Banns 1653-60 (Ptd DCRS 2 vols 1908-29); CB 1601-1837
    index only (DRO); CMB 1601-35 with index (DCRS/WSL); M 1601-1837 (Boyd);
    M 1790-1837 (Pallot); Extr CB 1601-1723 M 1601-1753 (Vol 3, BG/PCL)
<u>Cop (Mf)</u> Extr CM 1601-1837 (IGI); C 1601-1837 (Mf I SLC)
<u>MI</u> Ch extr (Ptd S.Cornish *Short Notes on the Church and Parish of Ottery
    St Mary*: n.d.: 20-3); Incledon 534 (NDA)

OTTERY ST MARY St John, Tipton. Erected 1840. Parish created 1841 from
Ottery St Mary. United 1933 with VENN OTTERY. Now with OTTER VALE
<u>OR</u> C 1840-1905 B 1834-49 (DRO)

OTTERY ST MARY St Philip and St James, Escot. Erected 1838. Parish created
1844 from Ottery St Mary, TALATON. Now with FENITON, BUCKERELL
<u>OR</u> C 1840-1923 M 1869-1978 B 1840-1884 (DRO)

OTTERY ST MARY St Michael the Archangel, West Hill. Erected 1846. Parish
created 1863 from Ottery St Mary. Now with OTTER VALE
<u>OR</u> CB 1846+ M 1869+ (Inc)

OTTERY ST MARY St James and St Anne, Alfington. Erected 1849-52. Parish
created 1882 from Ottery St Mary. Now with OTTER VALE
<u>OR</u> M 1884-1974 (DRO)

OTTERY ST MARY St Edward the Confessor, Wiggaton. Chapel-of-ease erected
1893. Now with OTTER VALE

OTTERY ST MARY (RC) St Anthony, Mill Street. New chapel 1935

OTTERY ST MARY (Presb/Ind/Cong, later URC) Jesu Street. Licensed 1672
[*Cong. Year Book* 1851] Batt's Lane [1882 Return]
<u>OR</u> CB 1746-1837 (RG 4/2029,2100 PRO); C 1746-1938 M 1839-1937 B 1746-1955;
    unfit for production; M 1906-47 (DRO)
<u>Cop (Mf)</u> CB 1746-1837 (Mf DCRS/WSL, SG); Extr C 1746-1837 (IGI); C 1746-1837
    (Mf I SLC)

OTTERY ST MARY (Ind) Yonder Street. Erected 1700. [1851 Religious Census]

OTTERY ST MARY (Ind) Meternite. Part of house, erected c.1836
[1851 Religious Census]

OTTERY ST MARY (Ind) West Hill [1851 Religious Census] [1882 Return]

OTTERY ST MARY (Wes) Mill Street. Erected 1829 [1882 Return] fl *c.*1970
<u>OR</u> for c.1809-37 see AXMINSTER, BARNSTAPLE, EXETER (RG 4/512,954,1207,1208
    PRO)

PAIGNTON St John the Baptist, Church Street [Haytor Hundred; Totnes Union] [1960] *see also* MARLDON
OR C 1559-1994 M 1559-1992 B 1559-1925 (DRO)
BT CMB 1597-1602, 1609-10, 1614, 1616, 1618, 1629, 1636, B 1644-61,
    CMB 1681-84, 1687-91, 1693-95, 1698-1702, 1704-06, 1730 (1731-1812 ?);
    CB 1821-23, 1826, 1828, 1833-36 M 1820-23, 1826, 1828, 1833-36 (DRO)
Cop CMB 1559-1827 (DCRS/WSL)
Cop (Mf) (Torquay SP); Extr CM 1559-1837 (IGI); CM 1559-1837 (Mf I SLC)
MI Ch 1971-78 (Torquay Central Lib); (I, DFHS); Ch 1874 (Ts SG);
    Extr (Whitmore MS, SG)

PAIGNTON St Mary the Virgin, Collaton St Mary. Parish created 1864 from Paignton St John. Now with STOKE GABRIEL
OR C 1865-1959 M 1866-1976 B 1866-1947 (DRO)

PAIGNTON St Andrew, Sands Road. Erected 1875; new building 1892. In parish of Paignton St John
OR C 1875+ ?; no MB (Inc)

PAIGNTON Christchurch, Torquay Road. Erected 1888. Parish created 1889 from Paignton St John
OR C 1888+ Banns 1967+ M 1889+ Confirmations 1937-94; no burials (Inc)

PAIGNTON St Michael. Mission church opened 1896; closed 1978. Redundant. Owned by Housing Association
OR C 1913-74 (DRO)

PAIGNTON St Paul, Torquay Road, Preston. Erected 1909. Rebuilt 1912, 1939. Parish created 1948 from Paignton Christchurch
OR C 1908+ M 1948+ B 1969+ (Inc)

PAIGNTON St Boniface, Belfield Road. Opened 1961, in parish of Paignton St John
OR C 1961+; no MB (Inc)

PAIGNTON St George, Barn Road, Goodrington. Erected 1938.
OR (Inc)

PAIGNTON R.A.F. Chaplaincy
OR C 1941-44, 1954-56 (AFCC)

PAIGNTON (RC) Blagdon. Domestic chapel of Blount family. fl *c*.1719
OR none known

PAIGNTON (RC) St Mary's Hill 1882-98, then Sacred Heart. New church 1931
OR C 1882+ M 1891+ B 1882+ Confirmations 1890+ (Inc)

PAIGNTON (RC) St Peter Chanel, Foxhole

PAIGNTON (Bapt) Erected 1837 [1851 Religious Census]

PAIGNTON (Bapt) Barnshill [1882 Return]

PAIGNTON (Bapt) Winner Street f 1886

PAIGNTON (Bapt) Preston, Old Torquay Road f 1928

PAIGNTON (Bapt) Roselands Christian Fellowship f 1994

PAIGNTON (Ind/Cong, later URC) f 1818 [1851 Religious Census] [1882 Return];
Cecil Road, formerly Spratts Lane, erected 1823; sold to Bible Christians
1884. Later Dartmouth Road
OR ZC 1818-37 B 1826-36 (RG 4/2536 PRO)
Cop (Mf) C 1818-37 B 1826-36 (Mf DCRS/WSL, SG); Extr ZC 1818-37 (IGI);
        ZC 1818-37 (Mf I SLC)

PAIGNTON (URC) Smallcombe Road, Foxhole f 1954

PAIGNTON (URC) Central Church, Tor Hill Road f 1974

PAIGNTON (Wes) [1882 Return]
OR for c.1811-37 see BRIXHAM (RG 4/842 PRO)

PAIGNTON (Wes) Palace Avenue. Erected 1890. fl c.1970
OR C 1845-1935 (DRO)

PAIGNTON (Wes) St Michael's, Merritt Road. Erected 1911. fl c.1970
OR C 1966, 1984 (DRO)

PAIGNTON (Bible Christian) Cecil Road, Southfield. Purchased 1884 from Cong
(erected 1823) fl c.1970

PAIGNTON (U Meth) Preston Chapel
OR C 1911-64 (DRO)

PAIGNTON (Meth) Grange Road, Goodrington. Erected 1966

PANCRASWEEK or PANCRASWYKE or WEEK ST PANCRAS St Pancras [Black Torrington
Hundred; Holsworthy Union] [526] Chapelry in BRADWORTHY. United 1959 with
PYWORTHY. Now also with BRIDGERULE
OR C 1655-1977 M 1655-1975 B 1653-1977 (DRO)
BT CMB 1611, 1627, 1636, 1638-39, 1668-74, 1676-82, 1695-97, 1699-1700,
    1708, 1714 (1715-1812 ?); CMB 1813-37 CB 1819-41 M 1819-37 (DRO)
Cop M 1813-37 (Ptd DFHS); CMB 1653-1837 (DCRS/WSL)
Cop (Mf) Extr C 1654-1837 M 1655-84, 1696-1837 (IGI); C 1654-1837 M 1655-84,
        1696-1837 (Mf I SLC)
MI Extr (Whitmore MS, SG)

PANCRASWEEK (Wes) Lana Farm. Erected 1838 [1882 Return] fl c.1970
OR for c.1817-37 see HOLSWORTHY (RG 4/1210 PRO)

PARKHAM St James [Shebbear Hundred; Bideford Union] [923]
Now with HARTLAND COAST
OR C 1538-1843 M 1537-1598, 1629-1978 B 1538-1871 (NDRO)
BT CMB 1597-1601, 1602-03, 1608, 1610, 1612, 1614, 1617, 1668, 1670, 1672,
    1674, 1678-79, 1682-83, 1685, 1688-91, 1694-97, 1699-1702, 1704,
    1707-08, 1710-12, 1714-15 (1716-1812 ?); CMB 1813-15, CB 1821-38, 1840
    M 1821-37 (DRO)
Cop CMB 1537-1812 (Ptd DCRS: 1906); M 1812-37 (DCRS/WSL, SG); M 1538-1837
    (Boyd); M 1790-1812 (Pallot)
Cop (Mf) (Appledore SP); Extr C 1537-1812 M 1813-37 (IGI); C 1537-1812
        M 1813-37 (Mf I SLC)
MI (Ptd DCRS, as above); (I, NDA)

PARKHAM (RC) Domestic chapel of Risdon family from 16th cent. Moved to
Harberton early 18th cent.
OR None known

PARKHAM (Wes) Erected 1833 [1851 Religious Census]
OR for c.1807-37 see BARNSTAPLE CIRCUIT, BIDEFORD (RG 4/854,955 PRO)

PARKHAM (Wes) Holwell. Erected 1823 [1851 Religious Census] [1882 Return]
Closed 1972. Now a house
OR C 1927-61 (NDRO)

PARKHAM (Wes) Erected 1888. fl c.1970

PARKHAM (Bible Christian/Meth) Goldworthy. Erected 1834 [1851 Religious
Census] Rebuilt 1854 ? [1882 Return] Closed 1972
OR C 1959-67 (NDRO)

PARRACOMBE St Helen (or St Petrock or St Peter) [Shirwell Hundred;
Barnstaple Union] [409] Redundant. Churches Conservation Trust
OR C 1687-1997 M 1687-1992 B 1687-1979 (NDRO)
BT CMB 1597-1601, 1607-08, 1610, 1613-14, 1620, 1625, 1631, 1635, 1668,
    1670-72, 1674, 1678-79, 1682, 1684, 1687, 1689-91, 1694-97, 1699-1700,
    1703-04, 1712, 1714-15 (1716-1812 ?); CB 1813-37, 1840-59, 1863-66
    M 1814-36 (DRO)
Cop CMB 1597-1683 from BT, 1687-1837 (Ptd DCRS 1917); M 1597-1837 (Boyd);
    M 1790-1837 (Pallot)
Cop (Mf) Extr C 1597-1836 M 1598-1837 (IGI); C 1597-1836 (Mf I SLC)
MI (I, DFHS); Ch, cy (Ptd Dwelly 47-70); Incledon 640 (NDA)

PARRACOMBE Christ Church, Erected 1878. Now parish church. Now with NORTH
DEVON COAST
MI Ch, cy (Ptd Dwelly 44-7)

PARRACOMBE (Wes) Erected 1839 [1851 Religious Census] [1882 Return]
fl c.1970
OR for c.1807-37 see BARNSTAPLE CIRCUIT (RG 4/954 PRO)

PATHFINDER VILLAGE   see WHITESTONE

PAYHEMBURY St Mary the Virgin [Hayridge Hundred; Honiton Union]   [542]
Now with BROADHEMBURY, PLYMTREE
OR C 1559-1562, 1679-1944 M 1593-1754, 1813-1978 B 1678-1991 (DRO)
M 1559-91 lost
BT CMB 1608, 1610, 1614, 1617, 1629, 1634, 1638, 1663, 1666-67, 1679-70,
    1672, 1675, 1678, 1683, 1685, 1687, 1690, 1694-95, 1697, 1703
    (1704-1812 ?); CB 1813-46, 1850, 1854 M 1813-46 (DRO)
Cop B 1800-37 (Ptd DFHS); B 1800-37 (SG)
Cop (Mf) (Colyton SP)
MI Incledon 232 (NDA)

PEATCOTT   see LYDFORD

PENNYCROSS   see PLYMOUTH

PETER TAVY or PETERTAVY or TAVY ST PETER St Peter [part Lifton Hundred;
part Roborough Hundred; Tavistock Union]   [500] see also BUCKLND MONACHORUM
St John, Horrabridge. Now with MARY TAVY, LYDFORD, BRENT TOR
OR C 1674-1868 M 1679-1977 B 1679-1868 (DRO)
BT CMB 1612, 1614, 1617-20, 1624, 1633, 1663, 1666, 1669-72, 1674-75,
    1676?, 1677-82, 1684, 1686, 1690, 1694-97, 1699-1700 (1701-1812 ?);
    CB 1813-30 M 1813, 1815, 1817-30 (DRO)

PETER TAVY cont.
<u>Cop</u> M 1679-1754 (I, Ptd, edit M.Brown, Dartmoor Press 1999); M 1679-1837
(DFHS); B 1674-1996 (I, PWDRO); Extr C 1675-1799 M 1722-34
B 1682-1789 (Vol 20, BG/PCL)
<u>Cop (Mf)</u> (Tavistock SP)
<u>MI</u> (Ptd DRMI 10: 1998); (I, DFHS)

PETER TAVY (Wes) Erected 1834 [1851 Religious Census]; rebuilt 1881
[1882 Return] fl *c*.1970
<u>OR</u> for *c*.1808-37 *see* TAVISTOCK (RG 4/341 PRO)

PETERSMARLAND St Peter [Shebbear Hundred; Torrington Union]   [356]
Rebuilt 1865. Now with TORRIDGE
<u>OR</u> C 1696-1913 M 1697-1980 B 1696-1997 (NDRO)
<u>BT</u> CMB 1602, 1607, 1610, 1623?, 1627, 1638, 1674, 1682-83, 1686, 1690-91,
1694-97, 1699, 1702-03, 1712, 1714-15 (1716-1812 ?); C 1813-25, 1828-36,
1838-42 M 1813-18, 1820-25, 1828-36 B 1813-25, 1828, 1830-36, 1838-42
(DRO)
<u>Cop (Mf)</u> C 1696-1913 M 1697-1980 B 1696-1812 (Mfc SG)

PETERSMARLAND (Bible Christian/Meth) House [1851 Religious Census]
Chapel erected 1870. fl *c*.1970

PETERSMARLAND (Bible Christian) Henry Stevens' cottage, Swellaton
[1882 Return]

PETHERWIN, NORTH [Black Torrington Hundred from 1844; Launceston Union
(Cornwall)] [1044] In Devon 1844-1966, see NIPR Vol 8 Part 4 Cornwall

PETROCKSTOWE St Petrock [Shebbear Hundred; Torrington Union]   [581] Now with
TORRIDGE
<u>OR</u> C 1597-1860 M 1597-1979 B 1597-1908 (NDRO)
<u>BT</u> CMB 1602, 1607, 1614, 1617, 1619, 1632, 1668, 1670, 1674-75, 1679, 1682,
1694-95, 1697, 1699-1700, 1702-04, 1706, 1709-12, 1714-15 (1716-1812 ?);
none listed after 1812 (DRO)
<u>Cop (Mf)</u> C 1597-1860 M 1597-1979 B 1597-1908 (Mfc SG)
<u>MI</u> Incledon 1069 (NDA)

PETROCKSTOWE (Wes) Erected 1834 [1851 Religious Census] [1882 Return]
New chapel 1934. fl *c*.1970
<u>OR</u> for *c*.1819-37 *see* BIDEFORD (RG 4/955 PRO)

PETROCKSTOWE (Bible Christian) Brandis Hill. Erected 1830 [1851 Religious
Census]; a building [1882 Return]

PETTON   *see* BAMPTON

PILTON St Mary the Virgin [Braunton Hundred; Barnstaple Union 1835-94]
[1819] United 1945 with ASHFORD. Now with BARNSTAPLE
<u>OR</u> C 1569-1948 M 1569-1965 B 1566-1946 (NDRO)
<u>BT</u> CMB 1597-1602, 1607-08, 1610-14, 1617, 1668, 1670, 1674, 1678-79,
1682-83, 1688-89, 1691, 1694-97, 1699-1700, 1702-05, 1707-09, 1712,
1714-16, 1718-23, 1725-28, 1732-43, 1745, 1747-54, 1756, 1762-1812;
CB 1813-56 M 1813-37 (DRO)
<u>Cop</u> B 1813-37 (Ptd DFHS); B 1813-37 (SG); CMB 1566-1899 (I, WSL);
C 1569-1884 M 1569-1899 B 1566-1860 (NDA, DLS); CMB 1569-1884 (WSL)
<u>MI</u> Incledon 1 (NDA)

PILTON (Wes)
OR for c.1807-37 see BARNSTAPLE CIRCUIT (RG 4/954 PRO)

PIMLICO   see TORQUAY

PINHOE St Michael and All Angels [Wonford Hundred; St Thomas Union]   [517]
United with BROADCLYST
OR C 1561-1687, 1813-1952 M 1561-1687, 1754-1959 B 1561-1687, 1813-1938
    (DRO)
BT CMB 1606, 1611, 1616-18, 1625-26, 1630, 1635, 1638, 1664, 1669-73, 1675,
    1678-79, 1683, 1690, 1696-97, 1699, 1701 (1702-1812 ?); CB 1813-38
    M 1813-23, 1825-37 (DRO)
Cop M 1687-1837 (DFHS, SG, Phil Ms); M 1687-1837 (Boyd)
Cop (Mf) C 1813-60 M 1754-1837 B 1813-1901 (Mfc SG)

PINHOE Hall Church. Licensed building in parish of Pinhoe

PINHOE (Cong ?/URC) Old Pinn Lane f 1886

PLYMOUTH

For the purposes of this volume the churches are grouped according to their
descent from the parishes of PLYMOUTH St Andrew, PLYMOUTH Charles,
STOKE DAMEREL and EGG BUCKLAND

PLYMOUTH ST ANDREW group

PLYMOUTH St Andrew, Royal Parade [Roborough Hundred; Plymouth Incorporation
1898-1930] [18884] United 1930 with Plymouth St Catherine. A new parish was
formed in 1954 from these and Plymouth Holy Trinity, St Saviour, and parts
of others. Now with St Paul, Stonehouse
OR C 1581-1968 M 1581-1981, 1988-97 B 1581-1896; baptisms of French
    Huguenot children 1695-1728 (PWDRO)
BT CMB 1608, 1610-11, 1614, 1617, 1624, 1629-30, 1634, 1638, 1663-64,
    1669-72, 1678-79, 1684, 1686, 1688-90, 1695-96, 1708-09, 1712-15,
    1719-37, 1744-51, 1753-74, 1785-97, 1799-1811; CMB 1813-16, 1818,
    1822-32, 1834-36 CB 1838-41, 1843-70, 1872-73, 1877 (DRO)
Cop CMB 1581-1618 C 1619-33 (Ptd DCRS 1954); CMB 1581-1633 (DRO);
    M 1581-1654 (Ptd Phil 2: 1915); CMB 1581-1837 (WSL); CMB 1618-1745
    (DCRS/WSL); Extr CMB 1683-1714 (DCRS/WSL); C 1781-1805 (I SG);
    B 1581-1818 (SG); C 1745-98: surnames only, no dates (Ptd A.Witwick
    'Plymouth St Andrew's baptism surname index' DFH 26-28 supplements:
    1983); M 1653-74 (DFHS); M 1581-1674 (Boyd); CMB 1581-1642, 1653-57
    C 1745-1816, 1851-96 B 1798-1812 (I, PWDRO); M 1798-1812, 1837-1955 with
    index (PWDRO); CMB 1751-98, C 1745-98 (PCL)
Cop (Mf) C 1745-98 (Mfc, I, from DFHS); CMB 1581-1674 C 1745-98, 1813-42
         M 1754-1837 B 1813-43 (Mfc SG); C 1745-98 (I, Mfc CFHS); B 1745-92
         (I, Mfc DFHS); Extr C 1581-1633 M 1581-1744 (IGI); C 1581-1633
         M 1581-1744 (Mf I SLC)
MI Extr (Ptd J.B.Rowe The Ecclesiastical History of Old Plymouth: 1876);
    Westwell Street burial ground 1897 (PWDRO); MI, including Bedford Street
    burial ground (PWDRO)

PLYMOUTH St George, (East) Stonehouse. Chapelry in Plymouth St Andrew; separate parish 1746. United 1954 with Stonehouse St Paul. *see also* Plymouth St Peter, Stonehouse St Matthew
OR C 1863-87, 1941-54 M 1852-94 B 1813-27 (PWDRO) Earlier registers destroyed in bombing 1941, but see copies below
BT CMB 1762, 1764-73, 1775-1800, 1802-11; C 1813-40 M 1813-37 B 1813-17, 1820-40 (DRO)
Cop CB 1697-1812 M 1697-1786 (C of A; Mf PWDRO); M 1697-1812 (DFHS, SG); M 1697-1812, 1858-61, 1904-40 with indexes (PWDRO); M 1786-1812 from BT (I, PWDRO); B 1813-37 (I, PWDRO)
Cop (Mf) C 1813-40 M 1813-37 B 1813-17, 1820-40 from BT (Mfc DRO); Extr M 1697-1812 (IGI); M 1697-1812 (Mf I SLC)
MI (I, DFHS); Cy 1952 (Ts SG, PWDRO); transcript of removed graves 1770-1907 (PWDRO); (PCL)

PLYMOUTH St Paul, Durnford Street, Stonehouse. Chapel-of-ease to St George, erected 1830; separate parish 1883
OR C 1873-1971 M 1884-1976 (PWDRO)

PLYMOUTH St Matthew, Clarence Street, Stonehouse. Parish created 1876 from St George. Entered Plymouth St Peter 1954
OR CM 1876-1964 (PWDRO)

PLYMOUTH St Budeaux, Crownhill Road, Devonport. Chapelry of St Budeaux in Plymouth St Andrew [669] Separate parish 1822-50. *see also* Devonport St Boniface
OR C 1538-1892, 1902-21, 1942-50 M 1539-1955 B 1538-1988 (PWDRO)
BT CMB 1609, 1613-14, 1617, 1633-34, 1641?, 1690, 1694, 1699, 1702, 1708-09, 1712-15, 1719-23, 1725-37, 1743-51, 1753-73, 1775-1808 (1809-12 ?); CMB 1813-21 C 1822-42, 1846-47, 1849-51, 1853-54, 1857-61 M 1822-36 B 1822-39, 1841-42, 1846-47, 1849-51, 1853-54, 1857-61 (DRO)
Cop M 1539-1837 (Ptd A.Chiswell 'St Budeaux Marriages' DFH 2-5 supplements: 1977-78); M 1539-1837 transcribed A.Chiswell 1971 (Ts SG); CMB 1538-1864 (WSL); M 1813-37 (Ptd DFHS); M 1539-1789; M 1539-1837 indexed by male spouse (DFHS); M 1837-1955 with index (PWDRO)
Cop (Mf) Extr C 1599-1848 M 1539-1653, 1792-1850, 1861-75 (IGI); C 1599-1848 M 1539-1653, 1792-1850, 1861-75 (Mf I SLC)
MI (I, DFHS); 1966 (PWDRO); Extr (Whitmore MS, SG)

PLYMOUTH Holy Trinity, Crownhill, Devonport. Erected 1845. Chapel-of-ease to St Budeaux
OR C 1898-1939 M 1902-39 (PWDRO)

PLYMOUTH St Catherine, Lockyer Street. Chapel-of-ease erected 1823. Parish created 1897 from Plymouth St Andrew, with which reunited 1930. Demolished 1957
OR C 1897-1956 M 1936-41 (PWDRO)
Cop M 1936-41 with index (PWDRO)

PLYMOUTH Holy Trinity, Southside Street. Erected 1842, parish created 1854 from Plymouth St Andrew. United with St Saviour 1930
OR C 1865-1941 M 1852-1938 (PWDRO)
Cop C 1919-40 M 1852-1938 with indexes (PWDRO)

PLYMOUTH Christ Church, Eton Place. Erected and parish created 1846 from Plymouth St Andrew. Closed 1965
OR C 1847-1965 M 1847-1964 (PWDRO)
Cop M 1847-1963 with index (PWDRO)

PLYMOUTH St James the Less, Clarendon Place, Citadel Road. Parish created
1847 from Plymouth St Andrew; consecrated 1861. Destroyed by enemy action in
1940s.
OR M 1941 (PWDRO) No other registers survive
Cop M 1941 with index (PWDRO)

PLYMOUTH St. Michael, West Hoe. Chapel-of-ease to St James the Less.
Erected 1891
OR M 1948-84 (PWDRO)
Cop M 1948-84 with index (PWDRO)

PLYMOUTH St Peter, Wyndham Square (Eldad). Proprietary chapel erected 1828.
Purchased by Church of England and re-named St Peter. Parish created 1847
from Plymouth St Andrew, St George, East Stonehouse. Rebuilt 1882
OR C 1849-1937 M 1851-1980 (PWDRO)
Cop M 1851-1952 with index (PWDRO)

PLYMOUTH All Saints, Harwell Street. Erected 1874. Parish created 1875 from
Plymouth St Peter, with which reunited 1958. Demolished
OR C 1875-1979 M 1875-1979 (PWDRO)
Cop M 1875-1966 with index (PWDRO)

PLYMOUTH St Saviour, Lambhay Hill. Chapelry in Plymouth Holy Trinity.
Erected 1870. Separate parish 1883. Reunited 1930 with Holy Trinity
OR C 1871-1958 M 1874-1954 (PWDRO)
Cop C 1871-1917 (PWDRO)

PLYMOUTH St Pancras, Honicknowle Lane, Pennycross (or Weston Peverell)
Chapelry in Plymouth St Andrew. Separate parish 1898.
OR C 1634-1970 M 1636-1752, 1874-1973 B 1634-1946 (PWDRO) Noted in 1831:
    'within the parish of Axmouth, and not being fitted up for Divine
    Service, the family to whom the chapel belongs, only have been buried
    here'. No marriages after 1752
BT pre-1812, see Plymouth St Andrew; C 1813, 1815, 1833-37 B 1813, 1815,
    1827, 1833-36 (DRO)
Cop CB 1634-1812 M 1636-1752 (DCRS/WSL, SG); M 1874-1973 with index (PWDRO)
Cop (Mf) Extr C 1634-1812 M 1636-1752 (IGI); C 1634-1812 (Mf I SLC)
MI Ch n.d. (Ts SG)

PLYMOUTH St Boniface, St Budeaux Square, Devonport. Erected 1913 ? Parish
created 1916 from St Budeaux. Now with St Philip Weston Mill as North
Devonport
OR C 1901-78 M 1916-80 (PWDRO)

PLYMOUTH St Philip, Bridwell Road, Weston Mill. Parish created 1933 from
St Budeaux, Devonport St Boniface, NORTH KEYHAM. Now with Devonport
St Boniface as North Devonport
OR C 1898-1944 M 1925-64 (PWDRO)
Cop M 1925-40 with index (PWDRO)

PLYMOUTH St Chad, Whitleigh. Parish created 1956 from St Budeaux, with
assets transferred from St Chad, Devonport see below
OR C 1952-54; 1951-93 (PWDRO)

PLYMOUTH St Francis, Little Dock Lane, Honicknowle. Parish created 1956 from
St Budeaux, St Pancras Pennycross
OR C 1939-73 M 1940-88 (PWDRO)

PLYMOUTH St Aidan, Ernesettle. Parish created 1958 from St Budeaux

PLYMOUTH CHARLES group

PLYMOUTH Charles Church, Norley Street [12196] Erected 1640-57. Parish
created 1641 from Plymouth St Andrew. United 1954 with Plymouth St Luke,
1964 with St Matthias. Redundant. Monument to the War Dead
OR C 1645-1962 M 1644-1962 B 1646-1932 (PWDRO)
BT CMB 1663?, 1664, 1666, 1670, 1677-79, 1688-90, 1694-96, 1701, 1708-09,
1712-15, 1720-27, 1729-37, 1743-51, 1753-72, 1774-1800, 1802-11;
CMB 1813-38 CB 1845-52, 1854-55 (DRO)
Cop C 1653-63 (Ptd J.Whitmarsh 'Charles Church, Plymouth: extracts from a
memorandum book' *Miscellanea Genealogica et Heraldica* NS 4 1884);
M 1653-1874 (Phil Ms); M 1813-37 (Ptd DFHS); CMB 1644-53 (I, PWDRO);
M 1837-1942 with index (PWDRO); Charles with St Luke M 1922-62 with
index (PWDRO)
Cop (Mf) C 1645-1840 M 1644-1837 B 1646-1841 (Mfc SG)
MI Cy 1951, 1955 and n.d (Ts SG); MI and list of removed graves c.1941
(PWDRO); (PCL); 1956 (PWDRO)

PLYMOUTH St Luke, Tavistock Place. Formerly proprietary chapel (Charles
Chapel). Erected 1828. Parish created 1874 from Plymouth Charles, with which
reunited 1954
OR C 1874-1950 M 1874-1921 (PWDRO)
Cop M 1874-1921 with index (PWDRO)

PLYMOUTH St John the Evangelist, Exeter Street, Sutton-on-Plym.
Erected 1844 ? Parish created 1855 from Plymouth Charles
OR C 1850-1948 M 1855-1967 (PWDRO)
Cop C 1850-1948 (I, PWDRO); M 1855-1967 with index (PWDRO)

PLYMOUTH Emmanuel, Compton Gifford, Mannamead. Chapelry and tything of
Compton Gifford in Plymouth Charles [229] Erected 1870. Separate parish
1871. United with St Paul, Efford, as North Sutton
OR C 1870-1927 M 1872-1941 (PWDRO)
Cop M 1872-1902 with index (PWDRO)

PLYMOUTH St Paul, Torridge Way, Efford. Daughter church to Plymouth Emmanuel
in the parish of North Sutton

PLYMOUTH St Jude, Beaumont Road. Erected 1876. Parish created 1877 from
Plymouth Charles
OR C 1877-1954 M 1877-1977 (PWDRO)
Cop M 1877-1926 with index (PWDRO)

PLYMOUTH St Matthias. Tavistock Road. Erected 1887. Parish created 1889 from
Plymouth Charles, St Luke, Christ Church, Emmanuel Compton Gifford. United
1964 with Plymouth Charles
OR C 1888-1968 M 1890-1971 (PWDRO)
Cop M 1890-1939 with index (PWDRO)

PLYMOUTH St Augustine, Lipson Vale. Parish created 1905 from Plymouth
Charles, St Matthias, St Jude, Emmanuel Compton Gifford. Redundant
OR C 1900-93 M 1905-72 (PWDRO)
Cop M 1905-72 with index (PWDRO)

PLYMOUTH St Simon, Salisbury Road. Erected 1907. Parish created 1908 from
Plymouth St Jude
OR (Inc)
Cop M 1908-90 (I, PWDRO)

PLYMOUTH St Gabriel, Peverell Park. Erected 1908. Parish created 1910 from Plymouth Emmanuel Compton Gifford, St Pancras Pennycross
OR (Inc)

PLYMOUTH St Mary, Cattedown. Parish created 1911 from Sutton on Plym, with which reunited 1954. Redundant.
OR C 1898-1956 M 1912-54 (PWDRO)

STOKE DAMEREL group

PLYMOUTH St Andrew, Paradise Road, Stoke Damerel [Roborough Hundred; Stoke Damerel Incorporation until 1898] [34883] Mother church of the DEVONPORT parishes. The name Devonport was given in 1824 to the Plymouth Docks area.
OR C 1595-1954 M 1595-1940 B 1595-1957 (PWDRO)
BT CMB 1614, 1624, 1631, 1664, 1670, 1675-76, 1678-82, 1687, 1689-90, 1694-97, 1699, 1719-30, 1732-37, 1743-51, 1753-1812; CMB 1813-28 (DRO)
Cop C 1811-12 (Ptd J.Henwood *Stoke Damerel Baptisms 1811-12 an index*: 1997);
     C 1810-12 (DFHS); B 1813, 1814, 1815 (Ptd DFHS); CMB 1595-1801
     (DCRS/WSL); M 1595-1782 (Boyd); CMB 1595-1707 index only (DRO);
     CMB 1595-1707 C 1720-24, 1746-51, 1780, 1810-20 (I, PWDRO); M 1755-80,
     1805-08, 1837-1940 with indexes (PWDRO); B 1707-10 (PWDRO); B 1723-24
     (I, PWDRO)
Cop (Mf) C 1596-1719, 1746-58, 1813-40 M 1597-1734, 1746-1854 B 1506-1722,
         1746-58, 1813-37 (Mfc SG); Extr C 1595-1801 M 1595-1837 (IGI);
         C 1595-1801 M 1765-86, 1808-37 (Mf I SLC)
MI (I, DFHS); (Ptd M.Selley, V.Blight *Monumental Inscriptions Names Index:*
     Stoke Damerel: 1995); (PWDRO); graves removed from additional cemetery
     at Milehouse (I, PWDRO); stones from Milehouse, now at Hole Mill,
     Branscombe, Seaton (Ptd DFH 89: Feb 1999: 29-33)

PLYMOUTH St James the Great, Keyham Road, Morice Town. Parish created 1847 from Stoke Damerel. Erected 1849-51. Abolished 1954
OR C 1847-1943 M 1851-1941 (PWDRO)
Cop M 1851-1941 with index (PWDRO)

PLYMOUTH St Chad, Devonport. Kelly College Mission, Moon Street, made a conventional district of St James the Great, Devonport, from 1933. After war damage to St James some events took place at St Chad, until 1954. Assets transferred from 1957 to new parish of St Chad, Whitleigh: *see above*
OR C 1929-54 (PWDRO)

PLYMOUTH St Mary, James Street, Devonport. Parish created 1846 from Stoke Damerel. Erected 1850. Entered Devonport St Aubyn 1958
OR C 1847-1957 M 1852-1957 (PWDRO)
Cop M 1852-1957 with index (PWDRO)

PLYMOUTH St Paul, Morice Square, Devonport. Parish created 1846 from Stoke Damerel. Erected 1849. Entered Devonport St Aubyn 1958
OR C 1847-1941 M 1851-1937 (PWDRO)
Cop C 1847-1941 M 1851-1937 with indexes (PWDRO)

PLYMOUTH St Stephen, George Street, Devonport. Parish created 1846 from Stoke Damerel. Erected 1852. Entered Devonport St Aubyn 1958
OR C 1848-1944 M 1920-41 (PWDRO)
Cop C 1848-1941 M 1920-41 with indexes (PWDRO)

PLYMOUTH St Michael, Albert Road, Devonport. Erected 1845. Parish created
1873 from Stoke Damerel
OR (Inc)

PLYMOUTH St. Michael, Stoke, Devonport. Erected 1845. Separate parish 1873
OR C 1873-1969 M 1873-1960 (PWDRO)

PLYMOUTH St Aubyn, Chapel Street, Devonport. Proprietary chapel erected
1771-72, Parish created 1882 from Stoke Damerel and Devonport St Paul.
Reconstituted 1958 to include Devonport St John the Baptist, St Mary,
St Paul, St Stephen
OR C 1878-1919, 1937-56 M 1883-1962 (PWDRO)
Cop M 1915-62 with index (PWDRO)

PLYMOUTH St John the Baptist, Duke Street, Devonport. Erected 1779 ? Parish
created 1887 from Stoke Damerel, Devonport St Aubyn. Entered Devonport
St Aubyn 1958
OR C 1887-1943 M 1887-1942 (PWDRO)

PLYMOUTH St Barnabas, Stuart Road, Devonport. Erected 1886. Parish created
1904 from Stoke Damerel
OR C 1886-1957 M 1904-67 B 1950-73 (PWDRO)
Cop M 1904-39 with index (PWDRO)

PLYMOUTH St Mark, Cambridge Road, Ford. Erected 1874-82. Parish created 1885
from Stoke Damerel; Devonport St Michael, St James; Plymouth St Andrew.
OR C 1875-1965 M 1886-1968 (PWDRO)

PLYMOUTH St Clement, Warleigh Avenue. Erected 1913. Chapel-of-ease to St
Mark, Ford

PLYMOUTH St Thomas, Royal Navy Avenue, North Keyham, Devonport. Parish
created 1929 from Devonport St Mark, Ford
OR C 1929-68 M 1915-59 (PWDRO)

PLYMOUTH St. Anne, Swilly. Mission church to St Mark, Ford c.1930-1959,
replaced by St James the Less, Ham
OR C 1938-42 (PWDRO); C 1942-59 (Inc, St James, Ham)

PLYMOUTH St James the Less, Ham. Parish created 1957 from St Mark Devonport,
St Mark Ford, St Pancras Pennycross, St Philip Weston Mill
OR (Inc)

PLYMOUTH St Bartholomew, Browning Road, Devonport Mission chapel in Stoke
Damerel parish. Moved to Outland Road. Parish created 1965 from Stoke
Damerel, Devonport St Barnabas, Plymouth St Pancras Pennycross
OR C 1881-1920 (PWDRO)
Cop C 1899-1918 with index (PWDRO)

EGG BUCKLAND group

PLYMOUTH St Edward, Egg Buckland [Roborough Hundred; Plympton St Mary Union]
[1117] Rebuilt 1864
OR C 1653-1972 M 1652-1984 B 1653-1908 (PWDRO)
BT CMB 1611, 1613?, 1614, 1616, 1618, 1626, 1635, 1663-64, 1666, 1668-72,
   1674, 1676-77, 1679-82, 1686, 1688, 1697, 1743-51, 1753-59, 1761-80
   (1781-1812 ?); CB 1813-56 M 1813-38 (DRO)

PLYMOUTH St Edward, Egg Buckland, cont.
Cop M 1813-37 (Ptd DFHS); B 1813-37 (Ptd DFHS); C 1749 from BT (DFHS);
  M 1837-1950 with index (PWDRO)
MI (I, DFHS); Cy, index (Ptd DFH 17: Jan 1981: 6); n.d. (PWDRO); (PCL)

PLYMOUTH St Mary the Virgin, Federation Road, Laira. Erected c.1911-15 ?
Parish created 1931 from EGG BUCKLAND, PLYMOUTH St Augustine, and extra-
parochial place Laira Green
OR (Inc)

PLYMOUTH St Anne, Glenholt. St Anne's Mission f 1950s, Woodford Road.
Attached to EGG BUCKLAND. Church in Glenholt Road erected 1955. From 1970s
in parish of BICKLEIGH near Plymouth. Now with ROBOROUGH united benefice
OR C, Funerals (Inc) No marriages or burials

PLYMOUTH Church of the Ascension, Crownhill. Parish created 1958 from Egg
Buckland, St Pancras Pennycross, St Budeaux, TAMERTON FOLIOT
OR (Inc)

PLYMOUTH HMS Drake St Nicholas. Dedicated 1907. Royal Naval Chaplaincy
OR CM 1907+ (Inc)

PLYMOUTH St John and St James, HMS Thunderer, RNEC Manadon
OR C 1945-95 (MoD)

PLYMOUTH Royal Marines - Plymouth Division
OR ZMD 1862-1920 (MoD)

PLYMOUTH St Catherine, The Citadel Chapel erected 1668, rebuilt 1845. Under
Board of Ordnance [1851 Religious Census]
MI (I, DFHS)

PLYMOUTH Royal Naval Hospital, Stonehouse Chapel erected c.1860 [Kelly 1889]
BT B 1813, 1814, 1824-26, 1830, 1835, 1837 (DRO)
Cop B 1813 (I, PWDRO)
MI *Royal Naval Hospital, Stonehouse: Notes on burials and M.I.s* 1989

PLYMOUTH Dockyard Church, Stonehouse [Kelly 1889]

PLYMOUTH Dockyard Chapel, Devonport [Kelly 1889]

PLYMOUTH Military Chapel, Devonport [Kelly 1889]

PLYMOUTH Raglan Barracks, Devonport [Kelly 1889]

PLYMOUTH Royal Naval Hospital. No Place Field burial ground opened 1824 for
R.N.Hospital; used until 1897. Site became part of St Dunstan's Abbey School
1956.
OR B 1887-1966 (PWDRO) Earlier register lost
MI 1870-1966 (I, PWDRO)

PLYMOUTH Mount Batten R.A.F. Chaplaincy
OR C 1954-72 (AFCC)

PLYMOUTH Great Western Docks. Extra-parochial place attached 1954 to
Plymouth St Andrew, St Peter

PLYMOUTH Lighthouse. Extra-parochial place

PLYMOUTH (RC) Mission f 1793 at Plymouth Dock, Devonport. Chapel, Stoke
Damerel, registered 1801. St Mary, East Stonehouse: erected 1818 [1851
Religious Census] Cathedral Church of St Mary and St Boniface, Wyndham
Street. Erected 1856-58 [1882 Return]
OR CMB 1793+ Confirmations 1800+ (Inc) Confirmations 1847, 1856, 1858-60,
    1863-1935 (Plymouth Diocesan Archives)

PLYMOUTH (RC) Naval Chapel, HMS Monmouth, Devonport 1856-1902

PLYMOUTH (RC) St Michael and St Joseph, James Street, Devonport f 1860 [1882
Return]
OR C 1861+ M 1863+ B 1861+ Confirmations 1862+ (Inc); Confirmations 1862+
    (Plymouth Diocesan Archives)

PLYMOUTH (RC) St Teresa, Tothill Lane [Beaumont Road] f 1871, succeeded by
Holy Cross 1881
OR C 1873+ M 1894+ B 1894+ Confirmations 1890+ (Inc, Holy Cross);
    Confirmations 1882+ (Plymouth Diocesan Archives)

PLYMOUTH (RC) Our Most Holy Redeemer, Ocean Street, Keyham. Erected 1902

PLYMOUTH (RC) St Edward the Confessor, Home Park Avenue, Peverell Erected
1910

PLYMOUTH (RC) St Paul, Pemros Road, St Budeaux. Erected 1933

PLYMOUTH (RC) St Peter, Crownhill Road 1937

PLYMOUTH (RC) The Holy Family, Beacon Park Road 1939

PLYMOUTH (RC) Christ the King, Armada Way 1962

PLYMOUTH (RC) Our Lady of Mount Carmel, Pike Road, Efford 1964

PLYMOUTH (RC) St Thomas More, Bampfylde Way, Southway 1964

PLYMOUTH (RC) Our Lady of the Ships, HMS Drake, Devonport

PLYMOUTH (RC) Chapel of Christ the King, HMS Thunderer, Manadon

PLYMOUTH (Bapt) Catherine Street f 1620

PLYMOUTH (Bapt) f 1637 Pig Market (Frankfort Gate); rebuilt 1751; to Hows
Lane 1789; to George Street 1845 [1851 Religious Census] [1882 Return]
George Street bombed 1941. Rebuilt Notte Street
OR Z 1786-1837 B 1787-1837 (RG 4/1215,1216 PRO) Other records destroyed by
    bombing, 1941
Cop (Mf) Z 1786-1837 B 1787-1837 (Mf DCRS/WSL, SG); How Street:
         Extr Z 1786-1837 (IGI)
MI (PWDRO)

PLYMOUTH (Bapt) Liberty Street and Pembroke Street, Devonport. f 1781.
Pembroke Baptist Chapel [1851 Religious Census] Later at Crownhill, Berwick
Avenue. Pembroke Street [1882 Return] Demolished
OR Z 1779-1821 (RG 4/963 PRO)
Cop Surnames 1779-1821 (Ptd A Chiswell: DFH 23: 1982); Z 1779-1810 (SG, PCL)
Cop (Mf) Z 1779-1810 (Mf DCRS/WSL, SG); Extr Z 1779-1813 (IGI)

PLYMOUTH (Bapt) Morice Square Chapel, Devonport f 1784. Purchased Morice Square from Independents 1799 and continued their register [1851 Religious Census] [1882 Return] Destroyed by bombing 1941. Now at Ham Drive
OR ZC 1770-1837 (RG 4/960 PRO); Z 1781-1806 C 1785-94 (RG 8/10) Other records lost by bombing 1941
Cop Z 1785-1837 (SG, PCL); C 1785-1805 (Mf DCRS/WSL)
Cop (Mf) Z 1785-1837 (Mf DCRS/WSL); Z 1770-1837 (Mf SG); Extr Z 1774-1837 (IGI)

PLYMOUTH (Bapt) Ebenezer Chapel, Union Street, Stonehouse f 1816 [1851 Religious Census]
OR Z 1817-37 (RG 4/2854 PRO)
Cop (Mf) Z 1817-37 (Mf DCRS/WSL); Z 1817-37 (Mf SG); Extr Z 1817-37 (IGI)

PLYMOUTH (Bapt) Providence, Home Park, Stoke Damerel f.1817 [1851 Religious Census]

PLYMOUTH (Open Communion Bapt) Hope Chapel, Fore Street, Devonport f 1855 [1882 Return] To Peverell Park Road, registered 1926

PLYMOUTH (Bapt) Ford, Alfred Road f 1868

PLYMOUTH (Bapt) Mutley, Mutley Plain f 1869 [1882 Return]

PLYMOUTH (Bapt) Hooe, Hooe Road f 1876

PLYMOUTH (Bapt) York Street [Kelly 1889]

PLYMOUTH (Bapt) Alexander Road, Ford. Registered 1894

PLYMOUTH (Bapt) Emmanuel, North Road. Registered 1899

PLYMOUTH (Bapt) Alfred Road, Ford. Registered 1899

PLYMOUTH (Bapt) St Budeaux, Fleetmoor Road 1902

PLYMOUTH (Bapt) Wolseley Road, St Budaeux. Registered 1904. Later a garage

PLYMOUTH (Bapt) Salisbury Road f 1906

PLYMOUTH (Bapt) Portland Chapel, Portland Villas. Registered 1925

PLYMOUTH (Bapt) Estover
OR M 1948-80 (DRO)
Cop M 1948-80 with index (PWDRO)

PLYMOUTH (Presb/Unit) f 1662. Erected Bilbury Street (Treville Street). Norley Street 1823. Rebuilt 1832 [1851 Religious Census] Demolished by bombing 1941. Notte Street 1958
OR ZC 1672-1835 B 1662-95 (RG 4/4091,2537,2159 PRO); other records destroyed by enemy action in 1940s
Cop (Mf) ZC 1672-1835 B 1662-95 (Mf DCRS/WSL, SG); Extr C 1672-97, 1704-1835 (IGI); C 1672-97, 1704-1835 (Mf I SLC)
MI Treville Street (PWDRO)

PLYMOUTH (Presb/Ind) f Old Marshalls 1662; to Batter Street 1704
[1851 Religious Census] Higher Batter Street [1882 Return] Closed 1923
OR ZC 1704-1837 B 1768-1837 (RG 4/1091,1217,1218 PRO); B 1768-1818 (PWDRO);
   and see IGI, below
Cop (Mf) C 1704-1837 M 1760-94 B 1768-1837 (Mf DCRS/WSL, SG);
         Extr C 1704-1837, 1860-1936 M 1802-38 (IGI); C 1704-1837 (Mf I SLC)

PLYMOUTH (Cong/URC) Old Tabernacle, Bretonside (Sherwell Chapel) Erected
1746. Closed 1801. Princes Street, registered 1822 [1851 Religious Census]
[1882 Return] Closed 1932. Destroyed in Second World War. Re-formed as
Pilgrim URC
OR C 1763-1837 (RG 4/961,838 PRO); C 1763-1915 M 1870-1915 B 1907-09
   (PWDRO); Pilgrim URC C 1950-79 M 1955-63 B 1950-63 (PWDRO)
Cop C 1763-1837 (SG, PCL); Sherwell C 1763-1817 with index (PWDRO); Princes
   Street C 1817-1915 M 1870-1915 B 1907-10 with index (PWDRO); Pilgrim
   C 1950-79 B 1950-63 with index (PWDRO)
Cop (Mf) C 1763-1837 (Mf DCRS/WSL, SG); C 1763-1837 (Mf SG); Princes Street
         or Church of Christ: Extr C 1763-1837 (IGI); C 1763-1837 (Mf I SLC)

PLYMOUTH (Ind/Cong) Corpus Christi, Union Place/Street, Stonehouse f 1780.
Erected 1833 [1851 Religious Census] Closed
OR ZC 1786-1837 (RG 4/120 PRO)
Cop (Mf) ZC 1786-1837 (Mf DCRS/WSL, SG); Extr C 1786-1800, 1818-37 (IGI);
         C 1786-1800, 1818-37 (Mf I SLC)

PLYMOUTH (Cong) Morice Square, Devonport f 1784. Building sold to Baptists
1799, and registers continued by them q.v. Closed
OR Z 1781-1806 C 1785-94 (RG 8/10 PRO)
Cop (Mf) C 1785-1805 (Mf DCRS/WSL); ZC 1781-1806 (Mf SG); Extr ZC 1781-1806
         (IGI); ZC 1781-1806 (Mf I SLC)

PLYMOUTH (Presb/Ind/Cong) Emma Place, Stonehouse. f 1787 from Batter Street
[1851 Religious Census] Closed after Second World War
OR ZC 1794-1836 B 1794-1835 (RG 4/450 PRO); C 1849-1940 M 1868-1939
   B 1891-1921 (PWDRO)
Cop C 1849-81, 1891-1940 M 1868-81, 1891-1939 B 1891-94, 1900-21 with index
   (PWDRO)
Cop (Mf) ZC 1794-1836 B 1794-1835 (Mf DCRS/WSL, SG); Extr ZC 1794-1836
         (IGI); ZC 1794-1836 (Mf I SLC)
MI (I, DFHS); 19th cent (PWDRO)

PLYMOUTH (Presb/Unit) Devonport f 1790. Erected George Street 1791. Sold
1806; now the Old Chapel public house. Granby Street 1829 [1851 Religious
Census] Christ Church, Duke Street 1864-1917
OR C 1828-35 (RG 4/524 PRO)
Cop C 1828-35 (SG)C 1836-37 (PCL)
Cop (Mf) C 1828-35 (Mf DCRS/WSL, SG); Extr C 1828-35 (IGI)

PLYMOUTH (Ind/Cong) New Tabernacle, Norley's Lane (Norley Street). f 1797 by
secession from Old Tabernacle. Rebuilt 1833 [1851 Religious Census] Closed
1954
OR ZC 1798-1837 (RG 4/1090 PRO)
Cop (Mf) ZC 1798-1837 (Mf DCRS/WSL, SG); Extr ZC 1798-1837 (IGI);
         ZC 1798-1837 (Mf I SLC)

PLYMOUTH (Ind) Rehoboth, Charles parish. Pre-1800 [1851 Religious Census]

PLYMOUTH (Prot Ind) Bethleham Chapel, Stoke Damerel. Erected 1808
[1851 Religious Census]

PLYMOUTH (Ind/Cong) Mount Street, Devonport f 1809 by secession from New Tabernacle. Erected 1810 [1851 Religious Census] [1882 Return] Closed
OR ZC 1809-37 (RG 4/962,581 PRO)
Cop Mount Street ZC 1808-37 (SG); ZC 1809-18, 1816-23 (PCL)
Cop (Mf) Mount Street ZC 1809-37 (Mf DCRS/WSL, SG); Granby or Mount Street
       Chapel: Extr ZC 1809-37 (IGI); ZC 1809-37 (Mf I SLC)

PLYMOUTH (Ind/Cong, later URC) Salem, Devonport. f 1817. 1856 Wycliffe Chapel, Navy Row (Albert Road) Morice Town [1882 Return] Bombed 1941. United with Pilgrim URC
OR C 1826-37 (RG 4/525, 520 PRO); C 1922-48 M 1923-47 B 1923-41 (PWDRO)
Cop Navy Row, Morice Town ZC 1826-37 (SG); C 1826-37 (PCL); C 1922-48
       M 1923-47 B 1923-41 with index (PWDRO)
Cop (Mf) C 1826-37 (Mf DCRS/WSL, SG); Extr C 1826-37 (IGI); C 1826-37
       (Mf I SLC)

PLYMOUTH (Ind/Cong) Mount Zion, Ker Street, Devonport f 1823 [1882 Return] Closed
OR C 1824-37 (RG 4/580 PRO)
Cop C 1824-37 (SG, PCL)
Cop (Mf) C 1824-37 (Mf DCRS/WSL, SG); Extr C 1824-37 (IGI); C 1824-37
       (Mf I SLC)

PLYMOUTH (Cong) Portland Place, Morice Town. Erected c.1825 [1851 Religious Census]

PLYMOUTH (Ind) Bethesda, Charles parish. Erected c.1830 [1851 Religious Census]

PLYMOUTH (Cong) Rehoboth, Buckwell Lane, later Trinity, York Street f 1833. Closed
OR ZC 1833-37 (RG 4/2101 PRO)
Cop (Mf) ZC 1833-37 (Mf DCRS/WSL, SG); Extr ZC 1823-37 (IGI); ZC 1823-37
       (Mf I SLC)

PLYMOUTH (Ind Diss) Ebenezer, Granby Street. Erected 1846 [1851 Religious Census]

PLYMOUTH (Cong) Union Chapel, Courtenay Street. f 1848 from Batter Street. [1851 Religious Census] [1882 Return] Bombed 1941
OR Records lost in bombing

PLYMOUTH (Cong/URC) Laira United, Old Laira Road f 1850; united with Meth 1994

PLYMOUTH (Ind/Cong) Temperance Hall, Fore Street, Devonport. Erected 1850 [1851 Religious Census]

PLYMOUTH (Ind) House at Compton Gifford 1850 [1851 Religious Census]

PLYMOUTH (Ind) House, Mount Street f 1851 [1851 Religious Census]

PLYMOUTH (Presb) Eldad f Devonport 1857. Erected 1862 [1882 Return]
Moved to Hartley 1938
OR Location unknown
Cop (Mf) = ? Plymouth Presbyterian Church Extr C 1860-75 (IGI); C 1860-75
       (Mf I SLC)

PLYMOUTH (Cong, later URC) Trinity, Tor Lane, Compton Gifford f 1858

PLYMOUTH (Cong/URC) Sherwell Cong Church, Tavistock Road, erected 1862-64 [Kelly 1889] Succeeded New Tabernacle

PLYMOUTH (Presb) Wyndham Street Erected 1869; rebuilt 1883 [Kelly 1889]

PLYMOUTH (Cong) Laira. Registered 1915

PLYMOUTH (URC) Powisland Drive, Derriford. f 1955

PLYMOUTH (Huguenot) Plymouth f c.1681. Used St Andrew's Church. Own church erected Hows Street 1733. Closed by 1762; members joined Batter Street Presbyterian church. Sold to Baptists 1810
OR C 1733-78, 1791-1807 M 1734, 1740 B 1733-34 (RG 4/4623 PRO); and see PLYMOUTH St Andrew
Cop C 1733-78, 1791-1807 M 1734, 1740 B 1733-34 (Ptd C.E.Lart Registers of the French Churches of Bristol, Stonehouse and Plymouth: Huguenot Soc of London 20: 1912)
Cop (Mf) French Episcopal Church Extr C 1733-78, 1791-1807 (IGI); C 1733-78, 1791-1807 (Mf I SLC)

PLYMOUTH (Huguenot) Stonehouse. Used St George's Church, East Stonehouse until 1691. Separated from Plymouth 1691; own church 1692; reunited with Plymouth 1785, when Stonehouse church sold
OR C 1692-1710, 1722-91 M 1693-1710, 1720-36, 1747-48 B 1692-1708, 1743-88 (RG4 4565, 4566, 4567, 4577 PRO)
Cop C 1692-1710, 1722-91 M 1693-1710, 1720-36, 1747-48 B 1692-1708, 1743-88 (Ptd C.E.Lart Registers of the French Churches of Bristol, Stonehouse and Plymouth: Huguenot Soc of London 20: 1912)
Cop (Mf) French Episcopal Church: Extr C 1692-1710, 1722-91 (IGI); C 1692-1710, 1722-91 (Mf I SLC)

PLYMOUTH (Moravian) Plymouth. Mitre Inn. f c.1768. Amalgamated with Devonport 1805

PLYMOUTH (Moravian) Devonport. Cherry Garden Street c.1768 until 1771, then James Street. Rebuilt 1844 [1851 Religious Census] [1882 Return] [Kelly 1889] Closed 1916. Demolished c.1960
OR ZC 1785-1834 (RG 4/526 PRO); ZC 1785-1914 M 1872-1904 (Moravian Church House, Muswell Hill, London)
Cop ZC 1785-1836 (SG, PWDRO, PCL)
Cop (Mf) ZC 1785-1836 (Mf DCRS/WSL, SG); Extr C 1785-87, 1804-34 (IGI); C 1785-87, 1804-34 (Mf I SLC)

PLYMOUTH (Wes) Morice Street, Devonport. f 1766. Erected 1808 [1851 Religious Census] [1882 Return]
OR ZC 1787-1837 (RG 4/864,865 PRO); C 1839-1944 (PWDRO)
Cop ZC 1787-1837 (SG); M 1787-1837 (DFHS); ZC 1787-1821 (PCL)
Cop (Mf) ZC 1787-1837 (Mf DCRS/WSL, SG); Extr C 1787-1837 (IGI); C 1787-1837 (Mf I SLC)

PLYMOUTH (Wes) Ker Street, Devonport. Erected 1785-86 [1851 Religious Census] [1882 Return] Demolished
OR C 1841-1930 (PWDRO)
Cop C 1841-1930 with index (PWDRO)

PLYMOUTH (Wes) Wesley Chapel, Buckwell Lane (Buckwell Street). Erected 1794 [1851 Religious Census] [1882 Return]

PLYMOUTH (Wes) Old Tabernacle, Britonside. Erected pre-1800 [1851 Religious Census]

PLYMOUTH (Wes) Gloucester Street, Morice Town. Erected 1811 [1851 Religious Census] Marine Town, Devonport [1882 Return] Destroyed in Second World War
OR M 1925-41 (PWDRO)
Cop M 1925-41 with index (PWDRO)

PLYMOUTH (Wes) Crownhill. Registered 1812, rebuilt 1871. fl c.1970
OR C 1863-1956 (PWDRO)
Cop C 1863-1956 with index (PWDRO)

PLYMOUTH (Wes) Ebenezer, Saltash Street. Erected 1815 [1851 Religious Census] [1882 Return] Rebuilt 1940. Later Plymouth Central Hall. fl c.1970
OR ZC 1813-37 B 1817-37 (RG 4/1325,1092 PRO); C 1837-63 (RG 8/8B PRO); C 1817-1909 (PWDRO)
Cop B 1817-38 with index (PWDRO)
Cop (Mf) CB 1813-63 (Mf DCRS/WSL, SG); Extr C 1813-63 (IGI); C 1813-63 (Mf I SLC)

PLYMOUTH (Wes) Edgecumbe Street, Stonehouse. Registered 1813. Rebuilt 1857
OR C 1866-1875, 1913-36 (PWDRO)
Cop C 1866-75, 1913-36 M 1899-1977 with indexes (PWDRO)

PLYMOUTH (Wes) Union Street, Stonehouse. Erected 1813; rebuilt 1857. Closed 1985
OR M 1899-1977 (PWDRO)

PLYMOUTH (Wes) Knackersknowle. Erected 1817 [1851 Religious Census] [1882 Return]

PLYMOUTH (Wes) Stoke Damerel. Erected 1823 [1851 Religious Census]

PLYMOUTH (Wes) Cattedown. Erected 1827. Rebuilt 1850 [1851 Religious Census] [1882 Return] Rebuilt 1897

PLYMOUTH (Wës) Salem, Salem Street. Erected 1828 [1851 Religious Census] [1882 Return]
OR C 1831-78 (RG 8/9 PRO)
Cop (Mf) Z 1831-78 (Mf DCRS/WSL); ZC 1831-78 (Mf SG); Extr C 1831-78 (IGI); C 1831-78 (Mf I SLC)

PLYMOUTH (Wes Meth Assn) Morice Town. Purchased 1837 [1851 Religious Census]

PLYMOUTH (Wes Meth Assn) Honicknowle. Erected 1839 [1851 Religious Census]

PLYMOUTH (Wes) Devonport Wes and Meth Circuit
Cop C 1839-1944 (I, SG, PWDRO)

PLYMOUTH (Wes) Foundry, Stonehouse Lane, Erected 1847 [1851 Religious Census]

PLYMOUTH (Wes) Binham Mill. Erected 1849 [1851 Religious Census]

PLYMOUTH (Wes) Temperance Hotel, Fore Street. Erected 1850 [1851 Religious Census]

PLYMOUTH (Wes) King Street. Erected 1866 [1882 Return] Bombed 1941. Rebuilt
in The Crescent
OR C 1929-39 (PWDRO)
Cop C 1929-39 with index (PWDRO)

PLYMOUTH (Wes) Mutley Plain [1882 Return]
OR C 1872-1977 M 1899-1977 (PWDRO)
Cop C 1872-1977 M 1899-1977 with index (PWDRO)

PLYMOUTH (Wes) Ebenezer, Cambridge Road, Ford. Registered 1874 [1882 Return]
[Kelly 1889] Bombed 1940s

PLYMOUTH (Wes) Belmont. Devonport Road. Succeeded Stoke Chapel. Erected 1876
[1882 Return] Rebuilt 1990
OR C 1909-51 M 1899-1986 (PWDRO)
Cop C 1909-51 M 1899-1986 with index (PWDRO)

PLYMOUTH (Wes) Ebrington Street, formerly Ham Street. Replaced Backwell
Lane. Registered 1879. Later used as a restaurant
OR M 1899-1937 (PWDRO)
Cop M 1899-1937 with index (PWDRO)

PLYMOUTH (Wes) Mutley Plain. Erected 1881. Closed 1977

PLYMOUTH (Wes) Wesley, Ham Street [1882 Return] [Kelly 1889]; see Ebrington
Street, above

PLYMOUTH (Wes) Millbrook Cottage, St Budeaux [1882 Return] = ? (Meth)
Millbrook Chapel, Devonport
OR C 1855-1907 M 1907-84 (PWDRO)

PLYMOUTH (Wes) St Levan, Stuart Road, Stoke. Erected 1888. Closed post-1945

PLYMOUTH (Wes) Johnstone Terrace. Keyham. Registered 1890. Replaced by
Admiralty Street 1903

PLYMOUTH (Wes) Zion, Old Laira Road, Laira. Erected 1892. Rebuilt 1906.
fl c.1970
OR M 1982-88 (PWDRO)
Cop M 1982-88 with index (PWDRO)

PLYMOUTH (Wes) Peverell Park Road. f 1896; rebuilt 1905. fl c.1970

PLYMOUTH (Wes) Revel Road, Compton. Erected 1900, rebuilt 1939. fl c.1970

PLYMOUTH (Wes) Keyham, Devonport
OR C 1902-60 (PWDRO)
Cop C 1902-60 with index (PWDRO)

PLYMOUTH (Wes) Victoria, Admiralty Street, Keyham, Devonport. Erected 1903.
Rebuilt 1982
OR M 1953-76 (PWDRO)
Cop M 1953-76 with index (PWDRO)

PLYMOUTH (Wes) Mount Gould. Erected 1904. fl c.1970
OR C 1904-48 (PWDRO)

PLYMOUTH (Wes) Beauchamp Road, Pennycross. Registered 1907

PLYMOUTH (Wes) Budwell Road, St Budeaux. Registered 1907

PLYMOUTH (Wes) Hope Chapel (later Central Hall) Fore Street, Devonport.
Registered 1925. Destroyed in war. Rebuilt 1956. Closed 1986
OR M 1951-85 (PWDRO)
Cop M 1951-85 with index (PWDRO)

PLYMOUTH (Wes) Stirling Road, St Budeaux. Registered 1939. Rebuilt 1957.
fl c.1970

PLYMOUTH (Wes/Meth) King Street, The Crescent. Erected 1957. fl c.1970

PLYMOUTH (Bible Christian) Siloam, Union Place, Stonehouse. Erected 1819
[1851 Religious Census]

PLYMOUTH (Bible Christian) Devonport Circuit
OR ZC 1820-37 (RG 4/334 PRO)
Cop ZC 1820-37 (SG, PCL)
Cop (Mf) ZC 1820-37 (Mf DCRS/WSL, SG); Extr ZC 1820-37 (IGI); ZC 1820-37
(Mf I SLC)

PLYMOUTH (Bible Christian) Ebenezer, King Street, Devonport. Erected 1845
[1851 Religious Census] [1882 Return]

PLYMOUTH (Bible Christian/U Meth) Zion, Zion Street. Erected 1847
[1851 Religious Census] [1882 Return]
OR C 1908-15 M 1937-46 (PWDRO); see also Embankment Road
Cop C 1908-38 M 1937-40 with index (PWDRO)

PLYMOUTH (Bible Christian) Haddington Road Chapel, Morice Town, Devonport.
Registered 1868 [1882 Return]

PLYMOUTH (Bible Christian/U Meth) Greenbank Road. Erected 1886. Closed 1976
OR C 1883-1976 M 1938-76 (PWDRO)
Cop C 1959-76 M 1938-41, 1944-70 with index (PWDRO)

PLYMOUTH (Bible Christian) East Street. Registered 1885 [Kelly 1889]

PLYMOUTH (Bible Christian/U Meth) Embankment Road. Erected 1898. Closed 1982
OR C 1920-38 M 1930-82 (PWDRO); see also Zion Street
Cop M 1930-82 with index (PWDRO)

PLYMOUTH (Bible Christian/Meth) St George's Terrace, Stoke. Registered 1907.
Rebuilt 1955. fl c.1970

PLYMOUTH (Prim Meth) Herbert Street, Devonport. Registered 1859 [Kelly 1889]
Closed 1952. Demolished
OR C 1901-52 M 1923-41 (PWDRO)
Cop C 1903-52 M 1923-41 with indexes (PWDRO)

PLYMOUTH (Prim Meth) Granby Street, Devonport. Registered 1862 [1882 Return]

PLYMOUTH (Prim Meth) Hotham Place, Millbridge. Erected 1877 [1882 Return]
Closed 1988
OR M 1950-88 (PWDRO)
Cop M 1950-88 with index (PWDRO)

PLYMOUTH (Prim Meth) Ebrington Street [1882 Return] [Kelly 1889]

PLYMOUTH (Prim Meth) Morice Town [1882 Return]

PLYMOUTH (Prim Meth) Camden Street. Registered 1906

PLYMOUTH (Prim Meth) Coburg Street. Registered 1908. Closed
OR M 1909-35 (PWDRO)
Cop M 1909-35 with index (PWDRO)

PLYMOUTH (Prim Meth) Barton Avenue. Registered 1910. Closed post-1935

PLYMOUTH (Wes Meth Assn/UMFC) Hope Chapel, Ebrington Street. Registered 1863
[1882 Return] [Kelly 1889] Bombed 1941

PLYMOUTH (UMFC) Gloucester Street, Morice Town. Registered 1864.
Re-registered for Calvinists 1866

PLYMOUTH (UMFC) Albert Road Chapel, Morice Town, Devonport. Registered 1867;
former Wes.Meth Assn. chapel [1882 Return] [Kelly 1889] Demolished after
Second World War

PLYMOUTH (UMFC/Meth) Butt Park Road/Carew Avenue, Honicknowle. Erected 1901.
fl *c.*1970 Honicknowle Methodist Church
OR M 1981-95 (PWDRO)
Cop M 1981-95 with index (PWDRO)

PLYMOUTH (U Meth) Halcyon Road, North Prospect. Erected 1929. fl *c.*1970

PLYMOUTH (Meth) Millbridge Methodist Church, Devonport, formerly Albert Road
Cop C 1909-88 with index (PWDRO)

PLYMOUTH (Meth) Cattedown
OR C 1936-67 (PWDRO)

PLYMOUTH (Meth) Uxbridge Drive, Ernesettle. Erected 1955 fl *c.*1970

PLYMOUTH (Meth) Whitleigh
OR C 1951-93 (PWDRO)

PLYMOUTH (Meth/C of E/URC/RC) Christ Church, Estover f 1994

PLYMOUTH (Calv) Trinity Chapel, York Street. Erected 1826 [1851 Religious
Census]

PLYMOUTH (Ind Calv) Zion, Fore Street. Erected 1834 [1851 Religious Census]

PLYMOUTH (Calv) Octagon Street. Registered 1839

PLYMOUTH (Calv) Burlington Street. Erected 1840 [1851 Religious Census]

PLYMOUTH (Supralapsarian Calv)) Portland or Portland Villas Chapel or
Mr Bubb's Chapel. Erected 1844 [1851 Religious Census] [Kelly 1889]

PLYMOUTH (Calv) Mays Cross. Registered 1845

PLYMOUTH (Calv) Ebenezer Chapel, Gloucester Street, Morice Town. Registered
1866 [1882 Return]

PLYMOUTH (Catholic Apostolic Church) Central Hall, Plymouth St Andrew
[1851 Religious Census]; Princess Street [Kelly 1889]

PLYMOUTH (Latter Day Saints) Heydon's Public Room, Fore Street, Devonport,
from 1851 [1851 Religious Census]

PLYMOUTH (Latter Day Saints) Odd Fellows Lodge Room, Russell Street.
Registered 1852

PLYMOUTH (Latter Day Saints) Ker Street/George Street. Registered 1856

PLYMOUTH (Latter Day Saints) Pembroke Street. Registered 1864. A building
lately known as 'The Billiard Room', Pembroke Street, Devonport [1882
Return]

PLYMOUTH (Latter Day Saints) Western College Road, Mannamead. Registered
1936

PLYMOUTH (Brethren/Exclusive Brethren) Raleigh Street, Plymouth, Erected
1831. Gospel Hall, Raleigh Street [Kelly 1889] Demolished

PLYMOUTH (Brethren) Ebrington Street. Erected 1840; closed by 1848

PLYMOUTH (Brethren/Open Brethren) Compton Street f 1845 by secession from
Raleigh Street

PLYMOUTH (Brethren) Knockersknowle, Egg Buckland. Erected 1849 [1851
Religious Census]

PLYMOUTH (Brethren) Park Street [Kelly 1889]

PLYMOUTH (Brethren) Albert Road, Devonport. Registered 1909

PLYMOUTH (Brethren) Wolseley Hall. Registered 1922

PLYMOUTH (S of F) Plymouth MM f 1668 ?
OR Z 1777-93 B 1777-95 (RG 6/274, 276 PRO)

PLYMOUTH (S of F) f 1654-55 on The Hoe; Bilbury Street 1675-1918 [1851
Religious Census] Treville Street [Kelly 1889]; Swarthmore, Mutley Plain
registered 1899
OR Z 1627-1793 M 1663-1795 B 1646-1791 (RG 6/352,1438,1480 PRO)
BT B 1865-68 (DRO)
MI Vennel Street burial ground 1762-1925 (RG 37/122 PRO); (PWDRO)

PLYMOUTH (S of F) Devonport. Meeting house 1777

PLYMOUTH (Dissenters) Trinity Dissenting Chapel, Citadel. Erected 1828
[1851 Religious Census]

PLYMOUTH (Christians) Providence, parish of St Andrew. Erected 1830
[1851 Religious Census]

PLYMOUTH (Christians) Compton Street. Erected 1848 [1851 Religious Census]

PLYMOUTH (Prot and Trinitarian) Princess Street. erected 1848
[1851 Religious Census]

PLYMOUTH (Second Adventist) St Peter's Street. Erected 1848
[1851 Religious Census] Later parish hall

PLYMOUTH (Protestant Evangelical Christians) School Room, Grosvenor Place,
Eldad [1882 Return]

PLYMOUTH (Protestant Evangelical Christians) Compton Street [1882 Return]

PLYMOUTH (Christian Mission) Central Hall, Central Street, Union Street
[1882 Return]

PLYMOUTH (United Christians) Christ Church, Duke Street [1882 Return]

PLYMOUTH (Protestant Dissenters or Salvation Army) Christian Mission, Mount
Street, Devonport [1882 Return]

PLYMOUTH (Salvation Army) Granby Street [Kelly 1889]

PLYMOUTH (Evang.Prot.) Cavendish Street [Kelly 1889]

PLYMOUTH (Jews) Synagogue, Catherine Street. f 1745, erected 1762
[1851 Religious Census] [1882 Return]
OR   Circumcision Register of Abraham Joseph 1784-1834 (Mocatta Library,
     University College, London)
Cop B in Hebrew Cemetery, adjacent to Ford Park (PWDRO)

PLYMOUTH (Jews) Chapel Street Synagogue, Devonport. Registered 1908. Bombed
1940s

PLYMOUTH Ford Park Cemetery
OR   (General ground) B 1855-70   (Church ground) 1853-1938 (PWDRO)
Cop B 1835-70 general ground 1853-72 church ground (I, PWDRO)
MI   (I, DFHS)

PLYMPTON St Mary, Market Road [Plympton Hundred; Plympton St Mary Union]
[2153] Former chapelry in Plympton St Maurice. Separate parish at an early
date
OR   C 1603-1977 M 1603-1975 B 1603-1973 (PWDRO)
BT   CMB 1610-11, 1614, 1617, 1619, 1623, 1626-27, 1629-30, 1633, 1663-64,
     1666, 1668, 1670-71, 1686, 1695, 1697, 1699, 1750-51, 1753-1800 (1801-12
     ?); CB 1813, 1815-35, 1838-63 M 1813, 1815-27, 1829-35 (DRO)
Cop M 1813-37 (Ptd DFHS); C 1684-1787 M 1869-1901 with indexes (PWDRO);
     C 1772-1909 M 1754-1901 B 1772-1873 (I, PWDRO); CMB 1603-1906 (WSL);
     M 1754-1812 indexed by male spouse (DFHS); C 1729-32 (C of A);
     Extr C 1603-1729 M 1612-1760 B 1605-1768 (Vol 7, BG/PCL)
Cop (Mf) M 1627-73 (Mf SG); CM 1684-1837 B 1684-1849 (Mfc SG);
        CMB Nov.1897-May 1899 (Mf SG); Extr C 1603-1728 M 1603-84 (IGI);
        C 1603-1728 M 1603-84 (Mf I SLC)
MI   Ch (Ptd Gent.Mag.1829 I: 512-4); Extr (Whitmore MS, SG)

PLYMPTON St Maurice (or Plympton Earle, or Plympton Morris) [804]
see also the chapelries of BRIXTON, SAMPFORD SPINEY and SHAUGH PRIOR
OR   C 1616-1963 M 1616-1971 B 1616-1958 (PWDRO)
BT   CMB 1610-11, 1613-14, 1623-24, 1633-34, 1677-81, 1684, 1689-90, 1695-96,
     1699, 1750-51, 1753-1801 (1802-12 ?); CB 1839-64 (DRO)

PLYMPTON St Maurice, cont.
Cop CMB 1616-1812 (WSL); CMB 1616-80 (PWDRO); M 1754-1812 indexed by male
    spouse (DFHS); M 1837-1941 with index (PWDRO); Extr C '1539'-1737,
    1749-1807 M 1616-43, 1748-1812 B 1617-1810 (Vol 6, BG/PCL)
Cop (Mf) CMB Nov.1897-May 1899 (Mf SG); Extr C 1616-1812 M 1616-32,
        1655-1812 (IGI); C 1616-1812 (Mf I SLC)
MI (I, DFHS); Ch (Ptd *Gent.Mag.* 1830 I: 302-3)

PLYMPTON All Saints, Sparkwell. Erected 1859. Separate parish from Plympton
St Mary 1884
OR (Inc)
Cop (Mf) CMB Nov.1897-May 1899 (Mf SG)

PLYMPTON Saltram House. Former home of Parker family, Earls of Morley. Now
National Trust. Chapel erected 1776

PLYMPTON (RC) Our Lady of Lourdes, Vicarage Road 1932

PLYMPTON (Ind) Longbrooke. Erected 1806 [1851 Religious Census]

PLYMPTON (Ind) Sparkwell. Erected 1826 [1851 Religious Census]

PLYMPTON (Cong) Lee Mill Bridge. Erected 1830 [1851 Religious Census]
[1882 Return] Closed 1967
OR ZC 1836-37 (RG 4/2538 PRO)
Cop (Mf) ZC 1836-37 (Mf DCRS/WSL, SG); Extr ZC 1836-37 (IGI)

PLYMPTON (Ind, now Cong Fed) Lee Mill, Plymouth Road f 1868

PLYMPTON (Cong Prot Diss) Mill Street Chapel, Ridgeway [1882 Return]

PLYMPTON (Wes) Underwood
OR for *c.*1820-36 *see* ASHBURTON CIRCUIT (RG 45/840 PRO)

PLYMPTON (Wes) Plympton St Mary. Erected *c.*1823 [1851 Religious Census]
OR for *c.*1801-37 *see* ASHBURTON CIRCUIT, PLYMOUTH Ebenezer (RG 4/1763,840,
    1325 PRO)

PLYMPTON (Wes) Ridgeway, Plympton St Maurice. Erected 1869 [1882 Return]
fl *c.*1970

PLYMPTON (Wes) Venton, Sparkwell. Erected 1873. fl *c.*1970
OR M 1972-93 (PWDRO)

PLYMPTON (Prim Meth) Plympton St Maurice. Building belonging to Mr W. Goss
[1882 Return]

PLYMPTON (UMFC/U Meth) Colebrooke. Erected 1868 [1882 Return] fl *c.*1970
OR M 1902-36 (PWDRO)
Cop M 1902-36 with index (PWDRO)

PLYMPTON (Meth) Greenway Avenue, Woodford. Erected 1959. fl *c.*1970

PLYMPTON (Who object to be designated) Mission Room, Underwood [1882 Return]

PLYMPTON (S of F) Part of PLYMOUTH MM. Meeting house 1792

PLYMPTON Plympton St Mary Poor Law Union Workhouse
OR Z 1868-1914 (PWDRO)

PLYMSTOCK St Mary and All Saints, Church Road [Plympton Hundred; Plympton St Mary Union] [3088] United with Hooe
OR C 1591-1919 M 1591-1933 B 1591-1904 (PWDRO)
BT CMB 1607, 1609-10, 1614, 1617-18, 1623, 1626, 1630, 1633, 1639, 1663-64, 1666, 1669-70, 1672, 1677, 1681, 1686, 1688, 1690, 1695, 1699-1700, 1730-37, 1743-44, 1746-51, 1753-75 (1776-1812 ?); CB 1813-42, 1852-54 M 1813-36, 1841-42 (DRO)
Cop M 1591-1812 (WSL, DFHS, SG, Phil Ms); M 1837-95 with index (PWDRO); M 1591-1812 (Boyd)
Cop (Mf) C 1592-1852 M 1592-1836 B 1592-1843 (Mfc SG)

PLYMSTOCK Church of the Good Shepherd, Oreston. Mission chapel erected *c.*1880
OR CM in Plymstock registers

PLYMSTOCK St John the Evangelist, Hooe. Erected and parish created 1855 from Plymstock, with which now united
OR C 1855-1958 M 1855-1969 B 1856-1964 (PWDRO)

PLYMSTOCK St Matthew, Sherford Road, Elburton. Parish created 1973 from Plymstock
OR (Inc)

PLYMSTOCK (RC) St Margaret Mary, Dean's Cross 1933; rebuilt 1961

PLYMSTOCK (Bapt) Hooe Cottage Meeting pre-1800 [1851 Religious Census]

PLYMSTOCK (Bapt) Hooe, preaching room. Pre-1809 [1851 Religious Census]

PLYMSTOCK (Bapt) Oreston. Erected *c.*1836 [1851 Religious Census]

PLYMSTOCK (Cong?/URC) Plymstock United (Norely Memorial), Plymstock Road 1928

PLYMSTOCK (Ind) n.d. [1851 Religious Census]

PLYMSTOCK (Wes) Oreston. Woburn Road. Erected 1816 [1851 Religious Census]; Refuge Chapel [1882 Return] Rebuilt 1888. fl *c.*1970.
OR for *c.*1787-1837 *see* PLYMOUTH Ebenezer, and Morice Street Devonport (RG 4/1325,864 PRO)

PLYMSTOCK (Wes) Elburton
OR for *c.*1801-37 *see* ASHBURTON CIRCUIT, PLYMOUTH Ebenezer (RG 4/1763,1325 PRO)

PLYMSTOCK (Wes) Hooe
OR for *c.*1813-37 *see* PLYMOUTH Ebenezer (RG 4/1325,1092 PRO)

PLYMSTOCK (Wes) Turnchapel. A building in the occupation of George Jackson [1882 Return]
OR for *c.*1813-37 *see* PLYMOUTH Ebenezer (RG 4/1325,1092 PRO)

PLYMSTOCK (Wes) Erected 1847 [1851 Religious Census]

PLYMSTOCK (Bible Christian) n.d. [1851 Religious Census]

PLYMSTOCK (Bible Christian) Springfield Road, Elburton. Erected 1868. fl *c.*1970

PLYMSTOCK (UMFC) Pomphlett Road. Erected 1909. fl c.1970

PLYMSTOCK (Prot Diss) Dean's Cross Chapel [1882 Return]

PLYMSTOCK Dissenters' burial ground
MI   (PWDRO)

PLYMTREE St John the Baptist [Hayridge Hundred; Honiton Union]   [439]
Now with BROADHEMBURY, PAYHEMBURY
OR   C 1538-44, 1560-1991 M 1538-44, 1560-1989 B 1538-1946 (DRO)
BT   CMB 1605, 1608, 1617, 1620, 1662-64, 1668-69, 1672, 1675, 1677?, 1678,
     1683, 1685, 1687, 1690 (1691-1812 ?); C 1813-56, 1858-59, 1862-64, 1866
     M 1813-18, 1820-27 B 1813-47, 1849-56, 1858-59, 1862-64, 1866 (DRO)
Cop CMB 1538-1837 (Ptd DCRS 1940); B 1813-37 (Ptd DFHS); B 1813-37 (WSL,
     SG); M 1579-1837 non parishioners (DFHS)
Cop (Mf) CMB 1538-1837 (I, Mfc CFHS); Extr CM 1538-1837 (IGI); CM 1538-1837
     (Mf I SLC)
MI   Incledon 718 (NDA)

PLYMTREE (Ind/Cong, later URC) Norman's Green f 1848 [1882 Return]
OR   M 1900-50, 1975-87 (DRO)

POLTIMORE St Mary the Virgin [Wonford Hundred; St Thomas Union]   [292]
Now with STOKE CANON, HUXHAM, REWE, NETHEREXE
OR   C 1718-1890 M 1718-1976 B 1718-1962 (DRO)   Noted in 1831: C 1694+
     M 1718+ B 1663-92, 1718+
BT   CMB 1614, 1617-18, 1621, 1624-25, 1630, 1641, 1663, 1667, 1669-72, 1675,
     1677-79, 1683, 1687, 1690, 1697 (1698-1812 ?); CB 1813-57 M 1814-27,
     1829-37 (DRO)
Cop CMB 1614-1716 from BT, 1718-1837 (DCRS/WSL); Extr C 1718-1806 M 1721-45
     B 1721-1809 (Vol 3, BG/PCL)
Cop (Mf) Extr C 1614-1837 M 1614-41, 1663-83, 1716-1837 (IGI); C 1614-1837
     M 1614-41, 1663-83, 1716-1837 (Mf I SLC)
MI   Extr (Whitmore MS, SG)

POOL, NORTH   see POOL, SOUTH

POOL, SOUTH St Nicholas and St Cyriac [Coleridge Hundred; Kingsbridge Union]
[567] United 1932 with CHIVELSTONE. Now with CHARLETON, BUCKLAND TOUT
SAINTS, EAST PORTLEMOUTH, CHIVELSTONE
OR   C 1664-1968 M 1665-1941 B 1664-1982 (DRO)
BT   CMB 1606, 1614, 1617, 1620, 1623, 1625, 1633, 1670-72, 1674, 1676,
     1678-81, 1686-87, 1689-90, 1695-97, 1699, 1700 (1701-1812 ?);
     CB 1813-34, 1836-38, 1840 M 1813-32, 1834, 1836 (DRO)
Cop M 1754-1812 indexed by male spouse (DFHS)
Cop (Mf) C 1664-1874 M 1665-1837 B 1664-1941 (Mfc SG)

POOL, SOUTH (Wes) North Pool
OR   for c.1813-37 see KINGSBRIDGE (RG 4/1088 PRO)

POOL, SOUTH (Wes)
OR   for c.1813-37 see KINGSBRIDGE (RG 4/1088 PRO)

PORTLEMOUTH, EAST St Winwalloe [Coleridge Hundred; Kingsbridge Union]   [427]
Now with CHARLETON, BUCKLAND TOUT SAINTS, SOUTH POOL, CHIVELSTONE
OR C 1563-1878 M 1594-1625, 1647-1983 B 1562-1978 (DRO)
BT CMB 1602, 1609, 1614-15, 1620, 1624-25, 1628, 1631, 1663-64, 1666,
    1669-77, 1680-81, 1686-88, 1690, 1696-97, 1699 (1700-1812 ?); C 1813-51
    M 1813-23, 1825-31, 1833-36 B 1813-25, 1827-51 (DRO)
Cop M 1754-1812 (DFHS)
Cop (Mf) C 1563-1669, 1692-1978 M 1594-1666, 1693-1836 B 1562-1670,
    1692-1978 (Mfc SG)

PORTLEMOUTH, EAST (Wes) Part of the old poorhouse [1851 Religious Census]

PORTLEMOUTH, EAST (Wes) Erected 1931. fl c.1970

PORTLEMOUTH, WEST   see MALBOROUGH

POSBURY   see CREDITON

POSTBRIDGE   see LYDFORD

POUGHILL St Michael and All Angels [West Budleigh Hundred; Crediton Union]
[331] Now with NORTH CREADY
OR C 1653-1908 M 1653-1837 B 1653-1812 (DRO) Noted in 1831: CMB 1567+
BT CMB 1603-04, 1613, 1624, 1630, 1663-64, 1667-70, 1672, 1675, 1678-79,
    1683, 1687, 1690, 1695-97, 1699 (1700-1812 ?); CB 1813-38 M 1813-37
    (DRO)
Cop CMB 1603-44 from BT, 1653-1837 (DCRS/WSL); Extr C '1537'-1811
    M '1538'-1747 B '1537'-1811 (Vol 4, BG/PCL)
Cop (Mf) (Tiverton SP); Extr C 1603-1837 M 1603-13, 1624-30, 1644-1837
    (IGI); C 1603-1837 M 1603-13, 1624-30, 1644-1837 (Mf I SLC)
MI (I, DFHS)

POUGHILL (Ind) A house [1851 Religious Census]; Meeting Room [1882 Return]

POUGHILL (Cong, now Cong Fed) Erected 1863

POUGHILL (Wes)
OR for c.1817-37 see HOLSWORTHY (RG 4/1210 PRO)

POUNDSGATE   see WIDECOMBE

POWDERHAM St Clement [Exminster Hundred; St Thomas Union]   [275]
Now with KENTON, MAMHEAD, COFTON, STARCROSS
OR C 1575-1705, 1734-1948 M 1559-1597, 1649-1719, 1734-1981 B 1558-78,
    1615-1979 (DRO)
BT CMB 1611, 1609, 1611, 1616, 1633, 1669-70, 1675?, 1677, 1679, 1683,
    1696-97 (1698-1812 ?); C 1813-15, 1837-50, 1852-58, 1860-61, 1863, 1881
    M 1813-16, 1818-26, 1828-33, 1835 B 1813-35, 1837-44, 1846-50, 1852-58,
    1860-61, 1863, 1881 (DRO)
Cop B 1785-1837 (Ptd DFHS); C 1575-1837 M 1559-1835 B 1558-1837 (DCRS/WSL,
    SG)
Cop (Mf) Extr C 1575-1847 M 1559-97, 1650-1700, 1715-19, 1734-1835 (IGI);
    C 1575-1847 (Mf I SLC)
MI (I, DFHS); Ch extr (Ptd Cresswell 133-5); Ch, cy 1932 (Ts SG)

POWDERHAM Powderham Castle. Seat of Earls of Devon. Chapel 1717

POWDERHAM (Presb) Licensed 1672; fl c.1690; closed by 1715

POWDERHAM (Wes)
OR for c.1813-37 see TEIGNMOUTH (RG 4/1220 PRO)

PRESCOTT   see CULMSTOCK

PRESTON   see PAIGNTON

PRINCETOWN   see LYDFORD

PRIXFORD   see MARWOOD

PUDDINGTON St Thomas à Becket [Witheridge Hundred; Crediton Union] [275]
Rebuilt 1838. Now with NORTH CREADY
OR C 1555-1752, 1790-1812 M 1555-1848 B 1555-1812 (DRO)
BT CMB 1606-08, 1610, 1634, 1668, 1670, 1672, 1674, 1679-80, 1682-83,
    1688-91, 1694-95, 1699-1700, 1702, 1712, 1714-15 (1716-1812 ?);
    C 1830-38, 1840, 1842 M 1831-33, 1835, 1837-38, 1840 B 1830, 1833-36,
    1838, 1840, 1842; unfit for production, except 1838-42 (DRO)
Cop C 1556-1812 Banns 1825-1935 M 1555-1848 B 1555-1812 (DRO); CMB 1555-1848
    (DCRS/WSL)
Cop (Mf) (Tiverton SP); CB 1555-1812 M 1555-1848 Banns 1759-1834 (Mfc SG)
MI (I, DFHS)

PUDDINGTON (Ind/Cong) Tristham Chapel fl 1729 [1851 Religious Census]
[1882 Return] Closed 1968
OR M 1906-65 (DRO)

PUTFORD, EAST Dedication unknown [Shebbear Hundred; Bideford Union] Chapelry
in BUCKLAND BREWER [209] later united with West Putford, and renamed Putford
1971. Rebuilt 1887. Redundant. Converted to farm building
OR C 1799-1964 M 1831-1947 B 1799-1953 (DRO) Noted in 1831: C 1671-1812
    MB 1671-1799. see DCRS copy and IGI, below, which appear also to
    include earlier, unlisted BTs.
BT CMB 1678-79, 1682-83, 1689, 1694-95, 1715? (1716-1812 ?); none listed
    after 1812 (DRO)
Cop CMB 1605-35 from BT, 1671-1799 (DCRS/WSL)
Cop (Mf) (Appledore SP); Extr C 1605-1799 M 1605-1770 (IGI); C 1605-1799
        M 1605-1770 (Mf I SLC)
MI (I, DFHS); Incledon 1051 (NDA)

PUTFORD, EAST (Wes)
OR for c.1817-37 see HOLSWORTHY (RG 4/1210 PRO)

PUTFORD, EAST (Bible Christian) Providence. Erected 1849. fl c.1970

PUTFORD, WEST St Stephen [Black Torrington Hundred; Bideford Union 1835-97;
Holsworthy Union 1897-1930] [400] United with East Putford. Renamed Putford
1971
OR CB 1668-1812 M 1668-1968 (DRO); CB 1813+ M 1968+ (Inc)
BT CMB 1614, 1624-25, 1629, 1634, 1663-64, 1668-72, 1674, 1676-82, 1684,
    1686-88, 1699-1700 (1701-1812 ?); CMB 1813-37 (DRO)
Cop CMB 1614-69 from BT, 1668-1812 (DCRS/WSL); M 1668-1812 (Boyd)
Cop (Mf) Extr C 1614-1812 M 1614-29, 1664-83, 1698-1811 (IGI); C 1614-1812
        M 1614-29, 1664-83, 1698-1811 (Mf I SLC)
MI (I, DFHS); Incledon 901 (NDA)

PUTFORD, WEST (Wes)
OR for c.1817-37 see HOLSWORTHY CIRCUIT (RG 4/1210 PRO)

PUTFORD, WEST (Wes) Sessacott. Erected 1843 [1851 Religious Census] [1882 Return]

PUTFORD, WEST (Bible Christian) Providence. Erected 1849 [1851 Religious Census] [1882 Return]

PYWORTHY St Swithun [Black Torrington Hundred; Holsworthy Union]   [700] United 1959 with PANCRASWEEK. Now also with BRIDGERULE
OR   C 1653-1977 M 1681-1992 B 1682-1891 (DRO)
BT   CMB 1610-11, 1614, 1616, 1619, 1633, 1639, 1673, 1679, 1695, 1699
     (1700-1812 ?); CMB 1813-34 (DRO)
Cop M 1813-37 (Ptd DFHS)
Cop (Mf) C 1653-1857 M 1681-1837 B 1682-1891 (Mfc SG)
MI   Extr (Whitmore MS, SG)

PYWORTHY (Wes) Lana Chapel. Erected 1840 [1851 Religious Census]; Monk's Farm [1882 Return]
OR   for c.1817-37 see HOLSWORTHY (RG 4/1210 PRO)

PYWORTHY (Bible Christian) Derril. Erected 1830 [1851 Religious Census] [1882 Return] fl c.1970

QUEEN'S NYMPTON or **QUEEN'S NYMET**   see MOLTON, SOUTH

RACKENFORD All Saints [Witheridge Hundred; South Molton Union]   [472] Now with EXE VALLEY
OR   C 1597-1686, 1703-1869 M 1561-1992 B 1577-1624, 1703-1947 (DRO)
BT   CMB 1606-07, 1610, 1612, 1614-15, 1621, 1628, 1631?, 1632, 1637, 1670,
     1674, 1679, 1684-85, 1688-89, 1691, 1694, 1700, 1704-07, 1710-11,
     1714-15 (1716-1812 ?); C 1813-32, 1861-66 M 1813-37 B 1813-20, 1822-52,
     1861-66 (DRO)
Cop C 1589-1699 M 1561-1700 B 1577-1699 (DRO)
Cop (Mf) (Tiverton SP)

RACKENFORD (Bible Christian) Ebenezer, Church Village. Erected 1848 [1851 Religious Census] [1882 Return] fl c.1970

RADDON   United benefice including THORVERTON, CADBURY, UPTON PYNE, BRAMPFORD SPEKE, NEWTON ST CYRES

RATTERY Blessed Virgin Mary [Stanborough Hundred; Totnes Union]   [506] Now with SOUTH BRENT
OR   C 1653-1865 M 1653-1992 B 1653-1993 (DRO)
BT   CMB 1609, 1614, 1618, 1630?, 1643, 1663-66, 1668, 1670-72, 1674-77,
     1679-81, 1684, 1686-88, 1690, 1695-96, 1699-1700 (1701-1812 ?);
     CB 1813-40 M 1813-35, 1837, 1839-40 (DRO)
Cop B 1800-37 (Ptd DFHS); CMB 1609-41 from BT, 1653-1837 (DCRS/WSL, WSL)
Cop (Mf) (Totnes SP); Extr C 1609-1837 M 1609-18, 1631-41, 1653-1837 (IGI);
     C 1609-1837 M 1609-18, 1631-41, 1653-1837 (Mf I SLC)

RATTERY (Wes)
OR   for c.1820-36 see ASHBURTON CIRCUIT (RG 4/840 PRO)

REVELSTOKE St Peter [Plympton Hundred; Plympton St Mary Union] [492]
Chapelry in YEALMPTON. Separate parish 1856. Church abandoned 1870s. Rebuilt
1882 on new site at Noss Mayo. Redundant. Churches Conservation Trust.
Now with NEWTON FERRERS
OR C 1649-1961 M 1654-1977 B 1652-1970 (PWDRO)
BT CMB 1611-12, 1614, 1617-18, 1620, 1623, 1639, 1677, 1682, 1690, 1699,
    1750-51, 1753-60, 1762-92 (1793-1812 ?); CB 1838-42 C 1844-57 B 1844-55,
    1857 (DRO)
Cop M 1838-1977 with index (PWDRO)
MI (I, DFHS)

REVELSTOKE (Wes) Noss Mayo. Erected 1870 [1882 Return] fl c.1970

REVELSTOKE (Brethren) n.d. [1851 Religious Census]

REWE St Mary the Virgin [part Hayridge Hundred; part Wonford Hundred;
St Thomas Union] [186] United 1937 with NETHER EXE. Now also with STOKE
CANON, HUXHAM, POLTIMORE
OR C 1675-1887 M 1686-1836 B 1686-1994 (DRO)
BT CMB 1609, 1611, 1614, 1616-17, 1620, 1622?, 1668, 1670, 1675, 1678,
    1683, 1685, 1689-90, 1696 (1697-1812 ?); C 1815, 1817-20, 1822-23,
    1838-60 M 1815-23 B 1815-20, 1822-23, 1838-60 (DRO)
Cop M 1686-1837 (SG, Phil Ms); CMB 1609-68 from BT, 1686-1837 (DCRS/WSL);
    M 1611-1837 (Boyd)
Cop (Mf) Extr C 1609-1837 M 1611-68, 1686-1836 (IGI); C 1609-1837 M 1611-68,
        1686-1836 (Mf I SLC)
MI (I, DFHS); Extr (Whitmore MS, SG)

REWE (Wes)
OR for c.1831-37 see EXETER Mint (RG 4/1208 PRO)

REXON CROSS   see BROADWOODWIDGER

RIDGEWAY   see PLYMPTON

RING ASH   see ASHREIGNEY

RINGMORE   see ST NICHOLAS

RINGMORE All Hallows [Ermington Hundred; Kingsbridge Union] [309]
United 1934 with KINGSTON. Now with MODBURY
OR C 1719-1860 M 1719-1836 B 1719-1792 (DRO) No earlier registers noted in
    1831
BT CMB 1602, 1608, 1614-15, 1618, 1621, 1628, 1630, 1634, 1642, 1663, 1666,
    1669-72, 1674-76, 1679-80, 1682, 1684, 1686-87, 1690, 1696-97, 1699,
    1750-52, 1754-59, 1761-83, 1785-95 (1796-1812 ?); C 1813-33 M 1813,
    1815-19, 1821-23, 1825-26, 1828, 1831-33 B 1813-33 (DRO)
Cop B 1764-1837 (Ptd DFHS); B 1764-1814 (WSL, SG); CMB 1616-1981 (WSL);
    CB 1719-1814 M 1717-1800; M 1754-1812 indexed by male spouse (DFHS)
Cop (Mf) Extr C 1719-1814 M 1719-1806 (IGI); C 1719-1814 M 1719-1806
        (Mf I SLC)

RINGMORE (Bapt) Erected 1832 [1851 Religious Census] [1882 Return]

RINGMORE (Wes)
OR for c.1820-36 see ASHBURTON CIRCUIT (RG 4/840 PRO)

RINGMORE (Wes) Challaborough
OR for c.1820-36 see ASHBURTON CIRCUIT (RG 4/840 PRO)

191

RINGSASH   see ASHREIGNEY

ROBOROUGH   see BICKLEIGH near Plymouth

ROBOROUGH (Ivybridge Deanery) United benefice including BICKLEIGH, GLENHOLT, SHAUGH PRIOR, LEE MOOR

ROBOROUGH St Peter [Fremington Hundred; Torrington Union]   [584]
Now with TWO RIVERS
OR C 1549-1857 M 1549-1972 B 1549-1933 (NDRO)
BT CMB 1597-1602, 1607, 1613, 1624, 1672, 1674, 1678-79, 1682-83, 1688-89,
     1691, 1694-97, 1699, 1702-04, 1707, 1709-12, 1714-15 (1716-1812 ?);
     C 1813-68 M 1813-38 (DRO)
Cop CMB 1549-1812 (DCRS/WSL); M 1549-1812 (Boyd)
Cop (Mf) Extr C 1550-1812 M 1549-1812 (IGI); C 1550-1812 M 1549-1812
     (Mf I SLC)

ROBOROUGH (Bible Christian) Ebberley Lodge. f 1838/9 [1851 Religious Census]
[1882 Return] fl c.1970

ROBOROUGH DOWN see BUCKLAND MONACHORUM

ROCK   see BUCKLAND MONACHORUM

ROCKBEARE St Mary with St Andrew [East Budleigh Hundred; St Thomas Union]
[530] Now with AYLESBEARE, FARRINGDON, CLYST HONITON, SOWTON
OR C 1645-1932 M 1645-1953 B 1645-1909 (DRO)
BT CMB 1606, 1614, 1625, 1630, 1662-64, 1666?, 1669, 1671-73, 1675,
     1678-79, 1683, 1687, 1690, 1695-97, 1699 (1700-1812 ?); CB 1813,
     1838-44, 1846-54 M 1813 (DRO)
Cop B 1813-37 (Ptd DFHS); B 1813-37 (WSL, SG); CMB 1645-1837 (DCRS/WSL, WSL)
Cop (Mf) Extr CM 1645-1837 (IGI); CM 1645-1837 (Mf I SLC)
MI (I, DFHS); Extr (Whitmore MS, SG); Incledon 258 (NDA)

ROCKBEARE (Ind) Marsh Green. Erected 1837 [1851 Religious Census]
[1882 Return]

ROCKBEARE (S of F) fl c.1696-1700. Part of TOPSHAM MM

ROMANSLEIGH St Rumon [Witheridge Hundred; South Molton Union]   [217]
Rebuilt 1868. Now with SOUTH MOLTON
OR C 1697-1993 M 1698-1959 B 1539-1995 (NDRO)
BT CMB 1602, 1607-08, 1610, 1614, 1630, 1634, 1668, 1670, 1674, 1679, 1683,
     1688, 1690-91, 1694-97, 1699-1700, 1707, 1711-12 (1713-1812 ?);
     C 1817-50 M 1817-22, 1824, 1826, 1829-31, 1833-36 B 1817, 1819-30,
     1832-50 (DRO)
Cop (Mf) C 1697-1812 M 1698-1836 B 1539-1804 (Mfc SG)
MI (I, NDA)

ROMANSLEIGH (Presb) fl c.1672-90

ROMANSLEIGH (Bible Christian) Rowley Cottage [1851 Religious Census]

ROOSDOWN   extra-parochial place, located in AXMINSTER [10]

ROSE ASH St Peter [Witheridge Hundred; South Molton Union]   [487]
Now with OAKMOOR
OR C 1591-1987 M 1591-1986 B 1591-1812 (DRO)
BT CMB 1607-08, 1612, 1614, 1617, 1629, 1632-33, 1668, 1670, 1674, 1679,
    1683, 1689, 1691, 1695-97, 1699-1700, 1706-07, 1709-10, 1711-12, 1714-15
    (1716-1812 ?); C 1813-50, 1852 M 1813-19, 1821, 1823-30, 1832, 1834-37
    B 1813-22, 1824, 1826-50, 1852 (DRO)
Cop CMB 1591-1837 (DCRS/WSL); M 1591-1836 (Boyd)
Cop (Mf) Extr C 1591-1837 M 1591-1646, 1660-1837 (IGI); C 1591-1837
    M 1591-1646, 1660-1837 (Mf I SLC)
MI (I, NDA); (I, DFHS)

ROSE ASH (Presb) fl c.1672-90

ROSE ASH (Wes) A room, Ash Moor [1851 Religious Census]; Ash Mill, erected
1867 [1882 Return] Closed 1984

ROSE ASH (Bible Christian) Hope, Rose Ash Moor. Erected 1858 [1882 Return]
fl c.1970

ROUNDSWELL   see BARNSTAPLE

ROUSDON   see AXMOUTH

ROWDEN   see SHEBBEAR

ST BUDEAUX   see PLYMOUTH

ST GILES IN THE HEATH [Black Torrington Hundred; Holsworthy Union 1837-52;
Launceston Union (Cornwall) 1852-1930; Truro Diocese from 1876] [357]
United 1973 with WERRINGTON, VIRGINSTOW
OR C 1653-1902 M 1653-1980 B 1653-1982 (CRO)
BT CMB terminal dates 1602-73, 1737-40, 1773-1812 (DRO); CMB terminal dates
    1684-1736, 1741-72 (CRO); C 1818, 1820-21, 1823-32 M 1818, 1821,
    1823-27, 1829-30, 1832 B 1818, 1820-21, 1823-26, 1828-32 (DRO)
Cop M 1813-37 (Ptd DFHS); M 1813-37 (Cornwall M Index); C 1733-1812
    M 1602-1812 B 1694-1812 (PWDRO); Extr M 1601-73 (SG); M 1602-73 from BT
    (Boyd); B 1813-37 (Cornwall B Index)
Cop (Mf) Extr C 1681-1804 (IGI); C 1681-1804 (Mf I SLC)

ST GILES IN THE HEATH (Bible Christian) Erected 1843 [1851 Religious
Census] Rebuilt 1879. fl c.1970
OR see LAUNCESTON Circuit

ST GILES IN THE WOOD St Giles [Fremington Hundred; Torrington Union] [894]
Now with TWO RIVERS
OR C 1556-1910 M 1556-1985 B 1556-1922 (NDRO)
BT CMB 1602, 1607, 1610-11, 1613, 1624, 1638, 1668, 1670, 1674, 1679,
    1682-83, 1688-91, 1693, 1699, 1702, 1704, 1707-12, 1714-15, 1717-23,
    1726-27, 1730, 1732-37, 1739, 1741-51, 1753-56, 1762-71 (1772-1812 ?);
    CB 1813-50 M 1813-37 (DRO)
Cop B 1813-37 (Ptd DFHS); B 1813-37 (WSL, DLS, SG); CMB 1555-1747
    (DCRS/WSL); M 1556-1747 (Boyd)
Cop (Mf) Extr C 1556-1743 M 1555-1743 (IGI); C 1556-1743 M 1555-1743
    (Mf I SLC)

ST GILES IN THE WOOD (Bapt) Kingscott. Erected pre-1801 [1851 Religious
Census]

ST GILES IN THE WOOD (Wes) Erected 1834 [1851 Religious Census]
[1882 Return]
OR for c.1819-37 see BIDEFORD (RG 4/955 PRO)

ST LEONARD   see EXETER

ST MARYCHURCH   see TORQUAY

ST NICHOLAS or SHALDON St Nicholas, Ringmore [Wonford Hundred; Newton Abbot
Union] [1178] Now a daughter church of St Peter, below
OR C 1616-1653, 1716-1904 M 1616-1653, 1716-1837 B 1616-1653, 1716-1936
    (DRO)
BT CMB 1633-35, 1639, 1663, 1665-67, 1668?, 1669, 1673, 1675, 1678-79,
    1683, 1687, 1690, 1695-97 (1698-1812 ?); CMB 1813-33 (DRO)
Cop CMB 1824-1928 (WSL)
Cop (Mf) (Torquay SP)
MI (I, DFHS)

ST NICHOLAS St Peter, Shaldon. Now the parish church, Erected 1893-1902

ST NICHOLAS (RC) St Ignatius of Loyola, Fore Street, Shaldon 1931

ST NICHOLAS (Bapt) Shaldon. Erected c.1800 [1851 Religious Census]

ST NICHOLAS (Cong) Ebenezer, Shaldon. Erected 1823 [1851 Religious Census]
OR ZC 1825-36 (RG 4/1327 PRO)
Cop (Mf) ZC 1825-36 (Mf DCRS/WSL, SG); 'Shaldon St Nicholas':
         Extr ZC 1825-36 (IGI); ZC 1825-36 (Mf I SLC)

ST NICHOLAS (Wes) Shaldon. Erected 1817 [1851 Religious Census]
[1882 Return]
OR for c.1813-37 see TEIGNMOUTH (RG 4/1220 PRO)

ST PANCRAS   see AXMOUTH Rousdon

ST PETROX   see DARTMOUTH

ST SAVIOUR   see DARTMOUTH

ST THOMAS THE APOSTLE   see EXETER St Thomas

SAINTHILL   see KENTISBEARE

SALCOMBE   see MALBOROUGH

SALCOMBE REGIS St Mary and St Peter [East Budleigh Hundred; Honiton Union]
[448] Now with SID VALLEY
OR C 1702-1995 M 1702-1991 B 1709-1975 (DRO) Noted in 1831: 'one old book
    of Bap Bur Marr but so torn and confused as to render it impossible to
    decide when the entries commence and terminate'
BT CMB 1609-11, 1614, 1617, 1620, 1624, 1629-30, 1669, 1672, 1675, 1678-79,
    1683 (1684-1812 ?); CMB 1813, 1815-35 C 1837, 1839, 1853-54, 1856-59
    B 1837, 1853-54, 1856-59 (DRO)
Cop B 1813-37 (Ptd DFHS); B 1813-37 (SG); CMB 1609-1700 (WSL); CMB 1609-1701
    from BT, 1690-1930 (DCRS/WSL); M 1609-1837 (Boyd)
Cop (Mf) (Colyton SP); Extr C 1609-1929 M 1609-30, 1669-1930 (IGI);
         C 1609-1875 M 1609-30, 1669-1875 (Mf I SLC)

SALCOMBE REGIS (Presb) fl c.1672-90

SAMPFORD COURTENAY St Andrew [Black Torrington Hundred; Okehampton Union]
[1217] Now with NORTH TAWTON, BONDLEIGH, HONEYCHURCH
OR C 1558-1888 M 1558-1955 B 1558-1812 (DRO)
BT CMB 1614 or 1617, 1629?, 1639, 1641, 1663-64, 1666, 1668-69, 1671-72,
    1674, 1676-79, 1686, 1694 (1695-1812 ?); CB 1813-53 M 1813-37 (DRO)
Cop C 1558-1840 Banns 1754-1812 M 1558-1837 B 1558-1812 (DRO)
Cop (Mf) (Okehampton SP)
MI Extr (Whitmore MS, SG)

SAMPFORD COURTENAY St Mary, Sticklepath. Chapel-of-ease. Now with BELSTONE

SAMPFORD COURTENAY (Presb) fl *c.*1672-90

SAMPFORD COURTENAY (Wes) Sticklepath. Erected 1816 [1851 Religious Census]
[1882 Return] fl *c.*1970
OR for *c.*1815-37 *see* OKEHAMPTON (RG 4/1089 PRO)

SAMPFORD COURTENAY (Bible Christian) Erected 1877. A building in the
occupation of H.Higman [1882 Return] fl *c.*1970

SAMPFORD COURTENAY (Meth) Sticklepath
OR C 1815-1880 1812 M 1839-1870 (DRO)

SAMPFORD COURTENAY (Evangelical) Sticklepath Community Church FIEC

SAMPFORD COURTENAY (S of F) Sticklepath fl 1691. Part of NORTH
TAWTON/CREDITON MM. Members said to have joined Wesleyans. Burial ground
amalgamated with Wes

SAMPFORD PEVERELL United benefice including SAMPFORD PEVERELL, UPLOWMAN,
HOLCOMBE ROGUS, HOCKWORTHY, BURLESCOMBE, HUNTSHAM, HALBERTON, ASH THOMAS

SAMPFORD PEVERELL St John the Baptist [Halberton Hundred; Tiverton Union]
[787] Now with SAMPFORD PEVERELL united benefice
OR C 1672-1883 M 1674-1972 B 1674-1860 (DRO)
BT CMB 1609, 1611, 1613, 1617, 1631-32, 1635, 1638, 1664, 1667-71, 1675,
    1678, 1685, 1687, 1690, 1696-97, 1699 (1700-1812 ?); CB 1813-38, 1840,
    1847-50 M 1813-38, 1847-49 (DRO)
Cop (Mf) (Tiverton SP)
MI Extr (Whitmore MS, SG)

SAMPFORD PEVERELL (Presb) fl *c.*1672-90

SAMPFORD PEVERELL (Wes) Erected 1803 [1882 Return] fl *c.*1970
OR C 1825-33 (RG 4/1326 PRO); B 1909-16 (DRO); for *c.*1806-37 *see also*
    CULLOMPTON, TIVERTON (RG 4/958,342 PRO)
Cop B 1909-16 (SG, Tiverton Museum)
Cop (Mf) C 1825-33 (Mf DCRS/WSL, SG); Extr C 1825-33 (IGI)

SAMPFORD SPINEY St Mary [Roborough Hundred; Tavistock Union] [366]
Chapelry in PLYMPTON ST MAURICE. Separate parish 1772. *see also* BUCKLAND
MONACHORUM St John, Horrabridge, with which now united.
OR C 1654-1660, 1704-1970 M 1654-1752, 1813-1987 B 1713-1989 (PWDRO)
Noted in 1831: CB 1659-1812
BT CMB 1608, 1611, 1614, 1616-17, 1619, 1631, 1633, 1639, 1664, 1666,
    1668-72, 1674-82, 1684, 1686, 1689-90, 1694-95, 1697, 1750-1811;
    C 1813-37 M 1813-15, 1817, 1820-37 B 1813-38, 1840, 1847-50 (DRO)

SAMPFORD SPINEY cont.
Cop M 1608-1754 (I, Ptd, edit M.Brown, Dartmoor Press 1999); CMB 1608-1811
(DFHS); B 1800-1900 (I, PWDRO); Extr C 1684-86 'very imperfect'
M 1691-1724 B 1674-1759 (Vol 20, BG/PCL)
Cop (Mf) (Tavistock SP)
MI (Ptd DRMI 1: 1998)

SAMPFORD SPINEY (Wes)
OR for *c*.1808-37 *see* TAVISTOCK (RG 4/341 PRO)

SAMPFORD ST SWITHUN *see* SANDFORD

SANDFORD or SAMPFORD St Swithin [Crediton Hundred; Crediton Union] [2011]
Chapelry in CREDITON. United 1928 with UPTON HELLIONS
OR C 1603-1906 M 1603-1991 B 1603-1856 (DRO)
BT CMB 1606, 1609, 1614, 1617, 1624, 1636, 1664-65, 1667-68, 1670-73, 1676,
1678, 1680-81, 1688, 1691, 1693, 1696-1706 (1707-1812 ?); CB 1813-49,
1851-54 M 1813-37, 1856 (DRO)
Cop CMB 1603-1837 (DCRS/WSL); B 1813-37 (Ptd DFHS); M 1603-1812 (Boyd);
Extr C 1603-77 M 1603-1704 B 1604-1812 (Vol 10, BG/PCL)
Cop (Mf) Extr CM 1603-1837 (IGI); CM 1603-1837 (Mf I SLC)
MI (I, DFHS); Extr (Whitmore MS, SG); Incledon 156 (NDA)

SANDFORD (Ind/Cong, later Cong Fed) Erected 1848 [1851 Religious Census];
a building, East Village [1882 Return]; British Schools [1882 Return];
Church Street (Cong Fed)

SANDFORD (Bible Christian) 'pre-1800' [1851 Religious Census]

SANDFORD (U Meth) East Village Chapel. Erected 1927. Closed 1972
OR M 1945-65 (DRO)

SANDFORD (U Meth) New Buildings. Erected 1935. fl *c*.1970

SATTERLEIGH St Peter [South Molton Hundred; South Molton Union 1835-94]
[58] *see* WARKLEIGH WITH SATTERLEIGH, Now with SOUTH MOLTON. Redundant.
Churches Conservation Trust
OR C 1574-1983 MB 1574-1989 (NDRO)
BT CMB 1606-08, 1610, 1617, 1620, 1632-33, 1670, 1674, 1680, 1683, 1688-89,
1698, 1700, 1712, 1714-16, 1718, 1722, 1726-29, 1732-34 (1735-1812 ?);
C 1813-21, 1823-39, 1841 M 1813, 1818, 1821, 1826, 1829, 1831, 1834-35
B 1813, 1816, 1818-19, 1821-23, 1826-27, 1829, 1832-35, 1837-38, 1840
(DRO)
Cop (Mf) CB 1574-1812 M 1574-1935 (Mfc SG)
MI (I, NDA); Incledon 1115 (NDA)

SATTERLEIGH (Presb) fl *c*.1672-90

SATTERLEIGH AND WALKLEIGH (Bible Christian) Meeth. Erected 1925. Closed 1982

SAUNTON   *see* BRAUNTON

SCORITTON   *see* BUCKFASTLEIGH

SEATON AND BEER St Gregory, Seaton [Colyton Hundred; Axminster Union 1836-94] [1803] Divided 1905 into parishes of SEATON and BEER
OR   C 1584-1932 M 1584-1972 B 1584-1952 (DRO)
BT   CMB 1611, 1614, 1616-17, 1620-21, 1624, 1629-31, 1669, 1671, 1679, 1683, 1687, 1690, 1696, 1699 (1700-1812 ?); C 1813-51, N 1813-38 B 1813-50 (DRO)
Cop M 1813-37 (Ptd DFHS); B 1813-37 (Ptd DFHS); B 1813-37 (SG); CM 1584-1837 B 1584-1861 (DCRS/WSL); M 1584-1837 (Boyd)
Cop (Mf) (Colyton SP); Extr C 1584-1838 M 1584-1837 (IGI); C 1584-1838 M 1584-1837 (Mf I SLC)
MI   Ch, cy (Ptd Pulman *Book of the Axe* 1875; reprint 1969); Cy extr 1909 (A.W.Matthews *Ye Olde Mortality* vol.8: MS SG); Incledon 397 (NDA)

SEATON AND BEER St Michael, Beer. Chapelry in Seaton and Beer; rebuilt 1877; separate parish 1905. Now with BRANSCOMBE
OR   C 1880-1923 M 1880-1981 B 1880-1978 (DRO)
MI   Cy (Ptd Pulman *Book of the Axe* 1875; reprint 1969); Incledon 405 (NDA)

SEATON AND BEER St Gregory, Seaton. Chapelry in Seaton and Beer; separate parish 1905

SEATON AND BEER (RC) St Augustine, Manor Road 1910; 1920; 1937

SEATON AND BEER (Bapt) 'A building in the occupation of William Moor, in the Square, Beer' [1882 Return]

SEATON AND BEER (Cong, later Cong Fed) Fore Street, Beer f 1700 [1851 Religious Census] Rebuilt 1855 [1882 Return]
OR   C 1788-1835 (RG 4/2401 PRO)
Cop C 1788-1835 (SG)
Cop (Mf) C 1788-1835 (Mf DCRS/WSL, SG); Extr C 1788-1835 (IGI); C 11788-1835 (Mf I SLC)

SEATON AND BEER (Cong, later URC) Cross Street, Seaton f 1825 [1851 Religious Census]

SEATON AND BEER (Wes) A house [1851 Religious Census]
OR   for *c.*1809-37 *see* AXMINSTER (RG 4.512 PRO)

SESSACOTT   *see* PUTFORD, WEST

SHALDON   *see* ST NICHOLAS

SHAUGH PRIOR St Edward [Plympton Hundred; Plympton St Mary Union]   [570] Chapelry in PLYMPTON ST MAURICE. Separate parish 1810. Now with ROBOROUGH united benefice
OR   C 1565-1962 M 1565-1973 B 1565-1993 (PWDRO)
BT   CMB 1602, 1607, 1613-14, 1618-19, 1663-64, 1671, 1686, 1696-97, 1699-1700, 1750-51, 1753-55, 1757-58, 1760-95 (1796-1812 ?); CMB 1813-14 CB 1818-21 C 1823, 1826-28, 1831, 1834, 1838-49 M 1816, 1818-20, 1826-27, 1832, 1834, 1838-40, 1842-43, 1845-46 B 1826-27, 1829, 1832, 1834, 1838-49 (DRO)
Cop M 1565-1754 (I, Ptd, edit M.Brown, Dartmoor Press 1999); B 1754-1812 (I, Ptd *ibid.* 1999); CMB 1565-1840 (C of A); M 1599-1837 with index (DFHS)
Cop (Mf) CMB Nov.1897-May 1899 (Mf SG)
MI   (Ptd DRMI 11: 1998)

SHAUGH PRIOR Lee Moor. House provided by mining company as mission chapel in parish of Shaugh Prior. Closed 1999
OR None

SHAUGH PRIOR (Presb) Licensed 1672; fl *c.*1690; closed by 1715

SHAUGH PRIOR (Wes/Meth) Lee Moor. Erected 1881. fl *c.*1970
OR C 1939-92 M 1907-93 B 1899-1995 (PWDRO)
Cop C 1939-92 M 1944-93 with index (PWDRO)

SHAUGH PRIOR (Wes) Norley Works. Erected 1835 [1851 Religious Census]
OR for *c.*1813-37 *see* PLYMOUTH Ebenezer (RG 4/1325 PRO)

SHAUGH PRIOR (Wes) Wotter. Erected 1940. fl *c.*1970

SHEBBEAR St Michael [Shebbear Hundred; Torrington Union] [1179]
see also chapelry of SHEEPWASH. Now with TORRIDGE
OR C 1576-1986 M 1576-1989 B 1576-1994 (NDRO) Noted in 1841: gap C 1742-55
BT CMB 1597-1602, 1604-07, 1610, 1612, 1617, 1619, 1629, 1668, 1670, 1674, 1678-80, 1682-83, 1685, 1690-91, 1694, 1696-97, 1700, 1702-05, 1707-12, 1714-16, 1751 (1752-1812 ?); CB 1813-39, 1841-45, 1848-49, 1854
M 1813-37 (DRO)
Cop B 1813-37 (Ptd DFHS); CMB 1597-1804 from BT, 1576-1862 (DCRS/WSL); CMB 1576-1837 (SG); M 1576-1812 (Boyd) ; B 1813-37 (DLS, WSL)
Cop (Mf) Extr CM 1576-1837 (IGI); CM 1576-1837 (Mf I SLC)
MI (I, DFHS); Ch 1931 (Ts SG); Cy extr 1965 (Ts SG); Ch: Harrington family (Ptd *Misc.Gen et Her*. NS iii: 1880: 347-8); Ch, cy: Hawking/Hocking 1965 (Ts SG); Extr (Whitmore MS, SG)

SHEBBEAR (Bapt) Caute Chapel. Erected 1843 [1851 Religious Census]

SHEBBEAR (Presb) fl *c.*1672-90

SHEBBEAR (Wes)
OR for *c.*1817-37 *see* HOLSWORTHY (RG 4/1210 PRO)

SHEBBEAR (Wes) New Inn. Erected 1840 [1851 Religious Census] fl *c.*1970

SHEBBEAR (Bible Christian/Meth) Ebenezer, Lake. Erected 1817, rebuilt 1841 [1851 Religious Census] [1882 Return] fl *c.*1970
OR ZC 1818-37 (RG 4/339 PRO); later registers (Minister)
Cop C 1818-45 B 1820-90 (DLS)
Cop (Mf) ZC 1818-37 (Mf DCRS/WSL, SG); Extr ZC 1818-37 (IGI); ZC 1818-37 (Mf I SLC)

SHEBBEAR (Bible Christian) Rowden. Erected 1832 [1851 Religious Census] [1882 Return] Rebuilt 1905. fl *c.*1970

SHEEPSTOR St Leonard [Roborough Hundred; Tavistock Union] [154] Chapelry in BICKLEIGH near Plymouth. Separate parish 1832. Now with YELVERTON, MEAVY, WALKHAMPTON
OR CB 1691-1812 M 1691-1837, 1839-1979 (PWDRO)
BT CMB 1610-11, 1614-20, 1630, 1638, 1641, 1666, 1668, 1670-72, 1679-80, 1682, 1694, 1697, 1699 (1700-1812 ?); C 1814-15, 1817-38 M 1815, 1820-21, 1824, 1827-28, 1835-38 B 1814, 1817-21, 1823, 1826, 1828-34, 1838-39 (DRO)

SHEEPSTOR cont.
Cop M 1610-1754 (I, Ptd, edit M.Brown, Dartmoor Press 1999); CMB 1610-82
from BT, 1691-1837 (DCRS/WSL); B 1772-1996 (I, PWDRO); M 1610-1837
(Boyd); Extr CMB 1697-1787 (Vol 17, BG/PCL)
Cop (Mf) (Tavistock SP); Extr CM 1610-1837 (IGI); C 1610-1837 (Mf I SLC)
MI (Ptd DRMI 7: 1988); Cy 1978 (Ts SG)

SHEEPWASH St Lawrence [Shebbear Hundred; Torrington Union] [446]
Chapelry in SHEBBEAR. Rebuilt 1881. Separate parish 1884. Now with TORRIDGE
OR C 1674-1898 M 1675-1989 B 1675-1945 (NDRO)
BT CMB 1602, 1607-08, 1610, 1612, 1617, 1641, 1668, 1678-79, 1683, 1689-91,
1694-97, 1700, 1702-05, 1707-10, 1715 (1716-1812 ?); CB 1813-38, 1840-48
M 1813-22, 1824-36 (DRO)
Cop B 1813-37 (Ptd DFHS); CMB 1602-1776 from BT, 1674-1838 (DCRS/WSL);
Extr CMB 1602-68, CMB 1674-1838 (SG); B 1813-37 (WSL, DLS, DFHS)
Cop(Mf) Extr C 1602-41, 1668-1838 M 1602-41, 1675-1742, 1753-1835 (IGI);
C 1602-41, 1668-1838 M 1602-41, 1675-1742, 1753-1835 (Mf I SLC)
MI (I, NDA); Extr (Whitmore MS, SG)

SHEEPWASH (Bapt) Erected 1827 [1851 Religious Census] Now with Halwill group

SHEEPWASH (Bible Christian) Sheepwash Town. Erected 1850 [1851 Religious
Census]

SHEEPWASH (Bible Christian) Jubilee. Erected 1866. fl c.1970

SHEEPWASH (S of F) Meeting house 1743

SHELDON St James the Greater [Hayridge Hundred; Honiton Union] [185]
Now with DUNKESWELL, LUPPITT
OR C 1715-1991 M 1715-1836 B 1715-1990 (DRO) No earlier registers noted in
1831
BT CMB 1608, 1610, 1626, 1633 or 1638, 1675, 1678, 1683, 1686-87, 1696-97,
1699, 1701, 1703-05, 1711, 1714, 1716, 1721-23, 1727, 1731-33, 1735-37,
1739-44, 1747-49, 1752, 1754, 1757-77, 1780-84, 1786-1800 (1801-12 ?);
C 1813-23, 1825-38 M 1813-16, 1820, 1822-23, 1825-29, 1831-36 B 1813-38
(DRO)
Cop (Mf) (Colyton SP); C 1715-1812 M 1715-1836 B 1715-1813 (Mfc SG)

SHELDON (Bapt) Baptist Preaching House [1882 Return]

SHELDON (Presb) fl c.1672-90

SHELDON (Prim Meth) Near the Turnpike Gate, Ringmore Road [1882 Return]

SHELDON (Who object to be designated) Christians' Meeting Room, Arch Street
[1882 Return]

SHELDON (Brethren) Gospel Hall, Arch Street [1882 Return]

SHERFORD St Martin [Coleridge Hundred; Kingsbridge Union] [511] Chapelry in
STOKENHAM, with which now united
OR C 1713-1878 M 1713-1907 B 1713-1946 (DRO) No earlier registers noted in
1831
BT CMB 1608, 1610, 1613-14, 1616, 1619, 1623, 1628, 1636, 1641, 1667-72,
1674-77. 1686, 1687?, 1690, 1695-97 (1698-1812 ?); CB 1813-35, 1844-46
M 1813-15, 1817-35 (DRO)

SHERFORD cont.
Cop Banns 1824-1929 (Ptd *Sherford Marriage Banns*: DFHS); B 1713-1996
    (I, PWDRO); M 1754-1812 indexed by male spouse; Extr Banns 1824-1929
    (DFHS)
Cop (Mf) C 1713-1838 M 1713-1837 B 1713-1846 (Mfc SG)

SHERFORD (Wes) Two chapels, erected 1824, 1828 [1851 Religious Census]
OR for *c.*1813-37 *see* KINGSBRIDGE (RG 4/1088 PRO)

SHERFORD (Calv) A house, Frogmore [1851 Religious Census]

SHERWOOD VILLA   Extra-parochial place [Crediton Hundred from 1858; Crediton
Union 1858-94]

SHILLINGFORD   *see* BAMPTON

SHILLINGFORD ABBOT   *see* EXMINSTER

SHILLINGFORD ST GEORGE St George [Exminster Hundred; St Thomas Union]   [89]
Now with DUNCHIDEOCK, IDE
OR C 1577-1975 M 1569-1991 B 1565-1812 (DRO)
BT CMB 1611, 1617, 1620, 1621?, 1626, 1633, 1636, 1639, 1641, 1663, 1671,
    1675, 1678-79, 1684, 1695-96 (1697-1812 ?); C 1813-14, 1816-26, 1828-37,
    1839-40, 1846-52, 1854-55 M 1817, 1823, 1829, 1831, 1834-35 B 1813-14,
    1817-26, 1828-33, 1835-37, 1839-40, 1846, 1849-52, 1854-55 (DRO)
Cop C 1577-1837 M 1569-1837 B 1565-1837 (DCRS/WSL, SG); M 1569-1836 (Boyd)
Cop (Mf) Extr C 1577-1837 M 1569-1753, 1765-1835 (IGI); C 1577-1837
    M 1569-1753, 1765-1835 (Mf I SLC)
MI (I, DFHS); Ch extr (Ptd Cresswell 141); Ch. cy 1929 (Ts SG);
    Extr (Whitmore MS, SG)

SHIPHAY COLLATON   *see* TORQUAY

SHIRWELL United benefice including SHIRWELL, LOXHORE, BRATTON FLEMING,
CHALLACOMBE, STOKE RIVERS, KENTISBURY, EAST DOWN, ARLINGTON

SHIRWELL St Peter [Shirwell Hundred; Barnstaple Union]   [688]
Now with SHIRWELL united benefice
OR C 1538-1970 M 1539-1836 B 1546-1971 (NDRO) C 1852-1970 B 1920-71 badly
    faded
BT CMB 1597-1601, 1607-08, 1610, 1612, 1619, 1623, 1631, 1634, 1636, 1644,
    1668, 1674, 1678-79, 1682, 1690-91, 1695-96, 1700, 1702, 1705, 1712,
    1714-15 (1716-1812 ?); C 1813-51 MB 1813-32, 1834-37 B 1838-47, 1849-51
    (DRO)
Cop CMB 1538-1772 (DCRS/WSL, NDA); M 1540-99 (SG); M 1601-1754 (Boyd)
Cop (Mf) Extr C 1538-1772 M 1539-1754 (IGI); C 1538-1772 M 1539-1754
    (Mf I SLC)
MI Incledon 430 (NDA)

SHIRWELL (Wes) A house [1851 Religious Census]
OR for *c.*1807-37 *see* BARNSTAPLE CIRCUIT, BIDEFORD (RG 4/954,955 PRO)

SHIRWELL (Wes) Shirwell Cross. Erected 1903. fl *c.*1970

SHOBROOKE St Swithin [West Budleigh Hundred; Crediton Union] [644]
Now with CREDITON
OR C 1539-1880 M 1539-1952, 1972-83 B 1539-1876 (DRO)
BT CMB 1609, 1619, 1624, 1629, 1636, 1638, 1666?, 1669-72, 1678, 1696
    (1697-1812 ?); CB 1813-44 M 1813-37, 1840 (DRO)
Cop B 1813-37 (Ptd DFHS); B 1813-37 (WSL, SG); CB 1538-1799 M 1538-1812
    (DCRS/WSL, WSL); M 1538-1812 (Boyd); Extr C 1541-1696 M 1539-1704
    B 1547-1711 (Vol 10, BG/PCL)
Cop (Mf) Extr C 1538-1799 M 1538-1638, 1654-1812 (IGI); C 1538-1799
    (Mf I SLC)
MI (I, DFHS)

SHOBROOKE All Saints, Efford. Mission church erected 1892. Closed 1975.
OR None

SHOBROOKE (Presb) Pennicot. Licensed 1672; fl c.1720; closed by 1772

SHOBROOKE (Wes) Erected 1815 [1851 Religious Census]

SHOBROOKE (Wes Reform) Erected c.1841 [1851 Religious Census]

SHOBROOKE (S of F) fl 1696, 1703

SHUTE St Michael [Colyton Hundred; Axminster Union] [617] Chapelry and
borough in COLYTON. Separate parish 1860. Now with STOCKLAND, DALWOOD,
KILMINGTON
OR C 1568-1901 M 1561-1978 B 1563-1883 (DRO)
BT CMB 1613-14, 1620, 1629-30, 1633, 1670-71, 1678-79, 1683, 1687, 1750,
    1756-58, 1761, 1764-71, 1773-1800, 1802-12; C 1813-14, 1817 M 1813, 1816
    B 1813, 1817 CMB 1820, 1823, 1827-28, 1830-33 CB 1836-40, 1842-47
    M 1836-37, 1840 (DRO)
Cop B 1813-37 (Ptd DFHS); B 1813-37 (WSL, SG); CMB 1561-1837 (WSL);
    C 1568-1837 M 1568-1878 (Colyton SP)
Cop (Mf) (Colyton SP); C 1568-1855 M 1561-1837 B 1563-1833 (Mfc SG)
MI Ch, cy (Ptd Pulman Book of the Axe 1875; reprint 1969); Cy 1909
    (A.W.Matthews Ye Olde Mortality vol.8: MS SG); Incledon 327 (NDA)

SHUTE St Mary at the Cross, Whitford. Chapel-of-ease erected 1908. Now in
parish of St Michael, Colyford

SHUTE (Ind) House, Painters Cross, 1849 [1851 Religious Census]

SHUTE (Bible Christian) House, Perhams Green 1840; house, Whiteford 1851
[1851 Religious Census] Erected 1857. fl c.1970

SHUTE (Bible Christian/U Meth) Mount Tabor, Whitford [1882 Return]
OR C 1949-63 (DRO)

SHUTE (Wes) Whitford
OR for c.1808-37 see TAVISTOCK (RG 4/341 PRO)

SID VALLEY United benefice including SIDMOUTH St Giles, SIDMOUTH All
Saints, WOOLBROOK, SALCOMBE REGIS, SIDBURY, SIDFORD

SIDBURY St Giles (formerly St Peter and St Giles) [East Budleigh Hundred;
Honiton Union] [1725] Rebuilt 1845. Peculiar of the Dean and Chapter of
Exeter until 1848. Now with SID VALLEY
OR C 1813-1907 M 1837-1927 B 1813-1863 (DRO) Noted in 1831: CMB 1559-1812.
    Destroyed by fire at vicarage 1850. M 1813-37 lost

SIDBURY cont.
BT CMB 1611, 1616, 1620, 1624, 1630, 1633-35, 1639, 1664?, 1669-70, 1678,
    1683 (1684-1812 ?); C 1813-32 M 1813-25, 1828-30 B 1813-31 (DRO)
Cop B 1813-37 (Ptd DFHS); B 1813-37 (SG); CMB 1609-1824 from BT (DCRS/WSL)
Cop (Mf) Extr C 1609-1824 M 1609-1721, 1738-75, 1791-1824 (IGI); C 1609-1824
    M 1609-1721, 1738-75, 1791-1824 (Mf I SLC)
MI Cy 1978 (Ts SG); Incledon 494 (NDA)

SIDBURY St Peter, Sidford. Chapel-of-ease opened 1873. Now with SID VALLEY
OR C 1950+ M 1980+ (Inc); M 1950-79 (DRO)

SIDBURY (Presb/Ind/Cong) fl.1672-1972. Rebuilt 1820 [1851 Religious Census]
OR ZC 1757-1836 B 1820-36 (RG 4/448 PRO); C 1844-1961 M 1846-1961
    B 1844-1972 (DRO)
Cop (Mf) C 1757-1836 B 1820-36 (Mf DCRS/WSL, SG); C 1844-1961 M 1846-1961
    B 1844-1972 (Mfc Colyton SP); Extr C 1757-1836 (IGI); C 1757-1836
    (Mf I SLC)

SIDBURY (Ind) Houses in Sidford and Barcombe [1851 Religious Census]

SIDBURY (Wes) House, Sidford [1851 Religious Census]

SIDBURY (Wes) Church Street, Sidford. Erected 1933. fl c.1970

SIDFORD see SIDBURY

SIDMOUTH St Giles and St Nicholas [East Budleigh Hundred; Honiton Union]
[3126] Re-named 1973 Sidmouth with Woolbrook. Now with SID VALLEY
OR C 1587-1964 M 1586-1972 B 1586-1979 (DRO)
BT CMB 1607-08, 1614, 1618?, 1620, 1625, 1629, 1631, 1634?, 1639, 1641.
    1662-64, 1669-70, 1672, 1675, 1677-78, 1683, 1685, 1687, 1690, 1695-97
    (1698-1812 ?); CMB 1813-16, 1818-39 (DRO)
Cop B 1813-37 (Ptd DFHS); CMB 1609-32 from BT, 1588-1666 M 1666-1801
    (DCRS/WSL); CMB Dec.1871-May 1872 (SG); B 1813-37 (SG)
Cop (Mf) Extr C 1586-1631 M 1586-1801 (IGI); C 1586-1631 M 1586-1801
    (Mf I SLC)
MI Cy, part of cemetery (I, DFHS); Ch, cy (Ptd H.Ormiston Catalogue of
    Tombstones and Monuments in Sidmouth Church and Churchyard: 1935);
    Ch 1928 (Ts SG)

SIDMOUTH All Saints. Erected 1837-40. Now with SID VALLEY
OR No information

SIDMOUTH St Francis of Assisi, Woolbrook Erected 1929-31. Now with SID
VALLEY
OR C 1931+ M 1961+ B 1986+ (Inc)

SIDMOUTH (RC) A mission 1845-47. Entries at Lyme [Dorset]; Most Precious
Blood, Radway Road 1935

SIDMOUTH (Bapt) f 1830; Emmanuel Baptist Church FIEC
OR M 1973-87 (DRO)

SIDMOUTH (Ind/Cong, later URC) f c.1650. Marsh Chapel erected 1810; rebuilt
1846 [1851 Religious Census] New building at Chapel Street 1846. Marsh
Chapel demolished 1967
OR C 1815-36 (RG 4/837 PRO); C 1815-1948, 1955+ M 1892+ B 1869-91;
    membership rolls 1816+ (Ch Sec)

SIDMOUTH (Ind/Cong) cont.
Cop (Mf) C 1815-36 (Mf DCRS/WSL, SG); Extr C 1815-36 (IGI); C 1815-36
(Mf I SLC)

SIDMOUTH (Presb/Unit) Higher or Old Meeting, Upper High Street f 1662.
Erected 1710 [1851 Religious Census]
OR C 1753-1836 B 1831-34 (RG 4/1219 PRO); CMB 1753-1978 M 1951-76 (DRO)
Cop (Mf) C 1753-1836 B 1831-34 (Mf DCRS/WSL, SG); Extr C 1753-1836 (IGI);
C 1753-1836 (Mf I SLC)

SIDMOUTH (Cong ? /URC) Primley Road f 1939

SIDMOUTH (Wes)
OR for c.1809-37 see AXMINSTER, BUDLEIGH (RG 4/512,517 PRO)

SIDMOUTH (Wes) Mill Street. Erected 1837 [1851 Religious Census] High Street
erected 1884. fl c.1970

SIDMOUTH (Brethren) n.d. [1851 Religious Census]

SIDMOUTH JUNCTION   see FENITON

SIGFORD   see ILSINGTON

SILVERTON St Mary [Hayridge Hundred; Tiverton Union]   [1389]
Now with BUTTERLEIGH, BICKLEIGH, CADELEIGH
OR C 1626-1904 M 1653-1655, 1678-1945 B 1626-1650, 1678-1684, 1754-1876
(DRO)
BT CMB 1620, 1625, 1630, 1638, 1644, 1662-63, 1664?, 1667, 1670, 1675,
1678, 1683, 1687, 1690, 1696-97 (1698-1812 ?); CB 1813-34, 1838
M 1813-34 (DRO)
Cop CMB 1620-67 from BT, 1626-1837 (DCRS/WSL, WSL)
Cop (Mf) Extr C 1620-1837 M 1620-25, 1653-1837 (IGI); C 1620-1837 M 1620-25,
1653-1837 (Mf I SLC)

SILVERTON (Presb) Licensed 1672; fl c.1716; closed by 1772

SILVERTON (Ind) Independent Preaching Room [1882 Return]

SILVERTON (Wes) Erected 1844 [1851 Religious Census]
OR for c.1806-37 see CULLOMPTON, EXETER Mint, TIVERTON (RG 4/958,1207,
342 PRO)

SILVERTON (UMFC/U Meth) Butterleigh Road. Erected 1914. fl c.1970

SILVERTON (Wes Free Church) Parsonage Lane [1882 Return]

SLAPTON St James the Greater [Coleridge Hundred; Kingsbridge Union]   [665]
Now with STOKENHAM
OR C 1634-1853 M 1634-1738, 1755-1971 B 1634-1883 (DRO)
BT CMB 1606, 1608, 1610, 1612, 1614-15, 1617, 1620, 1623, 1632, 1634, 1636,
1641, 1669, 1671, 1674, 1677, 1679-81, 1686, 1689-90, 1697
(1698-1812 ?); CB 1813-40 M 1813-29, 1831-36 (DRO)
Cop B 1813-37 (Ptd DFHS); B 1813-37 (SG); CMB 1605-41 from BT, 1755-1853
(DCRS/WSL); M 1754-1812 indexed by male spouse (DFHS); M 1616-1837
(Boyd)
Cop (Mf) Extr C 1606-1853 M 1606-1738, 1755-1837 (IGI); C 1606-1853
(Mf I SLC)
MI (I, DFHS)

SLAPTON (Wes)
OR for *c.*1811-37 *see* BRIXHAM CIRCUIT, KINGSBRIDGE (RG 4/842,1088 PRO)

SLAPTON (Prim Meth) Lower Chapel [1882 Return]

SOLDON CROSS *see* HOLSWORTHY

SOURTON St Thomas à Becket [Lifton Hundred; Okehampton Union] [625]
Chapelry in BRIDESTOWE; separate parish 1889. Now with OKEHAMPTON
OR C 1722-1872 M 1722-1951 B 1722-1920 (DRO) No earlier registers noted in
1831
BT CMB 1612, 1615-19, 1623, 1634, 1638, 1641, 1663-64, 1666, 1669-72, 1674,
1676-77, 1679-81, 1686, 1689-90, 1695-96 (1697-1812 ?); CB 1813-38,
1840-44 M 1813-37 (DRO)
Cop M 1722-54 (I, Ptd, edit M.Brown, Dartmoor Press 1999); B 1754-1812
(I, *ibid.* 1999)
Cop (Mf) (Okehampton SP)

SOURTON (Wes) Southerley [1882 Return]

SOUTH ALLINGTON   *see* CHIVELSTONE

SOUTH BRENT   *see* BRENT, SOUTH

SOUTH HUISH   *see* HUISH, SOUTH

SOUTH MILTON   *see* MILTON, SOUTH

SOUTH MOLTON   *see* MOLTON, SOUTH

SOUTH POOL   *see* POOL, SOUTH

SOUTH TAWTON   *see* TAWTON, SOUTH

SOUTH ZEAL   borough in NORTH TAWTON

SOUTHERLEY   *see* SOURTON

SOUTHLEIGH St Lawrence [Colyton Hundred; Honiton Union] [320]
Included the borough of Wiscombe. Now with COLYTON
OR C 1778-1902 M 1754-1757, 1812-1978 B 1778-1995 (DRO) Noted in 1831:
CMB 1718-1812, but this may be an error for 1778-1812
BT CMB 1611, 1634, 1663-64, 1666?, 1667, 1669-70, 1672, 1675, 1677, 1683,
1686-87, 1690-91, 1694-97, 1699 (1700-1812 ?); none listed after 1812
(DRO)
Cop B 1800-37 (Ptd DFHS); B 1800-37 (SG); M 1759-1812 (Colyton SP)
Cop (Mf) (Colyton SP)
MI (I, DFHS); Cy 1909 (A.W.Matthews *Ye Olde Mortality* vol.8: MS SG); Extr
(Whitmore MS, SG); Incledon 631 (NDA)

SOUTHWAY *see* TAMERTON FOLIOT

SOWTON or CLYST FOMISON or CLYST ST MICHAEL St Michael and All Angels
[Wonford Hundred; St Thomas Union] [391] Rebuilt 1845. Now with AYLESBEARE,
ROCKBEARE, FARRINGDON, CLYST HONITON
OR C 1560-1882 M 1561-1836 B 1561-1919 (DRO)
BT CMB 1608, 1616-17, 1620, 1625, 1663, 1672?, 1675, 1678, 1687, 1697
(1698-1812 ?); CB 1813-33, 1835-36, 1847-49 M 1813-28, 1831-33, 1835-36
(DRO)

SOWTON cont.
Cop B 1800-37 (Ptd DFHS); B 1800-37 (SG); CMB 1566-1837 (DCRS/WSL);
    Extr CMB 1562-1765 (Vol 17, BG/PCL)
Cop (Mf) Extr C 1560-1837 M 1561-1836 (IGI); C 1560-1837 M 1561-1836
    (Mf I SLC)
MI (I, DFHS)

SOWTON Bishop's Court (Clyst) Medieval chapel of former palace of Bishops of
Exeter

SPARKWELL   see PLYMPTON

SPICELAND   see CULMSTOCK

SPLATT   see BROADWOODKELLY

SPREYTON St Michael [Wonford Hundred; Okehampton Union] [423]
OR C 1563-1992 M 1563-1989 B 1563-1963 (DRO)
BT CMB 1606, 1608, 1617-18, 1621, 1630, 1635, 1644, 1663, 1666-67, 1668?,
    1669-70, 1672, 1675, 1677-78, 1683, 1687, 1690, 1695-97, 1699, 1701
    (1702-1812 ?); CB 1813-43 M 1813-31, 1834-38, 1843 (DRO)
Cop CMB 1563-1837 (DCRS/WSL, WSL); M 1563-1837 (Boyd); Extr C 1564-1710
    M 1588-1709 B 1568-1714 (Vol 17, BG/PCL)
Cop (Mf) (Okehampton SP); Extr C 1563-1837 M 1563-1718, 1729-1837 (IGI);
    C 1563-1837 M 1563-1718, 1729-1837 (Mf I SLC)
MI Extr (Whitmore MS, SG)

SPREYTON (Bible Christian) Erected 1880. A building in the occupation of
Mr H.Duloe [1882 Return] fl c.1970

STABLE GREEN   see WINKLEIGH

STARCROSS   see DAWLISH

STAVERTON St Paul de Leon [Haytor Hundred; Totnes Union] [1055] Peculiar of
the Dean and Chapter of Exeter until 1848. Now with BROADHEMPSTON, WOODLAND,
LANDSCOVE, LITTLEHEMPSTON
OR C 1614-1909 M 1614-1963 B 1614-1975 (DRO)
BT CMB 1614, 1616-17, 1624, 1633, 1636 (1637-1812 ?); CB 1813-46 B 1813-37
    (DRO)
Cop B 1813-37 (Ptd DFHS); B 1813-37 (SG); CMB 1614-1837 (DCRS/WSL);
    M 1614-1812 (Boyd); Extr C 1614-67 B 1614-1811 (Vol 16, BG/PCL)
Cop (Mf) (Totnes SP); Extr CM 1614-1837 (IGI); CM 1614-1837 (Mf I SLC)
MI Extr (Whitmore MS, SG)

STAVERTON St Matthew, Landscove. Erected 1849-50. Parish created 1852 from
Staverton. Now with BROADHEMPSTON, WOODLAND, STAVERTON, LITTLEHEMPSTON
OR CMB 1851+ (Inc)

STAVERTON (RC) Kingston House. Former chapel of Rowe family [Hosking]

STAVERTON (Presb) Licensed 1672; closed by 1715
OR see ASHBURTON

STAVERTON (Wes)
OR for c.1801-36 see ASHBURTON CIRCUIT (RG 4/1763,840 PRO)

STAVERTON (Wes) Wolston Green. Erected 1841 [1851 Religious Census] [1882 Return] Rebuilt 1956. fl *c*.1970
OR for *c*.1801-36 *see* ASHBURTON CIRCUIT (RG 4/1763,840 PRO)

STEIGNTON, KING'S or STEIGNTON REGIS *see* KINGSTEIGNTON

STIBB CROSS *see* LANGTREE

STICKLEPATH *see* BARNSTAPLE

STICKLEPATH *see* SAMPFORD COURTENAY

STOCKLAND [Dorset] Transferred to Devon 1844. see NIPR *Dorset*

STOCKLEIGH ENGLISH St Mary the Virgin [West Budleigh Hundred; Crediton Union] [144] Now with NORTH CREADY
OR CB 1610-1812 M 1610-1975 (DRO)
BT CMB 1663-64, 1667, 1669-73, 1675, 1678-79, 1683, 1687, 1690, 1695-97, 1700 (1701-1812 ?); C 1813-19, 1822-27, 1844-55, 1876 M 1816, 1818-19, 1821, 1823-24, 1826, 1828-32, 1834 B 1813-16, 1819-35, 1837, 1844-52, 1854-55, 1876 (DRO)
Cop CMB 1606-08 from BT, 1610-1837 (DCRS/WSL)
Cop (Mf) (Tiverton SP); Extr C 1606-1837 M 1606-1834 (IGI); C 1606-1837 M 1606-1834 (Mf I SLC)
MI (I, DFHS); Extr (Whitmore MS, SG)

STOCKLEIGH POMEROY St Mary the Virgin [West Budleigh Hundred; Crediton Union] [238] Now with NORTH CREADY
OR C 1602-1657, 1675-1812 M 1558-1837 B 1663-1812 (DRO) Noted in 1831: CMB 1556-1646, 1675+
BT CMB 1606, 1613-14, 1617, 1624, 1629-31, 1663, 1668-69, 1672-73, 1675, 1678, 1683, 1688, 1690, 1695-97, 1700 (1701-1812 ?); CB 1813-38 M 1813-15, 1817-24, 1826-37 (DRO)
Cop CMB 1558-1837 (DCRS/WSL)
Cop (Mf) (Tiverton SP); Extr C 1602-1837 M 1560-1837 (IGI); C 1602-1837 M 1560-1837 (Mf I SLC)
MI (I, DFHS); Extr (Whitmore MS, SG)

STOKE *see* HARTLAND

STOKE CANON St Mary Magdalene [Wonford Hundred; St Thomas Union] [446] Peculiar of the Dean and Chapter of Exeter until 1848. Now with POLTIMORE, REWE, HUXHAM and NETHEREXE
OR C 1654-1865 M 1656-1837 B 1655-1920 (DRO)
BT CMB 1615, 1620, 1629?, 16?6, 1641, 1672, 1697 (1698-1812 ?); CB 1813-44 M 1813-21, 1823-27, 1829-36 (DRO)
Cop B 1813-37 (Ptd DFHS); B 1813-37 (WSL, SG); CMB 1608-72 from BT, 1654-1837 (DCRS/WSL); CMB 1654-1837 (WSL); M 1616-1837 (Boyd)
Cop (Mf) Extr C 1608-1837 M 1608-41, 1656-1837 (IGI); C 1608-1837 M 1608-41, 1656-1837 (Mf I SLC)
MI (I, DFHS)

STOKE DAMEREL *see* PLYMOUTH

STOKE FLEMING St Peter [Coleridge Hundred; Kingsbridge Union] [725] Now with BLACKAWTON, STRETE
OR C 1538-1602, 1639-42, 1670-1901 M 1538-1603, 1671-1968 B 1539-1627, 1670-1863 (DRO)

STOKE FLEMING cont.
BT CMB 1611, 1614, 1616, 1620, 1627, 1629, 1635, 1666, 1668-69, 1671-72, 1674-77, 1679-82, 1684, 1686-87, 1689-90, 1695, 1698 (1699-1812 ?); CB 1813-57 M 1813-36 (DRO)
Cop CMB 1611-69 from BT, 1538-1837 (DCRS/WSL); Extr 'several sequences' of CMB 1543-1799 (Vol 5 BG/PCL)
Cop (Mf) (Torquay SP); C 1538-1602, 1639-42, 1670-1853 M 1538-1603, 1671-1836, B 1539-1627, 1670-1863 (Mfc SG); Extr C 1538-1837 M 1538-1635, 1666-1837 (IGI); C 1538-1837 M 1538-1635, 1666-1837 (Mf I SLC)
MI (Ptd W.H.Rogers *The monumental brasses found in the churches of Stoke Fleming, St Saviour's and St Petrock's Dartmouth*: 1906); (PCL)

STOKE FLEMING (Ind/Cong) Erected 1840 [1851 Religious Census] [1882 Return]

STOKE GABRIEL St Gabriel [Haytor Hundred; Totnes Union] [718]
Peculiar of the Bishop of Exeter until 1848. Now with COLLATON
OR C 1539-1961 M 1539-1974 B 1540-1947 (DRO)
BT CMB 1611-14, 1617, 1629, 1633-36, 1661, 1663-79, 1681-83, 1685-86, 1687?, 1688, 1690-1704, 1706 (1707-1812 ?); CB 1813-36 M 1813-35 (DRO)
Cop B 1813-37 (Ptd DFHS); B 1813-37 (WSL, SG); CMB 1539-1844 (DCRS/WSL); M 1539-1837 (Boyd); Extr CMB 1554-1635 C 1637-1754 M 1641-1753 B 1636-1775 (Vol 6, BG/PCL)
Cop (Mf) (Torquay and Totnes SPs); Extr C 1539-1855 M 1540-1837 (IGI); C 1539-1855 (Mf I SLC)
MI Extr (Whitmore MS, SG)

STOKE GABRIEL Waddleton Oratory. Proprietary chapel at Waddleton Court, erected 1868 by Goodson family

STOKE GABRIEL (Bapt) Erected 1820 [1851 Religious Census] [1882 Return]

STOKE GABRIEL (Wes) Erected 1836 [1851 Religious Census]
OR for *c.*1811-37 *see* BRIXHAM, PLYMOUTH Ebenezer (RG 4/842,1325 PRO)

STOKE RIVERS St Bartholomew [Shirwell Hundred; Barnstaple Union] [270]
Now with SHIRWELL
OR CB 1553-1812 M 1556-1837 (NDRO)
BT CMB 1597-1602, 1608, 1610, 1613, 1627-28, 1630, 1638, 1644, 1668, 1672-73, 1678-79, 1682-83, 1688-91, 1694-97, 1700, 1702-04, 1712, 1714-15 (1716-1812 ?); C 1813-50 M 1813-28, 1830-31, 1833-39, 1841-43 B 1813-51 (DRO)
Cop CMB 1553-1744 (DCRS/WSL); M 1556-1744 (Boyd)
Cop (Mf) CB 1553-1812 M 1556-1837 (Mfc SG); Extr C 1553-1744 M 1556-1744 (IGI); C 1553-1744 M 1556-1744 (Mf I SLC)
MI (I, DFHS); Ch, cy 1972 (Ts SG)

STOKE RIVERS (Bapt) A house [1851 Religious Census] Erected 1855 [1882 Return]

STOKE RIVERS (Wes)
OR for *c.*1807-37 *see* BARNSTAPLE CIRCUIT (RG 4/954 PRO)

STOKEINTEIGNHEAD St Andrew [Wonford Hundred; Newton Abbot Union] [621]
Now with COMBEINTEIGNHEAD, HACCOMBE
OR C 1538-1930 M 1539-1964 B 1538-1887 (DRO)
BT CMB 1606, 1611, 1616-17, 1620, 1624, 1633, 1635, 1639, 1670, 1672, 1675, 1678-79, 1683, 1687, 1690, 1695, 1697, 1699 (1700-1812 ?); CMB 1813-33 CB 1835-47 M 1835-36, 1838-39 (DRO)

STOKEINTEIGNHEAD cont.
Cop B 1800-37 (Ptd DFHS); B 1800-37 (SG); CMB 1538-1837 (DCRS/WSL)
Cop (Mf) (Torquay SP)
MI (Ptd J.Whittemore 'Monumental brass at Stokeinteignhead church': DCNQ 33
(8): 1977: 300-302); Incledon 124 (NDA)

STOKEINTEIGNHEAD (Bible Christian U Meth)
OR C 1911-32 (DRO); *see also* NEWTON ABBOT Circuit
Cop (Mf) Extr C 1538-1837 M 1538-1836 (IGI); C 1538-1837 M 1538-1836
(Mf I SLC)

STOKENHAM St Michael and All Angels [Coleridge Hundred; Kingsbridge Union]
[1609] *see also* chapelries of CHIVELSTONE and SHERFORD. Now with SHERFORD,
BEESANDS, SLAPTON
OR C 1578-1923 M 1574-83, 1605-1934 B 1570-81, 1605-1935 (DRO)
BT CMB 1597-1602, 1610, 1614, 1617-18, 1620, 1622, 1633-34, 1663, 1666,
1669-72, 1675-77, 1679, 1681, 1682?, 1684, 1687-90, 1696, 1699, 1702,
1708-09, 1712, 1714-15, 1730, 1732, 1733 (1734-1812 ?); CB 1813-39
M 1813-36 (DRO)
Cop C 1578-91 M 1574-82 B 1570-80 (DRO, DCRS/WSL, SG); M 1754-1812 (DFHS);
M 1578-82 (Boyd); Extr CMB 1585-90 C 1620-53, 1662-1709 M 1608-51,
1660-1728 B 1606-52, 1662-1804 (Vol 17, BG/PCL)
Cop (Mf) C 1578-1867 M 1574-1837 B 1570-1883 (Mfc SG); Extr C 1578-91
M 1574-82 (IGI); C 1578-91 M 1574-82 (Mf I SLC)
MI (I, DFHS); (Ptd W.Roberts *Records of Family Names in Stokenham:*
Monumental Inscriptions from all burial grounds in the parish: 1981);
Ch, cy 1980 (Ts SG)

STOKENHAM St Andrew, Beesands. Mission church erected 1883
OR C (Inc)
MI Ch extr 1980 (Ts SG)

STOKENHAM (Presb/Ind/Cong) Stokenham and Chivelstone, Ford Chapel f 1662.
Licensed 1672. Closed
OR ZCB 1772-1837 (RG 4/834 PRO)
Cop (Mf) ZCB 1772-1837 (Mf DCRS/WSL, SG); Extr ZC 1772-1837 (IGI);
ZC 1772-1837 (Mf I SLC)
MI Burial ground (Ts 1980)

STOKENHAM (Cong, later Cong Fed) Torcross f 1829 [1851 Religious Census]

STOKENHAM (Bible Christian) Ebenezer, Chillington. Erected 1850
[1851 Religious Census] [1882 Return] fl *c.*1970
MI Meth burial ground: 1980 (Ts SG); (I, DFHS)

STOKENHAM (Bible Christian) Zion, Hallsands. Erected 1851 [1851 Religious
Census]; a Building or Chapel in the occupation of James Hinks, Hallsends
[1882 Return]

STOKENHAM (Brethren) A barn. 1851 [1851 Religious Census]

STONEHOUSE, EAST   *see* PLYMOUTH

STOODLEIGH St Margaret [Witheridge Hundred; Tiverton Union] [524]
Now with EXE VALLEY
OR C 1603-1861 M 1598-1991 B 1597-1953 (DRO)
BT CMB 1668, 1670, 1672, 1674, 1678-79, 1683, 1688-91, 1694-96, 1699-1700,
1702?, 1703-07, 1710, 1712, 1714-15 (1716-1812 ?); C 1813-44 M 1813-17,
1820-21, 1823-37, 1839 B 1813-16, 1818-21, 1823-26, 1828-44 (DRO)
Cop (Mf) (Tiverton SP)

STOW ST JAMES   see JACOBSTOWE

STOW ST MARTIN   see TAMERTON FOLIOT

STOWFORD St John [Lifton Hundred; Tavistock Union] [463]
Now with MARYSTOWE, CORYTON, LEW TRENCHARD, THRUSHELTON
OR CB 1707-1992 M 1709-1981 (PWDRO) No earlier registers noted in 1831
BT CMB 1607, 1610, 1617, 1629-31, 1633, 1641, 1644, 1663-64, 1666, 1669-73,
1676-77, 1679-80, 1688, 1690, 1699-1700 (1701-1812 ?); CB 1813-27,
1828-35, 1837 M 1813-14, 1816-17, 1820-27, 1829-34, 1837 (DRO)
Cop M 1709-54 (I, Ptd, edit M.Brown, Dartmoor Press 1999); B 1813-37
(Ptd DFHS); B 1800-1900 (I, PWDRO); B 1813-37 (WSL, SG)
Cop (Mf) (Tavistock SP)

STOWFORD (Bapt) f 1840. Porte Park Hill [1882 Return] Halwill Group.

STOWFORD (Bible Christian) A house [1851 Religious Census]; Zion, Portgate.
Erected 1861 [1882 Return] fl c.1970
OR see LAUNCESTON Circuit

STRETE or STREET   see BLACKAWTON

SUTCOMBE St Andrew [Black Torrington Hundred; Holsworthy Union] [491]
OR CB 1653-1931 M 1653-1979 (DRO)
BT CMB 1597-1601, 1613, 1617, 1619?, 1623-24, 1636, 1629, 1634, 1639-41,
1663-64, 1666, 1669-81, 1695, 1699 (1700-1812 ?); CB 1813-38, 1840
M 1813-6 (DRO)
Cop B 1813-00 (Ptd DFHS); B 1800-37 (SG); CMB 1597-1670 from BT, 1654-1875
(DCRS/WSL);
Cop (Mf) Extr C 1597-1601, 1613-41, 1654-75, 1685-1765, 1775-94, 1803-16,
1844-72 M 1597-1613, 1623-41, 1677-71, 1685-1753, 1767-90, 1811-14,
1823-68 (IGI); C 1597-1601, 1613-41, 1654-75, 1685-1765, 1775-94,
1803-16, 1844-72 (Mf I SLC)
MI (I, DFHS); Extr (Whitmore MS, SG)

SUTCOMBE (Wes) Upcott. Erected 1837 [1851 Religious Census] [1882 Return]
OR for c.1817-37 see HOLSWORTHY (RG 4/1210 PRO)

SUTCOMBE (Bible Christian) Sutcombe Mill. Erected 1837 [1851 Religious
Census] [1882 Return]

SUTCOMBE (Bible Christian) Erected 1868. fl c.1970

SUTTON ON PLYM   see PLYMOUTH

SUTTON, NORTH   see PLYMOUTH

SWIMBRIDGE St James the Apostle [South Molton Hundred; Barnstaple Union]
[1511] Peculiar of the Bishop of Exeter until 1848. Now with WEST BUCKLAND,
LANDKEY
OR C 1562-1957 M 1563-1956 B 1562-1886 (NDRO)
BT CMB 1603, 1607, 1610, 1611, 1614, 1629, 1634, 1636, 1638, 1643, 1662-67,
    1669-71, 1674, 1678-1705, 1730 (1731-1812 ?); CB 1813-54, 1863-64
    C 1866, 1872-76, 1878 M 1813-36 B 1872-96, 1878 (DRO)
Cop CMB 1562-1850 (DCRS/WSL, NDA)
Cop (Mf) Extr C 1562-1850 M 1563-1850 (IGI); C 1562-1850 M 1563-1850
    (Mf I SLC)
MI (I, NDA); Incledon 69 (NDA)

SWIMBRIDGE Holy Name, Stone Cross, Gunn. Chapel-of-ease in Swimbridge,.
Opened 1873
OR None. *see* Swimbridge

SWIMBRIDGE St Thomas, Cobbaton. Chapel-of-ease erected 1866-67. Closed 1975.
Now a house. Memorials in church removed to St James, Swimbridge and
St Peter, West Buckland.
OR None. *see* Swimbridge

SWIMBRIDGE (Bapt) Station Hill. Erected 1837 [1882 Return] Closed 1999
OR None at church
MI MI 1839-1981, index and plan (Ch Sec, NDRO)

SWIMBRIDGE (Wes) Erected 1812 [1851 Religious Census]
OR for *c.*1807-37 *see* BARNSTAPLE CIRCUIT, BIDEFORD, LANDKEY
    (RG 4/954,955,1213 PRO)

SWIMBRIDGE (Wes) Cobbaton [1882 Return]

SWIMBRIDGE (Wes) [1882 Return] Erected 1898. fl *c.*1970

SYDENHAM DAMEREL St Mary [Lifton Hundred; Tavistock Union] [296] United
1938 with LAMERTON. Now also WITH MILTON ABBOT, DUNTERTON
OR C 1540-1994 M 1539-1938 B 1540-1978 (PWDRO)
BT CMB 1610, 1626, 1629, 1634, 1663, 1666, 1668-69, 1671-72, 1674-81, 1684,
    1686, 1688-90, 1695, 1697, 1699-1700 (1701-1812 ?); CMB 1813-24
    CB 1827-39, 1841-43 M 1827-29, 1831-39, 1841-42, 1844 (DRO)
Cop M 1813-37 (Ptd DFHS); M 1539-1754 (I, Ptd, edit M.Brown, Dartmoor Press
    1999); Extr C 1540-1794 M 1555-1738 B 1540-1807 (Vol 3, BG/PCL)
Cop (Mf) (Tavistock SP); C 1540-1870 M 1539-1837 B 1540-1812; with gaps
    (Mfc SG); Extr C 1540-1717 M 1542-1717 (IGI)

SYDENHAM DAMEREL (Bible Christian) Providence, South Sydenham. erected 1832
[1851 Religious Census]; Sydenham Chapel [1882 Return]

SYDENHAM DAMEREL (Bible Christian/U Meth) Erected 1926. fl *c.*1970

SYMONSBOROUGH   *see* HEMYOCK

TADDIPORT   *see* LITTLE TORRINGTON

TALATON St James the Apostle [Hayridge Hundred; Honiton Union] [479]
see also OTTERY ST MARY St Philip and St James, Escot. Now with WHIMPLE,
CLYST ST LAWRENCE
OR C 1621-1886 M 1621-1979 B 1621-1837 (DRO)
BT CMB 1611, 1614, 1616, 1620, 1624, 1638, 1666, 1669-70, 1675, 1678, 1683,
    1686, 1695-97, 1699, 1717 (1718-1812 ?); CB 1813-44, 1846-54 M 1813-16,
    1818-28, 1830-36 (DRO)
Cop B 1800-37 (Ptd DFHS); B 1800-37 (SG); CMB 1621-1837 (DCRS/WSL, WSL);
    M 1621-1837 (Boyd)
Cop (Mf) Extr C 1631-1837 M 1621-1836 (IGI); C 1621-1837 (Mf I SLC)

TALATON (Presb) Licensed 1672; fl c.1690 ?; closed by 1715

TAMERTON FOLIOT St Mary [Roborough Hundred; Plympton St Mary Union]   [1061]
see also PLYMOUTH Crownhill
OR C 1794-1897 M 1794-1948 B 1794-1850 (PWDRO) Noted in 1831:
    'all previous Registers were accidentally destroyed by fire'
BT CMB 1611, 1614, 1617, 1619, 1631, 1633, 1663-64, 1668-70, 1672, 1675-82,
    1684, 1687-90, 1697, 1750-51, 1753-95 (1796-1812 ?); CB 1813-69
    M 1813-37 (DRO)
Cop M 1813-37 (Ptd DFHS); C 1611-1794 M 1611-1795 from BT (PWDRO);
    M 1754-1840; M 1614-1837 indexed by male spouse (DFHS)
Cop (Mf) C 1794-1897 M 1794-1837 B 1794-1850; with gaps (Mfc SG)
MI Cy 1975 (Ts SG)

TAMERTON FOLIOT Holy Spirit, Southway. Parish created 1971 from Tamerton
Foliot
OR (Inc)

TAMERTON FOLIOT Maristow (Stow St Martin or Martinstow). Home of Lopes
family (Lord Roborough) Chapel 1877-79

TAMERTON FOLIOT (Wes) Erected c.1805 [1851 Religious Census]
OR for c.1787-1837 see PLYMOUTH Ebenezer; Morice Street Devonport
    (RG 4/864,1325,1092 PRO)

TAMERTON FOLIOT (Wes) Fore Street. Erected 1877. Salem [1882 Return]
fl c.1970

TAPHOUSE   see TEDBURN ST MARY

TAVISTOCK St Eustachius [Tavistock Hundred; Tavistock Union] [5602]
Now with Gulworthy
OR C 1614-1955 M 1614-1980 B 1614-1934 (DRO)
BT CMB 1602, 1606, 1608, 1611-14, 1616-17, 1620, 1624, 1630, 1632?, 1633,
    1635, 1638-39, 1663-64, 1666-72, 1675-79, 1686, 1688-90, 1694-95,
    1720-30, 1732-37, 1743-51, 1753-99, 1801-11; CMB 1813-31, 1833-36 (DRO)
Cop CMB 1614-1781 (DRO); M 1813-37 (Ptd DFHS); M 1614-1754 (I, Ptd, edit
    M.Brown, Dartmoor Press 1999); M 1754-1840 (DFHS); B 1813-82
    (Tavistock Lib); B 1813-82 (I, PWDRO); B Plymouth Road cemetery
    1882-1901 (I, PWDRO); Extr C 1614-1800 M 1614-1784 B 1614-1781 (Vol 20,
    BG/PCL)
Cop (Mf) (Tavistock SP); C 1761-1840 M 1745-1837 B 1761-1856 (Mfc SG)
MI (I, DFHS)

TAVISTOCK St Paul, Gulworthy. Parish created 1858 from Tavistock,.Now with
Tavistock St Eustachius
OR C 1858-1948 M 1859-1978 B 1859-1915 (DRO)
Cop B 1859-1916 (I, PWDRO)

TAVISTOCK Fitzford. Chapel Erected 1866-67. Taken over by RCs 1951
OR C 1867-1944 (DRO)

TAVISTOCK (RC) Our Lady of the Assumption 1951

TAVISTOCK (Ind/Cong later URC) Brook Street f 1796 [1851 Religious Census]
[1882 Return] Later Russell Street
OR ZC 1796-1837 (RG 4/451 PRO); C 1796-1911 M 1868-1975 B 1867-1907 (DRO)
Cop (Mf) ZC 1796-1837 (Mf DCRS/WSL, SG); C 1796-1811 M 1868-1909 B 1867-1907
    (Tavistock SP); Extr ZC 1796-1837 (IGI); ZC 1796-1837 (Mf I SLC)

TAVISTOCK (Presb/Unit) Abbey Chapel, Bedford Square f 1660. Licensed 1672
[1851 Religious Census] Closed 1959. Chapel later used by Brethren
OR C 1692-1837 (RG 4/2030 PRO); C 1862-1961 B 1874-1949 (DRO)
Cop (Mf) ZC 1692-1837 (Mf DCRS/WSL, SG); C 1862-1961 B 1874-1949
    (Tavistock SP); Extr C 1692-1837 (IGI); C 1692-1837 (Mf I SLC)

TAVISTOCK (Wes) Circuit
OR C 1809-42 (copy); 1837-1962, 1899-1914, 1918-72 (DRO)

TAVISTOCK (Wes)
OR ZC 1808-37 B 1832-37 (RG 4/341 PRO); Chapel Street M 1860-83 (DRO);
for *c.*1800-37 *see also* PLYMOUTH Ebenezer; Morice Street Devonport
(RG 4/864,1325 PRO)
Cop (Mf) ZC 1808-37 B 1832-37 (Mf DCRS/WSL, SG); Extr C 1808-37 (IGI);
    C 1808-37 (Mf I SLC)

TAVISTOCK (Wes) Barley Market Street erected 1814 or 1817 [1851 Religious
census]; Chapel Street erected 1858 [1882 Return] fl *c.*1970

TAVISTOCK (Wes) Morwellham. Erected 1820 [1851 Religious Census]
Rebuilt 1861 [1882 Return] fl *c.*1970

TAVISTOCK (Wes) Lamboon. Erected 1849 [1851 Religious Census]

TAVISTOCK (Wes) Ogbear. Erected 1850 [1851 Religious Census] [1882 Return]

TAVISTOCK (Wes) Russell Street. Erected 1838 [1851 Religious Census]

TAVISTOCK (Bible Christian) Mill House. Erected 1843. Closed 1983

TAVISTOCK (Bible Christian) Bannawell Street. Erected 1847 [1851 Religious
Census] [1882 Return] Used by Brethren from 1911; later in commercial use

TAVISTOCK (Bible Christian) Circuit
OR C 1859-1931 (DRO)

TAVISTOCK (UMFC) Morwellham [1882 Return]

TAVISTOCK (Free Meth/Wes Assn/U Meth) Russell Street [1882 Return]
OR C 1905-10, 1931-63 M 1919-61 (DRO)

TAVISTOCK (S of F) f 1702. Meeting house 1740; existed 1785. Lapsed. New
meeting house and burial ground 1835 [1851 Religious Census] Dolvin Road
[1882 Return] Now Canal Road
BT B 1865 (DRO)

TAVISTOCK (Brethren) in former Bible Christian Chapel, Bannawell Street, from 1911; in former Abbey Chapel after 1959

TAVISTOCK Poor Law Union Workhouse
OR Z 1866-1945 D 1866-1919 (DRO)

TAVISTOCK Dolvin Road Cemetery
Cop B 1834-82 (I, PWDRO)

TAVY ST MARY   see MARY TAVY

TAWSTOCK St Peter [Fremington Hundred; Barnstaple Union] [1348]
see also STICKLEPATH. Now with TWO RIVERS
OR C 1538-1988 M 1538-1995 B 1538-1847 (NDRO)
BT CMB 1597-1602, 1604-07, 1610-14, 1624, 1643-44, 1667, 1672?, 1674,
    1678-79, 1683, 1685, 1688, 1690 or 1691, 1695-97, 1699-1700, 1704-09,
    1711-12, 1714-16, 1718-23, 1725-30, 1732-39, 1741-42, 1745-51, 1753,
    1755-56, 1762-70 (1771-1812 ?); CMB 1813-22, 1824-36 (DRO)
Cop C 1538-1837, 1874-1979 M 1540-1836 B 1538-1837, 1848-1978 (NDA)
Cop (Mf) C 1805-93 M 1754-1966 B 1795-1847 (Mfc SG)
MI (I, NDA); Ch, cy (Ptd C.Wrey List of Flagstones, Mural Tablets and
    Monuments and some Epitaphs from the Churchyard: n.d.); (Ptd A.Messenger
    'The heraldry of Tawstock church': TDA 83: 1951: 130-71)

TAWSTOCK Holy Trinity, Harracott. Chapel-of-ease erected 1844. Closed 1960s.
Now a house
OR C 1842-1893 M 1843 (NDRO)

TAWSTOCK (RC) Tawstock Court. Domestic chapel of Wrey family. Erected c.1827
[1851 Religious Census] Mission moved to Barnstaple. Closed 1862
OR Barnstaple register 1836+ now missing

TAWSTOCK (Bapt) Providence, Hiscott. Erected 1830 [1851 Religious Census]
[1882 Return] Sold to Bible Christians 1859

TAWSTOCK (Bapt) Eastacombe. Erected 1817 [1851 Religious Census]
[1882 Return] later used by Brethren

TAWSTOCK (Wes)
OR for c.1807-37 see BARNSTAPLE CIRCUIT (RG 4/954 PRO)

TAWSTOCK (Bible Christian) Hiscott. Purchased 1859 [1882 Return] fl c.1970.
Later used by Brethren. Closed. Now a house

TAWSTOCK (Bible Christian/U Meth) Chapelton. Erected 1830 [1851 Religious
Census] Rebuilt 1916. fl c.1970

TAWSTOCK (Brethren) in former Eastacombe and Hiscott chapels (Bapt)

TAWTON, BISHOP'S or TAWTON EPISCOPI St John the Baptist [South Molton
Hundred; Barnstaple Union] [1641] see also chapelry of LANDKEY. Now with
BARNSTAPLE
OR C 1558-1917 M 1587-1990 B 1587-1952 (NDRO)
BT CMB 1607-08, 1610?, 1614-15, 1629, 1634-35, 1639?, 1663-66, 1669, 1674,
    1678-80, 1682, 1685-86, 1688-1716, 1718-58, 1777-78, 1780-1804
    (1805-12 ?); CB 1813-53 M 1813-37, 1838-40 (DRO)

TAWTON, BISHOP'S cont.
Cop B 1813-37 (Ptd DFHS); C 1558-1857 M 1587-1857 B 1587-1866 (NDA);
   CMB 1558-1840 (DCRS/WSL); B 1813-37 (SG)
Cop (Mf) Extr C 1558-1840 M 1587-1840 (IGI); C 1558-1840 M 1587-1840
   (Mf I SLC)
MI Ch cy 1975 (SG); Incledon 338 (NDA)

TAWTON, BISHOP'S St John the Baptist, Newport. Parish created 1847 from
Bishop's Tawton. Now with BARNSTAPLE
OR C 1830-1921 M 1847-1986 B 1895-1977 (NDRO)
BT C 1854-57 (DRO)

TAWTON, BISHOP'S Herner Chapel. Chapel-of-ease to Bishop's Tawton,
erected 1888
OR M 1890-1947 (NDRO)

TAWTON, BISHOP'S (Bapt) Erected 1850 [1851 Religious Census] [1882 Return]

TAWTON, BISHOP'S (Bapt) A building, Newport [1882 Return]

TAWTON, BISHOP'S (Wes) Newport, Newport Road. Erected 1911. fl *c.*1970

TAWTON, BISHOP'S (Wes)
OR for *c.*1807-37 *see* BARNSTAPLE CIRCUIT, LANDKEY (RG 4/954,1213 PRO)

TAWTON, BISHOP'S (Bible Christian) Erected 1936, fl *c.*1970

TAWTON, NORTH or CHAPING TAWTON St Peter [North Tawton and Winkleigh
Hundred; Okehampton Union] [1788] Now with BONDLEIGH, SAMPFORD COURTENAY,
HONEYCHURCH
OR C 1538-1958 M 1538-1973 B 1538-1961 (DRO)
BT CMB 1607-08, 1623, 1628-29, 1668, 1670, 1672, 1679, 1682-83, 1686,
   1689-91, 1694, 1696-97, 1699-1700, 1703, 1707-08, 1710-12, 1714-15, 1751
   (1752-1812 ?); CMB 1814-15, 1817-20, 1822-35 (DRO)
Cop C 1538-1838 Banns 1754-99 MB 1538-1837 (DRO); Extr CMB 1538-1667
   C 1669-71 M 1635-1793 B 1637-69 (Vol 2, BG/PCL)
Cop (Mf) (Okehampton SP); Extr C 1538-1843 M 1538-1837 B 1538-1866 (Mfc SG)
MI Extr (Whitmore MS, SG)

TAWTON, NORTH (Ind/Cong, later URC) f 1810. Erected 1833 [1851 Religious
Census] Fore Street
OR ZC 1812-36 (RG 4/452 PRO)
Cop (Mf) C 1812-36 (Mf DCRS/WSL, SG); Extr C 1812-36 (IGI); C 1812-36
   (Mf I SLC)

TAWTON, NORTH (Bible Christian) Bethel, Barton Lane. Erected 1842
[1851 Religious Census] [1882 Return] Barton Street. Erected 1898. fl *c.*1970

TAWTON, NORTH (S of F) North Tawton MM f 1668; replaced *c.*1691 by
CREDITON MM

TAWTON, NORTH (S of F) f pre-1669; closed by 1688 ?

TAWTON, SOUTH St Andrew [Wonford Hundred; Okehampton Union]   [1937]
Now with BELSTONE
<u>OR</u> C 1541-1885 M 1558-1964 B 1558-1908 (DRO)
<u>BT</u> CMB 1607, 1609, 1618, 1630, 1635-36, 1641, 1663-64, 1667, 1669-72, 1675,
   1678-79, 1687, 1690, 1695-96, 1699, 1701, 1703-04, 1711, 1713-16,
   1720-21 (1722-1812 ?); none listed after 1812 (DRO)
<u>Cop</u> CMB 1540-1738 (DCRS/WSL); Extr CMB 1541-1837 (Ptd, edit. M.Brown:
   Dartmoor Press: 1998); Extr C 1540-1725 by family M 1559-1727
   B 1558-1730 (Vol 2, BG/PCL)
<u>Cop (Mf)</u> (Okehampton SP); C 1541-1837 M 1558-1837 B 1558-1866 (Mfc SG);
   Extr C 1540-1738 M 1558-1738 (IGI); C 1540-1738 M 1558-1738
   (Mf I SLC)
<u>MI</u> (Ptd DRMI 23: 1998); Ch 1945 (MS, SG); Extr (Whitmore MS, SG)

TAWTON, SOUTH St Mary. South Zeal. Chapel rebuilt 1713. Now licensed
building in parish of South Tawton
<u>OR</u> None

TAWTON, SOUTH (Ind) Zeal f c.1831. No building [1851 Religious Census]

TAWTON, SOUTH (Wes)
<u>OR</u> for c.1815-37 see OKEHAMPTON (RG 4/1089 PRO)

TAWTON, SOUTH (Wes) South Zeal. Erected 1846 [1851 Religious Census]
<u>OR</u> for c.1815-37 see ASHBURTON CIRCUIT, OKEHAMPTON (RG 4/840,1089 PRO)

TAWTON, SOUTH (Bible Christian) Ebenezer Shelley Hill, South Zeal. Erected
1866 [1882 Return] fl c.1970

TAWTON, SOUTH (Bible Christian) Whiddon Down. Erected 1906. fl c.1970

TAWTON, SOUTH (Bible Christian) Gooseford n.d. [1851 Religious Census]

TEDBURN ST MARY St Mary [Wonford Hundred; St Thomas Union]   [821]
Now with NORTH KENN
<u>OR</u> C 1559-1883 M 1558-1837 B 1559-1879 (DRO)
<u>BT</u> CMB 1610, 1616, 1623-24, 1628, 1630, 1632, 1644, 1667-70, 1675, 1677-79,
   1683, 1687, 1690, 1699, 1701 (1702-1812 ?); CB 1813-41, 1843-46,
   1850-53, 1855, 1857-60 M 1813-37 (DRO)
<u>Cop</u> CMB 1557-1837 (DCRS/WSL); CMB 1557-1943 (WSL); M 1558-1708 (Boyd);
   Extr C 1606-1753 M 1624-91 B 1571-1773 (Vol 2, BG/PCL)
<u>Cop (Mf)</u> Extr C 1557-1837 M 1558-1837 (IGI); C 1557-1837 M 1558-1837
   (Mf I SLC)
<u>MI</u> (I, DFHS); Ch extr (Ptd Cresswell 149-51); Cy 1978 (Ts SG)

TEDBURN ST MARY (UMFC/U Meth) Taphouse, Dunsford Road [1882 Return]
Erected 1930. fl c.1970

TEIGNGRACE St Peter and St Paul [Teignbridge Hundred; Newton Abbot Union
[160] Rebuilt 1787. Now with HIGHWEEK
<u>OR</u> C 1685-1990 M 1684-1851 B 1688-1812 (DRO)
<u>BT</u> CMB 1613-14, 1618, 1630, 1664, 1668, 1671?, 1672, 1676, 1682, 1686, 1695
   (1696-1812 ?); CB 1813-35 M 1813, 1816-17, 1819-23, 1825-26, 1829-33
   (DRO)
<u>Cop</u> CMB 1613-86 from BT, 1683-1914 (DCRS/WSL);
<u>Cop (Mf)</u> Extr CM 1683-1914 (IGI); CM 1683-1875 (Mf I SLC)
<u>MI</u> (I, DFHS)

TEIGNMOUTH St Michael the Archangel, East Teignmouth [Exminster Hundred; Newton Abbot Union] [1810] Chapelry in DAWLISH. Separate parish 1777. Peculiar of the Dean and Chapter of Exeter 1777-1848. Rebuilt 1823. Now with HALDON
OR C 1665-1979 M 1666-1971 B 1666-1927 (DRO)
BT CMB 1606, 1608, 1613-14, 1617, 1620, 1633, 1635-36, 1639, 1641, 1678, 1690 (1691-1812 ?); CMB 1813-19 CB 1821-61 M 1821-37 (DRO)
Cop B 1813-37 (Ptd DFHS); B 1813-37 (WSL, SG); CMB 1606-41 from BT, 1665-1837 (DCRS/WSL); B 1881-1904 (DFHS)
Cop (Mf) Extr C 1606-1837 M 1606-20, 1633-41, 1666-1837 (IGI); C 1606-1837 (Mf I SLC)
MI Ch extr (Ptd Cresswell 160-2)

TEIGNMOUTH St James, West Teignmouth [Exminster Hundred; Newton Abbot Union] [2878] Chapelry in BISHOPSTEIGNTON. Separate parish 1842. Peculiar of the Bishop of Exeter 1842-48. Now with HALDON
OR CB 1706-1877 M 1706-1869 (DRO) No earlier registers noted in 1831
BT CMB 1615, 1617, 1624, 1633-36, 1641, 1666-68, 1670, 1674-75, 1678-80, 1682-86, 1688-98, 1700-06, 1731 (1732-1812 ?); CB 1813-41 M 1813-18, 1820-37 (DRO)
Cop CMB 1615-1705 from BT, 1706-1837 (DCRS/WSL)
Cop (Mf) Extr C 1615-1837 M 1615-41, 1666-1837 (IGI); C 1615-1837 M 1615-41, 1666-1837 (Mf I SLC)
MI Ch extr (Ptd Cresswell 166-71); Incledon 97 (NDA)

TEIGNMOUTH St Nicholas see ST NICHOLAS

TEIGNMOUTH (RC) A mission for French émigrés 1794-1815. Room in a house, occupied by Mr Prouse, served from Ugbrooke [1851 Religious Census]; Our Lady and St Charles 1854-78 then Our Lady and St Patrick [1882 Return]
OR Early entries in UGBROOKE registers; C 1857+ M 1870+ NB 1858+ Confirmations 1869+ (Inc) Confirmations 1864+ (Plymouth Diocesan Archives)

TEIGNMOUTH (RC) St Scholastica's Abbey, Dawlish Road; Benedictine Nuns. f Dunkirk, Flanders 1662; moved to Hammersmith, London 1795; to Teignmouth 1862. Closed 1990
OR B 1828-1985 (St Mary's Convent, Buckfast) Early entries refer to Hammersmith. Confirmations 1892-1934 (Plymouth Diocesan Archives)

TEIGNMOUTH (Bapt) Fore Street f 1821

TEIGNMOUTH (Bapt/Brethren) Ebenezer, Bitton Park Road. Opened 1824 as Bapt church; congregation later joined Brethren. Renamed Gospel Hall

TEIGNMOUTH (Cong, later URC) Zion f 1790 [1851 Religious Census] Dawlish Road f 1807
OR C 1804-36 B 1809-36 (RG 4/453 PRO)
Cop (Mf) C 1804-36 B 1809-36 (Mf DCRS/WSL, SG); Extr C 1804-36 (IGI); C 1804-36 (Mf I SLC)

TEIGNMOUTH (Presb) fl c.1672-90

TEIGNMOUTH (Wes) Circuit and Chapel
OR ZC 1813-37 B 1824-33 (RG 4/1220 PRO); C 1813-1820, 1837-1899 B 1838-53 (DRO)
Cop (Mf) ZC 1813-37 (Mf DCRS/WSL, SG); Extr ZC 1813-37 (IGI); ZC 1813-37 (Mf I SLC)

TEIGNMOUTH (Wes) Somerset Place. Erected 1845 [1851 Census] [1882 Return]
fl *c.*1970

TEIGNMOUTH (Wes) Fore Street, Shaldon. Erected 1867. fl *c.*1970

TEIGNMOUTH (Prim Meth) West Teignmouth
OR C 1870-1956 (DRO)

TEIGNMOUTH (Prim Meth) Market Room, over the Old Market [1882 Return]

TEIGNMOUTH (Prim Meth) Primitive Methodist School Chapel, Parson Street
[1882 Return]

TEIGNMOUTH (British and Foreign Bible Society) Bethel, Duke of Somerset's
Quay [1882 Return]

TEIGNMOUTH (Brethren) West Teignmouth since 1800 [1851 Religious Census]
Meeting Room, Bitton Street [1882 Return]

TEIGNMOUTH East and West Teignmouth Cemetery
BT 1856, 1860-62 (DRO)

TEIGNTON DREW   *see* DREWSTEIGNTON

TEIGNTON EPISCOPI   or TEIGNTON, BISHOP'S *see* BISHOPSTEIGNTON

TEIGNTON REGIS   or TEIGNTON, KING'S see KINGSTEIGNTON

TEIGNWEEK   *see* HIGHWEEK

TEMPLETON St Margaret [Witheridge Hundred; Tiverton Union] [222]
Peculiar of the manor of Templeton. Used for clandestine marriages before
1754. United 1924 with LOXBEARE. Now with EXE VALLEY
OR C 1556-1812 M 1578-1837 B 1578-1809 (DRO)
BT None listed before 1812; CB 1815-31, 1833-36 M 1815-16, 1819-20,
    1822-26, 1828-31, 1834-36 (DRO)
Cop (Mf) (Tiverton SP)

TEMPLETON (Ind) n.d. [1851 Religious Census]

TEMPLETON (Bible Christian) n.d. [1851 Religious Census]; Templeton Bridge
[1882 Return]

TETCOTT Holy Cross [Black Torrington Hundred; Holsworthy Union] [293]
Now with ASHWATER, HALWILL, BEAWORTHY, CLAWTON, LUFFINCOTT
OR C 1596-1812 M 1599-1836 B 1599-1812 (DRO)
BT CMB 1611, 1613, 1624, 1627, 1634, 1663, 1669-72, 1674-82, 1694-97, 1699
    (1700-1812 ?); CB 1813-34, 1836, 1838, 1842 M 1814, 1817-28, 1830-34,
    1836 (DRO); CB 1813-33, 1838-40 M 1813-14, 1816, 1818, 1820, 1822-23,
    1826-27, 1829, 1831-33, 1838-40 (DRO)
Cop M 1813-37 (Ptd DFHS); CMB 1597-1837 (DCRS/WSL); M 1599-1836 (Boyd)
Cop (Mf) Extr C 1597-1837 M 1599-1836 (IGI); C 1597-1837 M 1599-1836
    (Mf I SLC)
MI Extr (Whitmore MS, SG)

TETCOTT (Bible Christian) Zion n.d. [1851 Religious Census] [1882 Return]
Rebuilt 1899 ? fl *c.*1970

THELBRIDGE St David [Witheridge Hundred; Crediton Union] [219]
Rebuilt 1871-74. Now with WITHERIDGE, MESHAW, EAST WORLINGTON, WEST
WORLINGTON
OR C 1632-1945 M 1632-1846 B 1632-1991 (NDRO)
BT CMB 1607-08, 1610, 1614, 1618, 1630, 1668, 1674, 1678-79, 1683, 1688,
  1694, 1697, 1699, 1707, 1712, 1714-15 (1716-1812 ?); none listed after
  1812 (DRO)
Cop CMB 1633-1837 (DCRS/WSL)
Cop (Mf) (Tiverton SP); Extr C 1633-1837 M 1635-39, 1654-1837 (IGI);
  C 1633-1837 M 1635-39, 1654-1837 (Mf I SLC)
MI (I, NDA); Incledon 170 (NDA)

THORNBURY St Peter [Black Torrington Hundred; Holsworthy Union] [546]
Now with BLACK TORRINGTON, BRADFORD, COOKBURY, HIGHAMPTON
OR C 1653-1994 M 1656-1797, 1813-1836 B 1652-1992 (DRO)
BT CMB 1610, 1614, 1619, 1629, 1664, 1666, 1668-72, 1674-78, 1680-81, 1688,
  1694-96, 1699 (1700-1812 ?); CB 1813-36, 1838-39 M 1813-17, 1819-36
  (DRO)
Cop CMB 1600-1813 from BT, 1652-1837 (DCRS/WSL); CMB 1652-1837 (SG)
Cop (Mf) Extr C 1600-1837 M 1600, 1614-24, 1652-1837 (IGI); C 1600-1837
  M 1600, 1614-24, 1652-1837 (Mf I SLC)
MI Incledon 1030 (NDA)

THORNBURY (Presb) fl *c.*1672-90

THORNBURY (Wes)
OR for *c.*1817-37 *see* HOLSWORTHY (RG 4/1210 PRO)

THORNBURY (Wes) Holsworthy Beacon. Erected 1835 [1851 Religious Census]
[1882 Return] Rebuilt 1882. fl *c.*1970

THORNBURY (Wes) Woodacott Cross. Erected 1820 [1851 Religious Census]
Rebuilt 1891. fl *c.*1970

THORNCOMBE [Dorset] [Axminster Hundred until 1844; Axminster Union 1836-94]
[1368] Moved from Dorset to Devon 1844; back to Dorset 1896. *see* NIPR
Dorset

THORNHILLHEAD *see* BUCKLAND BREWER

THORVERTON St Thomas of Canterbury [Hayridge Hundred; Tiverton Union]
[1455] *see also* chapelry of NETHEREXE. Now with RADDON
OR C 1730-1917 M 1725-1968 B 1725-1918 (DRO) Registers damaged by flooding
  1821. No earlier volumes noted in 1831
BT CMB 1606, 1610-11, 1615, 1617, 1620-21, 1628-29, 1632, 1641?, 1662,
  1667, 1669-71, 1675, 1678-79, 1683, 1687, 1695-97 (1698-1812 ?);
  CB 1813-51 M 1813-37 (DRO)
Cop CMB 1606-1837 (WSL); M 1606-1750 from BT (Boyd)
Cop (Mf) CMB 1606-70 from BT 1720-1837 (Mf DCRS/WSL); Extr C 1606-1837
  M 1606-41, 1662-97, 1713-1837 (IGI); C 1606-1837 M 1606-41,
  1662-97, 1713-1837 (Mf I SLC)
MI (I, DFHS); Extr (Whitmore MS, SG)

THORVERTON Raddon Chapel. Medieval. Rebuilt 1896, removed 1925

THORVERTON (Bapt) Berrysbridge Road f 1831; erected 1834 [1851 Religious
Census]; chapel purchased from Presbyterians [1882 Return]
OR Thorverton and Brampford Speke C 1832-1938 (DRO)

THORVERTON (Presb) f 1715. Declined by 1800. Sold to Baptists 1831

THORVERTON (S of F) f by 1688; part of CULLOMPTON MM;   EXETER MM by 1698; closed *c.*1700

THROWLEIGH St Mary the Virgin [Wonford Hundred; Okehampton Union]   [460]
Now with CHAGFORD, GIDLEIGH
OR C 1653-1988 M 1654-1989 B 1653-1985 (DRO)
BT CMB 1606, 1610, 1614, 1620, 1626, 1630, 1636, 1664, 1667-70, 1672, 1675,
    1677-78, 1683, 1685, 1687, 1690, 1696-97, 1699, 1701 (1702-1812 ?);
    CMB 1813-38 (DRO)
Cop CMB 1606-36 from BT, 1653-1837 (DCRS/WSL, WSL, Okehampton SP
    Extr CMB 1653-1837 (Ptd, edit. M.Brown: Dartmoor Press: 1998)
Cop (Mf) (Okehampton SP); Extr C 1606-1837 M 1606-36, 1654-1837 (IGI);
    C 1606-1837 M 1606-36, 1654-1837 (Mf I SLC)
MI (Ptd DRMI 23: 1998)

THROWLEIGH (Bible Christian/Meth) Providence. Erected 1839 [1851 Religious
Census] [1882 Return] fl *c.*1970
MI (Ptd DRMI 23: 1998)

THRUSHELTON St George [Lifton Hundred; Tavistock Union]   [353]
Chapelry in MARYSTOWE, United 1922 with LEW TRENCHARD. Now also with
MARYSTOWE, CORYTON, STOWFORD
OR C 1654-1992 M 1654-1976 B 1654-1927, 1960-91 (PWDRO)
BT CMB 1614, 1627, 1633, 1635, 1663, 1669, 1671-72, 1675-77, 1680-81, 1686,
    1689, 1690?, 1697, 1700 (1701-1812 ?); CB 1813-39 M 1813-26, 1828-36
    (DRO)
Cop B 1800-1900 (I, PWDRO); Extr C 1663-90 M 1665 B 1664-1710
    (Vol 8, BG/PCL)
Cop (Mf) (Tavistock SP)

THRUSHELTON (Wes) Broadleydown. Erected 1836. fl *c.*1970
OR for *c.*1815-37 *see* OKEHAMPTON (RG 4/1089 PRO)

THRUSHELTON (Wes) Axworthy
OR for *c.*1815-37 *see* OAKHAMPTON (RG 4/1089 PRO)

THURLESTONE All Saints [Stanborough Hundred; Kingsbridge Union]   [466]
Now with SOUTH MILTON
OR C 1558-1986 M 1558-1994 B 1558-1933 (DRO)
BT CMB 1614-15, 1620, 1663-64, 1666, 1668-73, 1675-76, 1678, 1680-81, 1685,
    1687, 1690, 1696, 1699-1700 (1701-1812 ?); CB 1813-37, 1819-38
    M 1813-37, 1819-23, 1825-26, 1828-37 (DRO)
Cop M 1754-1812 indexed by male spouse (DFHS)
Cop (Mf) C 1558-1878 M 1558-1837 B 1558-1812 (Mfc SG)

THURLESTONE (Wes) Buckland [1882 Return]   Erected 1908. Closed 1971

THURLESTONE (Wes) House 1841 [1851 Religious Census]
OR for *c.*1813-37 *see* KINGSBRIDGE (RG 4/1088 PRO)

TINHAY   *see* LIFTON

TIPTON ST JOHN   *see* OTTERY ST MARY

TIVERTON St Peter [Tiverton Hundred; Tiverton Union] [9766]
see also chapelry of COVE. Now with CHEVITHORNE, COVE
OR   C 1560-1983 M 1560-1987 B 1560-1928 (DRO)
BT   CMB 1605?, 1607, 1613, 1617, 1625, 1630, 1632?, 1635, 1667-69, 1672,
     1675, 1678, 1683, 1687, 1690, 1695-97, 1701, 1703-05, 1711, 1713-37,
     1739-48, 1750, 1752-54, 1757-77, 1779-1803, 1805-12; CMB 1813-36 (DRO)
Cop CMB 1605-1812 from BT (DCRS/WSL); Extr CB 1559-1616 M 1559-1615
     (Vol 12, BG/PCL)
Cop (Mf) (Tiverton SP); Extr C 1605-1812 M 1605-35, 1667-1812 (IGI);
          C 1605-1812 (Mf I SLC)
MI   (I, DFHS); Ch, cy (Ptd E.Chalk *A History of the Church of St Peter,
     Tiverton*: 1905); Extr (Whitmore MS, SG); Incledon 726 (NDA)

TIVERTON St Paul, Westexe. Parish created 1856 from Tiverton St Peter
OR   C 1857-1944 M 1857-1981 (DRO)

TIVERTON St Thomas, Chevithorne. Erected 1843. Parish created 1889 from
Tiverton St Peter, with which now united
OR   C 1843-1881 M 1890-1979 B 1843-1914 (DRO)

TIVERTON St Catherine, Withleigh. Erected 1846. Parish created 1890 from
Tiverton St Peter. Now with EXE VALLEY
OR   C 1846+ M 1886+ B 1856+ (Inc)

TIVERTON St George, Fore Street. Erected 1730. Parish created 1896 from
Tiverton St Peter
OR   C 1889-1971 M 1890-1972 B 1890-1926 (DRO)

TIVERTON St Andrew, Blundells Road. Parish created 1960 from Tiverton
St Peter, St George
OR   (Inc)

TIVERTON Blundells School Chapel
MI   (Ptd *British Archivist* I: 1913: 63-7)

TIVERTON Waldron's Almshouses, Well Brook Street. Chapel *c.*1579

TIVERTON Greenway's Almshouses, Gold Street. Tudor chapel [1851 Religious
Census]

TIVERTON (RC) St John. Erected 1837 [1851 Religious Census]
OR   C 1856+ M 1888+ B 1858+ Confirmations 1850, 1863+ (Inc) No earlier
     registers known

TIVERTON (RC) St James 1967

TIVERTON (Bapt) Newport Street f by 1628. Licensed 1672. Erected 1697,
rebuilt 1730, 1876. Burial ground from 1816 [1851 Religious Census]
[1882 Return]
OR   Z 1767-1837 B 1816-37 (RG 4/1221 PRO); C 1687-1845 (DRO)
Cop (Mf) Z 1767-1837 B 1816-37 (Mf DCRS/WSL, SG); Extr Z 1767-1837 (IGI)

TIVERTON (Bapt) New School House, The Works [1882 Return]

TIVERTON (Presb/Ind/Cong, later URC) f 1660. Licensed 1672. St Peter's
Street. Erected 1787, rebuilt 1831 [1851 Religious Census] [1882 Return]
OR   ZC 1766-1837 (RG 4/1764,2031 PRO) None at church
Cop (Mf) ZC 1766-1837 (Mf DCRS/WSL, SG); Extr ZC 1766-1837 (IGI);
          ZC 1766-1837 (Mf I SLC)

TIVERTON (Ind) Bolham. Erected 1849 [1851 Religious Census] [1882 Return] Closed. Now a house

TIVERTON (Ind/Cong later URC) Chapel Street, Elmore. Erected 1843 [1851 Religious Census]

TIVERTON (now Cong Fed) Nomansland f 1864

TIVERTON (Wes) Circuit
OR C 1838-1931 (DRO)
Cop (Mf) C 1838-1931 (Mfc Tiverton SP)

TIVERTON (Wes) St. Peter Street. f c.1752. Erected 1814 [1851 Religious Census] [1882 Return] fl c.1970
OR ZC 1812-37 B 1834-37 (RG 4/342 PRO); M 1845-1869 B 1834-1899 including (DRO); for c.1807-37 see also BARNSTAPLE CIRCUIT, BIDEFORD, CULLOMPTON, PLYMOUTH Morice Street Devonport (RG 4/954,955,958,864 PRO)
Cop B 1834-99 (SG, Tiverton SP)
Cop (Mf) ZC 1812-37 (Mf DCRS/WSL, SG); Extr ZC 1812-37 (IGI)

TIVERTON (Wes) Chevithorne. Erected 1813 [1851 Religious Census] Rebuilt 1888. fl c.1970

TIVERTON (Bible Christian/U Meth/Meth) Erected 1844 [1851 Religious Census]; Ham Place, St Andrew Street [1882 Return]
OR C 1844-1958 M 1936-57 (DRO)
Cop (Mf) C 1844-1958 (Mfc Tiverton SP)

TIVERTON (S of F) f 1656; existed 1680. Part of CULLOMPTON MM

TIVERTON (New Jerusalem) f 1846, meeting in Baptist chapel erected 1836 [1851 Religious Census]

TIVERTON Burial Board
OR B 1855-1899 (DRO)

TIVERTON Registration district
OR M notices 1837-1970 (DRO)
Cop (Mf) M notices 1837-1970 (Mf Tiverton SP)

TIVERTON Poor Law Union Workhouse
OR D 1906-49 (DRO)

TOPSHAM St Margaret [Wonford Hundred; St Thomas Union] [3184]
Peculiar of the Dean and Chapter of Exeter until 1848
OR C 1600-1914 M 1600-1961 B 1600-1965 (DRO)
BT CMB 1606, 1608, 1610-11, 1616, 1619?, 1625, 1630, 1643 (1644-1812 ?); CMB 1813-14, 1816 CB 1818-77, 1887 M 1818-37 (DRO)
Cop CMB 1600-1837 (Ptd DCRS 1938); B 1813-37 (Ptd DFHS); CMB 1837-1914 (DCRS/WSL); B 1813-37 (SG); M 1600-1744 (Boyd); M 1790-1837 (Pallot)
Cop (Mf) Extr CM 1600-1914 (IGI); CM 1600-1875 (Mf I SLC)
MI (I, DFHS); Ch, cy (Ptd DCRS, as above); (Ptd J.Dallas 'The heraldry of Devonshire churches: Topsham: Notes and Gleanings, Devon and Cornwall 4: 1891: 157-9); Extr (Whitmore MS, SG)

TOPSHAM St Luke, Countess Wear Erected 1838. Parish created 1844 from Topsham
OR C 1844-1956 M 1845-1970 B 1847-1948 (DRO)
MI (I, DFHS)

TOPSHAM (RC) Countess Wear House. Served from Topsham

TOPSHAM (RC) Holy Cross, Station Road 1920; 1925; 1936

TOPSHAM (Ind/Cong, later Cong Fed) Victoria Road f 1804. Erected 1839.
[1851 Cong Year Book] Associated with Point in View, WITHYCOMBE RALEIGH
OR ZC 1808-37 (RG 4/4473 PRO)
Cop ZC 1808-37 (Ptd DCRS 1938)
Cop (Mf) ZC 1809-36 (Mf DCRS/WSL); ZC 1809-36 (Mf SG); Extr ZC 1809-36
     (IGI); ZC 1809-36 (Mf I SLC)
MI Cong (I, DFHS)

TOPSHAM (Presb/Unit) Unity Chapel f 1662 ?; licensed 1672. Erected 1723-27,
1890 [1851 Religious Census] Closed
OR ZC 1744-1837 B 1771-1837 including Gulliford, Woodbury entries
     (RG 4/1222 PRO); C 1744-1883 M 1844-1870 B 1771-1887 (DRO)
Cop ZC 1774-1837 B 1771-1837 (Ptd DCRS 1938); B 1852-84 (Ptd A Coles
     Gulliford Chapel burial ground: 1998)
Cop (Mf) C 1744-1837 B 1771-1837 (Mf DCRS/WSL, SG); Extr C 1744-55,
     1771-1837 (IGI); C 1744-55, 1771-1837 (Mf I SLC)

TOPSHAM (Wes) pre-1800 [1851 Religious Census]
OR for *c*.1809-37 *see* AXMINSTER, EXETER Mint (RG 4/512,1207,1208 PRO)

TOPSHAM (Wes) St Nicholas, Fore Street [1882 Return] Erected 1967. fl *c*.1970

TOPSHAM (S of F) Topsham MM f *c*.1668-69. United with EXETER MM 1702.

TOPSHAM (S of F) Topsham f 1654. New meeting house 1712. Closed 1782 and
sold to Wes. Burial ground sold to Wes 1844. *see also* COLATON RALEIGH,
Grindle burial ground
OR Z 1642-1708 M 1665-1706 B 1658-1707 (RG 6/1374 PRO)
Cop Z 1642-1794 M 1665-1719 B 1658-1833; entries after 1706-08 from sources
     at Friends House, London (Ptd DCRS 1938)

TORBAY   The merged urban areas of TORQUAY, PAIGNTON and BRIXHAM

TORBRYAN Holy Trinity [Haytor Hundred; Newton Abbot Union]   [257]
Now with IPPLEPEN. Redundant. Churches Conservation Trust
OR C 1564-1980 M 1564-1973, 1980-82 B 1564-1811 (DRO)
BT CMB 1614, 1624, 1635?, 1636, 1669-72, 1674-75, 1677, 1679, 1682, 1690,
     1695, 1699-1700, 1750-80 (1781-1812 ?); C 1813-38 M 1813, 1815-18,
     1820-26, 1828-37 B 1813-18, 1820-22, 1824-38 (DRO)
Cop CMB 1564-1837 (WSL); Extr CMB 1566-1863 (Vol 16, BG/PCL)
Cop (Mf) (Torquay SP); Z 1653-64 C 1715-1812 M 1653-64, 1715-1838
     B 1653-54, 1715-1811 (Mfc SG)

TORBRYAN (Wes)
OR for *c*.1820-36 *see* ASHBURTON CIRCUIT (RG 4/840 PRO)

TORCROSS   *see* STOKENHAM

TORMOHUN   *see* TORQUAY

TORQUAY

For the purposes of this volume the town of Torquay includes the ancient
parishes of TORMOHUN, ST MARYCHURCH and COCKINGTON and the churches formed
from them

TORQUAY St Saviour, Tormohun [Haytor Hundred; Newton Abbot Union 1836-1924]
[3582] *see also* Torquay St John, St Luke. Closed. Transferred to Greek
Orthodox Church
OR C 1637-1966 M 1637-1987 B 1637-1895 (DRO)
BT CMB 1612-14, 1618, 1623, 1625, 1630, 1632, 1636, 1664, 1669-72, 1675,
1677, 1681-82, 1689, 1695, 1699-1700 (1701-1812 ?); CB 1813-38 M 1813-36
(DRO)
Cop M 1813-37 (Ptd DFHS); B 1813-37 (Ptd DFHS); C 1637-1739 MB 1637-1743
(DCRS/WSL, SG); B 1813-37 (SG); Extr C 1638-1810 M 1637-1834 B 1643-1812
(Vol 5, BG/PCL)
Cop (Mf) (Torquay SP); C 1637-1849 M 1637-1837 B 1637-1842 (Mfc SG);
Extr C 1637-1739 M 1637-1743 (IGI); C 1637-1739 M 1637-1743
(Mf I SLC)
MI (Ptd H.Leathers *Memorial Inscriptions: St Mary Magdalene, Upton, and St
Saviour, Torquay*: 1974)

TORQUAY All Saints, Bampfylde Road. Chapel-of-ease erected 1884-90. Replaced
St Saviour as parish church

TORQUAY St Mary the Virgin, St Marychurch [Haytor Hundred; Newton Abbot
Union 1836-1924] [1204] *see also* chapelries of COFFINSWELL and
KINGSKERSWELL. Rebuilt 1861
OR C 1641-1956 M 1641-1972 B 1641-1953 (DRO)
BT CMB 1614, 1620, 1624, 1628-29, 1632, 1635, 1641, 1705 (1706-1812 ?);
CMB 1813-31, 1834 (DRO)
Cop M 1813-37 (Ptd DFHS); B 1813-37 (Ptd DFHS); B 1813-37 (SG);
Extr C 1641-1729 M 1641-1756 B 1655-1790 (Vol 5, BG/PCL)
Cop (Mf) (Torquay SP); CMB 1641-1812 (Mfc SG)
MI (I, DFHS); (Ptd H.Leathers *Memorial inscriptions...St Mary the
Virgin...St Marychurch*: 1975); Cy 1975 (Ts SG)

TORQUAY St George and St Mary, Cockington [Haytor Hundred; Newton Abbot
Union 1836-1928] [223] Former curacy in Tormohun. Peculiar of the Manor of
Cockington until 1848
OR C 1628-1923 M 1632-1915 B 1632-1907 (DRO)
BT CMB 1612-14, 1618, 1623, 1629, 1635-36, 1665, 1669, 1688, 1695-97, 1700,
1750-80 (1781-1812 ?); CMB 1815, 1817, 1822 (DRO)
Cop M 1813-37 (Ptd DFHS); B 1780-1834 (Ptd DFHS); B 1780-1834 (SG);
Extr C 1628-1811 M 1635-1804 B 1633-1805 (Vol 5, BG/PCL)
Cop (Mf) (Torquay SP)
MI Extr (Whitmore MS, SG)

TORQUAY St Matthew, Chelston. Erected 1896-1904, in parish of Cockington
OR No information

TORQUAY St Peter, Queensway, Chelston. Now with Cockington
OR No information

TORQUAY St John the Evangelist, Montpellier Road, Torquay. Parish created
1861 from Tormohun. Erected 1861-71. Now with Christ Church, Ellacombe
OR C 1862-1959 M 1862-1973 (DRO)

TORQUAY St Michael, Market Street, Pimlico. Erected 1877
<u>OR</u> C 1877-1966 M 1947-66 (DRO) catalogued with Torquay St John

TORQUAY St Mary Magdalene, Upton. Erected and parish created 1848 from
Tormohun. *see also* Torquay St John, St Luke, St James
<u>OR</u> C 1849-1956 M 1849-1983 B 1850-1906, 1928, 1936 (DRO)
<u>MI</u> (Ptd H.Leathers *Memorial Inscriptions: St Mary Magdalene, Upton, and St
Saviour, Torquay*: 1974); Ch, cy 1974 (Ts SG); Extr (Ptd D.Seymour
Upton, The Heart of Torquay: 1963)

TORQUAY St James, Upton. Parish created 1910 from St Mary Magdalene, Upton
<u>OR</u> C 1911-65 (DRO)

TORQUAY St Mark, Torwood. Erected and parish created 1857 from Tormohun,
St Marychurch. Redundant. Used by Torbay Operatic and Dramatic Society.
<u>OR</u> CM 1857-1979 (DRO)

TORQUAY Christ Church, Ellacombe. Erected and parish created 1868 from
St Mary Magdalene Upton. Now with Torquay St John
<u>OR</u> C 1868-1973 M 1868-1974 (DRO)

TORQUAY St. Barnabas' Mission, Stentifords Hill. Chapel-of-ease to Christ
Church, Ellacombe. Erected 1878. Closed
<u>OR</u> C 1912-57 (DRO) catalogued with Christ Church, Ellacombe

TORQUAY All Saints, Cary Avenue, Babbacombe. Erected 1868-74. Parish created
1868 from St Marychurch. Erected 1873
<u>OR</u> C 1867-1964 M 1868-1980 (DRO)

TORQUAY St Luke, Torquay. Erected 1863. Parish created 1869 from St Saviour
Tormohun, St Mary Magdalene Upton
<u>OR</u> C 1888-1968 M 1930-40 (DRO)

TORQUAY St Matthias, Babbacombe Road, Ilsham. Erected 1858. Parish created
1880 from Torwood. Now parish of St Matthias, St Mark and Holy Trinity
<u>OR</u> M 1877-1995 (DRO)

TORQUAY Holy Trinity, Torwood Erected 1895, Torwood Gardens replacing
Meadfoot Road. Parish created 1896 from Torwood. Redundant. Now a sports
hall
<u>OR</u> C 1930-79 M 1896-1966, 1971-79 (DRO)

TORQUAY St John the Baptist, Shiphay Collaton. Parish created 1956 from
St Marychurch, St Saviour Tormohun, KINGSKERSWELL
<u>OR</u> C 1951-72 M 1952-71 (DRO)

TORQUAY St Martin, Barton Hill Road. Parish created 1960 from St Marychurch,
KINGSKERSWELL

TORQUAY (Free Church of England) Babbacombe Road, St Marychurch 1849, by
secession from parish church [1851 Religious Census] building used by Cong
from 1904

TORQUAY (RC) St Saviour, Torre Abbey, Tormohun f 1644, chapel of Cary
family. Converted from guest-hall of former Torre Abbey 1779 [1851 Religious
Census] Closed 1854. Succeeded and registers continued by The Assumption,
below
OR C 1785+ M 1789+ D 1788+ Confirmations 1793+ (Inc, The Assumption)
Cop C 1788-1853 M 1789-1852 D 1788-1848 (SG, Plymouth Diocesan Archives);
    C 1788-1852 D 1788-1848 (Catholic FHS)

TORQUAY (RC) The Assumption, Banner Cross, Abbey Road 1853
OR C 1854+ M 1856+ D 1857+ Confirmations 1859+ (Inc) Confirmations 1859+
   (Plymouth Diocesan Archives)

TORQUAY (RC) Our Lady Help of Christians and St Denis, St Marychurch 1865;
1969 [1882 Return]
OR C 1866+ M 1871+ D 1866+ Confirmations 1868+ (Inc)

TORQUAY (RC) St John Fisher and St Thomas More, Hele Road 1935

TORQUAY (RC) Holy Angels, Sherwell Rise, Chelston 1938

TORQUAY (RC) St Vincent, St Vincent Road

TORQUAY (Bapt) Barton, St Marychurch. Erected pre-1800 [1851 Religious
Census] [1882 Return]; Happaway Road f 1958

TORQUAY (Bapt) Christian Assembly Room, South Street, Tormohun. Erected 1820
[1851 Religious Census]

TORQUAY (Bapt) Ebenezer, Temperance Street f 1832. Erected 1837/40
[1851 Religious Census] replaced 1863 at St Marychurch Road, Upton Vale
[1882 Return]

TORQUAY (Bapt) Zion, Pimlico. Erected 1850 [1851 Religious Census]

TORQUAY (Bapt) Hele Road, St Marychurch. Sunday School Centenary Memorial
Room [1882 Return]; church 1959

TORQUAY (Ind/Cong) Lower Union Lane or Carey Street f 1824 [Cong Year Book
1851] Closed
OR ZC 1834-37 (RG 4/454 PRO)
Cop (Mf) ZC 1834-37 (Mf DCRS/WSL); C 1834-37 (Mf SG); Extr C 1834-37 (IGI);
         C 1834-37 (Mf I SLC)

TORQUAY (Cong) Belgrave Church, Tor Hill [1882 Return]
OR C 1867-1942 M 1868, 1892-1905 B 1892-93 (DRO)

TORQUAY (Presb/Unit) f 1883. Montpellier Road erected 1912

TORQUAY (Scottish Presbyterian) St Andrew, Torwood Gardens. Erected 1863
[1882 Return] Church sold 1951 to Christian Scientists. Closed
OR Location unknown
Cop (Mf) 'St Andrew Scotch Church': Extr C 1863-1950 (IGI); C 1863-1950
         (Mf I SLC)

TORQUAY (Ind) Union Street, Tormohun. Erected c.1836 [1851 Religious Census]

TORQUAY (Ind/Cong) Abbey Road. f 1844 by secession from Carey Street.
Erected 1847 [1851 Religious Census]

TORQUAY (URC) Furrough Cross, Babbacombe Road f 1981

TORQUAY (Cong Fed) Holy Trinity, Parkhill Road f 1984

TORQUAY (Wes) Barton, St Marychurch. Erected 1802 [1851 Religious Census]
[1882 Return]
OR for c.1813-37 *see* TEIGNMOUTH (RG 4/1220 PRO)

TORQUAY (Wes) George Street. Erected 1807 [1851 Religious Census]
OR ZC 1813-37 (RG 4/1223 PRO); for c.1811-37 *see also* BRIXHAM, KINGSBRIDGE,
TEIGNMOUTH (RG 4/842,1088,1220 PRO)
Cop (Mf) ZC 1813-37 (Mf DCRS/WSL); Extr ZC 1813-36 (IGI); ZC 1813-36
(Mf I SLC)

TORQUAY (Wes) St Marychurch
OR for c.1811-37 *see* BRIXHAM, TEIGNMOUTH (RG 4/842,1220 PRO)

TORQUAY (Wes) Tormohun
OR for c.1813-37 *see* TEIGNMOUTH (RG 4/1220 PRO)

TORQUAY (Wes) Wesley Church, Babbacombe Road. Erected 1874 [1882 Return]
Closed 1981. Now used by Elim Pentecostal church
OR C 1879-1982 M 1876-1983 (DRO)

TORQUAY (Wes) Union Street. Erected 1879 [1882 Return] Closed 1974

TORQUAY (Wes) Warren Hill [1882 Return]

TORQUAY (Wes) St Marychurch Road, Victoria Park [1882 Return] Erected 1889.
fl c.1970

TORQUAY (Wes) Old Mill Road, Chelston. Erected 1908. fl c.1970

TORQUAY (Bible Christian) *see* NEWTON ABBOT

TORQUAY (Bible Christian) Circuit
OR C 1849-1909 (DRO)
Cop (Mf) C 1849-1909 (Mfc Torquay SP)

TORQUAY (Bible Christian) Zion, Masons Row, Tormohun. Erected 1849
[1851 Religious Census] Zion, Torre Hill [1882 Return]

TORQUAY (Bible Christian) Ebenezer, Albert Place, St Marychurch
[1882 Return]

TORQUAY (Prim Meth) St Marychurch Chapel; Babbacombe, St Marychurch [1882
Return]
OR C 1862-65 (DRO)

TORQUAY (Prim Meth) Market Street, Ellacombe. Erected 1878 [1882 Return]
Closed 1973

TORQUAY (Meth New Conn) Chelston Chapel
OR C 1904-34 (DRO)
Cop (Mf) C 1904-34 (Mfc Torquay SP)

TORQUAY (U Meth) Torquay and Newton Abbot Circuit
OR C 1914-47 (DRO)
Cop (Mf) C 1914-47 (Mfc Torquay SP)

TORQUAY (Free Meth/U Meth) Zion Chapel
OR C 1914-54 M 1935-54 (DRO)
Cop (Mf) C 1948-54 (Mfc Torquay SP)

TORQUAY (Meth) St Andrew's. Torridge Avenue, Shiphay. Erected 1953.
fl c.1970

TORQUAY (Meth) St George's, Fore Street, Barton. Erected 1954. fl c.1970

TORQUAY (S of F) St John's Place 'not a settled meeting' [1851 Religious
Census]; Warren Road erected 1854 [1882 Return] Now Tor Hill Road

TORQUAY (Brethren) Room, Temperance Street 1844 [1851 Religious Census];
Albert Place, St Marychurch [1882 Return]

TORQUAY (Brethren) Warren Road. erected 1852. Building in the occupation of
Leonard Strong, Warren Road, Warren Hill [1882 Return] Closed. Later used
as auction rooms

TORQUAY (Who object to be designated) The Room, Banner Cross Steps, Abbey
Road [1882 Return]

TORQUAY (Christian) Salem, Braddon Place, Tormohun [1851 Religious Census]

TORQUAY Cemetery
OR (Consecrated) B 1854-1960 (Unconsecrated) B 1852-1974 (DRO)

TORRE   see TORQUAY

TORRIDGE United benefice including SHEBBEAR, BUCKLAND FILLEIGH, SHEEPWASH,
LANGTREE, NEWTON ST PETROCK, PETROCKSTOWE, PETERSMARLAND, MERTON, HUISH

TORRIDGE ESTUARY United benefice including BIDEFORD, NORTHAM, WESTWARD HO!,
APPLEDORE, LANDCROSS, LITTLEHAM, WEARE GIFFARD

TORRINGTON Poor Law Union Workhouse
OR Z 1872-1935 D 1871-1914 (DRO)

TORRINGTON, BLACK St Mary [Black Torrington Hundred; Holsworthy Union]
[1083] Now with BRADFORD, COOKBURY, THORNBURY, HIGHAMPTON
OR C 1547-1936 M 1547-1978 B 1548-1879 (DRO)
BT CMB 1598-1601, 1604-07, 1614, 1618, 1619 or 1629, 1634, 1638-39, 1663 or
    1675, 1664, 1668-71, 1672, 1674, 1676-81, 1690, 1694, 1696-97, 1699
    (1700-1812 ?); CM 1813-15, 1817-21, 1831, 1833-34 (DRO)
Cop CMB 1598-1641 from BT (Ptd Granville); CMB 1601-1793 from BT, 1547-1837
    with index (DCRS/WSL); CMB 1545-1837 (SG); C 1837-48 B 1837-79 (I SG);
    M 1762-1813 (DFHS)
Cop (Mf) Extr CM 1547-1837 (IGI); CM 1547-1837 (Mf I SLC)
MI Extr (Whitmore MS, SG); Incledon 46 (NDA)

TORRINGTON, BLACK (Wes) Brandis Corner [1882 Return]
OR for c.1817-37 see HOLSWORTHY (RG 4/1210 PRO)

TORRINGTON, BLACK (Bible Christian) Rehoboth. Erected 1839 [1851 Religious
Census]

TORRINGTON, BLACK (Bible Christian/U Meth) Emmanuel, Chilla. Erected 1840
[1851 Religious Census] Rebuilt 1893. fl c.1970
OR B 1896-1933 (DRO)

227

TORRINGTON, BLACK (Bible Christian) Hope, Church Village. Erected 1842 [1851 Religious Census] [1882 Return] Rebuilt 1893. fl *c.*1970

TORRINGTON, GREAT St Michael [Fremington Hundred; Torrington Union] [3093] Blown up by Cromwellian troops, 1645; rebuilt 1651. Now with LITTLE TORRINGTON, FRITHELSTOCK
<u>OR</u> C 1616-1975 M 1616-1978 B 1616-1970 (NDRO)
<u>BT</u> CMB 1597-1602, 1607, 1612-14, 1629-30, 1634, 1668-71, 1674-75, 1678-80, 1685, 1688-89, 1691-92, 1694-97, 1699-1700, 1704-05, 1707, 1709-12, 1714-16, 1740-42, 1745-56, 1762, 1764-1812; CB 1813-46 M 1813-37 (DRO)
<u>Cop</u> CMB 1597-1837 (DCRS/WSL); Extr 17th cent (Ptd S.H.Parsons' Records of Great Torrington': *New England Historical and Genealogical Register* 7: 1853)

TORRINGTON, GREAT (RC) Holy Family 1965

TORRINGTON, GREAT (Bapt) New Street f 1820; erected 1828 [1851 Religious Census] [1882 Return]
<u>OR</u> Z 1814-1838 (NDRO)
<u>Cop</u> Z 1814-38 (NDA, DLS)

TORRINGTON, GREAT (Bapt) Kingscott. f 1833 from New Street
<u>OR</u> *see* New Street

TORRINGTON, GREAT (Presb/Cong/URC) Howe Chapel, Castle Street f 1662; licensed 1672. Rebuilt 1811 [1851 Religious Census] [1882 Return]
<u>OR</u> C 1858-1993 M 1859-1993 B 1867-1958 (NDRO)

TORRINGTON, GREAT (Cong Fed) Gas Lane n.d.

TORRINGTON, GREAT (Cong) Calf Street, a room [1851 Religious Census]

TORRINGTON, GREAT (Cong) Well Street, a room [1851 Religious Census]

TORRINGTON, GREAT (Wes) Mill Street. Erected 1832 [1851 Religious Census]
<u>OR</u> for *c.*1819-37 *see* BIDEFORD (RG 4/955 PRO)

TORRINGTON, GREAT (Wes) Windy Cross. Erected 1832/1861 [1882 Return] fl *c.*1970

TORRINGTON, GREAT (Bible Christian) Erected 1843 [1851 Religious Census]
<u>OR</u> Circuit C 1837-67 (NDRO)

TORRINGTON, GREAT (Meth) Torrington and other places
<u>OR</u> C 1902-62 (NDRO)

TORRINGTON, GREAT (Bible Christian) South Street Chapel [1882 Return]

TORRINGTON, GREAT (S of F) Meeting house 1743, Mill Street ?

TORRINGTON, GREAT Cemetery
<u>OR</u> B 1870-1903 (NDRO)

TORRINGTON, LITTLE St Giles [Shebbear Hundred; Torrington Union] [572]
Now with GREAT TORRINGTON, FRITHELSTOCK
OR C 1672-1949 M 1672-1968 B 1672-1897 (NDRO)
BT CMB 1597-1602, 1607, 1610, 1612-14, 1617, 1624, 1628-29, 1632, 1636,
    1670-71, 1674, 1678-79, 1683-85, 1688-90, 1692, 1694, 1696-97,
    1699-1700, 1702, 1704, 1707-12, 1714-15 (1716-1812 ?); CB 1813-46
    M 1813-36 (DRO)
Cop CMB 1597-1671 from BT, 1672-1812 (DCRS/WSL); M 1672-1812 (Boyd)
Cop (Mf) Extr C 1597-1812 M 1598-1812 (IGI); C 1597-1812 M 1598-1812
    (Mf I SLC)

TORRINGTON, LITTLE Hospital of St Mary Magdalen, Taddiport f 1345;
refounded 1665. Hospital disappeared.
OR None

TORRINGTON, LITTLE (Ind/Cong) Taddiport [1851 Religious Census]

TORRINGTON, LITTLE (Wes) Erected 1840 [1851 Religious Census] [1882 Return]

TORWOOD *see* TORQUAY

TOTNES United benefice including TOTNES, BRIDGETOWN, BERRY POMEROY,
DARTINGTON, BROOKING

TOTNES St Mary [Coleridge Hundred; Totnes Union] [3442]
Now with BRIDGETOWN, BERRY POMEROY, DARTINGTON, BROOKING
OR C 1560-1900 M 1556-1939 B 1556-1908 (DRO)
BT CMB 1602, 1605-06, 1608-09, 1613-16, 1618, 1620, 1624-25, 1628-29, 1631,
    1635, 1666, 1670?, 1671?, 1674-77, 1679?, 1680, 1684, 1688-90, 1695-96,
    1699 (1700-1812 ?); CB 1813-50, 1852-69 M 1813-36 (DRO)
Cop CMB 1556-1812 (DCRS/WSL); CMB 1651-1850 (I, WSL); C 1560-1740
    M 1556-1751 B 1556-1735; CMB 1700-1850, Workhouse C 1837-50, banns of
    non-residents, marriages elsewhere, and non-events (Ts SG); M 1741-54 of
    non-residents (DFHS SG); M 1801-12 (WSL); M 1601-91 (Boyd);
    Extr CMB 1556-1691 C 1692-1730 M 1654-1751 B 1691-1732 (Vol 18, BG/PCL)
Cop (Mf) (Totnes SP); Extr C 1560-1812 M 1556-1812 (IGI); C 1560-1812
    (Mf I SLC)
MI Extr (Whitmore MS, SG)

TOTNES St John the Evangelist, Bridgetown. Erected 1832. Originally in BERRY
POMEROY. Now with TOTNES, BERRY POMEROY, DARTINGTON, BROOKING
OR C 1844-1878 M 1845-1869, 1895-1925 B 1844-1888 (DRO) *and see* BERRY
    POMEROY

TOTNES (RC) Follaton House f 1788. Domestic chapel of Cary family
[1851 Religious Census] [1882 Return] Served from PLYMOUTH 1866-67, NEWTON
ABBOT 1873-76, TEIGNMOUTH 1876-77. BUCKFAST ABBEY 1884+. Closed 1902
OR C 1845-58 D 1853-58 Confirmations 1856-58 (Plymouth Diocesan Archives);
    C 1871+ M 1935+ B 1929+ (Inc, Totnes St Mary and St George); *see also*
    DARTMOUTH register 1782-1814

TOTNES (RC) St Mary and St George, South Street 1902

TOTNES (Bapt) Zion, behind the walls. Erected 1847 [1851 Religious Census]
[1882 Return] Fore Street LEP CURRENT

TOTNES (Bapt) A large room in the Gate House [1882 Return]

TOTNES (Presb/Ind/Cong, now URC) Fore Street f 1662. Ashburton Road, erected
1793, rebuilt 1841 [1851 Religious Census] [i882 Return]
OR ZC 1794-1837 (RG 4/1224 PRO); C 1794-1870, 1876-1879 (DRO)
Cop (Mf) ZC 1794-1856 (Mf Totnes Lib); ZC 1794-1837 (Mf SG);
      Extr ZC 1794-1837 (IGI); ZC 1794-1837 (Mf I SLC)

TOTNES (Wes) Totnes Ashburton Circuit
OR C 1802-1857 (DRO); for *c.*1801-37 *see also* ASHBURTON CIRCUIT,
    KINGSBRIDGE, PLYMOUTH Ebenezer (RG 4/1763,840,1088,1325 PRO)
Cop (Mf) C 1802-57 (Mf Totnes Museum)

TOTNES (Wes) Erected pre-1800 [1851 Religious Census]; Fore Street.
Erected 1901. fl *c.*1970

TOTNES (Wes) On the Plains [1882 Return]

TOTNES (S of F) Bridgetown fl 1692, 1708; meeting house in Totnes 1715.
EXETER or KINGSBRIDGE MM ? Now at Ticklemore Street

TOTNES (Brethren) Gospel Hall, junction of Plymouth Road and High Street
[1882 Return]

TOTNES Burial Board. Town Cemetery
OR B 1856-57 (DRO)
Cop B 1856-92 (I, Ms SG)

TOWNSTAL *see* DARTMOUTH

TRENTISHOE St Peter [Braunton Hundred; Barnstaple Union] [128]
Rebuilt 1861. Now with NORTH DEVON COAST
OR C 1695-1987 M 1697-1947 B 1696-1812 (NDRO)
BT CMB 1597-1601, 1607-08, 1610, 1613, 1629-31, 1667-68, 1670, 1674,
    1678-79, 1681-83, 1689-90, 1694-96, 1702-03, 1706, 1709, 1712, 1714-16,
    1718-23, 1725-28, 1731-42, 1745-54 (1755-1812 ?); C 1813-16, 1841-46,
    1856-59, 1861-68 M 1813-17, 1822-23, 1825-31, 1833-35, 1837, 1842-45
    B 1813-16, 1819-20, 1822-24, 1826-29, 1832-33, 1836-37, 1841-43, 1845,
    1856-59, 1861-68 (DRO)
Cop M 1697-1812 (Ptd Phil 1: 1909); CMB 1695-1812 (NDA, WSL); CMB 1695-1836
    (DCRS/WSL); M 1697-1812 (Great Card Index, SG); M 1695-1812 (Boyd);
    M 1790-1812 (Pallot)
Cop (Mf) Extr C 1695-1875 M 1697-1873 (IGI); C 1695-1875 M 1697-1873
    (Mf I SLC)
MI (I, DFHS); Ch, cy (Ptd Dwelly 17-43); Incledon 664 (NDA)

TRUSHAM St Michael the Archangel [Exminster Hundred; Newton Abbot Union]
[207] Now with CHRISTOW, ASHTON, BRIDFORD
OR C 1559-1959 M 1559-1837 B 1560-1978 (DRO)
BT CMB 1609, 1615, 1619, 1624, 1633, 1635-36, 1638, 1669-72, 1675, 1677?,
    1683, 1688, 1690, 1695-97, 1699 (1700-1812 ?); C 1813-56, 1850-62, 1876
    M 1813-46 B 1813-23, 1825-56, 1860-62, 1876 (DRO)
Cop Extr C 1570-1732 M 1605-84 B 1579-1697 (Vol 6, BG/PCL)
MI Extr (Whitmore MS, SG)

TUPPERIDGE *see* HUISH, NORTH

TWITCHEN St Peter [South Molton Hundred; South Molton Union] [170] Chapelry
in NORTH MOLTON. Separate parish before 1850. Now with SOUTH MOLTON
OR C 1715-1991 M 1708-1946 B 1711-1989 (DRO) No earlier registers noted in
    1831. *see* NORTH MOLTON
BT CMB 1602, 1607, 1610, 1619, 1635, 1638, 1668, 1670, 1672, 1675, 1678-79,
    1683, 1689-91, 1694-97, 1700, 1703-04, 1710-12, 1714-15 (1716-1812 ?);
    C 1813-32, 1834-36, 1838-75 M 1 813, 1818-19, 1829-30, 1834-36
    B 1813-20, 1822-36, 1840-42, 1844-75 (DRO)
Cop B 1813-37 (Ptd DFHS); B 1813-37 (SG); C 1715-1850 M 1708-1850
    B 1711-1850 (DCRS/WSL, NDA); M 1736-1836 (DFHS)
Cop (Mf) Extr C 1715-1850 M 1708-1850 (IGI); C 1715-1850 (Mf I SLC)
MI (I, NDA); (I, DFHS)

TWITCHEN (Wes) Erected 1860. 'Building occupied by John Lyddon'
[1882 Return]

TWO RIVERS United benefice including NEWTON TRACEY, ALVERDISCOTT, HUNTSHAW,
YARNSCOMBE, HORWOOD, TAWSTOCK, ATHERINGTON, HIGH BICKINGTON, BEAFORD,
ROBOROUGH, ST GILES IN THE WOOD

TYTHECOTT (Bapt) f 1840 Torridge Fellowship

UFFCULME St Mary the Virgin [Bampton Hundred; Tiverton Union] [2082]
Peculiar of the Prebend of Uffculme, Salisbury Cathedral *c.*1543-1833
OR C 1542-1958 M 1538-1753, 1783-1990 B 1538-1975 (DRO)
BT CMB 1591-97, 1603-06, 1614-38, 1661-66, 1668-74 (Wiltshire RO);
    CB 1813-53 M 1813-36 (DRO)
Cop M 1538-1837 (Ptd Phil 1: 1909); B 1813-37 (Ptd DFHS); CMB 1538-1837
    (DCRS/WSL, WSL); M 1538-1837 (Great Card Index, SG); B 1813-37 (SG);
    M 1538-1837 (Boyd); M 1790-1837 (Pallot); Extr C 1545-1709 M 1540-1734
    B 1538-1695 (Vol 10, BG/PCL)
Cop (Mf) (Tiverton SP); Extr C 1542-1837 M 1538-1753, 1783-1837 B 1591-1638,
    1661-74 (IGI); C 1542-1837 M 1538-1753, 1783-1837 (Mf I SLC)
MI (I, DFHS)

UFFCULME St Stephen, Ashill. Erected 1882 as chapel-of-ease to Uffculme

UFFCULME Bradfield Chapel. Erected 1875 as chapel-of-ease to Uffculme
OR C 1876-1928, 1940 M 1876-1931 B 1876-1957 (DRO)

UFFCULME (Bapt) Conniger Lane. Erected 1725 [1851 Religious Census] [1882
Return] Prescott, Culmstock and Chapel Hill f 1743. Chapel Hill rebuilt 1815
OR *see* CULMSTOCK

UFFCULME (Bapt) Ashill [1882 Return]

UFFCULME (Presb/Cong) Uffculme and Culmstock. Crosslands or Cold Harbour
Chapel f 1663. Rebuilt 1720 [1851 Religious Census] Crosslands, or
Coldharbour, or Independent Chapel [1882 Return]; later Commercial Road
OR ZC 1790-1837 (RG 4/455 PRO)
Cop (Mf) ZC 1790-1837 (Mf DCRS/WSL, SG); Extr ZC 1790-1837 (IGI);
    ZC 1790-1837 (Mf I SLC)

UFFCULME (Unit) Bridewell f 1792, closed by 1830. Private chapel, Clarke
family

UFFCULME (Wes)
OR for *c.*1806-37 *see* CULLOMPTON, TIVERTON (RG 4/958,342 PRO)

UFFCULME (S of F) fl *c*.1662-71. Part of CULLOMPTON MM

UGBOROUGH St Peter [Ermington Hundred; Totnes Union] [1467]
Now with ERMINGTON
OR C 1538-1966 M 1538-1990, 1993-97 B 1542-1953 (PWDRO)
BT CMB 1608-10, 1612-14, 1617, 1624, 1626, 1632-34, 1668, 1671-72, 1674,
    1676-78, 1684, 1686, 1689-90, 1694-97, 1699 (1700-1812 ?); CMB 1813-19,
    1821-23, 1829-30 CB 1834-35, 1837-42 M 1835, 1837-40 (DRO)
Cop CMB 1538-1837 (DCRS/WSL); C 1852-1913 (I, PWDRO); M 1539-1837 (Boyd);
    Extr C 1539-1729 M 1541-1694 B 1542-1680, 1690-1807 (Vol 15, BG/PCL)
Cop (Mf) (Totnes SP); Extr CM 1538-1837 (IGI); CM 1538-1837 (Mf I SLC)
MI (Ptd DRMI 17: 1998)

UGBOROUGH (Presb) fl *c*.1672-90

UGBOROUGH (Ind) Erected *c*.1830 [1851 Religious Census]

UGBOROUGH (Wes) Bittaford. Erected 1914. fl *c*.1970

UGBROOKE   *see* CHUDLEIGH

UMBERLEIGH   *see* CHITTLEHAMPTON

UNDERWOOD   *see* PLYMPTON

UP EXE   tithing of REWE [100]

UPHAM   *see* CHERITON FITZPAINE

UPLOWMAN St Peter [part Halberton Hundred; part Tiverton Hundred; Tiverton
Union] [335] Now with SAMPFORD PEVERELL
OR C 1662-1874 M 1662-1978 B 1662-1930 (DRO)
BT CMB 1607, 1610, 1613, 1616, 1619, 1630, 1634, 1662, 1667-69, 1675, 1678,
    1683, 1689, 1696-98, 1701 (1702-1812 ?); C 1813-38, 1840-48 M 1813-21,
    1823-36 B 1813-38, 1840-41, 1843-48 (DRO)
Cop CMB 1607-34 from BT, 1662-1837 (DCRS/WSL)
Cop (Mf) (Tiverton SP); Extr C 1606-1837 M 1607-30, 1662-1837 (IGI);
        C 1606-1837 (Mf I SLC)

UPLOWMAN (Presb) fl *c*.1672-90

UPLOWMAN (Wes) Whitnage. Erected 1899. fl *c*.1970

UPLYME St Peter and St Paul [Axminster Hundred; Axminster Union] [975]
Now with AXMOUTH
OR C 1710-1977 M 1710-1952 B 1684-1970 (DRO) No earlier registers noted in
    1831
BT CMB 1613-14, 1620, 1624, 1631, 1669, 1672, 1675, 1678, 1684-85, 1687,
    1690, 1695-97, 1699 (1700-1812 ?); CMB 1813-36 (DRO)
Cop M 1813-37 (Ptd DFHS); B 1813-37 (Ptd DFHS); B 1813-37 (SG)
Cop (Mf) (Colyton SP); C 1710-1841 M 1710-1838 B 1710-1857 (Mfc SG)
MI Cy extr 1909 (A.W.Matthews *Ye Olde Mortality* vol.8: MS SG); Incledon 349
    (NDA)

UPLYME (Wes)
OR for *c*.1809-37 *see* AXMINSTER (RG 4/512 PRO)

UPOTTERY St Mary the Virgin [Axminster Hundred; Honiton Union] [940]
Now with YARCOMBE. MEMBURY, COTLEIGH
OR   C 1560-1931 M 1576-1678, 1703-1971 B 1559-1680, 1703-1948 (DRO)
BT   CMB 1611, 1615, 1617, 1620-21, 1625, 1669, 1678, 1685, 1687, 1690, 1696,
     1699 (1700-1812 ?); CMB 1813-37 (DRO)
Cop M 1813-37 (Ptd DFHS); B 1813-37 (Ptd DFHS); B 1813-37 (SG);
     CMB 1559-1837 (DCRS/WSL); M 1576-1837 (Boyd)
Cop (Mf) (Colyton SP); C 1559-1843 M 1576-1831 B 1559-1862 (Mfc SG);
          Extr C 1559-1837 M 1576-1678, 1702-1837 (IGI); C 1559-1837
          M 1576-1678, 1702-1837 (Mf I SLC)
MI   Incledon 226 (NDA)

UPOTTERY (Bapt) f 1652 at Luppitt. Moved in 17th cent. [1851 Religious
Census] Rebuilt 1859

UPOTTERY (Presb) fl c.1715-72 ?

UPOTTERY (Ind) Roldge. Erected c.1846 [1851 Religious Census]

UPTON   see TORQUAY

UPTON HELLIONS St Mary the Virgin [West Budleigh Hundred; Crediton Union]
[152] United 1928 with SANDFORD
OR   C 1678-1927 M 1679-1925 B 1678-1928 (DRO)
BT   CMB 1611, 1613-14, 1630, 1635, 1668-72, 1675, 1678, 1683, 1687, 1690,
     1695-96 (1697-1812 ?); C 1838-51 B 1838-51, 1853-55 (DRO)
Cop CMB 1611-78 from BT, 1676-1837 (DCRS/WSL)
Cop (Mf) Extr C 1613-1837 M 1611-30, 1668-1836 (IGI); C 1613-1837 M 1611-30,
          1668-1836 (Mf I SLC)

UPTON HELLIONS (Wes)
OR   for c.1818-31 see EXETER Mint (RG 4/1207 PRO)

UPTON PYNE Church of Our Lady [Wonford Hundred; St Thomas Union] [514]
Now with RADDON
OR   C 1673-1865 M 1688-1838 B 1688-1921 (DRO)
BT   CMB 1612, 1617, 1620, 1624, 1628, 1630, 1636, 1638, 1644, 1664, 1667-69,
     1672-73, 1683, 1687, 1690, 1694, 1696, 1699 (1700-1812 ?); CB 1813-40,
     1842-44, 1847-49 M 1813-38 B 1813-40, 1842-44, 1847-49 (DRO)
Cop CMB 1612-87 from BT, 1673-1837 (DCRS/WSL); CMB 1669-1837 (WSL)
Cop (Mf) Extr C 1612-1837 M 1620-44, 1664-75, 1687-1837 (IGI); C 1612-1837
          M 1620-44, 1664-75, 1687-1837 (Mf I SLC)
MI   Extr (Whitmore MS, SG)

VAULTERSHORNE   see MAKER

VENN   see CHURCHSTOW

VENN OTTERY or FEN OTTERY St Gregory [East Budleigh Hundred; Honiton Union]
[133] Chapelry of HARPFORD. Separate parish at an early date. United 1933
with TIPTON ST JOHN. Now with OTTER VALE
OR   C 1596-1946 M 1591-1837 B 1587-1946 (DRO)
BT   CMB 1606, 1609, 1611, 1613-14, 1620, 1630, 1638, 1666-69, 1671-73, 1675,
     1677-79, 1683, 1685, 1687, 1690, 1697 (1698-1812 ?); C 1813-39, 1845-51
     M 1813-15, 1818, 1822-25, 1827-29 (DRO)

VENN OTTERY cont.
Cop ZCMB 1596-1680 (Ptd F.B.Dickinson 'The early register of the parish of
Fenn Ottery': TDA 33 1901); CMB 1587-1837 (DCRS/WSL)
Cop (Mf) Extr C 1596-1837 M 1591-1837 (IGI); C 1596-1837 M 1591-1837
(Mf I SLC)
MI Incledon 679 (NDA)

VENTON *see* DARTINGTON or DREWSTEIGNTON, or PLYMPTON, or WIDECOMBE
or WINKLEIGH

VIRGINSTOW [Lifton Hundred; Holsworthy Union 1837-52; Launceston Union
(Cornwall) 1852-1930; Truro Diocese from 1876] [136] Rebuilt 1851-52.
United 1973 with WERRINGTON, ST GILES ON THE HEATH
OR C 1730-1970 M 1730-1967 B 1730-1982 (CRO) No earlier registers noted in
1831
BT CMB 1609, 1616-17, 1629, 1632, 1639, 1668-72, 1674-83, 1687-88, 1690,
1694-95, 1697, 1699 (1700-1812 ?) (DRO)
Cop M 1813-37 (Cornwall M Index); M 1813-37 (I, PWDRO); C 1668-1833
M 1668-1810 B 1668-1899 (PWDRO); B 1813-37 (Cornwall B Index)
MI (Ptd CFHS)

VIRGINSTOW (UMFC) Ebenezer. Erected 1862. fl *c.*1970
OR *see* LAUNCESTON Circuit

WADDLETON *see* STOKE GREGORY

WALKHAMPTON St Mary the Virgin [Roborough Hundred; Tavistock Union] [691]
see also BUCKLAND MONACHORUM St John Horrabridge. Now with YELVERTON, MEAVY,
SHEEPSTOR
OR C 1674-1857 M 1675-1983 B 1676-1996 (PWDRO)
BT CMB 1607, 1609, 1614, 1616, 1618-19, 1624, 1630, 1633, 1663, 1666,
1668-72, 1674, 1677, 1680-81, 1683-84, 1686-87, 1696-97, 1699
(1700-1812 ?); CMB 1813-24, 1826-34 C 1842-66 B 1842-65 (DRO)
Cop M 1607-1754 (I, Ptd, edit M.Brown, Dartmoor Press 1999);
Extr CMB 1674-1837 (Ptd, *ibid.* 2 vols 1998); C 1675-1800 M 1675-1810
B 1676-1793 (DFHS); CMB 1675-1800 (WSL); B 1793-1900 (I, PWDRO);
Extr C 1675-1761 M 1677-1751 B 1676-1766 (Vol 17, BG/PCL)
Cop (Mf) (Tavistock SP)
MI (Ptd DRMI 4: 1998)

WALKHAMPTON (Wes) Erected pre-1820 [1851 Religious Census] [1882 Return]
OR for *c.*1808-37 *see* TAVISTOCK (RG 4/341 PRO)

WALKHAMPTON (Wes) Erected 1902. Closed 1983
OR M 1912-81 (PWDRO)
Cop M 1912-81 with index (PWDRO)

WALKHAMPTON (Bible Christian) Erected *c.*1847 [1851 Religious Census]

WARKLEIGH with SATTERLEIGH St John [South Molton Hundred; South Molton Union
1835-94] [283] Now with SOUTH MOLTON
OR C 1538-1932 MB 1538-1993 (NDRO)
BT CMB 1597-1601, 1608, 1610, 1617, 1623, 1629, 1635, 1670, 1672, 1674,
1684, 1687, 1689-91, 1694, 1696, 1697?, 1714-16, 1718, 1720-22, 1726-28,
1730, 1733-36 (1737-1812 ?); C 1814-33, 1836-42 M 1815-16, 1820-23,
1826-33, 1836-37 B 1814-35, 1837-41 (DRO)
Cop Extr CMB 1539-1734 (Vol 12, BG/PCL)
Cop (Mf) C 1538-1932 MB 1538-1812 (Mfc SG)
MI (I, NDA); Incledon 332 (NDA)

WASHFIELD St Mary the Virgin [West Budleigh Hundred; Tiverton Union] [453]
Now with EXE VALLEY
OR C 1554-1874 M 1554-1979 B 1554-1951 (DRO)
BT CMB 1613, 1615, 1617, 1624, 1626, 1630, 1634, 1635?, 1664, 1666?, 1667,
    1670, 1675, 1678, 1683, 1685, 1696-97, 1717 (1718-1812 ?); CB 1813-51,
    1873-74 M 1813-18, 1820-33, 1835-38 (DRO)
Cop B 1800-37 (Ptd DFHS); B 1800-37 (SG); Extr C 1559-1809 M 1575-1745
    B 1554-1806 (Vol 17, BG/PCL)
Cop (Mf) (Tiverton SP)

WASHFORD PYNE St Peter [Witheridge Hundred; Crediton Union] [174]
Rebuilt 1883-87. Now with NORTH CREADY
OR C 1588-1739 M 1587-1732, 1754-1836 B 1586-1742 (DRO)
BT CMB 1607, 1613-14, 1644, 1668, 1674, 1678, 1682-83, 1688, 1690-91,
    1694-95, 1699-1700, 1714-15 (1716-1812 ?); C 1813-36, 1838-40, 1842,
    1844-48 M 1813-15, 1817, 1819-22, 1825-31, 1833-36 B 1813-30, 1832-36,
    1838-40, 1842, 1844-48 (DRO)
Cop (Mf) (Tiverton SP)
MI (I, DFHS)

WASHFORD PYNE (Bible Christian/Meth) Providence, Hele Lane, Black Dog.
In school purchased 1956. fl *c.*1970

WAYTOWN   *see* INWARDLEIGH

WEAR, COUNTESS WEAR   *see* TOPSHAM

WEARE GIFFARD Holy Trinity [Shebbear Hundred; Torrington Union] [547]
Now with TORRIDGE ESTUARY
OR C 1583-1617, 1711-1959 M 1584-87, 1616-67, 1711-1837 B 1583-1631,
    1711-1933 (NDRO)
BT CMB 1607-08, 1610-12, 1614, 1644, 1668, 1672, 1674, 1678-79, 1682-83,
    1688-91, 1695-97, 1700, 1702, 1704, 1706-07, 1710-12, 1714-16
    (1717-1812 ?); CB 1813-40 M 1813-37 (DRO)
Cop B 1813-37 (Ptd DFHS); B 1813-37 (DFHS, SG); CMB 1583-1812 (DCRS/WSL);
    M 1655-1837 (DFHS); M 1583-1812 (Boyd)
Cop (Mf) (Appledore SP); Extr C 1583-1812 M 1584-87, 1615-1812 (IGI);
        C 1583-1812 M 1584-87, 1615-1812 (Mf I SLC)
MI Incledon 1099 (NDA)

WEARE GIFFARD (Wes) Gammaton Chapel. Erected 1835. [1851 Religious Census]
[1882 Return] fl *c.*1970
OR M 1929-70 (NDRO)

WEARE GIFFARD (Wes) Huxwill. Erected 1836 [1851 Religious Census]

WEARE GIFFARD (Wes) Erected 1853. 'The outskirts of Wear Wood' [1882 Return]
Closed 1972

WEARE GIFFARD (Prim Meth) Gammaton Chapel, Exwell Estate, near Gifford [1882
Return]

WEEK ST GERMANS   *see* GERMANSWEEK

WEEK ST MARY [Cornwall] (Bible Christian/U Meth)
OR Circuit registers contain some Devon references: C 1838-1934 (CRO)

WEEK ST PANCRAS   *see* PANCRASWEEK

WEEK, HIGH   *see* HIGHWEEK

WELCOMBE St Nectan [Hartland Hundred; Bideford Union]   [258]
Now with HARTLAND COAST
OR C 1777-1992 M 1757-1786, 1813-1836 B 1778-1992 (NDRO) Noted in 1831:
    CMB 1653-1812
BT CMB 1607-08, 1610, 1614, 1617, 1624, 1631, 1636, 1670, 1672, 1676, 1680,
    1683, 1689-90, 1692, 1698, 1701, 1705-06, 1709-12, 1714-15
    (1716-1812 ?); C 1813-34, 1836-41 M 1813-18, 1828-34, 1836 B 1813-14,
    1816-20, 1822-23, 1825-34, 1836-40 (DRO)
Cop CMB 1757-1837 (WSL); M 1607-1837 (NDA); M 1757-1837 (DLS)
Cop (Mf) (Appledore SP); C 1777-1812 M 1757-86, 1813-36 B 1778-1812 (Mfc SG)
MI (I, NDA)

WELCOMBE (Wes)
OR for *c.*1817-37 *see* HOLSWORTHY CIRCUIT (RG 4/1210 PRO)

WELCOMBE (Wes) Lower Darracott. Erected 1836. Closed 1971
OR M 1927-42 (NDRO)

WEMBURY St Werbergh [Plympton Hundred; Plympton St Mary Union]   [652]
OR C 1611-1980 M 1612-1989 B 1611-1895 (PWDRO)
BT CMB 1614, 1620, 1630, 1633, 1635, 1639, 1686, 1688-90, 1695-97, 1699
    (1700-1812 ?); CMB 1813-27 CB 1829-43, 1845 M 1829-37 (DRO)
Cop CMB 1611-1837 (DCRS/WSL); CB 1611-1772 M 1612-1753 with index (PWDRO);
    M 1612-1750 (Boyd)
Cop (Mf) Extr C 1611-1837 M 1612-1837 (IGI); C 1611-1837 M 1612-1837
    (Mf I SLC)
MI (I, DFHS); Ch, cy extr (Ptd A.Jewers 'Wembury church': *Western Antiquary*
    9: 1890: 177-81); Cy index (Ptd DFH 8: Oct 1978)

WEMBURY Wembury Manor. Chapel erected 1682

WEMBURY Hele Almshouses. Chapel 1682

WEMBURY HMS Cambridge. Royal Naval Chaplaincy

WEMBURY (Wes)
OR for *c.*1813-37 *see* PLYMOUTH Ebenezer (RG 4/1325 PRO)

WEMBURY (Wes) Down Thomas. Erected 1832 [1851 Religious Census]; a building
in the occupation of George Jackson [1882 Return] Rebuilt 1900. Closed 1971
OR C 1939-58 (PWDRO); for *c.*1787-1837 *see* PLYMOUTH Morice Street and
    Ebenezer (RG 4/864,1325 PRO)
Cop C 1939-58 with index (PWDRO)

WEMBURY (Bible Christian) Neighton n.d. [1851 Religious Census]

WEMBWORTHY St Michael [North Tawton and Winkleigh Hundred; Crediton Union]
[378] Now with CHULMLEIGH, CHAWLEIGH, CHELDON, EGGESFORD, BURRINGTON
OR C 1674-1876 M 1674-1947 B 1674-1812 (DRO)
BT CMB 1607, 1634, 1668, 1670, 1672, 1674, 1678-79, 1683, 1685, 1688-91,
    1694-96, 1699-1700, 1708, 1712, 1714-15, 1735, 1738-39, 1741, 1745-56,
    1762, 1764-1812; CMB 1813-37 (DRO)
Cop Extr CMB 1674-1750 (SG); Extr CMB 1674-1750 (Vol 18, BG/PCL)
MI Extr (Whitmore MS, SG)

WEMBWORTHY (Ind) Unity Chapel [1882 Return]

WERRINGTON St Martin of Tours [part Black Torrington Hundred, part East Hundred (Cornwall); part Helston Union, part Launceston Union (Cornwall); Truro diocese from 1876] [661] Rebuilt on new site 1742. Transferred to Cornwall 1966. United 1973 with ST GILES ON THE HEATH, VIRGINSTOW
OR C 1653-1982 M 1653-1980 B 1653-1967 (CRO)
BT CMB terminal dates 1608-73, 1737-40, 1773-1812 (DRO); CMB terminal dates 1676-1736, 1741-72 (CRO); CMB 1813-36 (DRO)
Cop M 1654-1812 (Ptd Phil 1: 1909); C 1773-1812 M 1608-1812 B 1773-1812 (PWDRO); CMB 1654-1812 (WSL); M 1813-27 (I, WSL,PWDRO); M 1813-37 (Cornwall M Index); M 1608-54 (Great Card Index, SG); CMB 1653-1743, 1714-37 (I, CFHS); M 1608-1812 (Boyd); M 1790-1812 (Pallot); B 1813-37 (Cornwall B Index)
Cop (Mf) Extr C 1670-1719 M 1720-1805 (IGI); C 1670-1719 M 1720-1805 (Mf I SLC)

WERRINGTON (Wes) Lady Cross. Erected 1879 [Kelly 1889]

WERRINGTON (Wes) Yeolmbridge. Erected 1834 [1851 Religious Census]

WERRINGTON (Bible Christian) Bridgetown. Erected 1837 [1851 Religious Census] [Kelly 1889]

WERRINGTON (Bible Christian) Simmons House f 1849 [1851 Religious Census]

WERRINGTON (Bible Christian) Bullipit Down, house f 1849 [1851 Religious Census]

WEST ALVINGTON   *see* ALVINGTON, WEST

WEST ANSTEY   *see* ANSTEY, WEST

WEST BUCKLAND   *see* BUCKLAND, WEST

WEST DOWN   *see* DOWN, WEST

WEST EXE   see TIVERTON

WEST HILL   *see* OTTERY ST MARY

WEST OGWELL   *see* OGWELL, WEST

WEST PORTLEMOUTH   *see* MALBOROUGH

WEST PUTFORD   *see* PUTFORD, WEST

WEST TEIGNMOUTH   *see* TEIGNMOUTH, WEST

WEST WORLINGTON   *see* WORLINGTON, WEST

WESTEXE   *see* TIVERTON

WESTLEIGH   *see* BURLESCOMBE

WESTLEIGH St Peter [Fremington Hundred; Barnstaple Union]   [408]
OR C 1560-1915 M 1561-1988 B 1560-1679, 1698-1916 (NDRO)
BT CMB 1607-08, 1610-12, 1614, 1624, 1629, 1634, 1638, 1668, 1670, 1672,
    1674, 1678-79, 1682, 1684, 1688-90, 1692, 1694-97, 1699-1701, 1704-09,
    1712, 1714-15 (1716-1812 ?); CB 1813-35 M 1813-28, 1830-35 (DRO)
Cop C 1560-1873 M 1561-1873 B 1559-1875 (DCRS/WSL, NDA); CB 1698-1886
    M 1698-1762 (DRO); C 1820-29 M 1812-37 (SG); M 1561-1757 (Boyd)
Cop (Mf) (Appledore SP); Extr C 1560-1697 M 1561-1643, 1654-97 (IGI);
        C 1560-1697 M 1561-1643, 1654-97 (Mf I SLC)
MI (I, NDA); Incledon 788 (NDA)

WESTLEIGH (Wes) Erected 1847 [1851 Religious Census] [1882 Return]
OR C 1923-65 (NDRO); M 1923-45 (DRO); for c.1807-37 see BARNSTAPLE CIRCUIT,
    BIDEFORD (RG 4/954,955 PRO)

WESTLEIGH (Wes) Eastleigh Chapel. Erected 1863 [1882 Return]   Closed 1976.
Now a house
OR C 1926-74 M 1927-75 (NDRO)

WESTON MILL   see PLYMOUTH

WESTON PEVERELL   see PLYMOUTH St Pancras, Pennycross

WESTWARD HO !   see NORTHAM

WESTWOOD   see CLYST, BROAD

WHIDDON   see LEW, NORTH

WHIDDON DOWN   see TAWTON, SOUTH

WHIMPLE St Mary [Cliston Hundred; St Thomas Union]   [739]
Now with TALATON, CLYST ST LAWRENCE
OR C 1653-1955 M 1653-1966 B 1653-1984 (DRO)
BT CMB 1607, 1613, 1625, 1663-64, 1667, 1669-73, 1675, 1678-79, 1682?,
    1683, 1697, 1690, 1699, 1701, 1717 (1718-1812 ?); CB 1813-43 M 1813-37
    (DRO)
Cop B 1813-37 (Ptd DFHS); B 1813-37 (WSL, SG); CMB 1653-1836 (DCRS/WSL, WSL)
Cop (Mf) Extr C 1653-1836 M 1654-1836 (IGI); C 1653-1836 M 1654-1836
        (Mf I SLC)
MI (Ptd J.Dallas 'The heraldry of Devonshire churches: St Mary's, Whimple:
    Notes and Gleanings, Devon and Cornwall 5: 1892: 3-6); Incledon 575
    (NDA)

WHIMPLE (Ind) Independent Church [1882 Return]

WHIPTON   see EXETER

WHITCHURCH St Andrew [Roborough Hundred; Tavistock Union]   [791]
see also BUCKLND MONACHORUM St John, Horrabridge
OR C 1560-1973 M 1559-1987 B 1562-1941 (PWDRO)
BT CMB 1606, 1610, 1612-14, 1616-18, 1620, 1630?, 1663-64, 1668-72,
    1674-81, 1684, 1689, 1695-97, 1700 (1701-1812 ?); CB 1838-41 M 1840-41
    (DRO)
Cop B 1813-37 (Ptd DFHS); B 1750-1900 (I, PWDRO); B 1813-37 (WSL, SG)
Cop (Mf) (Tavistock SP); C 1560-1860 M 1559-1838 B 1562-1881 (Mfc SG)
MI (Ptd DRMI 5, 6: 1998); Ch, cy 1975 (Ts SG)

WHITCHURCH (Meth) Ebenezer
OR M 1940-54 (DRO)

WHITCHURCH (Bible Christian) Unity Chapel. Erected 1850 [1851 Religious
Census] Rebuilt 1861 [1882 Return] fl c.1970

WHITCHURCH (Wes Meth Assn) [1851 Religious Census]

WHITESTONE St Catherine [Wonford Hundred; St Thomas Union]   [643]
Now with NORTH KENN
OR C 1594-1913 M 1594-1981 B 1594-1882 (DRO)
BT CMB 1615-16, 1624, 1629-30, 1632, 1635?, 1636, 1638, 1641, 1662-63,
    1666, 1669-73, 1678 (1679-1812 ?); CB 1813-80, 1885 M 1813-36 (DRO)
Cop C 1594-1605, 1611-41, 1645-1913 M 1594-1602, 1608-09, 1612-41, 1646-51,
    1654-1912 B 1594-1605, 1611-41, 1645-1882 (DRO); CMB 1594-1837
    (DCRS/WSL); CMB 1594-1913 (WSL)
Cop (Mf) Extr CM 1594-1837 (IGI); CM 1594-1837 (Mf I SLC)
MI (I, DFHS); Ch extr (Ptd Cresswell 175); (Ptd H.F.Williams 'Arms in
    St Catherine's Church, Whitestone: DCNQ 28: 1959-61: 233-6)

WHITESTONE St John the Evangelist, Pathfinder Village. f 1981 in parish of
Whitestone
OR see Whitestone St Catherine

WHITESTONE (Wes) Erected c.1838 [1851 Religious Census]; Slades
[1882 Return] Erected 1897. Closed 1974
OR for c.1818-31 see EXETER Mint (RG 4/1207 PRO)

WHITFORD   see SHUTE

WHITLEIGH   see PLYMOUTH

WIDECOMBE IN THE MOOR St Pancras [Haytor Hundred; Newton Abbot Union]   [959]
Now with MOORLAND
OR C 1570-1893 M 1573-1992 B 1560-1928 (DRO)
BT CMB 1597-1602, 1613, 1624, 1626-27, 1663-64, 1666-72, 1674-75, 1677-78,
    1681-82, 1688-89, 1695, 1699-1700, 1702, 1708-09, 1712-15, 1719-30,
    1732-37, 1743 (1744-1812 ?); CMB 1813-18, 1820-33, 1835-37 CB 1839-43
    (DRO)
Cop C 1570-1837 M 1573-1837 B 1560-1837 (Ptd DCRS 1938); M 1573-1754
    (I, Ptd, edit M.Brown, Dartmoor Press 1999); C 1570-1837 (I, SG);
    Extr C 1601-1730 M 1573-1677 B 1566-1647 (Vol 9, BG/PCL)
Cop (Mf) (Okehampton and Totnes SPs); Extr C 1560-1837 M 1573-1837 (IGI);
        C 1560-1837 M 1573-1837 (Mf I SLC)
MI (Ptd DCRS, as above); (Ptd DRMI 19: 1998); (I, DFHS)

WIDECOMBE IN THE MOOR St John the Baptist, Leusdon. Erected 1863. Parish
created 1864 from Widecombe. Now with MOORLAND
OR CMB 1864+ (Inc)
MI (Ptd DRMI 19: 1998)

WIDECOMBE IN THE MOOR (RC) Chapel of the White Knights Crusade, Venton.
Private chapel erected 1908 by Miss Olive Parr (Beatrice Chase) [Kelly 1930]

WIDECOMBE IN THE MOOR (Ind/Cong) Watergate. Erected 1834 [1851 Religious
Census]

WIDECOMBE IN THE MOOR (Wes)
OR for c.1801-36 see ASHBURTON CIRCUIT (RG 4/1763,840 PRO)

WIDECOMBE IN THE MOOR (Wes) Dunstone. Erected 1833-34 [1851 Religious Census] [1882 Return]   fl *c.*1970
OR   for *c.*1820-36 *see* ASHBURTON CIRCUIT (RG 4/840)

WIDECOMBE IN THE MOOR (Wes) Poundsgate. Erected 1854 [1882 Return]
fl *c.*1970

WIDECOMBE IN THE MOOR (Wes) Uppacott. Erected 1834 [1851 Religious Census]

WIDECOMBE IN THE MOOR (Wes) Venton
OR   for *c.*1820-36 *see* ASHBURTON CIRCUIT (RG 4/840 PRO)

WIDWORTHY St Cuthbert [Colyton Hundred; Honiton Union]   [278]
Now with COLYTON
OR   C 1540-1954 M 1540-1973 B 1540-1993 (DRO)
BT   CMB 1616-17, 1620, 1629, 1633?, 1636?, 1667-70, 1672, 1675, 1677-78,
     1685, 1687, 1690 (1691-1812 ?); CB 1813-49 M 1813-37 (DRO)
Cop CMB 1540-1840 (DCRS/WSL, WSL)
Cop (Mf) (Colyton SP); Extr C 1544-1840 M 1548-1837 (IGI); C 1544-1840
         M 1548-1837 (Mf I SLC)
MI   (I, DFHS); Ch (Ptd *Gent.Mag.*: 1791 II: 609-10); Incledon 486 (NDA)

WIGGATON   *see* OTTERY ST MARY

WILLAND St Mary the Virgin [Halberton Hundred; Tiverton Union]   [321]
OR   C 1670-1968 M 1670-1989 B 1671-1941 (DRO)
BT   CMB 1607, 1610, 1614, 1616, 1624, 1633-34, 1635?, 1667, 1668?, 1669-71,
     1675, 1677?, 1678-79, 1683, 1685, 1687, 1690, 1695-96 (1697-1812 ?);
     CMB 1813-17 CB 1819-44, 1847, 1851-57, 1859-63 M 1819-34, 1836-37,
     1843-44 (DRO)
Cop CMB 1607-71 from BT, 1670-1837 (DCRS/WSL)
Cop (Mf) (Tiverton SP); Extr C 1607-1837 M 1607-35, 1667-1837 (IGI);
         C 1607-1837 M 1607-35, 1667-1837 (Mf I SLC)
MI   Incledon 1092 (NDA)

WILLAND (Wes) Erected 1825 [1851 Religious Census]
OR   for *c.*1806-37 *see* CULLOMPTON, TIVERTON (RG 4/958,342 PRO)

WILLAND (Wes) Gables Road. Erected 1899
OR   C 1981-90 (DRO)

WILLSWORTHY   hamlet in PETER TAVY [86 in 1821]

WILMINGTON   *see* OFFWELL

WINKLEIGH All Saints [North Tawton and Winkleigh Hundred; Torrington Union]
[1596]
OR   C 1585-1886 M 1569-1914 B 1569-1944 (NDRO)
BT   CMB 1597-1812 with gaps; CB 1815-22, 1827-32, 1834 M 1815-22, 1827-30,
     1832, 1834 (DRO)
Cop CMB 1569-1837 (DCRS/WSL); Extr M 1609-1717 B 1585-1649 (Vol 17, BG/PCL)
Cop (Mf) Extr C 1585-1837 M 1569-1837 (IGI); C 1585-1837 M 1569-1837
         (Mf I SLC)
MI   Ch: vicars only (Ptd *Notes and Queries* 167: 1934: 168-9)

WINKLEIGH (Ind/Cong) Hollacombe. Erected 1829 [1851 Religious Census]
[1882 Return]

WINKLEIGH (Wes) Erected *c*.1816 [1851 Religious Census] [1882 Return]
OR for *c*.1815-37 *see* OKEHAMPTON (RG 4/1089 PRO)

WINKLEIGH (Bible Christian) Zion. Erected 1839 Siloam [1882 Return]

WINKLEIGH (Bible Christian/U Meth) Peniel Chapel, Stable Green. Erected 1840
[1851 Religious Census] Rebuilt 1863 [1882 Return] Closed 1912-20

WINKLEIGH (Bible Christian) Siloam [1882 Return]

WINKLEIGH (Bible Christian) Erected 1883. fl *c*.1970

WISCOMBE   *see* SOUTHLEIGH

WITHERIDGE with CREACOMBE St John the Baptist [Witheridge Hundred; South
Molton Union] [1263] Now with THELBRIDGE, MESHAW, EAST WORLINGTON,
WEST WORLINGTON
OR C 1586-1836 M 1586-1965 B 1586-1852 (NDRO)
BT CMB 1607-1812 with gaps; CMB 1813-15, 1817-20 CB 1824-48 M 1824-25,
    1827-48 (DRO)
Cop CMB 1585-1837 (DCRS/WSL, SG); CMB 1585-1772 (NDRO); CMB 1646-1837 (WSL);
    M 1646-1837 (Phil Ms); M 1646-1837 (Boyd)
Cop (Mf) (Tiverton SP); Extr CM 1585-1837 (IGI); CM 1595-1837 (Mf I SLC)
MI (I, NDA); (I, DFHS)

WITHERIDGE (Ind/Cong, later Cong Fed) Fore Street. Erected 1839
[1851 Religious Census]

WITHERIDGE (Ind) House, Drayford [1851 Religious Census]

WITHERIDGE (Bible Christian) Providence. Erected 1834 [1851 Religious
Census] [1882 Return]

WITHERIDGE (Bible Christian) Erected 1859. fl *c*.1970

WITHLEIGH   *see* TIVERTON

WITHYCOMBE RALEIGH   *see* EXMOUTH

WOLBOROUGH   *see* NEWTON ABBOT

WOLSTON GREEN   *see* STAVERTON

WONFORD   *see* EXETER

WOODACOTT   *see* THORNBURY

WOODBURY   *see* AXMINSTER

WOODBURY with EXTON, St Swithun [East Budleigh Hundred; St Thomas Union]
Peculiar of the Vicars Choral of Exeter [1673]
OR C 1557-1959 M 1557-1991 B 1575-1954 (DRO)
BT CMB 1610-42, 1727-28 with gaps; CMB 1813, 1818, 1821, 1823, 1833
    C 1835-36, 1838-44 M 1836, 1838 B 1835, 1837-47, 1849-58 (DRO)
Cop B 1813-37 (Ptd DFHS); B 1813-37 (WSL, SG); CMB 1557-1837 (DCRS/WSL);
    Extr CMB 1657-1764 (WSL); Extr C 1557-1733; 1612-34 M 1557-1731;
    1589-1714 B 1575-1751; '1533'-1711 (Vols 11,19 BG/PCL)
Cop (Mf) Extr CM 1557-1837 (IGI); CM 1557-1837 (Mf I SLC)
MI (I, DFHS)

WOODBURY St Andrew, Exton. Chapel-of-ease [Kelly 1889] Now with WOODBURY

WOODBURY Holy Trinity, Woodbury Salterton. Parish formed 1845 from WOODBURY, AYLESBEARE, COLATON RALEIGH. Now with CLYST ST MARY, CLYST ST GEORGE
<u>OR</u> M 1845-1972 (DRO)

WOODBURY (Free C of E) Christ Church. Erected 1851 by seceders from parish church. Later used by Brethren

WOODBURY (Presb/Unit) Gulliford f 1662. Erected 1689; rebuilt 1774 [1851 Religious Census]; Lympstone 1820-pre-1900. Closed c.1888.
see also TOPSHAM
<u>OR</u> ZC 1773-1837 B 1786-1835 (RG 4/1226 PRO); B 1852-84 (Ptd A Coles
      Gulliford Chapel burial ground: 1998) *and see* Gulliford entries in
      TOPSHAM registers (DRO)
<u>Cop (Mf)</u> C 1773-1837 B 1786-1835 (Mf DCRS/WSL, SG); Extr ZC 1773-1837
      (IGI); ZC 1773-1837 (Mf I SLC)
<u>MI</u> 1743-1888 with surname index (Ptd A Coles *Gulliford Chapel burial
      ground*: 1998)

WOODBURY (Free Church) Erected 1828 [1851 Religious Census]

WOODBURY (Brethren) in former Christ Church

WOODLAND St John the Baptist [Haytor Hundred; Newton Abbot Union] [237] Chapelry in IPPLEPEN. Separate parish 1754. United 1938 with BROADHEMPSTON, STAVERTON, LANDSCOVE, LITTLEHEMPSTON
<u>OR</u> CB 1560-1812 M 1560-1835 (DRO); CB 1812+ M 1835+ (Inc)
<u>BT</u> CMB 1610-1811 with gaps; CB 1813-43 M 1813-36 (DRO)
<u>Cop</u> Extr C 1560-1713 M 1570-1732 B 1560-1735 (Vol 16, BG/PCL)
<u>Cop (Mf)</u> (Totnes SP)

WOODLAND (Wes)
<u>OR</u> for c.1801-36 see ASHBURTON CIRCUIT (RG 4/840,1763 PRO)

WOODLEIGH St Mary [Stanborough Hundred; Kingsbridge Union] [279] Now with MODBURY
<u>OR</u> C 1635-1938 M 1663-1836 B 1663-1812 (DRO) Noted in 1831 that earlier
      registers had been destroyed by fire in 1662
<u>BT</u> CMB 1606-1812 with gaps; none post-1812 (DRO)
<u>Cop (Mf)</u> (Totnes SP)

WOODLEIGH (RC) Wood Barton. Monastery of French Cistercian monks. Settled 1902, closed 1921

WOODLEIGH (Wes)
<u>OR</u> for c.1813-37 *see* KINGSBRIDGE (RG 4/1088 PRO)

WOOLACOMBE   *see* MORTEHOE

WOOLBROOK   *see* SIDMOUTH

WOOLFARDISWORTHY EAST St Mary [Witheridge Hundred; Crediton Union] [226] Rebuilt 1845. Now with NORTH CREADY
<u>OR</u> C 1643-1812 M 1657-1739, 1754-1973 B 1656-1812 (DRO)
<u>BT</u> CMB 1608, 1610, 1614, 1619, 1635, 1670, 1672, 1674, 1678-79, 1682-83,
      1688-91, 1694-97, 1699-1700, 1704-12, 1714-15 (1716-1812 ?); C 1813-27,
      1829-37 M 1813, 1815-16, 1818-21, 1824-29, 1835-36 B 1813-26, 1828-35,
      1837 (DRO)

WOOLFARDISWORTHY EAST cont,
Cop (Mf) (Tiverton SP)
MI I (DFHS)

WOOLFARDISWORTHY WEST or WOOLSERY All Hallows [Hartland Hundred; Bideford
Union] [840] Now with HARTLAND COAST
OR C 1723-1985 M 1723-1989 B 1723-1993 (NDRO) Registers from 1538 lost in
    fire 1789
BT CMB 1607-08, 1614, 1617, 1623, 1630-32, 1644, 1670-72, 1674, 1678,
    1682-83, 1685, 1689-91, 1695, 1697, 1699, 1705, 1708, 1710, 1712, 1715
    (1716-1812 ?); CB 1813-40, 1842-44 C 1847-48, 1850, 1852 M 1813-36
    B 1847-50, 1852 (DRO)
Cop CMB 1608-1722 from BT, 1723-1812 (DCRS/WSL); M 1723-1812 (Boyd)
Cop (Mf) (Appledore SP); C 1723-1846 M 1723-1837 B 1723-1885 (Mfc SG);
       Extr C 1607-1812 M 1607-32, 1670-99, 1710-1812 (IGI); C 1607-1812
       M 1607-32, 1670-99, 1710-1812 (Mf I SLC)
MI (I, NDA)

WOOLFARDISWORTHY WEST St Anne, Bucks Mills. Erected 1861. Parish created
1862 from WOOLFARDISWORTHY WEST and PARKHAM. Now with HARTLAND COAST
OR C 1862+ B 1863+ (Inc); M 1862-1989 (NDRO)
MI (I, NDA)

WOOLFARDISWORTHY, WEST (Presb) fl c.1672-90

WOOLFARDISWORTHY, WEST (Wes) Alminstone Cross ? Erected 1836 [1851 Religious
Census] [1882 Return] fl c.1970
OR for c.1817-37 see BIDEFORD, HOLSWORTHY (RG 4/955,1210 PRO)

WOOLFARDISWORTHY, WEST (Wes) Bucks Mills. Erected 1836 [1851 Religious
Census] [1882 Return]
OR C 1923-43 (NDRO)

WOOLFARDISWORTHY, WEST (Bible Christian) Woolsery, Erected 1835
[1851 Religious Census] Rebuilt 1857. fl c.1970

WOOLSERY   see WOOLFARDISWOPRTHY, WEST

WORLINGTON   see INSTOW

WORLINGTON, EAST St Mary [Witheridge Hundred; South Molton Union] [292]
Rebuilt 1879. Now with WITHERIDGE, THELBRIDGE, MESHAW, WEST WORLINGTON
OR C 1725-1968 M 1725-1990 B 1725-1987 (NDRO) No earlier registers noted in
    1831
BT CMB 1607-08, 1610, 1615, 1621, 1627, 1629, 1672, 1674, 1678-83, 1688-90,
    1696, 1699-1700, 1702, 1704, 1706, 1709-12, 1714-15, 1717-22, 1725-28,
    1731-32, 1734-39 (1740-1812 ?); C 1813-45 M 1813-36 B 1813-41, 1843-44
    (DRO)
Cop CMB 1725-1851 (DCRS/WSL); C 1725-1884 MB 1725-1850 (WSL, SG)
Cop (Mf) Extr C 1725-1851 M 1725-1850 (IGI); C 1725-1851 M 1725-1850
        (Mf I SLC)
MI (I, NDA); Extr (Whitmore MS, SG)

WORLINGTON, EAST (Bible Christian) Erected 1842 [1851 Religious Census]

WORLINGTON, EAST (Bible Christian) Sharon, Thornham Cross. Erected 1849
[1882 Return] fl c.1970

WORLINGTON, EAST (Bible Christian) Siloam, North Lake. Erected 1905. fl *c.*1970

WORLINGTON, WEST St Mary [Witheridge Hundred; South Molton Union 1835-85] [187] Now with WITHERIDGE, THELBRIDGE, MESHAW, EAST WORLINGTON
OR C 1694-1812 M 1694-1846 B 1681-1812 (NDRO)
BT CMB 1607-08, 1610, 1614, 1621, 1623-24, 1630, 1635, 1667-78, 1672, 1674, 1678, 1670, 1682-83, 1685, 1690-91, 1694, 1696, 1699, 1704, 1707, 1709, 1711, 1714-15 (1716-1812 ?); C 1813-40, 1842 M 1813-35 B 1813-15, 1817-40, 1842 (DRO)
Cop CM 1693-1850 B 1681-1850 (DCRS/WSL, SG)
Cop (Mf) Extr C 1694-1850 M 1693-1850 (IGI); C 1694-1850 M 1693-1850 (Mf I SLC)
MI (I, NDA); Extr (Whitmore MS, SG)

WORLINGTON, WEST (Ind) Town Living farm house [1851 Religious Census]

WOTTER   *see* SHAUGH PRIOR

YARCOMBE St John the Baptist [Axminster Hundred; Chard Union (Somerset) 1836-94; Honiton Union 1894-1930]   [804] Now with MEMBURY, UPOTTERY, COTLEIGH
OR C 1545-1875 M 1539-1958 B 1539-1869 (DRO)
BT CMB 1610, 1617, 1625, 1630, 1633, 1669, 1678, 1685, 1687, 1690, 1717 (1718-1812 ?); CB 1813-42 M 1813-38 (DRO)
Cop M 1813-37 (Ptd DFHS); B 1813-37 (Ptd DFHS); B 1813-37 (SG); CMB 1539-1837 (DCRS/WSL)
Cop (Mf) (Colyton SP); Extr C 1545-1837 M 1539-1837 (IGI); C 1545-1837 M 1539-1837 (Mf I SLC)
MI Incledon 230 (NDA)

YARCOMBE (Bapt) Marsh Chapel f 1827 [1882 Return]
OR M 1923-24 (DRO)

YARCOMBE (Bapt) Four Elms. Erected 1829 [1851 Religious Census]

YARNSCOMBE St Andrew [Hartland Hundred; Torrington Union]   [498] Now with TWO RIVERS
OR C 1653-1998 M 1653-1978 B 1653-1983 (NDRO)
BT CMB 1606-07, 1610-11, 1614, 1624, 1626?, 1627, 1629, 1631?, 1643, 1668, 1670, 1674, 1678-79, 1683, 1689-90, 1695-97, 1699-1700, 1704-05, 1710, 1712, 1714-15 (1716-1812 ?); CMB 1813-34, 1838 CB 1871-77 (DRO)
Cop CMB 1653-1812 (DCRS/WSL); M 1653-1812 (Boyd)
Cop (Mf) C 1653-1888 M 1653-1837 B 1653-1812 (Mfc SG); Extr C 1607-1812 M 1606-1812 (IGI); C 1607-1812 M 1606-1812 (Mf I SLC)
MI (I, NDA); Incledon 583 (NDA)

YARNSCOMBE (Wes)
OR for *c.*1820-36 *see* ASHBURTON CIRCUIT (RG 4/840 PRO)

YARNSCOMBE (Bible Christian/U Meth) Erected 1908. fl *c.*1970

YEALMPTON St Bartholomew [Plympton Hundred; Plympton St Mary Union]   [1262] Rebuilt 1850. *see also* chapelry of REVELSTOKE. Now with BRIXTON
OR C 1600-1923 M 1600-1943 B 1600-1883 (PWDRO)
BT CMB 1606, 1610, 1614, 1617, 1620, 1624-26, 1633, 1639, 1669?, 1677, 1684, 1686, 1688-90, 1695, 1697, 1699 (1700-1812 ?); CB 1813-39, 1841-50, 1852-54 M 1813-37 (DRO)

YEALMPTON cont.
Cop CMB 1600-50 (DRO, WSL, SG)
Cop (Mf) CMB 1600-1850 (Mf DCRS/WSL); Extr C 1600-1850 M 1600-09, 1628-1837
       (IGI); C 1600-1850 M 1600-09, 1628-1837 (Mf I SLC)

YEALMPTON (RC) Kitley. Domestic chapel, Bastard family 1852-56
OR C 1852-56 (Plymouth Cathedral)

YEALMPTON (Wes) n.d. [1851 Religious Census] [1882 Return]
OR for c.1813-37 see PLYMOUTH Ebenezer (RG 4/1325 PRO)

YEALMPTON (Wes) Ford Road. Erected 1909. fl c.1970

YEALMPTON (Prim Meth) Building belonging to Mr Nathaniel Battershill,
Dunstone [1882 Return]

YEALMPTON ('Providence') Lower Chapel [1882 Return]

YEALMPTON (Prot. Christian) n.d. [1851 Religious Census]

YEALMPTON (S of F) Lyneham. fl 18th cent. Part of PLYMOUTH MM

YELVERTON   see BUCKLAND MONACHORUM

YEOFORD   see CREDITON

YEOLMBRIDGE   see WERRINGTON

ZEAL MONACHORUM St Peter [North Tawton and Winkleigh Hundred; Crediton
Union] [747]
OR C 1594-1986 M 1594-1663, 1678-1968 B 1594-1895 (DRO)
BT CMB 1602, 1605, 1607-08, 1610-11, 1617, 1620, 1624, 163?, 1667-69,
    1674-75, 1678, 1690, 1694-95, 1712, 1714-15 (1716-1812 ?); C 1814-33,
    1835-38 M 1814-33, 1835-37 B 1814-15, 1817-33, 1835-38 (DRO)
Cop B 1813-37 (Ptd DFHS); B 1813-37 (WSL, SG); CMB 1594-1837 (DCRS/WSL);
Cop (Mf) Extr CM 1594-1837 (IGI); CM 1594-1837 (Mf I SLC)
MI (I, DFHS); Ch, cy (Ptd Dwelly 135-49)

ZEAL MONACHORUM (Ind/Cong, now Cong Fed) f 1848; [1851 Cong Year Book];
a building [1882 Return]

ZEAL MONACHORUM (Brethren) A cottage upon Shapcott Farm [1882 Return]

ZEAL, SOUTH   see TAWTON, SOUTH